INDEPENDENT
FORCE

INDEPENDENT FORCE

The War Diary of the
Daylight Bomber Squadrons
of the Independent Air Force
6th June – 11th November 1918

KEITH RENNLES

GRUB STREET · LONDON

To
John Wilfred Archibald Rennles
Eric John Rennles
Ronald Peter Chamberlain

Published by
Grub Street
The Basement
10 Chivalry Road
London SW11 1HT

British Library Cataloguing in Publication Data
Rennles, Keith
 Independent force: the war diary of the daylight bomber
 squadrons of the Independent Air Force, 6th June – 11 November 1918
 1. Great Britain. Royal Air Force. Independent Force – History
 2. World War, 1914-1918 – Aerial operations, British – Campaigns – Germany
 3. World War, 1914-1918 –
 I. Title
 940.4'48

ISBN 1 902304 90 X

Typeset by Pearl Graphics, Hemel Hempstead

Printed and bound in Great Britain by
Biddles Ltd, Guildford and King's Lynn

CONTENTS

ACKNOWLEDGEMENTS

The idea for this book came out of the blue, and was suggested to me while talking to a friend about aviation in the Great War. It seemed for years that the 'Fighter Boys' had always got the limelight, while the 'mud movers' in their less glamorous role (although probably more dangerous), were seldom written about. Although I had contributed material to several books in the Grub Street range, writing my own book seemed quite a daunting task as I set to it in the summer of 1995. Despite the irregularity of the records and the passage of time, hopefully presented here is an account of bombing in its infancy, and the dangers it involved for the brave men of the I.A.F. tasked with carrying it out.

I have been assisted along the way by several people, some unfortunately no longer with us, and I would especially like to thank the following for their help with information and photographs.

Norman Franks, Mike O'Connor, The Beater Collection via the late Don Neate, the late Jack Bruce/Stu Leslie, Frank Cheesman, Mike Armstrong, Stewart Taylor, the late Neal O'Connor, Ronda Rennles, Barry Grey, Ray Sturtivant, Ralph Barker, Hal Giblin, Brad King, Victoria Rennles, The Public Records Office Kew, The Imperial War Museum, Lambeth, Cross & Cockade International, The Royal Air Force Museum, Hendon, Sterling Financial Print Ltd for the jacket design, W.J.Sanderson Collection via Canada's Aviation Hall of Fame, and last but by no means least John Davies and his staff at Grub Street.

PROLOGUE

Azelot, 31st July 1918

The damp blanket of morning dew began to melt away, as the first rays of sunlight reached out to touch the quiet morning calm that was Azelot aerodrome. What noise there had been came muted from the aircraft hangars, as the aircraft mechanics prepared the aeroplanes.

The noise increased as the fronts of the hangars were opened and the de Havillands were pushed out. Most aircraft look ungainly on the ground, and these 'Nines' were no less so.

Once outside, with the morning sun streaming in from the distant horizon, the huge bombs were brought out on four-wheeled trolleys. At least, huge for the time; some 112lb bombs, several 230lb monsters. Grunting and heaving, the mechanics lifted bodily the bombs to the underside of the fuselage, fixing them in place. It would be up to the pilots to release them once over the day's target.

Under the ever watchful eyes of the flight sergeant mechanics, the final preparations were made. The gentlemen would be out soon and everything must be ready. Already most of the NCO observer/gunners had arrived, breakfasted and kitted out for the day.

Minutes ticked by. The officers arrived. Flight sergeants stood upright, reporting all was well; all was ready. The Flight Commander acknowledged the men's usual good and efficient work. Other pilots and observers huddled together, holding subdued and somewhat nervous conversations, while drawing a faint glow from a last cigarette. One or two disappeared to empty an equally nervous bladder. A quarter of a century later, in another war, men would do this against a tail wheel, much to the chagrin of their ground crews, for it tended to corrode the metal, but in 1918, there was a more gentlemanly approach.

At last came the order to climb aboard and start engines. Dressed in thick, somewhat cumbersome Sidcot flying suits, scarves, warm gloves, 'fug' boots and flying helmets, the pilots settled themselves into cockpits, while the gunners clambered into their rear positions. Armourers handed up the Lewis guns to the gunners, who then clipped them to the Scarfe rings and tested free movement. An ammunition drum was locked into place, while others, spares, were handed up and stowed in their special places inside the rear cockpits.

The Flight Commander signalled. The propellers were turned, petrol being sucked into carburettors, then with a shout, contact, the props were swung. Each aircraft's 230 horse-power Siddeley Puma engine burst into life, making the airframe tremble and vibrate. Each pilot throttled up, listening for any faltering sound, but all roared away valiantly.

The Flight Commander waved to his ground crew who ducked down, grasped the ropes of the wheel chocks and pulled them away. His 'Nine' rolled forward, rocking gently on the uneven grass of the airfield. Bringing it into wind he throttled up again, and the bomber inched forward, gathered speed and headed across the take-off area. The others began to follow. One by one the two-seaters rose into the morning sky, and, forming up, headed east, towards the lines, towards Germany, towards Saarbrücken – towards the enemy.

The men on the ground watched them, hands and arms protecting eyes from the glare of the rising sun.

All were silent. They would have to wait several hours before they expected to see them return. In the meantime, they knew the Squadron could expect anti-aircraft fire, more than likely attacks from German fighters, both Home Defence units and front-line Jastas, and have to fight their way through. These were the thoughts in the minds of both the men in the aeroplanes as well as those on the ground.

However, most of the watchers would not see 'their' aircraft again. Of the small force that were now almost dots on the eastern horizon, less then half would return.

FOREWORD

On the 10th of November 1918 at 14.30, 99 and 104 Squadrons of the Independent Air Force, dropped a ton of high explosive on the German aerodrome at Morhange. This action bought to a close the first daylight strategic bombing campaign against Germany.

Bombing Imperial Germany, especially direct attacks against industry and communications, was not a new phenomen confined to the last year of The Great War. The Royal Naval Air Service, notably 3 Wing in late 1916, up until April 1917, were engaged in a bombing offensive together with the French Air Service against targets in western Germany, using aircraft, mostly the Sopwith 1½ Strutter, which were unsuitable for long-range bombing. These attacks were not, and could not, be wholly successful, and in general terms were of little military significance, and used resources which could have perhaps been better employed elsewhere, with regard to damage to the German war effort. However, they did show that targets could be reached and bombed within Germany itself. The Germans, of course, had already been adopting flying bomb raids against Britain using Zeppelin and Schutz-Lanz airships. But by their very nature, these were almost totally indiscriminate rather than in any sense strategic.

Later, sight of German multi-engined Gotha bombers over England in broad daylight in 1917, to early 1918, dropping their deadly cargo on military targets and civilians alike, gave more weight to the call for retaliatory strikes against Germany's homeland. The incursion of enemy bombers began to ring warning bells in the British War Cabinet, as public opinion called for revenge attacks, while many in the Army and Navy were demanding the resumption of attacks on Germany's war industries. The Army wanted production stopped, or certainly hindered, while the Navy, concerned with the massive loss in ships to German submarines, wanted U-boat production hit.

After the second daylight Gotha bomber raid on London, on Saturday 7th July 1917, Lieutenant-General Jan Christian Smuts, a South African soldier and statesman, and a member of the War Cabinet, was appointed by Lloyd George the Prime Minister to compile a report on the nation's air policy and organization. This report was to become more commonly known as the Smuts Report. While compiling it, General Smuts was informed by Lord Cowdray, then President of the Second Air Board, that there would be a surplus of aircraft available in 1918, after all requirements had been met for the Army and Navy. In Lord Cowdray's opinion these surplus aircraft could be the nucleus of a bomber force, with which to attack Germany, and her industries. General Smuts consistently sought the opinion and advice of Lieutenant-General Sir David Henderson, Director General of Military Aeronautics, while compiling his report, and later, in his efforts to see that the two main recommendations were carried out. These were firstly, that a separate Air Ministry and Air Force should be set up, independent of the Army and Navy; and secondly, that a strategic bomber force should be formed within the Air Force to attack Germany and her war production.

The British War Cabinet approved in principle the recommendations laid out in the Smuts Report, for the formation of a separate Air Ministry, and Air Force. However, the War Cabinet delayed its decision on a new branch within the armed services, fearful of the disruption these changes would cause. Opinion in Parliament, however, was strongly in favour of a separate Air Service, the bill (Air Force [Constitution] Act, 1917) passing though Parliament quickly, and receiving Royal Assent on 29th November 1917.

The first Air Council came into being in January 1918. Lord Rothermere was appointed Secretary of State for the Air Force, and Major-General Hugh Trenchard was made Chief of the Air Staff. Sir David Henderson also joined the newly formed Air Council as Vice-President, and the three men set about planning the formation of the new service. By the middle of March 1918, friction between Trenchard and Lord Rothermere became unbearable, culminating in the resignations of Trenchard and Rothermere from the Air Council. (Trenchard handed in his resignation on the 19th of March, two days before the expected German offensive Operation Michael, even though Rothermere told him that he himself would be resigning shortly. Trenchard later said that he tried to withdraw his resignation when he learned that the Royal Air Force was in crisis, but subsequent research into correspondence with Rothermere would suggest otherwise. Rothermere eventually gave in to Trenchard and accepted his resignation on the 13th of April. Major-General Frederick H.Sykes was appointed to replace Trenchard, as Chief of Air Staff, and Sir William Weir replaced Lord Rothermere as Secretary of State for the Air Force. When Sir David Henderson heard of the appointment of Sykes he resigned from the first Air Council (Henderson had had Sykes banished from the Royal Flying Corps in 1915 after arguments between the two men), leaving Sir William Weir and General Sykes to lead the second Air Council, and finish the organization of the Royal Air Force.

Frederick Sykes was probably the most likely man within the Air Ministry to accomplish this feat. Sykes' revolution in airpower thinking began in 1911. When most were sceptical of the importance aircraft would play in any future war, Sykes embraced the advantages of being airborne above the battlefield. As commander of the Military Wing of the Royal Flying Corps, he organized, trained and equipped the R.F.C. and it was due to his forward thinking that the R.F.C. was able to enter the war in August 1914.

On 1st April 1918, unhappily 'All Fools Day', the Royal Flying Corps and the Royal Naval Air Service were amalgamated to form the Royal Air Force. This made little initial difference to the men in the fighting squadrons but it was a historic date in the future annals of military aviation.

Sir William Weir and Major-General Sykes, both keen advocates of strategic bombing, did not under-estimate the difficult task that lay ahead if strategic bombing was going to help win the war. In order to overcome some of these difficulties, the second Air Council set up a Strategic Council, containing specialist officers whose advice they would seek in deciding a plan for the long awaited bombing offensive against Germany. The first meeting of the Strategic Council was held on the 22nd of April 1918; subsequent meetings were held discussing aircraft and aerodromes to be used, specific ordnance for certain targets, as well as the 'surplus aircraft' promised by Lord Cowdray in 1917. The second Air Council remained hopeful that a strategic campaign could be waged against Germany, and on the 13th of May 1918 notified the War Cabinet that . . .

'. . . The time has arrived, to constitute an Independent Force of the Royal Air Force, for the purpose of carrying out bombing raids on Germany, on a large scale. This will be organized as a separate command of the British Royal Air Force under Major-General H.M.Trenchard, who will work directly under the Air Ministry.'

The War Cabinet gave approval for the Air Council's policy, and the Independent Air Force (or I.A.F.) was officially formed at midday, on the 6th of June, 1918.

CHAPTER 1

THE BEGINNING

By 1918, the fourth year of the Great War, aeroplanes and their power, which had started out so falteringly in 1914, had developed and grown out of all proportion. What had begun in those early days as basically an instrument for reconnaissance had now turned into a powerful war machine. Reconnaissance continued, but now the aeroplane helped direct artillery fire, co-operated with ground forces during battles, and bombed front line troops and rear lines of communications, railways and supply dumps. Single-seaters flew fighting patrols, engaged hostile aircraft and observation balloons as well as strafing and bombing ground targets in the battle areas.

Ideas and strategies had also developed, so that by 1917, bombing aircraft were increasingly active against long-range targets, not only in France and Belgium, but western Germany too. These first raids into Germany had commenced, tentatively, back in 1914 but had not been sustained; the Royal Naval Air Service for example bombed the Zeppelin sheds at Düsseldorf on 22nd September. By late 1917, with increasing strength in bombing aircraft, something new was envisaged.

Although the Independent Air Force came in to being on the 6th of June 1918, it was really little more than VIII Brigade Royal Air Force, consisting of two night and one day bomber squadrons. These squadrons operated out of the already well established French aerodrome of Ochey, fifteen miles south-west of Nancy, under the command of Brigadier-General Cyril L.N.Newall. Newall at 34 years of age had entered the Army from Sandhurst in 1905 and after serving in India had transferred to the R.F.C. in 1914. He had been a staff officer since 1916.

These squadrons had been engaged in bombing targets just behind German front lines in direct support of the land offensives, as well as targets in south-west Germany, since October 1917. Added to this force came two more day bomber squadrons on May 20th and 23rd 1918. VIII Brigade now consisted of five squadrons, two of night bombers, 100 Squadron flying FE2cs, and 216 Squadron, with Handley Page 0/100s. The three day squadrons were 55 with the de Havilland 4, and the two recent arrivals, 99 and 104 Squadrons, both equipped with the new de Havilland 9.

When Sir William Weir, now Air Minister, appointed Hugh Trenchard as Commander-in-Chief of The Independent Air Force[1] he had visions not only of a British bomber force, but a multi-national one involving the Americans, and if they were willing or could be persuaded, the French. However French opposition to the idea of strategic bombing came straight from the top in the form of General M.Duval, Chief of French Air Staff. Duval's reasoning was that all bomber resources should be used in attacking German armies in the field, as opposed to targets in far off Germany itself. In trying to appease the French, Sir William conceded that any request by the French armies in the field, under General Ferdinand Foch, would receive direct bomber support.

Trenchard arrived in Nancy on 20th May 1918, cynical of his new appointment and sceptical of the ability of this new bomber force about to come under his command (the appointment of Trenchard as Commander-in-Chief of The Independent Air Force was really his last chance for a big command after turning down several other posts). Trenchard's enthusiasm for his post grew once he saw the amount of work already undertaken regarding the building of new aerodromes and other essential facilities for the

---

[1] Trenchard had turned down Inspector General Overseas; Commander-in-Chief, Middle East; Inspector General in England; Commander of the 8th Brigade; and Commander of the R.A.F. in the Field; Trenchard actually asked Weir to make him G.O.C. of the Air Force with a seat on the Air Council. Weir declined such a position and told Trenchard to accept the Independent Air Force and that was his last offer. Field Marshal Haig had offered his old friend Trenchard a Brigade but Weir refused to let Trenchard go and was adamant he should not have to yield to Trenchard's request.

expanding bomber force. However the construction and positioning of these new aerodromes posed some serious problems for him.

The Strategic Council was set up to determine the best way of inflicting maximum damage on German war industries. Once a target had been selected, it was up to the Strategic Council to determine how many aircraft, and how many bombs it would take to destroy it. The first meeting was held by the council on 22nd April 1918. Planning of the I.A.F. raids fell to Lieutenant-Colonel R.C.M.Pink, a man who was under no allusions as to the difficulty of the task which lay ahead. The targets drawn up by The Strategic Council for bombing Germany ran along a rough line Cologne-Frankfurt-Stuttgart. This imaginary line was approximately one hundred and twenty-five miles from the then present front line, and with the limitations of day and night bombers of the period, all aircraft would have to be stationed in the mountainous and wooded area around Nancy to be within effective range. The airfield sites given to the Independent Air Force by the French Army required immense labour. This included the elimination of deep furrows and high ridges, as well as levelling and drainage; thirty-six miles of drains alone were required for the building of just one aerodrome.

Work had not only been started on the aerodromes, railheads were being built where fuel trains arriving from Rouen could stop and unload their cargo into large storage tanks. From these it would be pumped to the aerodromes along underground pipes. Ammunition trains were detailed to arrive at Courbain where four bomb dumps had been established. From here trucks would ferry all ordnance including bombs, anti-aircraft shells for airfield defence and machine-gun ammunition, right down to Very light flare cartridges, to the relevant aerodromes. An extensive telephone network was created connecting all aerodromes with each other. Also connected was the 17th century château at Autigny-la-Tour that Trenchard had requisitioned for his Headquarters, and as accommodation for his small personal staff.

The Air Ministry's hopeful prediction was that by July 1919, the Independent Air Force would comprise no fewer than twenty-eight day bomber, and forty-two night bomber squadrons with which to 'obliterate targets' one by one. Most of these bombing squadrons were to be based in the Nancy region, so construction at various stages of completion of fourteen other aerodromes took place right up until the Armistice. Had the War continued and these predictions come to fruition, German towns may well have seen much devastation.

The main daylight bomber base of the Independent Air Force was at Azelot, twelve miles south of Nancy. The three daylight bomber squadrons available to Trenchard on 6th June were situated here, as the 41st Wing R.A.F., until the Armistice. The first de Havilland squadron to arrive at Azelot was 104 on 20th May, flying in straight from St Omer, one of the main stopping-off points for all new squadrons arriving in France from England. Both 55 and 99 did not arrive from their old aerodrome of Tantonville, until 5th June. The facilities at Azelot consisted of twenty-eight hangars for the aircraft, as well as accommodation to house personnel from five squadrons. Petrol facilities and ordnance dumps were complete, and the landing surfaces were deemed to be in very good condition. 41st Wing Headquarters was located at Lupcourt.

Despite the future promise of a much larger force, 110 Squadron, flying the new de Havilland 9a, was the fourth and last daylight bomber squadron Trenchard would receive before the Armistice. But it did not arrive at the new aerodrome of Bettoncourt until 1st September. Also stationed at Bettoncourt arriving on 22nd September, were the Sopwith Camels of 45 Squadron, recently moved from the Italian Front. These two Squadrons were to become 85th Wing R.A.F. When 45 Squadron swapped their Camels for Sopwith Snipes plus the addition of long-range tanks, it was hoped that the Snipes would be able to escort the day bombers to and from their targets. However, the change of aircraft did not materialise until after the Armistice (January 1919), so 45 Squadron were used purely for attacking any enemy aircraft which crossed the lines. The facilities at Bettoncourt were much the same as at Azelot, with accommodation for personnel of five squadrons, twenty-five hangars for the aircraft but unlike Azelot, they had their Wing Headquarters on the airfield itself.

The night bomber contingent of the Independent Air Force between 6th June and 11th November 1918, consisted of five squadrons.[2] 97 Squadron R.A.F. left Netheravon airfield situated fifteen miles north of Salisbury in Wiltshire, equipped with Handley Page 0/400. They arrived at Xaffévillers airfield, twenty-five miles south-east of Nancy on 3rd August. 100 Squadron had been flying its night-flying FE2cs out of Ochey as part of the Force since its formation on 6th June. It moved to Xaffévillers on 10th August swapping

---

[2] For the history of these Handley Page night bombers, see *Handley Page Bombers* by Chaz Bowyer.

its FE2cs for Handley Page 0/400s. 215 Squadron, formerly 15 Naval Squadron, based at Coudekerque south of Dunkirk, were already equipped with the Handley Page 0/100. Redesignated on 1st April 1918 as 215 Squadron R.A.F. with the amalgamation of the R.F.C. and R.N.A.S. they later moved to Netheravon on 23rd April where they exchanged their Handley Page 0/100s in May, for the new 0/400s. On 13th May they left Andover for Alquines, fifteen miles south of Calais. Arriving at Xaffévillers on 19th August, they completed the 83rd Wing R.A.F. stationed at Xaffévillers.

No.115 Squadron R.A.F. equipped with 0/400s arrived at Castle Bromwich from Netheravon on 17th July 1918. From here they left to join the Independent Air Force arriving at the new airfield of Roville-aux-Chenes on 29th August. 216 Squadron R.A.F., formerly 16 Naval Squadron, were already based in France by January 1918 flying Handley Page 0/100s out of Ochey. Converting to 0/400s in March they changed aerodromes on 30th March moving to Villesneux, thirty miles south-south-east of Reims. On 1st April they were redesignated 216 Squadron R.A.F. On 9th May they moved to Ochey, becoming part of the Independent Air Force on 6th June. Moving to Autreville aerodrome on 26th August situated twenty miles south-west of Nancy, they stayed here until moving to their last aerodrome of the war at Roville-aux-Chenes on 28th September, where together with 115 Squadron they made up the 85th Wing R.A.F. with its headquarters at Roville château.

The aircraft that equipped the daylight squadrons of The Independent Air Force originated from the well known de Havilland aircraft company. 55 Squadron were equipped throughout the campaign with the de Havilland 4, a tried and tested bombing and reconnaissance platform. Although its maiden flight took place in August 1916, by the end of the hostilities it was still the best daylight bomber available to the I.A.F. In June 1918, 55 Squadron were flying the de Havilland 4 powered by the Rolls-Royce Eagle VI and VII engines, giving an approximate speed of 102mph at 15,000ft. In September they refitted with the Rolls-Royce Eagle VIII engine which gave a better performance of 126mph at 15,000ft. The squadron had been using this faster engine in limited numbers, on its special long-distance reconnaissance aircraft. One of these special reconnaissance aircraft was also experimentally fitted with the larger wings from a de Havilland 9a, but no noticeable improvement in performance was achieved. The de Havilland 4 had an air endurance of only three and a quarter hours, far too short to reach long-distance targets in Germany. However, 55 Squadron rectified this problem itself with the addition of extra fuel tanks giving an improved endurance of five hours.

The de Havilland 9 was the workhorse for both 99 Squadron and 104 Squadron throughout the air campaign against Germany. The de Havilland 9 embodied many major components from the successful DH 4, although its performance was considerably worse due to the shortage of Rolls-Royce Eagle engines, necessitating the installation of the less reliable Siddeley Puma engine. The under-powered engines not only gave the DH 9 a lower speed than its predecessor (approximately 105mph at 15,000ft) but was prone to serious failure, often weakening formations through aircraft dropping out when safety in numbers was critical. However, its endurance was a good four and a half hours and many crews did prefer the DH 9 to its predecessor. One new design feature incorporated in the 'Nine' was to have the front cockpit moved backwards, so pilot and observer back to back were almost touching, communication being improved considerably, especially when bombing and engaging enemy aircraft. One bonus for the pilot with this new seating arrangement, was that the observer tended to shield the pilot with his body from machine-gun fire from behind.

Due to the disappointing performance of the DH 9, attempts were made to fit the Rolls-Royce Eagle VIII engine to the de Havilland 9 airframe. This experimental aircraft was flown to Martlesham Heath for evaluation on 23rd February 1918, and on 9th March 1918 the de Havilland 9a was born. Although the prototype aircraft was flown with the Rolls-Royce Eagle engine, it was quickly decided, due to shortages, to fit the American Liberty 12 engine with its 400hp, giving an approximate speed of 105mph at 15,000ft. The first R.A.F. squadron to receive the new DH 9a was 110 Squadron, having their eighteen aircraft presented to them from money donated by The Nizam of Hyderabad, each aircraft bearing the name of its benefactor.

Armament in the de Havilland 4s of 55 Squadron varied. The majority of the aircraft had a single Vickers .303 machine gun for the pilot, but a small minority of aircraft had twin Vickers. This twin mounting was frowned upon by the more experienced pilots, as the increased weight and subsequent loss of performance far outstripped the usefulness of two forward-firing guns on bombing operations. The de Havillands of 99, 104 and 110 Squadron all had a single Vickers fitted on their aircraft, which were not ex-Naval machines, unlike the twin-firing guns in the DH 4s of 55 Squadron.

Firepower when needed was from the rear, and again two different choices were available to the observers of all squadrons. For solo reconnaissances one Lewis gun with three double drums of ammunition were carried. For bombing raids either one or two Lewis guns coupled together, the choice being left to the observer as one Lewis gun was much lighter and therefore easier to handle, so that it far outweighed the advantage of the increased volume of fire given by two guns. The other factor was whether the observer had enough brawn to man-handle two guns. Whether one or two guns were carried, the ammunition supply was limited, on account of weight, to six double drums. With the increased firepower of twin Lewis guns there was a danger of all the ammunition being expended early in a fight, which could prove disastrous as the Force could be engaged many times by hostile aircraft when hitting long-distance targets in western Germany, having to fight their way in and back out again.

The 230lb Mk III bomb was the heaviest used by the de Havilland squadrons of the Independent Air Force. This bomb had an armoured nose for maximum penetration, and a light metal casing which resulted in a large crater upon impact. The filling was of Amatol with a delayed action of up to fifteen seconds. The 112lb Mk I bomb was the most commonly used by the daylight squadrons. Two of these could be carried by each aircraft instead of only one of the heavier 230lb bombs. The filling was either Amatol or TNT, with a mercury detonator and Tetryl exploder; this bomb could also be delayed to explode up to fifteen seconds after impact. 40lb Incendiary bombs were sometimes dropped especially when attacking aerodromes, as hangars made of canvas and wood provided ideal kindling. The incendiaries contained a phosphorus mixture which was set to ignite by a timing ring seven hundred feet above the ground. Also used when attacking aerodromes was the 20/25lb Mk I Cooper bomb. The Cooper bomb was a heavy steel-cased fragmentation bomb filled with Amatol, particularly effective against personnel, transport and aircraft on the ground. Eight were carried by a single aircraft in the formation, four under each wing.

Apart from aborting machines formations as a whole were never less than twelve aircraft, except on special occasions when aircraft and pilots were hand picked due to ability and experience. Although twelve aircraft made up a bombing formation, six aircraft were found to be the maximum which could be readily controlled by one leader, therefore the formation was split into two groups of six. Each formation adopted an arrow-head as shown below:

```
1    Leader                          1
5    Deputy Leader            3           2
                        6        5           4
```

The first row (numbers 2 and 3) flew 50ft higher than the leader, the rear row (numbers 4, 5 and 6) flew 50ft lower than the leader. The leader and deputy leader were easily distinguishable as both carried streamers. Positions 2 and 3 were given at first to experienced pilots who, by keeping close to the leader, would hopefully hold the formation together. Of the rear row numbers 4 and 6 were the newer and less experienced pilots, with the number 5 position being taken by the more experienced deputy leader. As the fighting in the air grew more intense, most casualties were taken in the number 4 and 6 positions. To overcome this it was found better to place the more experienced pilots in the rear row, as they tended to drive the less experienced pilots (numbers 2 and 3) up to the leader, as they themselves would not straggle.

The second formation flying exactly as the first, flew either half-left or half-right astern of the leading formation, about 80 to 100ft above it. The choice of right or left depended on the position of the sun as enemy aircraft normally attacked from the rear and out of the sun. With this in mind the second formation flew on the side furthest from the sun to enable observers of the leading formation to fire at enemy aircraft attacking the second formation without being blinded by aiming towards the sun.

For long-distance raids against targets such as Cologne, Frankfurt and Darmstadt the fuel supply allowed only a direct outward and return route. To avoid delay in gaining position, formations formed up on the ground and took off in formation. The only difficulty was that number 5 in the formation was directly behind the leader and if as sometimes happened, the leader's engine failed in taking off, it was difficult for number 5 to avoid running into him. However, number 5 was usually an experienced pilot who delayed his take-off run and quickly gained position in the formation once in the air if nothing untoward had taken place. On several occasions three squadron formations totalling thirty-six aircraft or more took off from Azelot aerodrome. However the DH 9-equipped 99 and 104 Squadrons, found it extremely difficult to keep up with the faster de Havilland 4s of 55 Squadron. Several experiments with the larger formations were tried but they were never a success.

Although three different aircraft were used by the daylight squadrons of the Force, the endurance was pretty much the same. The de Havilland 9 and 9a had an endurance of approximately four and a half hours, whereas the de Havilland 4s of 55 Squadron with their extra fuel tanks had an endurance of five hours. For long-distance bombing raids such as on Cologne, careful calculation and constant checking of wind direction and strength was critical as all the bombers were at the limit of their range. In addition to the main objective, secondary targets on route were given, so that aircraft did not have to return with their bombs. Weather conditions were not the only danger that could influence a drop on the secondary target. Often stiff resistance from enemy fighters made continuation to a long-distance target inadvisable, especially if the formation had been weakened previously by aircraft dropping out through engine trouble, or the inevitable casualties.

When conditions were suitable, one hour was normally allotted for climbing over Allied territory which allowed the bombers to cross the lines at 14 to 15,000ft. This height would be maintained until bombs were released and if formations were not being attacked, height would be increased on the homeward journey. For the furthest raids one hour could not be spared for climbing, so the lines had to be crossed at 8-9,000ft making the heavily laden bombers easier targets for the German front line anti-aircraft fire. One wonders if the Germans ever worked out that if heading out at well below 10,000ft, the bombers were going for a deep penetration?

When flying at heights above 16,000ft it was advisable to use oxygen as altitude was maintained for considerable periods, two and a half to three and a half hours. Observers especially became unable to carry out their duties. Many photographic reconnaissances were aborted due to the breakdown of the oxygen supply. The oxygen apparatus provided failed so often that most pilots and observers simply took oxygen cylinders in their cockpits, and absorbed the gas as they thought fit direct from the cylinder through rubber tubing. When flying at height considerable inconvenience was caused due to frostbite. This was mainly overcome by copious application of whale oil to the exposed portions of the face and the wearing of chamois leather masks. Cold limbs and torso were kept warm by electrically heated clothing, which in the main was reliable and actually worked.

Bombs were dropped in formation, only the leader taking aim. The second formation closed up near the target and dropped their bombs simultaneously with the leading formation. On the whole this method was found to be satisfactory, especially if a good formation had been flown, this giving an excellent pattern of bursts on the target. Various types of bomb-sights were tried in the squadrons but nothing even moderately satisfactory was produced; leaders simply judged when to release their bombs and with experience good results were often achieved.

The outline of the Independent Air Force offensive against Germany was laid out in a top secret document titled: *The Scientific And Methodical Attack on Vital Industries*. This title was taken to mean that having considered the war industries of Germany as a whole, certain objectives were selected for two different reasons. Firstly their production was of great importance, if not essential, to enable the enemy to carry on the war, and secondly their location was within an area which would enable attacks more or less continuously.

The limit to which systematic attacks could be carried out stretched from the already mentioned line Cologne-Frankfurt-Stuttgart. Between the front line trenches and these towns (approximately one hundred and twenty-five miles) lay some of the most vital industries of Germany.

These were:
(a) Iron and coal mines.
(b) The iron ore basins where most of the blast furnaces were situated. Here iron ore was made into pig iron, which formed the basis of steel.
(c) Chemical production.
(d) Explosive production.
(e) Railway junctions and rolling stock.
(f) Aircraft and engine manufacture.
(g) Aerodromes.

Coal Industry
Although the mining and storing of the iron and coal presented a small and almost impossible target for the bombers, the machinery of the mines especially the pumping plant if destroyed or damaged would cause the mines to flood and work would cease. Therefore the objective for air attacks would be the surface electric power and steam plants which kept the mines dry and workable.

Iron Industry

Iron works were mainly situated close to the coal mines especially works with blast furnaces. These furnaces were thought to be very sensitive to bombing, and if damaged in a vital area, would be difficult and slow to repair. The iron industry was a particularly important target for the bombers. In the Lorraine area alone Germany extracted 80% of its iron, half of which was smelted on the spot. The blast furnaces offered a prominent landmark to both day and night squadrons; some works like the big Esch works had eight huge furnaces, and forty hot blast stove towers each over a hundred feet high. It was hoped that with enough squadrons attacking by day and night, the works could not hope to escape serious material damage, as well as sustaining casualties to the work force. When it was realised that not enough bombers would be available for an around-the-clock assault, it was decided to attack the blast furnaces only, as all the ore before becoming the finished product pig iron, had to pass through the furnaces.

Chemical Production

Chemical factories on the whole covered a large area comprising many buildings easily distinguishable by day. The biggest of these and the most frequently visited was the Badische Analin and Soda Fabrik factory situated near the towns of Mannheim and Ludwigshafen. It was hoped that if repeatedly attacked, chemical output at these factories would drop or stop altogether, seriously affecting other industries which relied heavily on chemicals for their war production.

Explosive Factories

Explosive and munitions factories unlike other industries tended to be small isolated buildings scattered widely within the area targeted by the Independent Air Force. The reason for this as in other parts of Germany was that all factories not previously engaged in the production of war materials were transformed to do so. Several large factories, previously not manufacturing munitions were adapted to manufacture shells, guns, rifles and other essential arms for the war effort. Intelligence on these larger transformed factories was scarce and it was hoped that once located, they also could be bombed for the obvious reasons.

Railways and Rolling Stock

It was generally admitted throughout Germany that its principal vulnerability lay in the lack of rolling stock with which to supply its armies. As far as munitions production was concerned Germany would always produce sufficient to carry on fighting. However, if the rolling stock which delivered the munitions was destroyed, it could not be supplied. Goods yards and shunting stations were therefore prime targets, as well as converging railway lines where large destruction of track could create bottlenecks of both men and materials. The main shunting stations and goods yards within the I.A.F. area were to be found at Thionville, Saarbrücken, Mannheim and Karlsruhe.

Aircraft and Engine Manufacture

With regard to engine manufacture so essential in transport and aircraft, the Daimler engine and the Bosch magneto works both situated at Stuttgart, and the Benz works at Mannheim provided excellent targets for bombing aircraft. These factories covered large areas and although easy to spot from the air, giving serious damage to, or knocking them out completely, was practically impossible with the small amount of aircraft available at the time; raids were therefore sent to hinder output rather than actually stop it.

Aerodromes

The presence of British bombing squadrons in the Nancy area would soon become apparent to the German Air Service. A German bombing offensive was envisaged against the various Independent Force aerodromes and with this in mind, bombing the German bomber and fighter bases would be started, with the aim of putting the German Air Service on the defensive as well as destroying its aircraft on the ground. No enemy day-bomber units (Bombengeschwaders) were located in the Lorraine area at the beginning of operations in June. Night-bomber units were believed to be in the area, and with the help of photography, spies, and escaped prisoners of war, the location of these aerodromes would hopefully be established as the year progressed.

Research into any Fighter, Bomber or Reconnaissance unit in the First World War throws up a number of problems. Most operational records can be found at The Public Records Office at Kew, that's if they exist at all. The quality of the remaining records depends upon the squadron being researched, and more importantly, the Recording Officer or clerk some eighty years ago doing a complete and thorough job. Unfortunately some records have been stolen over the years, some have been recovered, but what actually went missing is never certain, because of the large amount of files available. It would be nice just to open a file and read off all men, targets, aircraft serial numbers, casualties and any interesting narratives regarding a particular action, however very few such files exist.

Personnel involved in the bombing raids, for example 99 Squadron, are well documented, listing the pilot and observer as well as their initials from June 1918 right up to the Armistice. An older squadron such as 55 should in theory be well documented as well. However, many files on 55 Squadron, mainly in June and July, do not list the flight leaders let alone the rest of the crews. If for instance a pilot is known, an educated guess could be made as to the observer, but crews were often switched, especially between Flights due to sickness or wounds. Posting to Home Establishment also separated regular crews so for these reasons, observers and pilots have only been included where names exist on operational records, or in personal diaries and memoirs.

Aircraft serial numbers again fall roughly into the same context as pilots and observers. Again 99 Squadron list the aircraft serial number and the crew, 55 and 104 Squadrons however list neither. When aircraft were shot down, or so damaged that they were struck off squadron strength, the serial number is then often given. Diaries again list some aircraft, but usually only those flown that day, by the diarist.

Researching targets also poses a problem, especially when the main objective could not be reached and an alternative target was attacked. Secondary targets were allotted usually on or near the route being flown by the squadron. If this could not be reached or was obscured by cloud any target within the vicinity was a viable alternative. Records at squadron level often simply state "main target obscured by cloud, bombed railways at Metz instead". Main targets can be found sometimes by checking Wing records or reports, or orders sent direct to the squadrons with the prioritised target listed.

Casualties fortunately (and sadly) are well documented; however not all wounds were reported, especially by a busy Recording Officer. Often the cause of death is not always noted; personal extracts such as diaries or memoirs give a better insight into these unfortunate events, as well as the action beforehand. Records can sometimes be found in miscellaneous files stating where crews, who had been killed either side of the lines, were buried. Many letters exist in squadron correspondence files from families who have missing loved ones; although not appropriate for this book, they do give family addresses and usually Christian names, as well as nicknames.

Combat reports are a very good source of what actually happened, as the crews saw it, during the fighting with enemy aircraft. These reports sometimes give the colour and type of enemy aircraft, very handy in trying to establish the enemy units. Serial numbers of allied aircraft are sometimes given, especially if the crew made a claim, or were awarded a victory. Allied pilots and observers in general over-claimed throughout the war; observers in the I.A.F. were to a certain extent no exception. These combat reports were sent to Wing Headquarters who decided which claims were to be awarded and which were not. Brigades also received copies of these reports and sometimes credited crews with a victory, which Wing Headquarters had disallowed; victories were awarded to both pilot and observer regardless of who pulled the trigger. Obviously the aerial fighting took place over the German side of the lines, which posed problems regarding verifications. A German aircraft engaged in combat could be hit for example in the engine, or propellor, or the pilot could be wounded. Above home territory, the German pilot could simply leave the fight by spinning away, or diving, even with a stopped engine, and usually make an emergency landing on an aerodrome or field. Observers would have seen an enemy aircraft hit by machine-gun fire, diving or spinning away in their minds, out of control. Observers certainly wouldn't have had much time to watch it spin to the ground, or crash, especially if they were engaged by other German aircraft which was usually the case. This is not to say that I.A.F. did not shoot down any German aircraft. Over-claiming was due to the system without a precise set of rules for victories; willing your opponent to crash after seeing him spin away is another matter.

If all the German aircraft claimed in the combat reports were actually downed, then resistance to the I.A.F. would have been severely curtailed. To the contrary, however, German victories continued to mount as I.A.F. operations increased from June 1918. These victories usually required a wreck for verification, or reports from fellow pilots or ground observers. If victories were awarded they would usually be listed in the German *Nachrichtenblatt*, but not all victories are listed here. Jasta records and recent publications have helped in regard to these missing victories, and assist in piecing together a rather complex jigsaw. Merely matching a date, a German claim, and an allied aircraft is not enough. Firstly German pilots often called the De Havilland 9 a De Havilland 4 when making out their claims. This is not a serious problem when claims are matched against a map, and times taken into consideration. However joint bombing raids between squadrons were undertaken, also several different German Jasta or Kests were encountered on a single raid. In the general mêlée of a dogfight nothing is certain but it is feasible to list the majority of 'who got who' with a high degree of accuracy. German pilots sometimes landed near their victims, or met the occupants if they were alive in captivity. German records regarding victories on the whole are very accurate, wounded pilots or those killed are equally accurate, and when compared to claims by observers for downed aircraft, make very different reading.

It is not for present-day historians to diminish the achievements of these men whatever their nationality. However the amount of material available now, and the passing of time, enables a more realistic account to be told of what actually happened all those years ago.

Defence against these bombing formations of The Independent Air Force started with an extensive communication network (for the time) which connected anti-aircraft batteries, balloon observers, observation posts and various aerodromes with home defence Kampfeinsitzer Staffeln or more commonly known Kest units. Detection of incoming bomber raids usually started with forward observation posts situated on the highest ground near the front line. These observation posts were able to contact by telephone the 19th German Army Flakgruko Headquarters at Frankfurt. Here the information was passed to the relevant Flugzeug Abwehr Kanone or anti-aircraft unit, (flak was more commonly referred to as 'archie' by allied airman after a music hall song of the time). These anti-aircraft units were usually situated near major industrial towns or strategic railway junctions vital for supplies to factories and the front lines. Situated on the hills running alongside the River Saar were various batteries connected with each other by telephone. At the top of this line was Treves with fourteen guns, Bous with six, Dillingen with ten, Völklingen with eight and Saarbrücken at the end with twenty. Treves and Saarbrücken had the biggest batteries using barrage fire once aircraft were in range and their height established.

A second line of anti-aircraft batteries ran on the eastern side of the River Rhine to the eastern slopes of the Vosges Mountains. Cologne at the top had twenty-eight guns, Coblenz twelve, Frankfurt twenty, Mannheim-Ludwigshafen twenty-six, Kaiserslautern eight, Speyer six and Pirmasens eight. Of course, these were not the only anti-aircraft defences over which I.A.F. had to run. Anti-aircraft batteries at the front line were also a constant problem. Formations often came over at roughly the same height, and place, when crossing the front line, an easier target for the gunners, and seldom did formations change height on the return journey either due to fuel shortage or engine performance.

Although the formations of bombers could be under near constant fire from anti-aircraft batteries along their entire route, to and from the target, a second and more serious opponent were the German home defence units or Kests. The history of these units can be traced back to August 1916 with the creation of Kampfeinsitzer Staffel 1, or Kest 1, stationed at Mannheim. The number of Kest units started to grow and by April 1917 their number had increased to nine.

Kest 1a	Mannheim	became	Jasta 90	29.10.18
Kest 1b	Karlsruhe	became	Jasta 90	29.10.18
Kest 2	Saarbrücken	became	Jasta 82	29.10.18
Kest 3	Morchingen	became	Jasta 83	29.10.18
Kest 4a	Boblingen	became	Jasta 84	29.10.18
Kest 4b	Freiburg	became	Jasta 84	29.10.18
Kest 5	Freiburg	became	Jasta 85	29.10.18
Kest 6	Bonn	became	Jasta 86	29.10.18
Kest 7	Krefeld	became	Jasta 87	29.10.18
Kest 8	Neumünster	became	Jasta 88	29.10.18
Kest 9	Mainz	became	Jasta 89	29.10.18

Kest units tended to be equipped with a diversity of aircraft, and the personnel within those aircraft tended to be of differing experience also. Aircraft used by the Kests differed from Kest to Kest – combat reports from allied airmen and some surviving Kest records suggest a mixture of Pfalz DIII, Fokker DVII, Albatros DVa, Roland DVIb, Pfalz DVIII and two-seater DFW C with an onboard wireless set to help the Kest intercept the bomber raids. Personnel also varied with Kest leaders usually being former front line Jasta pilots who with knowledge of current fighter tactics, could share this knowledge with their less experienced colleagues. Other front line pilots were also sent to Kest units mostly to recover from fatigue or slight wounds while still keeping their hand in at air-to-air combat. Leutnant Willi Rosenstein is a good example of this, scoring two victories with Jasta 27, scoring one victory with Kest 1b before returning to the front and scoring another six victories with Jasta 40 before the war ended. These Kests had seen little or no action up to 1918 but their chance would soon be coming with the formation of the Independent Air Force.

Kest and anti-aircraft fire would be opposition enough for the daylight squadrons of the I.A.F. but their real test would come, if and when, they also came across some of the Jasta units stationed in the German 19th Army sector on the French front. Jasta units were moved about frequently, usually to where the fighting was thickest, or air supremacy was needed over the battlefield, and Jasta units in the I.A.F. sector were no exception. Moving into Montingen airfield near Metz on 14th June 1918 was Jasta 18. Jastas such as these were a great threat to the bomber formations, experienced as they were in splitting up formations and picking off stragglers. These pilots if allowed could decimate a bombing squadron which could be already short in numbers, due to engine failure, low on fuel and quite possibly on the return journey from a target, low on ammunition too.

The daylight squadrons of The Independent Air Force were up against a formidable opponent, well armed, well trained and waiting . . .

CHAPTER 2

OPERATIONS – JUNE 1918
The First Raids

Target: Factories, Station and Barracks at Coblenz

6th June	**Take Off:**	**04.30**
55 Squadron	**Returned:**	**09.48**

Formation 1
Capt F.Williams
2Lt W.J.Pace
2Lt C.R.Whitelock   photo machine
Lt A.Clarke
Lt E.H.Van der Reit
2Lt J.Cunliffe   ret e/t 05.50

Formation 2
Lt H.S.P.Walmsley
Lt C.A.Bridgland
Lt D.J.Waterous
2Lt W.Legge   ret e/t 06.15
2Lt J.R.Bell
Lt E.Blythe

Although it was now part of the new Independent Air Force, 55 Squadron, the most experienced at Azelot, started out as usual with both formations gaining height over their new airfield, and then heading north-west to cross the lines at Château-Salins at 14,000ft. Before crossing the lines, however, the first formation lost 2Lt Cunliffe and his observer due to engine trouble, while just over the lines 2Lt Legge and his observer departed company with the second formation, also due to engine trouble; both crews returned to Azelot.

The remaining ten DH4s led by Captain Frederick Williams, one of many experienced leaders in long-distance bombing within the ranks of 55 Squadron, headed north towards Saarlouis, which lay fifteen miles north-east of Saarbrücken and out of range of the town's formidable anti-aircraft defences. Also stationed at Saarbrücken was the German home-defence fighter unit, Kest 2; however, no enemy aircraft were seen and the formations headed north-west towards Coblenz. Keeping the Moselle river to their left for a distance of eighty miles, the two formations continued on.

Reaching Coblenz the formations closed up as slight but accurate anti-aircraft fire opened up from the twelve 9cm guns of the Coblenz battery. Despite the flak, eighteen 112lb bombs, and one 230lb bomb were released from 15,000ft. Several hits were observed on the buildings and houses adjacent to the railway tracks, while three bombs were seen to fall near the old fort which lay within the town. Both formations then turned south-west for the homeward trip, passing north of Treves then south of Luxembourg, re-crossing the lines near the French battle-torn town of Verdun, the scene of much bitter fighting for more than two years. The photographic machine flown by 2Lt Whitelock took 18 photographs of what proved a very successful first show for 55 Squadron as part of the I.A.F., against a long-distance target.

A commission sent after the war to assess bomb damage found that 55 had in fact found their mark, contrary to the German press release. An extract from the town Mayor's Report found that a single bomb had fallen on the building material depot of Bérger & Son. Damage was done to the reservoir tower behind the despatching office, for express goods, at the main railway station. Three bombs had fallen in the barracks north-west of the main station, causing damage to masonry and the officer's mess. Two bombs were also reported to have hit the Casino. Near misses were reported near the gas works and round the engine sheds and goods station. The German press release said "As a result of the effective work of the defences, no bombs fell within the town".

Target: Station and Sidings at Thionville

6th June			Take Off:	13.00
99 Squadron			Returned:	15.40

Formation 1

Capt W.D.Thom	Lt L.G.Claye	D5570		
Lt W.G.Stevenson	Lt T.W.Wiggins	C6153		
Lt K.D.Marshall	2Lt O.Bell	C6145		
Lt F.G.Thompson	2Lt S.C.Thornley	C6113	ret e/t 14.10	
Lt H.D.West	2Lt J.Levy	D5573	ret e/t 14.15	

Formation 2

Capt P.C.Purser	Lt R.F.Connell	C6149	ret e/t 14.35	
Lt V.Beecroft	2Lt D.G.Benson	C6202	joined 1st formation	
Lt E.A.Chapin	2Lt B.S.W.Taylor	D7223	ret e/t 15.15	
Lt W.J.Garrity	2Lt E.Beale	C1668	ret e/t 14.35	
Lt H.Sanders	Lt W.W.A.Jenkin	C6191	photo machine	
Lt S.M.Black	2Lt E.Singleton	C1669	ret e/t 15.00	

For their first show as part of the I.A.F. 99 Squadron were tasked with an attack on the vital railway station and shunting yards at Thionville. Led by Captain William Dorian Thom, both formations crossed the lines at Pont-à-Mousson.

Shortly after crossing the lines, the Siddeley Puma engines gave an indication of their unreliability as one by one, aircraft started to leave their formations. When approaching Metz, the straggling aircraft came under heavy but inaccurate anti-aircraft fire; adding to the confusion Lieutenants Chapin and Black aborted with engine trouble leaving just five aircraft out of an original eleven to carry on.

The two remaining aircraft in the second formation joined up with the three remaining machines in the first, and continued towards Metz. Bombing from 14,000ft the five DH 9s dropped ten 112lb bombs onto Thionville's station and sidings through scattered cloud. No damage was observed, and only six photographic plates were exposed over the target due to the weather. The single formation returned via Metz and re-crossed the lines at Pont-à-Mousson.

Target: Railway Sidings at Konz

7th June		Take Off:	06.00
55 Squadron		Returned:	08.50

Formation 1

Lt H.S.P.Walmsley		
Lt A.Clarke	photo machine	
Lt D.J.Waterous		
2Lt J.Cunliffe	ret e/t 06.25	
2Lt J.R.Bell		
2Lt J.B.McIntyre		

Formation 2

Lt M.G.Jones	ret e/t 06.15	
2Lt W.J.Pace		
2Lt C.R.Whitelock	ret e/t 07.05	
2Lt W.Legge		
Lt C.A.Bridgland		
Lt E.Blythe		

Both formations, led by Lt H.Walmsley took off and started to gain height over Azelot, but 2Lt Cunliffe and Lt Jones both returned while still over the field due to engine trouble. The remaining ten aircraft in two formations headed out towards the lines, 2Lt Whitelock returning due to engine trouble just before the lines were crossed south-east of Château-Salins, at 14,500ft. Flying west of Bolchen then heading north, the formations flew between the Moselle and Saar rivers until they met up at Konz.

Konz station and its railway sidings were a strategic junction for all rail supplies heading into Namur and Luxembourg. The sidings were usually filled with rolling stock containing either armaments or personnel, prime targets for the thirteen 112lb bombs, one 230lb bomb, and twelve 20lb Cooper bombs dropped from 15,000ft. Several bursts were observed on the sidings as the formations turned west, flying north of Luxembourg, then south-west, crossing the lines at Fresnes just east of Verdun. Altogether fifteen photographic plates were exposed, ten over the target. Both formations encountered heavy anti-aircraft fire from the fourteen flak guns of the Treves battery; fortunately all aircraft returned safely.

Target: Station and Sidings at Thionville

7th June			Take Off:	08.20
99 Squadron			Returned:	10.45
Formation 1				
Capt P.C.Purser	Lt R.F.Connell	C6149		
Lt V.Beecroft	2Lt D.G.Benson	D1668		
Lt S.M.Black	2Lt E.Singleton	D1669		
Lt H.Sanders	2Lt W.W.A.Jenkin	D1670		
Lt E.L.Doidge	2Lt W.B.Walker	D5568	ret damaged A.A.	
Lt E.A.Chapin	2Lt B.S.W.Taylor	C6202	ret e/t 09.45	
Lt K.D.Marshall	2Lt O.Bell	C6145	spare ret 09.40	

Due to engine trouble on the previous day's trip to Thionville, only one formation was sent to attack this target again. The same route as the previous day was taken, crossing the lines at Pont-à-Mousson where the spare machine piloted by Lt Marshall separated from the formation.

Not long after this Lt Chapin and 2Lt Taylor left the formation being unable to keep up while climbing to bombing height, their second engine failure in two days. The formation, now down to five machines, continued north over Metz. Heavy anti-aircraft fire from the Metz battery hit the lower wing of Lt Doidge and 2Lt Walker's aircraft forcing them to return reducing the formation to four.

These remaining four aircraft bombed Thionville with four 112lb and two 230lb bombs. Three bombs were seen to land in the centre of the station, one on the road bridge west of the station, and two in the river near the bridge. One enemy aircraft was seen east of Metz at 09.30 on the way to the target, while on the return, a two-seater was observed at 10.15 north-west of Hagondange. Two more enemy aircraft were spotted east of Metz at 10.20 but none of these engaged. The lines were re-crossed at Pont-à-Mousson without further incident.

CAPTAIN PHILLIP CHARLES PURSER was born on 4th January 1896. He started his training at Netheravon on 3rd January 1916 where he then joined 19 Squadron who were working up to proceed overseas. However judging by records, he joined 70 Squadron flying Sopwith 1½ Strutters on 14th June 1916. While with 70 Squadron he was awarded the Military Cross in October 1916, and was mentioned in despatches on 14th November 1916. On 14th December 1916 he arrived at Reading as an assistant flying instructor. He remained at Reading where he joined 41 Reserve Squadron until posted to 99 Squadron on 26th April 1918. Falling ill while with 99 Squadron, he was sent home and spent time at Hampstead Hospital before joining 141 Squadron on 16th April 1919. He also served with 117 and 106 Squadrons during 1919. His home address given during the war was 23 Arath Parade, Grantham, Lincs. He applied for the R.A.F. VR in October 1939, his address at the time being 205 Farmworld Road, Sutton Coldfield.

Target: Railway Station at Metz

8th June		Take Off:	04.35
104 Squadron		Returned:	07.15/55
Formation 1			
Capt J.B.Home-Hay	Lt C.C.Blizard		
Lt E.Cartwright	Lt A.G.L.Mullen		
Lt R.J.Gammon	2Lt P.E.Appleby		

Lt W.J.Rivett-Carnac	Sgt J.C.Wilderspin		
Lt O.J.Lange	Sgt G.A.Smith		ret e/t 05.00
Lt S.C.H.Pontin	2Lt J.E.Belfort		ret e/t 05.20

Formation 2			
Capt E.A.McKay	Capt R.H.Wetherall		
Lt G.C.Body	Lt L.G.Norden	C6262	
Lt M.J.Ducray	Lt R.K.Pollard	D1674	/W.I.A.
Lt J.Valentine	Sgt A.C.Wallace	D5658	
Lt C.L.Startup	2Lt K.C.B.Woodman	D5650	
Lt F.W.Mundy	Sgt E.H.Perrot		ret 06.35

The first show for 104 Squadron was a raid to the railway station at Metz. Although only a short trip over the lines compared to later trips made by the I.A.F., it was the first raid to be intercepted by enemy aircraft. The two separate formations gained height over the airfield, the first formation losing Lt Lange and Lt Pontin to engine trouble. The two formations headed out towards the lines crossing at Forêt B'le Pietre. Once over the lines the formation flew via Gorze and Peltre to approach Metz where they let loose four 112lb bombs and two 230lb bombs. The second formation crossed the lines at Regnéville at 13,000ft but before reaching the target Lt Munday managed to get his aircraft into a spin. He regained control but lost sight of the formation and had no option but to return home. The remaining five aircraft bombed Metz from 13,000ft letting loose six 112lb and two 230lb bombs. Two direct hits were observed on the station and sidings.

The first formation left Metz heading west returning via Malencourt and Conflans without any incident. The second formation while turning for home, noticed three enemy aircraft approaching from the north of Metz at 07.00. The enemy aircraft shadowed the formation and made three attacks, each being met by concentrated fire from 300 yards by Lts Norden, Pollard, Woodman and Sgt Wallace. After the third attack one enemy aircraft dived away steeply, apparently on fire and smoking, and was last seen gliding towards a wood at Villecey; the other two enemy aircraft withdrew. The squadron, however, had not got away unscathed, Lt Pollard receiving a bullet in his left arm. The combat had lasted for twenty minutes and the formation by this time had passed over Verny, and was approaching the lines at Pont-à-Mousson when the combat finished. The second formation landed without further incident. The four observers had fired off 1,434 rounds between them; the enemy aircraft was credited to all four observers as driven down.

RAYMOND KINGSLEY POLLARD was born on 5th March 1899. Between July 1916 and February 1917, he was an art student at the Technical Institute at Kingston-upon-Thames. Joining the Royal Flying Corps Pollard received his training at Reading and Hythe, before moving to 104 Squadron. Becoming a 2Lt on 7th June 1918, he was unfortunately wounded the next day and would take no further part in the war. He was treated at the Hospital at Balon until 5th August 1918. He was eventually certified as unfit for flying duties, and was put on the unemployed list on 15th February 1919. The family lived at The Oaks, Burleigh Road, Addlestone, Surrey, but Pollard gave his address during the war as 10 Grange Road, Ealing, W5. He was still living here in February 1928. He passed away on 31st May 1972. He was the first daylight casualty of the I.A.F.

Target: Factory, Station and Barracks at Coblenz
Secondary Target: Station and Sidings at Thionville

8th June		**Take Off:**	**04.35**
55 Squadron		**Returned:**	**07.47**
Formation 1			
Lt M.G.Jones			
Lt C.A.Bridgland			
2Lt W.J.Pace		photo machine	
2Lt W.Legge			
2Lt C.R.Whitelock			
2Lt J.Cunliffe			

Formation 2
Lt E.F.Van der Reit
Lt A.Clarke   photo machine
Lt D.J.Waterous
Lt E.Blythe   ret e/t 04.55
2Lt J.R.Bell
2Lt J.B.McIntyre

While both formations were gaining height over the airfield, Lt Blythe was compelled to land because of engine trouble. The remaining aircraft crossed the line at Nomeny at 14,500ft, keeping east of the Moselle river and west of Bolchen. Lt Jones leading the formation, decided that due to heavy cloud cover an attack on Coblenz was impractical, and elected instead to bomb the secondary target, Thionville railway station.

The formations climbed to 15,000ft and released fourteen 112lb, thirty-four 20lb and one 230lb bomb; no bursts were seen due to cloud. The formations turned south flying west of the Moselle river crossing the lines at Pont-à-Mousson. Heavy and accurate anti-aircraft fire was encountered from the Metz battery on the way in, and on the way home. The two photo machines took thirty photos, seventeen over the target, although the quality was hampered by cloud.

Target: Thionville Station and Sidings
Secondary Target: Railway and Factory at Hagondange

8th June			Take Off:	06.30
99 Squadron			**Returned:**	**09.50**
Formation 1				
Capt W.D.Thom	Lt L.G.Claye	C1670		
Lt W.G.Stevenson	2Lt T.W.Wiggins	D5570		
Lt K.D.Marshall	2Lt O.Bell	C6145		
Lt H.Sanders	Lt W.W.A.Jenkin	C6149		
Lt E.L.Doidge	2Lt W.B.Walker	D5562	photo machine	
Lt H.D.West	2Lt J.Levy	D5573		
Lt R.F.Freeland	2Lt R.E.Sothcott	C1666	ret e/t 07.15	
Formation 2				
Capt A.D.Taylor	Lt H.S.Notley	C6153	ret e/t 07.45	
Lt V.Beecroft	Lt D.G.Benson	C6278		
Lt F.G.Thompson	Lt S.C.Thornley	C6113		
Lt M.T.S.Papenfus	Lt A.L.Benjamin	C6191		
Lt J.W.Richards	2Lt E.J.Munson	D7223	ret e/t 09.20	
CW.J.Garrity	2Lt E.Beale	C1668	ret pilot sick 08.45	
Lt S.M.Black	2Lt E.Singleton	C1669	ret e/t 07.15	

With the recent unreliability of their engines, 99 Squadron decided to take two spare aircraft with them for the attack on the railway lines and sidings at Thionville. After gaining height over the airfield and heading off north to cross the lines at Pont-à-Mousson, aircraft started to drop out. Captain Taylor, leading the second formation, returned with engine trouble so the second formation joined with the first, led by Captain William Thom. Ironically, before this single formation crossed the lines, even the two spare aircraft piloted by Lieutenants Freeland and Black aborted with engine trouble, leaving the eleven remaining aircraft to carry on to the target.

As soon as the formation crossed into German territory a barrage of anti-aircraft fire commenced. At first it was inaccurate, but as the formation got nearer to Metz the barrage became heavier and more accurate. Lt Garrity turned for home, unable to continue due to sickness, while Lt Richards, unable to keep up with the formation due to engine trouble, was also compelled to abort. The flak barrage was growing in intensity, and with Thionville covered in cloud, Captain Thom decided to bomb Hagondange. The nine remaining aircraft making a single formation let loose eight 112lb and five 230lb bombs. Two bursts were observed near the railway north of the factory. The formation returned via Metz where an enemy aircraft was spotted at 09.15, but it stayed clear; and 99 Squadron re-crossed the lines at Pont-à-Mousson. Lt Doidge and 2Lt Walker managed to take eighteen photos over and around the target despite the archie.

Reconnaissance

8th June		Take Off:	07.15
55 Squadron		Returned:	11.00
Capt F.Williams	Capt W.H.Mason-Springgay A7837		

Crossed lines at Forêt-de-Parroy at 19,000ft taking twelve plates, took twelve plates over objective and re-crossed lines at Nomeny. Difficulties with photos due to cloud, one enemy aircraft seen over Saarburg.

Target: Railway and Factory at Hagondange

9th June		Take Off:	05.05
104 Squadron		Returned:	07.55

Formation 1

Capt J.B.Home-Hay	Lt C.C. Blizard	
Lt J.Valentine	Sgt A.C.Wallace	
Lt R.Gammon	2Lt P.E.Appleby	photo machine
Lt W.J.Rivett-Carnac	Sgt J.C.Wilderspin	
Lt E.Cartwright	Lt A.G.Mullen	
Lt McConchie	Lt R.A.C.Brie	ret e/t

Formation 2

Capt J.M.Heap	Sgt V.G.McCabe 263228	ret e/t
Lt F.W.Mundy	Sgt E.H.Perrot 88164	ret obs fainted
2Lt A.W.Robertson	Lt M.H.Cole	ret e/t
Lt C.G.Jenyns	2Lt H.C.Davis	ret e/t
Lt F.H.Beaufort	Lt C.G.Pickard	ret e/t
Lt O.J.Lange	Sgt G.A.Smith	

The second raid for 104 Squadron would be an attack on the factories and rail lines at Hagondange, situated between the vital rail junctions of Metz and Thionville on the western side of the River Moselle. Leading this raid as on the previous day would be Captain Jeffrey Batters Home-Hay.

Crossing the lines at Varneville, the two formations had quickly become one with the Siddeley Puma engines showing their usual unreliability. Captain Heap and Lt Beaufort turned for home both with leaking radiators, soon followed by Lt McConchie unable to climb and keep formation. Lt Jenyns returned with broken exhaust springs while Lt Mundy was forced to return after Sgt Perrot fainted. Lt Lange joined the first formation and the remaining six aircraft headed towards Conflans then north-east towards Thionville. From Thionville the formation turned south towards Hagondange encountering slight flak as they prepared to drop six 112lb and three 230lb bombs from 14,000ft. No enemy aircraft were encountered and all aircraft returned safely crossing the lines west of Pont-à-Mousson at Nomeny.

Lt Percival Ewart Appleby was busy taking eleven photos over and around the target area. Once developed they would show two hits on factory buildings near the railway station, and several hits in the surrounding fields. Lt Rivett-Carnac dropped a 230lb delayed action fuse bomb which, apparently according to records, hit a train. Air Ministry investigations concluded that the factory buildings mentioned were part of the Thyssen Works. One bomb had burst on a building damaging the corner of it considerably. They also noted that a single bomb had burst on the main railway line between Thionville and Metz.

EMILE HENRY PERROT was born in November 1891 in Guernsey. He joined the Royal Flying Corps on 8th August 1917 as a fitter, leaving his civilian job as a farm labourer. His records show that he received a gunshot wound to the right leg on 19th August 1917. He was taken on this day to the 82nd Stationery Hospital at Wimereux. From here he went to the Military Hospital at Bethnal Green, arriving on 27th August. On 1st January 1918 he was posted to the recruitment depot from where he again joined the R.F.C. On the creation of the Royal Air Force he was posted to 104 Squadron and was re-mustered AM3 on 3rd July 1918. On 24th June 1918 a medical board concluded that his "physical condition is unlikely to improve sufficiently to allow him to fly", so ended Perrot's brief flying career. The family address at this time was St Peters Port, Câtch, Guernsey. When looking through 104 Squadron records, it shows that all ranks below sergeant, who became observers like Perrot, were immediately made up to sergeant. It also shows that as soon as Perrot was stood down from flying, he was immediately reduced in rank as well. When 104 were short of observers, it appears they used air mechanics to fill gaps basically as aerial gunners. Bomb raid reports show Perrot's rank as 2AM when we know he was a sergeant (if only very temporary); unfortunately bomb raid reports are quite misleading at times in this way.

JEFFREY BATTERS HOME-HAY was born in Alloa, Scotland, on 31st January 1890. He emigrated with his widowed mother, three sisters and two brothers, to the Canadian Prairies shortly before the outbreak of World War I. He transferred to the R.F.C. in 1916, after infantry service with an Imperial Battalion of the Argyll and Sutherland Highlanders. Proud of his Scottish heritage, when opportunity allowed, he would proudly wear his kilt and sporran. After completing his flight training quickly, and tiring of instructing, he was posted to France in February 1917 and served for ten months with 53 Squadron, flying an RE8 on artillery observation work. Earning the Military Cross gazetted in July 1917, he received his medal in April 1917 from King George V at Buckingham Palace. He joined 104 Squadron in May 1918 where he was awarded the D.F.C. in September 1918. After the war he returned to Canada in 1919 and began to farm. In 1920 he was called to Ottawa to take part in the first Trans-Canada flight from Halifax to Vancouver. Later he was to fly on the regular Prairie Airways route between Winnipeg, Saskatoon, Moose Jaw and Regina. At one time he was the oldest commercial aviator in northern Canada. In the spring of 1952 he retired to his farm home at Kelington, Saskatchewan where he resided until his death at the age of sixty-six the following summer.

Captain Jeffrey Batters Home-Hay
D.F.C. gazetted 21st September 1918

This officer displayed admirable coolness and resource while leading a raid on an enemy railway station. His formation was heavily attacked by seven aeroplanes, but keeping it well in hand, he fought his way to his objective; proceeding well over the station, he successfully bombed it. In the course of the severe fighting two hostile machines were shot down out of control, one of which he himself brought down. He has taken part in eight other raids, and his consistent gallantry is a valuable asset in maintaining the morale of his new squadron.

Reconnaissance

9th June			**Take Off:**	**07.45**
55 Squadron			**Returned:**	**12.45**
Lt E.F.Van der Reit	Capt O.L.Beater	A7837		

Crossed lines at Forêt-de-Parroy at 19,000ft, went north to Homburg then south-west to Bolchen and Metz, re-crossed lines at Pont-à-Mousson. Sixteen plates exposed, reconnaissance not completed due to cloud. Although this reconnaissance seems pretty standard, reading the diary of Beater, you get a more in depth account of the actual events. Once airborne the oxygen supply wouldn't work. Beater broke the copper tube and proceeded to take gulps of oxygen before it ran out. After four and a half hours he began to feel "a bit done in" but had to keep his wits about him, as they had been shadowed by an enemy aircraft while over the lines. On returning to Azelot, Van der Reit made a bad landing and had to go around again after narrowly missing A Flight's hangar. To cap it all he also had a double exposure over Bolchen. The problems with oxygen at high altitude were very common. With the common failure of the oxygen, crews often used to take CO_2 cylinders in their cockpits and take air as and when required by sucking in through a piece of pitot tubing. On the whole the heated suits were of a pretty reliable nature, and the airmen usually applied whale oil, and wore chamois leather masks, to try and protect from frostbite. If the crews were operating at twenty thousand feet, they usually tried to take an hour to descend to avoid drowsiness, sickness and temporary deafness. For solo reconnaissance one Lewis gun was taken and three double drums of ammunition.

Reconnaissance

9th June			**Take Off:**	**08.00**
55 Squadron			**Returned:**	**11.20**
Capt F.Williams	Capt W.H.Mason-Springgay	B3967		

Crossed lines west of the Forêt-de-Parroy at 18,000ft, then flew to Dieuze then north to St.Avold. Flew south-east to Sarre-Union and Pfalzburg, re-crossed lines at Rambervillers. Forty-five plates exposed.

Reconnaissance

9th June			**Take Off:**	**08.15**
55 Squadron			**Returned:**	**12.00**
Lt C.A.Bridgland	2Lt E.R.Stewart	A7763		

Crossed lines at Nomeny at 19,000ft, went north-east to Boulay then south-west to Courcelles and Metz. Re-crossed the lines at Pont-à-Mousson. Eighteen plates exposed and seven enemy aircraft seen at 17,000ft over Metz.

Target: Factory and Railway Station at Dillingen

9th June			**Take Off:**	**08.50**
99 Squadron			**Returned:**	**11.40**
Formation 1				
Capt W.D.Thom	Lt L.G.Claye	C1670		
Lt K.D.Marshall	2Lt O.Bell	C6145		
Lt W.G.Stevenson	2Lt T.W.Wiggins	D7223		
Lt H.D.West	2Lt J.Levy	D5573		
Lt E.L.Doidge	2Lt W.B.Walker	D5568	photo machine	
Lt R.F.Freeland	2Lt R.E.Sothcott	C1666		
Lt H.Sanders	Lt W.W.A.Jenkin	C6196	spare m/c	
Formation 2				
Lt V.Beecroft	2Lt R.F.Connell	C6153		
Lt S.M.Black	2Lt E.Singleton	C1669		
Lt E.A.Chapin	2Lt B.S.W.Taylor	C1668		
Lt M.T.S.Papenfus	Lt A.L.Benjamin	C6191		
Lt F.G.Thompson	2Lt S.C.Thornley	C6113		
Lt J.W.Richards	2Lt E.J.Munson	C6278		

A short trip for 99 to Dillingen started with both formations gaining height over the field and heading north to cross the lines between Pont-à-Mousson and Château-Salins. Heavy and accurate archie was encountered as they crossed the lines but all thirteen machines were over, and Lt Sanders in the spare machine left the first formation and returned to Azelot. The remaining twelve DH9s carried on towards Dillingen which lay thirty miles north of the lines on the river Saar, north-west of Saarbrücken. Keeping to the east of Metz and its defences, the formations flew over Boulay aerodrome reporting on their return twenty-one T-shaped hangars, and eight large sheds.

Approaching Dillingen, the town's battery of ten 9cm guns opened fire but the flak was inaccurate as both formations dropped their mixed load of 230lb and 112lb bombs at 10.50am. Two bursts were observed on the southern portion of the factory, three bursts on the railway south-west of the factory, and three on the station itself, while two bursts were also observed on the town. Leaving the target area to the south the two formations headed straight for the lines spotting only one enemy aircraft at 8,000ft over Delme, before crossing the lines at Château-Salins with eighteen photos.

The raid to Dillingen looked on paper to be very successful, especially when compared to the three previous raids carried out by the Squadron. However out of thirty-two aircraft despatched to targets, fourteen returned before reaching the target and dropping their ordnance. However, after the Great War had finished, a commission was sent to investigate bomb damage caused to various German installations by the I.A.F. during their operations. Reporting on this raid, three bombs burst on the Dillingen Hüttenwerke, while ten bombs were reported to have fallen one and a half miles from the target. From such a grouping of bombs it would appear that an entire flight dropped on the flight leader's orders, and completely missed the target. Without diminishing the achievements of the pilots and observers of the I.A.F. in any way, this sort of occurrence illustrates the infancy of strategic bombing and highlights the fact that if a target was reached, even in numbers, it was not necessarily hit, or seriously damaged.

Target: Railways at Metz-Sablon

12th June 99 Squadron			Take Off: Returned:	04.55 07.30
Formation 1				
Capt A.D.Taylor	Lt H.S.Notley	C6153		
Lt F.G.Thompson	2Lt S.C.Thornley	C6133		
Lt J.H.Underwood	2Lt T.K.Ludgate	C6145		
Lt M.T.S.Papenfus	Lt A.L.Benjamin	C6202	photo machine	
Lt J.W.Richards	2Lt E.J.Munson	D7223		
Lt W.G.Stevenson	2Lt T.W.Wiggins	C6210		
Lt R.F.Freeland	2Lt R.E.Sothcott	C1679	ret e/t	
Lt V.Beecroft	2Lt D.G.Benson	C6278		
Formation 2				
Lt S.M.Black	2Lt E.Singleton	C1669		
Lt E.A.Chapin	2Lt B.S.W.Taylor	C2173		
Lt E.L.Doidge	2Lt W.B.Walker	C1670		
Lt H.Sanders	Lt W.W.A.Jenkin	C6149	photo machine	
Lt C.A.Vick	2Lt E.Beale	C1668		
Lt H.D.West	2Lt J.Levy	D5573		

Although only a short flight over the lines for their fifth raid, 99 Squadron took two spare aircraft, having had a sorry total of thirteen returns due to engine trouble and pilot sickness on the previous four raids. Crossing the lines at Pont-à-Mousson the two formations headed north, except Lt Freeland and his observer 2Lt Sothcott who headed south and home due yet again to engine trouble. The remaining thirteen machines encountered moderate but accurate archie as they approached their target, easily visible due to a triangular pattern of railway tracks. Dropping eight 230lb and eight 112lb bombs the formations headed for home. Six or more bomb bursts were observed on the town's barracks but none on the railway tracks. Leaving Metz, three enemy aircraft shadowed the formations but did not engage and all aircraft returned safely.

After the war the commission sent to investigate bomb damage concluded that 99 Squadron did hit the barracks this day. Five bombs landed behind the artillery barracks, wounding one soldier, one hit the blacksmiths while another hit the stables killing a horse. Dinner was also ruined when the Bavarian canteen received a direct hit and two near misses. Not earth-shattering results but the raids were beginning to be viewed more seriously by the Germans. They could not remain too complacent – the I.A.F. bombing might improve!

Target: Triangle of Railways at Metz-Sablon

12th June 104 Squadron		Take Off: Returned:	16.50 19.15
Formation 1			
Capt E.A.McKay			
Formation 2			
Capt J.M.Heap			

A return trip to the triangular railway junction at Metz-Sablon was delayed until the afternoon. Bright sunshine with a little cloud was ideal bombing weather, except for a thick layer of haze which had hung around for most of the day. Captain Evans Alexander McKay would be leading the two formations this time hoping to avoid any contact with enemy fighters, unlike the previous trip to Metz.

On this trip all twelve aircraft were to make it to the lines crossing at Bois-de-Pretre, however once over, number six in the first formation became lost and returned to Azelot with his load of two 112lb bombs. The remaining eleven aircraft continued to Metz where they encountered moderate anti-aircraft fire while dropping seven 230lb and seven 112lb bombs from 13,000ft. All bombs were seen to impact within the triangle of tracks, four hits being observed directly on the lines.

The eleven DH9s returned safely crossing the line at Nomeny without encountering any enemy aircraft. Upon landing, one DH9 crew was alarmed to find a 112lb bomb still hanging underneath their aircraft which did not drop due to the release cable or control being shot away, presumably by archie.

High over Cheneurières, on the Allied side of the lines, Lt Max Greville Jones and 2Lt Thomas Elison Brewer of 55 Squadron were engaged in a height test in DH4 A7650. What happened next is unclear but they were involved in a fight with a German photo-reconnaissance aircraft, and were unfortunately shot down. Both men were killed and buried in Charmes Cemetery. Max Greville Jones was a holder of the Military Cross, and was originally from the 1st Northumberland Fusiliers. He originated from Middlesborough and was twenty-three when he was killed. A capable leader with much experience, tragically he was due to go on a much deserved leave in a matter of days.

Note: Apart from the two formation leaders, records for the remaining crews have so far eluded the author.

Target: Railway Sidings at Coblenz
Secondary Target: Railway and Barracks at Treves

13th June			**Take Off:**	**04.50**
55 Squadron			**Returned:**	**08.50**
Formation 1				
Capt F.Williams				
Formation 2				
Lt E.H.Van der Reit				
2Lt W.Legge	2Lt A.McKenzie	A7466	K.I.A./K.I.A.	

The two formations gained height over the airfield, heading out north-west from Azelot to cross the lines at Verdun. Crossing over at 14,500ft, the bombers headed north-north-east towards Arlon situated on the Belgium and Luxembourg border. Here the formations again changed direction heading west towards Konz from where they would head north-west to reach Coblenz.

Upon reaching Konz, however, thick cloud banks north of Treves made continuation to Coblenz impossible; thick mist was also starting to form below obscuring the ground. Captain Frederick Williams decided to bomb the nearby railway and barracks at Treves instead. One 230lb, fourteen 112lb and twenty-four 20lb Cooper bombs were dropped from 15,000ft. E.D.Laeis & Co., a machine company situated next to the iron foundry was hit by a single bomb. Considerable damage was caused, this being reported to the commission sent to investigate bomb damage after the war.

Also above Treves at this time were seven fighters of Kest 2 flying out of Saarbrücken, and a running fight developed between these and the rear formation of DH4s. A German two-seater who had also joined the fight was shot in the engine, stopping its prop, and was last seen diving away. Another enemy aircraft was also seen to drop away with its engine stopped and eventually to crash. This aircraft was claimed by two observers, Lt Quinton and Sgt Boocock, both being credited with a shared out of control victory. In the unenviable sixth position of the rear formation was 2Lt W.Legge and his observer 2Lt A.McKenzie. They received considerable attention from the enemy fighters and were seen to drop out of formation apparently under control, although closely pursued by two enemy fighters. Their aircraft eventually caught fire and crashed south-east of Trier, both occupants being killed. Vizefeldwebel Kurt Handrock received official credit in the German *Nachrichtenblatt der Luftfahrtruppen* for William Legge from Leith, Edinburgh and Alexander McKenzie, also a Scot, from Blacklunans, Perthshire, his first and only victory. This all-Scottish crew were buried at Cologne, both men being twenty-three years of age.

The de Havilland formations, constantly harassed, continued south flying over Merzig which lay on the Saar river eventually crossing the lines at Château-Salins. Both formations had been under heavy but inaccurate anti-aircraft fire throughout the trip, their only respite from the flak being while engaged by the Kest 2 fighters.

Note: Apart from the two formation leaders and the casualties, other crew records so far have not been found.

Reconnaissance

13th June			Take Off:	07.45
55 Squadron			Returned:	11.40
Lt C.A.Bridgland	2Lt E.R.Stewart	A7837		

Crossed lines at 19,000ft over Pont-à-Mousson then north-east to Metz, Boulay, Saarlouis, Saarbrücken and Homburg. Then flew south-east over St.Avold, re-crossed lines at Château-Salins, thirty-eight plates taken.

Target: Iron and Steel Furnaces at Dillingen

13th June			Take Off:	08.05
99 Squadron			Returned:	11.05
Formation 1				
Capt A.D.Taylor	Lt H.S.Notley	C6153	ret e/t t/o C6113	
Lt W.G.Stevenson	2Lt T.W.Wiggins	C6210		
Lt C.A.Vick	2Lt E.Beale	D1668		
Lt E.L.Doidge	2Lt W.B.Walker	C6149		
Lt H.D.West	2Lt J.Levy	D5573		
Lt K.D.Marshall	2Lt O.Bell	C6145		
Formation 2				
Lt M.T.S.Papenfus	Lt A.L.Benjamin	C6278		
Lt R.F.Freeland	2Lt R.E.Sothcott	D1666		
Lt F.G.Thompson	2Lt S.C.Thornley	D1669		
Lt J.W.Richards	2Lt E.J.Munson	D7223		
Lt E.A.Chapin	2Lt B.S.W.Taylor	C2173		
Lt J.H.Underwood	2Lt T.K.Ludgate	C6202	ret e/t	

An eventful day awaited 99 Squadron as they took off for their second visit to Dillingen in four days. Situated on the north bank of the River Saar, Dillingen housed many potential targets for the I.A.F. However, this day 99 Squadron led by Captain A.D.Taylor were after the steel works, and in particular their huge blast furnaces. Ten minutes after take-off Captain Taylor returned to Azelot with a snapped magneto drive, Lt Underwood and his observer 2Lt Ludgate also returned with engine trouble. Lt Marthinus Papenfus, as deputy leader, was now in command of the two formations as they headed north to cross the lines at Château-Salins.

Captain Taylor and his observer Lt Notley jumped into DH9 C6113 upon landing and were soon airborne in the hope of rejoining the formation. Crossing the lines meantime, the formations encountered heavy archie as they headed north towards the target. Captain Taylor, unable to find the formations, reluctantly returned to Azelot.

Attacking from a lower altitude than normal, six 230lb and eight 112lb bombs were dropped by the bombers. The lower attack altitude seemed to have worked as five hits were reported on the Burbacher Huttonn Iron and Steel works, two direct hits on blast furnaces, one north of the Saar river and one to the south. Two bursts were reported on the railway south of the station, while another was seen to hit a building south-west of the station. Bursts were also observed in the town, several around the church. How low the formations were when they bombed is not clear but all ten aircraft returned safely to Azelot; three enemy aircraft were spotted but there was no engagement. Lt Marthinus Papenfus was awarded the DFC. for his actions on this day which read as follows:

Lt Marthinus Theunis Steyn Papenfus
D.F.C. gazetted 21st September 1918

This officer displayed excellent judgement in a recent raid. Keeping his formation well together, and, descending to a low altitude, he led them well over an enemy factory and so enabled them to use their bombs most effectively. The success of this operation was very largely due to his fine leadership. In addition, he has taken part in eighteen raids as deputy leader of the formation, invariably showing the greatest keenness and devotion to duty.

Target: Factories and Railways at Hagondange

13th June			**Take Off:**	**09.15**
104 Squadron			**Returned:**	**11.45**
Lt W.J. Rivett-Carnac	Sgt W.E.Flexman 242568	C6267	W.I.A./D.O.W.	

Once again twelve DH9s of 104 Squadron set out for the factories and railways at Hagondange. It was a clear morning as the aircraft set out to cross the lines at Brin. Only twenty-five minutes into the flight and three aircraft from the first formation had already returned with engine trouble, leaving the remaining nine to carry on to the target via Charlevilly and Flevy.

Reaching Hagondange they let loose six 230lb and four 112lb from 13,000ft; three bursts were observed on the factory and one on the railway. Five fighters from Jasta 65 led by Leutnant Otto Fitzner took off from their base at Mars-la-Tour, and started to engage the rear formation of DH9s while still over the target. In the ensuing fight two were seen to go down under control from the concentrated fire of the observers. Unteroffizier Rudolf Kassner was killed in action crashing at Amanweiler this day. Unfortunately 104 Squadron didn't get away unscathed. DH9 C6267 was riddled with machine-gun fire, the pilot 2Lt W.J.Rivett-Carnac being wounded in the foot, while his observer Sergeant Walter Edward Flexman was hit in the lung. Rivett-Carnac put his nose down and managed to force land at Toul behind Allied lines, and was taken to the Gama Hospital in Toul. Flexman, however, had died of his wounds. Although crash landing on the Allied side Ltn Heinrich Zempel of Jasta 65 was credited with a DH9 at Uckingen at 12.45, German time being one hour ahead and so making his claim most valid. The remaining eight DH9s returned via Doncourt and Spoonville re-crossing the lines at Limey. Eighteen photos were taken while 1640 rounds had been fired by the observers. Sergeant Walter Edward Flexman from Worcester, aged twenty, was buried in the I.A.F. Cemetery in Charmes.

Note: Records for missing crews were unable to be located by the author.

Target: Triangle of Railways at Metz-Sablon

23rd June			**Take Off:**	**18.15**
99 Squadron			**Returned:**	**21.20**
Formation 1				
Capt W.D.Thom	Lt L.G.Claye	D1670		
Lt K.D.Marshall	2Lt O.Bell	C6145		
Lt N.S.Harper	2Lt D.G.Benson	C6210		
Lt H.D.West	2Lt J.Levy	D5573		
Lt M.T.S.Papenfus	Lt A.L.Benjamin	C6153		
Lt F.G.Thompson	2Lt S.C.Thornley	C6113		
Lt J.W.Richards	2Lt E.J.Munson	D7223	spare m/c	
Formation 2				
Capt V.Beecroft	2Lt R.E.Sothcott	D1666		
Lt E.A.Chapin	2Lt B.S.W.Taylor	B7653		
Lt S.M.Black	2Lt E.Singleton	D1669		
Lt H.Sanders	Lt W.W.A.Jenkin	C6149		
Lt C.A.Vick	2Lt E.Beale	D1668		
Lt J.H.Underwood	Lt T.K.Ludgate	D1679	spare m/c ret e/t	

The weather for most of the day was cloudy with occasional rain showers, so it wasn't until the late afternoon that the first squadron from Azelot, 99, headed north towards Metz-Sablon in two separate formations. The spare machine in the second formation flown by Lt Underwood, returned with engine trouble before reaching the lines. Crossing the lines at Pont-à-Mousson, the spare machine for the first formation flown by Lt J.W.Richards, departed company and headed home. Both formations, with a full complement of six bombers each, dropped eight 230lb and eight 112lb bombs, but no hits were observed due to low cloud. Anti-aircraft fire over the target was moderate but very accurate, Lt H.D.West and 2Lt J.Levy receiving slight damage to their machine. The two formations turned south re-crossing the lines at Pont-à-Mousson without further incident.

CHARLES ALFRED VICK, from Montreal, Canada, was twenty-six and a former marine engineer with Canadian Vickers Ltd between 1915 and 1917. He joined 99 Squadron in May 1918 but was hospitalised on 30th June and lost his flying category. He finally had to relinquish his commission in September 1918 due to ill-health, but with the honorary rank of Lieutenant.

Target: Railway Triangle at Metz-Sablon

23rd June			**Take Off:**	**18.20**
104 Squadron			**Returned:**	**20.30**
Formation 1				
Capt J.B.Home-Hay				

Formation 2			
Capt E.A.McKay			
Lt M.J.Ducray	2Lt R.L.Phillips	D1674	crashed 18.45

On a day mostly overcast with occasional rain showers, 104 Squadron was tasked with their third trip to Metz and its triangular sprawl of railway tracks. Captain Home-Hay would again be leading, as the two formations gained height above the field before setting out to cross the lines at Regnéville. Before reaching the lines Lt Ducray was seen to drop out of formation with engine failure, crash landing his machine near Azelot aerodrome, the machine being struck off strength. Lt Ducray was injured in the crash but recovered, and again flew with the Squadron; Phillips, however, was not to fly with 104 Squadron again.

Once over the lines the formations were reduced to ten machines. Engine trouble was the culprit yet again, the offending machine landing at Azelot at 19.30, leaving four bombers in the second formation. Passing overhead Chambley, the formations turned towards Metz which was seen through a small gap in the clouds. Moderate flak was encountered as six 230lb and eight 112lb bombs were dropped from thirteen thousand feet, results were un-observed due to cloud cover. No enemy aircraft engaged the formations, but observers fired off 762 rounds at three enemy aircraft seen below the formation, as well as a single balloon.

Re-crossing the lines at Pont-à-Mousson, all ten machines returned safely to Azelot along with twenty-one photos which were taken.

Note: Apart from the two formation leaders and casualties, records do not give any other crews.

Target: Railway Station at Thionville
Secondary Target: Railway and Station at Metz-Sablon

23rd June	**Take Off:**	**18.45**
55 Squadron	**Returned:**	**20.55**
Formation 1		
Capt F.Williams		
Lt S.L.Dowswell		
2Lt J.R.Bell		
Lt A.Clarke		
Lt E.Blythe		
2Lt G.A.Sweet		

Formation 2
Lt E.H.Van der Reit

As Sunday evening service finished the weather cleared sufficiently to allow the squadrons to take off. Five minutes after doing so number six in the second formation returned with engine trouble, while the rest continued to climb. Clouds made the climb to altitude very difficult but once through the last layer, bursting into sunshine, Captain Williams led his formation to Pont-à-Mousson where he joined Lt Van der Reit and his formation at 14,500ft. The bombers continued north against a strong north wind which slowed them down. While passing Metz heavy anti-aircraft fire opened up which had so nearly claimed Lt West and 2Lt Levy of 99 Squadron half an hour earlier. According to Capt Williams: "a shell burst with a report like thunder and blew a big hole in my left hand outer plane." Before reaching Thionville, Captain Williams could see the target was completely covered in cloud, so swinging the formation around, he decided to attack the railway station at Metz-Sablon which he had observed through a hole in the clouds. Unfortunately he could also see the fire of the anti-aircraft guns as well.

Sixteen 112lb, one 230lb, twelve 25lb bombs and twelve 20lb Coopers were released, but again no bursts were observed due to cloud. One enemy aircraft attacked the rear formation near the target as the formations headed south for the fifteen mile journey back to the lines, carrying nine photographic plates which had been exposed over the target. They landed back at Azelot in the gathering gloom. The hostile aircraft did no damage.

ERNEST HENRY VAN DER REIT arrived at St.Omer pilots pool in September 1917 with forty-one hours flying time in his log book. He was posted from 49 Reserve Squadron at Spittlegate, near Grantham, after being delayed to receive medical treatment. During his delay he sat another course at the Aerial Gunnery School at Turnberry, before finally getting his orders to proceed overseas. Leaving 55 at the end of June for Home Establishment, he learnt that he had been awarded the D.F.C. His citation read as follows:

Lt Ernest Henry Van der Reit
D.F.C. gazetted 3rd August 1918

This officer has taken part in thirty-eight raids, showing consistent determination and skill. During one raid the formation, of which he was the leader, was attacked when over the objective, by twenty-five enemy planes, and a running fight ensued to our lines, a distance of forty miles. By his skilful and resolute leadership he brought his formation back safely, destroying two enemy aeroplanes.

Note: Records are again incomplete for crews on this raid.

Target: Landau Chemical Works near Mannheim
Secondary Target: Foundries at Dillingen, Station at Metz

24th June	**Take Off:**	**08.30**
55 Squadron	**Returned:**	**12.10**
Formation 1		
Capt B.J.Silly		
Formation 2		
2Lt J.R.Bell		

Both formations were detailed to bomb the important Landau chemical works near Mannheim, the first time this target became scheduled to be attacked by daylight squadrons of the Independent Force. The first formation led by Captain Benjamin Silly took off, gaining height over the field, then headed out towards the lines. The second formation led by 2Lt John Bell took off fifteen minutes later, but failed to rendezvous with the first group due to cloud. The first formation, unable to wait any longer at the rendezvous point if it was to reach Mannheim, headed out towards the lines. This formation had two machines drop out with engine trouble before crossing the lines at 14,000ft at Fôret-de-Parroy. Once over the lines it was apparent that Landau would be impossible to reach, as the ground to the north-east was totally obscured by cloud. The formation therefore headed towards Dillingen which was just visible through a gap in the clouds. On arrival amongst heavy but inaccurate anti-aircraft fire they dropped one 230lb bomb and six 112lb bombs; five photographs were taken but no hits were observed due to cloud.

Failing to rendezvous, the second formation crossed the lines independently at 14,000ft above cloud over Château-Salins. To the north-east cloud blocked the way to Landau as it had for the first formation. To the north-west however, the Moselle river was visible north of Thionville. The de Havillands headed towards Thionville passing over Metz where the ever present heavy and accurate anti-aircraft fire opened up. The bombers carried on towards Thionville but once past Metz, Thionville was no longer visible, so 2Lt Bell turned the formation around and prepared to bomb Metz instead. As they approached Metz for a second time, six Albatros scouts were spotted but they did not engage. The formation dropped one 230lb, eight

112lb and twelve 25lb bombs on Metz, then headed south towards the lines shadowed but unmolested by the Albatros scouts.

The anti-aircraft batteries had found the height of the formation, badly damaging the lead aircraft flown by Bell. Although his machine was badly hit, he managed to get it home where the DH was struck off strength. The intense flak also claimed another victim as several observers reported an Albatros hit and going down under control. Both formations arrived home at Azelot simultaneously without further incident.

Note: Records are again incomplete for crews and have so far eluded the author.

Target: Railway Factories at Dillingen
Secondary Target: Railway and Factories at Saarbrücken

24th June			Take Off:	08.30
104 Squadron			**Returned:**	**12.00**
Formation 1				
Capt J.M.Heap			ret e/t 09.55	
Formation 2				
Capt E.A.McKay	Capt R.H.Wetherall			
Lt O.J.Lange	Sgt G.A.Smith	D7229	W.I.A./W.I.A.	
Lt M.J.Ducray	2Lt K.C.B.Woodman	D1674	W.I.A./W.I.A.	

Tasked with the Iron and Steel works as well as the railways at Dillingen, 104 Squadron would take off twenty minutes before 99 Squadron also tasked with the same objective. Taking off in bright early morning sunshine, the two formations led by Captain Heap gained height and then headed out north-east, to cross the lines at Château-Salins. Once over the lines Captain Heap started to experience engine trouble, so firing a white Very light he turned for home. Unfortunately two crews in the first formation took this signal for a washout of the raid, and returned with him. The remaining three aircraft from the first formation, joined the second formation, as Captain McKay took on the lead in a sky increasingly filling with cloud.

Flying north towards Dillingen the landscape was almost completely covered by cloud, and with strength down to nine machines Captain McKay turned north-east at St Avold and decided to bomb Saarbrücken instead.

Over Saarbrücken the formation of nine was intercepted by four enemy aircraft described as either Albatros DIII or DVs, and the fight ensued as they dropped six 230lb and six 112lb bombs from 13,500 ft. Six bursts were observed on the railway, but due to the attention of the fighters no more bursts were seen. The attack was hard pressed by the fighters with several pilots and observers being wounded. One enemy aircraft was seen to dive in flames through the formation, narrowly missing two DH9s after closing in on the lead aircraft of Capt McKay and Capt Robert Hodgson Wetherall. Lt R.J.Searle, a native of South Africa, was credited with an out of control victory as the enemy aircraft spun away, while Captain Wetherall was credited with a destroyed. Although no DH9s were lost, several machines were shot up. Lt O.J.Lange and his observer Sgt G.A.Smith were both wounded, while 2Lt K.C.B.Woodman, an observer, was also wounded.

Re-crossing the lines at Arracourt Lt Lange and Sgt Smith nursed their crippled machine but to no avail, crash landing near Azelot. Smith who was the worse of the two was treated in Charmes Hospital. Oscar Jacob Lange, from Green Leaf Avenue, Chicago, Illinois, remained with 104 Squadron. Despite the firing of 1,244 rounds by observers, no German aircraft were reported lost this day amongst the Jastas, although the enemy fighters were probably from Kest 2, which was stationed at Saabrücken at this time.

Note: A white Very light was the signal to bomb the target. A green light was a signal to abort the raid, and a red Very light meant enemy aircraft. Perhaps Heap would have been better firing a green Very light. However, he may then have had two formations following him back. Lt Ducray was injured when he crashed his machine landing back at Azelot; whether Woodman was his observer is not clear in the available records concerning this raid, his machine however may well have been shot about inducing his crash.

This was CAPTAIN JOSEPH MILNE HEAP's last operation. From Birkenhead, Cheshire, this former railway engineering student had been born in March 1889, but received his education at McGill University, Montreal, pre-war. A Captain in the A.S.C., he had joined the R.F.C. in August 1916 and flown with No.2 Squadron between November 1916 and July 1917. After a period as an instructor, he'd been sent to 104 Squadron in May 1918. Hospitalised on 27th June 1918, he eventually had to leave the R.A.F. through ill-health in October 1919.

Target: Factory and Railway Station at Dillingen
Target: Factory and Railway at Saarbrücken

24th June			Take Off:	08.50
99 Squadron			Returned:	13.25/12.10

Formation 1

Capt A.D.Taylor	Lt H.S.Notley	C6153	
Lt F.G.Thompson	2Lt S.C.Thornley	C6113	
Lt J.H.Underwood	2Lt T.K.Ludgate	C6202	
Lt M.T.S.Papenfus	Lt A.L.Benjamin	D5568	
Lt H.D.West	2Lt J.Levy	C6210	
Lt R.F.Freeland	2Lt R.E.Sothcott	C1666	ret e/t10.50
Lt J.W.Richards	2Lt E.J.Munson	D7223	ret e/t spare m/c

Formation 2

Capt V.Beecroft	2Lt R.F.Connell	C6278	
Lt E.A.Chapin	2Lt B.S.W.Taylor	B7653	
Lt N.S.Harper	2Lt D.G.Benson	D5570	
Lt H.Sanders	2Lt W.W.A.Jenkin	C6149	photo machine
Lt C.A.Vick	2Lt E.Beale	C1668	
2Lt J.Whattam	2Lt T.W.Wiggins	C1679	ret e/t
Lt S.M.Black	2Lt E.Singleton	C1669	ret e/t spare m/c

On an overcast morning 99 Squadron was tasked with hitting the Iron and Steel works at Dillingen, as well as the important railway lines running through the town which connected the towns of Treves and Saarbrücken.

As normal two spare aircraft accompanied the formations as they headed north to cross the lines at Château-Salins. The unreliable Siddeley Puma engines again took their toll on both formations. Lt Richards and 2Lt Munson were the first to return home being unable to keep up with the formation, shortly followed by 2Lt Whattam and 2Lt Wiggins, then Lt Black and 2Lt Singleton from the second formation, both with engine trouble. The remaining eleven machines continued north being quickly reduced to ten, Lt Freeland and 2Lt Sothcott leaving the first formation with spark plug trouble, landing back at Azelot at 10.50.

The two formations continued north towards Saarbrücken looking down on an almost overcast landscape. The first, led by Captain Ashley Dudley Taylor turned north-west at Saarbrücken to follow the Saar river towards Dillingen. The second formation led by Captain Victor Beecroft was unable to spot Dillingen through the overcast and decided to bomb Saarbrücken just visible through a hole in the overcast. Three 230lb and four 112lb bombs were dropped with bursts observed on a railway shed south-east of the town, while another burst was observed in the centre of town, but no other bursts were seen due to cloud cover. Thirteen photos were taken by Lt Sanders and 2Lt Jenkin.

The first formation on reaching Dillingen encountered flak from the ten 9cm anti-aircraft guns of the town's battery. The flak was inaccurate as the five machines dropped three 230lb and four 112lb bombs but observed no hits due to cloud cover. Two enemy aircraft were spotted below the formation at 10,000ft but no engagement took place. The second formation returned from Saarbrücken without incident while the first had a more eventful return flight becoming lost and arriving home after four and a half hours in the air. They were thankful for their aircraft's endurance.

Target: Ammunition Factories at Karlsruhe

25th June			Take Off:	04.15
104 Squadron			Returned:	08.00

Formation 1
Capt J.B.Home-Hay

Lt S.C.M.Pontin	2Lt J.Arnold	C2170	P.O.W./P.O.W.

Formation 2

2Lt A.W.Robertson	Lt M.H.Cole	D1675	W.I.A.
Lt E.W.Mundy	2Lt H.A.B.Jackson	C6260	W.I.A./D.O.W.

With a high wind from the north-west and drifting banks of clouds, Captain Home-Hay led 104 Squadron east after gaining height over the field to cross the lines at Badonviller, just north of Raon-l'-Etape. Engine trouble hit the formations hard, as one by one machines returned leaving only eight DH9s to continue on to Karlsruhe. The eight remaining aircraft joined to make one formation as they headed east towards Saverne where another DH9 left the formation, dropping its 230lb bomb in the forests west of the town to enable it to get home. Later it was established the engine had been hit by flak before reaching Saverne.

Down to seven the formation continued north-east towards Haguenau. Following the Rhine north-east the formation arrived over Karlsruhe where they dropped six 112lb and four 230lb bombs. A direct hit was observed on the Metalurgie buildings while another explosion was observed near the railway. Two more bursts were seen, one on houses near the gas works, and another on the town's barracks.

Leaving Karlsruhe to the west the formation was being tailed by five enemy aircraft of Kest 1b which were stationed at Karlsruhe. Overhead Bitche, which lay south-east of Saarbrücken, a running fight ensued with the fighters. Lt Mundy was wounded in the right arm and leg while his observer 2Lt Jackson was shot through the stomach; 2Lt Robertson was also wounded although his observer Lt Cole survived unscathed. Lt Pontin and his observer 2Lt Arnold left the formation diving away with engine trouble. Sgt Willi Rössel was credited with this victory, his only one of the war. The fight continued and despite the wounded crew all six remaining aircraft returned to Azelot. The engagement was fierce with the observers expending 1660 rounds of ammunition and claiming two aircraft driven down. Observers managed to take thirty-four photos while also reporting Kest aircraft using incendiary rounds. Both Robertson and Mundy survived their wounds but unfortunately 2Lt Jackson had died from his. Both Pontin and Arnold survived to be prisoners of war managing to crash land their aircraft east of the Vosges. No German losses this day match any claims made by the observers. Photographs later revealed two bursts on the main station, several bursts on buildings to the east of the Cartoucherie, and two bursts in buildings west of the goods station.

Hugh Arthur Bruce Jackson came from Victoria in British Columbia, and was only nineteen years of age; he was buried at Charmes in the I.A.F. Cemetery. Anthony William Robertson received the D.F.C. for his actions, his citation read as follows:

2Lt Anthony William Robertson
D.F.C. gazetted 3rd August 1918
A very gallant and determined pilot. Whilst engaged in a long-distance bombing raid, the formation of which this officer was acting leader, was heavily attacked by hostile aircraft whilst over the objective. He took a leading and brilliant part in the action, and received a severe wound which paralysed his right arm. Despite this he succeeded in flying home.

Note: Robertson became leader of the second formation when his leader returned with engine trouble. However, when he and Mundy were the only two aircraft left in the second formation they joined the first led by Captain Home-Hay. Again poor records do not help regarding crews.

Target: Railway and Sidings at Offenburg

25th June			Take Off:	04.45
99 Squadron			Returned:	08.15

Formation 1

Capt W.D.Thom	Lt L.G.Claye	D1670	
Lt N.S.Harper	2Lt D.G.Benson	D5570	K.I.A./K.I.A.
Lt C.A.Vick	2Lt E.Beale	D1668	

Lt K.D.Marshall	2Lt O.Bell	C6145	
Lt H.Sanders	Lt W.W.L.Jenkin	C6149	/D.O.W.
Lt J.H.Underwood	2Lt T.K.Ludgate	C6203	ret pilot ill 06.15
Lt H.D.West	2Lt J.Levy	C6210	ret e/t 05.45

Formation 2			
Capt A.D.Taylor	Lt H.S.Notley	C6153	
Lt F.G.Thompson	2Lt S.C.Thornley	C6113	
Lt M.T.S.Papenfus	Lt A.L.Benjamin	C6278	
Lt J.W.Richards	2Lt E.J.Munson	D7223	
Lt S.M.Black	2Lt E.Singleton	D1669	
2Lt J.Whattam	2Lt T.W.Wiggins	B7653	crashed on return
Lt R.F.Freeland	2Lt R.E.Sothcott	D1666	ret e/t 05.20

Taking off fourteen strong, 99 Squadron headed east towards the lines for their first trip to Offenburg. Situated forty-five miles over the lines on the eastern side of the Rhine valley, Offenburg station was part of the extensive rail network running down this side of the Rhine from Cologne in the north, past Coblenz, Mainz and Karlsruhe right down to the Swiss border in the south. Crossing the lines at Raon-l'-Etape the fourteen DH9s were already down to eleven with Lt Freeland and 2Lt Sothcott and Lt West and 2Lt Levy both returning with engine trouble; Lt Underwood and 2Lt Ludgate also returned due to pilot sickness.

Approaching Offenburg accurate archie was encountered while seven enemy scouts were also spotted as the DH9s dropped seven 230lb and eight 112lb bombs on the station below. Wheeling round for the homeward leg the DH9s had to contend not only with the accurate flak but a running fight with the scouts of Kest 5 from their airfield at Freiburg. Lt N.S.Harper and 2Lt D.G.Benson in D5570 were seen to drop out of formation gliding down under control, and last observed south of Strasbourg on the west side of the Rhine followed by five enemy aircraft. The remaining ten DH9s made it back to Azelot where more bad luck awaited the crews as 2Lt Whattam and 2Lt Wiggins crashed on landing both escaping serious injury. Lt W.W.A.Jenkin, however, was not so lucky being already dead from an anti-aircraft wound to the head when lifted from the back cockpit.

Despite the attention of the fighters and flak, the photo machine crewed by Lt Sanders and Lt Jenkin managed to take eighteen plates in around the target area revealing several hits on tracks north of the station, and direct hits on an engine shed and barracks. It would appear from the amount of photos taken that Jenkin was hit leaving the target, or on the return journey crossing the lines. Although Lt Harper and 2Lt Benson were listed as missing in action, they unfortunately were killed, the one and only victory of Vizefeldwebel Heidfeld previously of Jasta 47w and now with Kest 5. The all-Canadian crew of Norman Stuart Harper, and Donald Good Benson, were buried at Niederzwehren in Germany. Harper was from Kamloops, British Columbia, while Benson aged twenty-one was from Aylmer West, Ontario. William Walter Lloyd Jenkin was buried in Charmes Cemetery; aged twenty he came from Liskeard in Cornwall.

Target: Ammunition Factories at Karlsruhe
Secondary Target:Railway and Factories at Saarbrücken

25th June		**Take Off:**	**05.32**
55 Squadron		**Returned:**	**08.40**
Formation 1			
Capt F.Williams	Capt R.P.Ward		
2Lt F.F.H.Bryan		forced landing e/t	

Formation 2			
Lt E.H.Van der Reit			
2Lt G.A.Sweet	2Lt C.R.F.Goodyear	B7866	K.I.A./K.I.A.
Lt D.J.Waterous			
2Lt J.Cunliffe		ret e/t 07.15	

After gaining height over the airfield, both formations headed out north-west towards the lines. Before reaching them, 2Lt Bryan dropped out of the first formation due to engine trouble, having to force-land at Bar-le-Duc which lay on the Allied side of the lines. The remaining machines crossed at Château-Salins at

14,500ft where a stronger than forecast wind and the sight of the Rhine valley covered in cloud, would mean a shorter trip than the one planned to Karlsruhe.

Captain Williams turned the formations north, and headed towards the factories and station at Saarbrücken. As the squadron approached, moderate but accurate anti-aircraft fire opened up as the formations let loose three 230lb, ten 112lb and twelve 25lb bombs, several good bursts being observed on the factories and railways, while ten photographic plates were exposed.

Leaving Saarbrücken to the west the Squadron were confronted by two enemy aircraft of Kest 2. The two Albatrosses caught up with the formations and flew alongside at a distance due to the observers' fire. Suddenly one Albatros pilot flew right into the second formation firing as he went, shooting down 2Lt Sweet and 2Lt Goodyear, in DH4 B7866 from a few yards range. A large piece of fabric and three-ply came off their machine as it fell out of formation, and they were seen going down out of control five miles west of Saarbrücken. Nine other enemy aircraft joined the fight harassing the remaining eight de Havillands all the way to the lines. Captain Williams recorded in his memoirs: "the Huns followed us to the lines, they might have followed us back to the aerodrome for all the opposition on our side of the lines". Offizierstellvertreter Gottlieb Vothknecht previously of Jastas 14 and 24 received official confirmation for George Sweet and Charles Goodyear. Both men were killed making this Vothknecht's third and last victory of the war. George Arscott Sweet from Hamilton, Ontario, and Charles Richards Frederick Goodyear aged nineteen from Wallasey in Cheshire, were both buried at Kalhausen in France.

Arriving back at Azelot Captain Williams was confronted by Major Alex Gray, Commanding Officer of 55 Squadron who pointed out the wind wasn't too strong on paper, and felt Williams had failed to reach the target through lack of determination, . . . Oh, to be home!

Photographs showed bursts near the Cavalry barracks and the gas works. German reports stated that four people were killed, eight seriously and eight slightly injured.

RICHARD PERCYVALE WARD was born on 21st August 1894. He first served with the Welsh Regiment before being seconded to the Royal Flying Corps. He went to the School of Aerial Gunnery at Hythe, and was promoted to Captain on 19th October 1917. A Military Cross was gazetted on 1st November 1917, followed by a Croix de Guerre which was awarded while serving with 55 Squadron. Posted to Home Establishment on 29th August 1918, Ward was awarded a D.F.C. which was gazetted a month later. After the war ended he returned to the Army and transferred to the 3rd Battalion Royal Welsh Fusiliers on 7th March 1919. His home address given during the war was 88 Marlboro Road, Donnybrook, Dublin. His D.F.C. citation read as follows:

Captain Richard Percyvale Ward (Royal Welsh Fusiliers)
D.F.C. gazetted 21st September 1918

Has been engaged on thirty-seven bombing raids, and on ten photographic reconnaissances, and has been in nearly all the raids in which severe fighting has taken place. Captain Ward has displayed the greatest coolness and courage in action, combined with ability and keenness in the work entrusted to him.

Note: Records are again lacking regarding crews.

Reconnaissance

25th June			Take Off:	07.15
55 Squadron			Returned:	11.45
Lt A.S.Keep	2Lt W.R.Patey	A7942		

Crossed lines at Pont-à-Mousson at 19,000ft and proceeded to Frescaty aerodrome (five large enemy aircraft out), Metzerwiege to Bettsdorf (new railway), Bolchen (one large machine on ground, two in air) then supposed aerodrome at Ham St.Avold, large dump at Walmen, re-crossed lines at Nomeny at 22,000ft, twelve plates exposed.

Reconnaissance

25th June			Take Off:	07.55
55 Squadron			Returned:	12.25
Capt B.J.Silly	Lt J.Parke	A7763		

Crossed lines at Blâmont at 19,000ft. Exposed plates at Mettingen, Pfalzburg and railway sidings through clouds. Re-crossed at Château-Salins, fourteen plates taken.

Target: Factory and Station at Karlsruhe

26th June				**Take Off:**	**10.00**
104 Squadron				**Returned:**	**14.00**
Formation 1					
Capt J.B.Home-Hay					
Lt C.G.Jenyns	Lt H.C.Davis	C6256		P.O.W./K.I.A.	
Formation 2					
Capt E.A.McKay				ret e/t 11.55	
Lt J.Valentine	Sgt A.C.Wallace	D5658			

Leading the mass raid on Karlsruhe by all three daylight squadrons, Captain Home-Hay had a hard job not only keeping his two formations together, but also managing to rendezvous with the two other units. Eventually the three squadrons headed east, 99 leading, and 55 flying higher and in front with 104 the tail enders. Engine trouble plagued 104 as it did 99 Squadron on this raid. Five of the second formation, and one of the first returned being unable to keep formation due to engine trouble, while number three in the first formation had already returned with a split radiator. Lt Valentine and his observer Sgt Wallace joined the first formation giving 104 a total of five machines.

Arriving over Karlsruhe at 13,500/15,500ft (two reports in the Public Records Office give very vague information regarding this raid, and both give two different bombing heights), 104 Squadron was down to three machines dropping two 230lb and two 112lb bombs observing hits on the railways. Fifteen enemy aircraft were reported over the objective but did not attack until the bombers turned for home.

The attention from so many hostile fighters forced the combined force of three Squadrons to fly directly back to the lines, crossing over Haguenau directly towards Raon-l'-Etape. 55 Squadron lost a machine to Kest 1b west of Haguenau on the return trip, fortunately 104 Squadron's three machines made it back to Azelot after prolonged attack by hostile scouts. Only three machines from 104 Squadron actually bombed Karlsruhe, so two machines went missing. Lt C.G.Jenyns and Lt H.C.Davis were shot down by Oberleutnant Hans Schlieter the CO of Jasta 70 at Schirmeck at 13:05 German time. The reason for two missing machines over Karlsruhe could be that 104 Squadron were intercepted as they crossed the lines, as Schirmeck is close to Raon-l'-Etape. The other reason is that Oberleutnant Schlieter recorded his victory at 13.05 German time, which was one hour ahead of British time and only two hours into the raid. A good reason for believing 104 Squadron was intercepted as they crossed the lines is the story of DH9 D5658 piloted by an American, Lt James Valentine, and Sgt Wallace. This aircraft was seen to fire a red Very light and glide away towards Soultz, which lay south of Colmar near the Swiss border, a considerable distance from Karlsruhe, the target, and the return journey taken by the three formations. If D5658 had engine trouble, one would have expected the crew to glide back over the lines, unless this path was blocked by enemy fighters. Reports of a DH9 forced to land by Swiss anti-aircraft fire could be a possibility as both crew eventually returned to operations along with their aircraft. The other possibility is that Valentine and Wallace simply got lost. Lt Davis was killed, while Lt Jenyns was wounded and became a prisoner of war. Harold Charles Davis from the 9th Essex Regiment was twenty-four when he was killed, and buried at Plaine in France.

CHARLES GAMBIER JENYNS was born on 1st August 1899. He attended Latterthwaite Church of England School, Oaklands Road, Bromley in Kent. From here he joined the London Stock Exchange as a clerk, and worked there from September 1914 to June 1917. He joined 104 Squadron on 9th January 1918, and was repatriated on 13th December 1918. In his records it states that he was wounded on the 26th when shot down. The family's address during the war was Broadwater, 56 Tweedy Road, Bromley in Kent.

Target: Railway and Workshops at Karlsruhe

26th June			Take Off:	10.00
99 Squadron			Returned:	14.00

Formation 1

Capt W.D.Thom	Lt L.G.Claye	D1670	
Lt R.F.Freeland	2Lt R.E.Sothcott	D5568	
Lt K.D.Marshall	2Lt O.Bell	C6145	
Lt J.W.Richards	2Lt E.J.Munson	D7223	ret vacuum control
Lt M.T.S.Papenfus	Lt A.L.Benjamin	C6153	
Lt H.D.West	2Lt J.Levy	C6210	

Formation 2

Lt H.Sanders	2Lt W.B.Walker	C6202	ret e/t
Lt E.A.Chapin	2Lt B.S.W.Taylor	C2173	ret obs sick
Lt S.M.Black	2Lt E.Singleton	D1669	ret e/t
Lt C.A.Vick	2Lt E.Beale	D1668	ret e/t
2Lt J.Whattam	2Lt T.K.Ludgate	C6196	ret e/t
Lt F.G.Thompson	2Lt S.C.Thornley	C6113	

Captain William Dorian Thom would be leading 99 Squadron with Lt Sanders leading the second formation for the massed attack on Karlsruhe, together with 55 and 104 Squadrons. (Captain Beecroft was unable to lead due to illness.) The formations had trouble at the rendezvous and 99 Squadron finally set off to cross the lines with 104 Squadron in tow. 55 Squadron were flying above and in front due to superior engine performance.

Heading east to cross the lines at Raon-l'-Etape the twelve DH 9s quickly became six as four machines from the second formation, including the lead flown by Lt Sanders, returned due to engine trouble. Lt Chapin also headed for home as his observer 2Lt Taylor fainted leaving Lt Thompson to join the first formation, however the seven soon became six after Lt Richards and 2Lt Munson returned with vacuum control problems.

Once over the lines the formations continued east until picking up the Rhine river where they turned north-west up the Rhine valley towards Karlsruhe. Approaching the town, the workshops were obscured by cloud so 99 Squadron dropped their three 230lb and six 112lb bombs on the railway and station. Bursts were observed on and near the sidings with several bursts near a powder factory. However, more attention was now being paid to four enemy scouts seen approaching. The scouts were more interested in 104 Squadron and as the six DH9s of 99 Squadron headed for home, five more enemy scouts were spotted near Haguenau but these also went after 104 Squadron. The DH9s of 99 Squadron returned safely to Azelot; Lt Benjamin managed two pictures of the Suffleheim Dumps near Karlsruhe before the camera jammed. Although only 50% of 99 Squadron's machines made it to Karlsruhe they were not alone; only twenty bombers out of a possible thirty-six from the three squadrons made it to the target.

A bomb damage assessment made after the war by the Air Ministry concluded that 99 Squadron had been on target. One bomb fell in the Shunting Station damaging the lines. Several bombs fell in and around the town's waterworks doing little damage. Explosions were also recorded in the Durlach Electricity Works and the Unterburg & Co Works causing no damage. Obviously this damage was attributed to all three squadrons of the I.A.F., and clearly illustrates how little impact could be made with the bombs of the time even when targets were reached in force.

Target: Railway and Workshop at Karlsruhe

26th June			Take Off:	10.10
55 Squadron			Returned:	14.10

Formation 1

Capt B.J.Silly

2Lt F.F.H.Bryan	Sgt A.Boocock	A8073	P.O.W./P.O.W.

Formation 2

2Lt J.R.Bell

2Lt E.J.Whyte			ret e/t 11.45

All three squadrons from Azelot were detailed to bomb the Karlsruhe workshops. It was hoped this would be one of many massed formation attacks of thirty-six bombers or more, which would shut down or at least seriously damage a target, for a considerable amount of time. The formation led by Captain Silly climbed over the field and headed out south-west to cross the lines already short of one machine, 2Lt E.J.Whyte returning through sickness.

Crossing the lines at Raon-l'-Etape, the formations continued east until picking up the Rhine valley where they then headed north-west, following the Rhine to Karlsruhe. The main target was the workshops, but they were obscured by cloud, so bombs were dropped on the station and railway lines instead. Good results were observed despite the heavy and accurate anti-aircraft fire, as sixteen 112lb, two 230lb, eight 25lb bombs and two 40lb phosphorous bombs fell onto the tracks and sidings.

As the formations turned for home ten enemy aircraft were seen to the north of the town. Kest 1b were stationed at Karlsruhe, and with prior warning of an attack through the improving network of home defence communications, the fighters had climbed up to the bombers' height, and were ready to attack. Kest 1b engaged the two flights in a running battle as they headed south-west, straight for the lines. As the bombers approached Haguenau, DH4 A8073 flown by 2Lt F.F.H.Bryan and his observer Sergeant A.Boocock was seen to go down under control, finally landing in a field south of Saverne. Both men survived and were taken prisoner.

Ltn Willi Rosenstein of Kest 1b claimed his third victory as the fight continued up to the lines. Rosenstein had learnt to fly pre-war and had already seen combat with Jasta 27. He would end the war with nine victories following his return to the Western Front with Jasta 40. The DH4s crossed the lines at Raon-l'-Etape without further loss, and despite the attentions of archie and fighters, had managed to take twenty-eight photographic plates.

Note: Records for this raid are incomplete, however 2Lt John Ross Bell was the leader of the second formation despite his rank and would rise up quickly through the hierarchy of 55 Squadron in the coming months.

Reconnaissance

26th June			Take Off:	15.30
55 Squadron			Returned:	19.00
Capt F.Williams	Capt R.P.Ward	A7942		

Crossed lines at Delme at 18,000ft, exposed plates over Bolchen (two enemy aircraft on ground, one at 17,000ft), then to St.Avold. Plates exposed at Genweiler-Saargemund aerodrome, Sarre-Union aerodrome, new railway from Mackweiler to Fleicheim aerodrome, and over Sarrebourg and Buhl. Forty-two plates exposed in all.

Target: Railway Workshops at Thionville

27th June		Take Off:	14.25
104 Squadron		Returned:	17.20
Formation 1			
Capt E.A.McKay	Capt R.H.Wetherall		
Lt G.C.Body	2Lt L.G.Norden		
2Lt O.J.Lange	Sgt V.G.McCabe 263228		
2Lt R.J.Searle	2Lt M.B.Cole		
Lt E.Cartwright	2Lt A.G.L.Mullen		
Lt T.L.McConchie	Lt R.A.C.Brie	ret e/t 16.20	

Leading the combined raid on the railway workshops at Thionville, Capt Evans Alexander McKay took five other DH9s of 104 Squadron, gained height above Azelot, and attempted to rendezvous with 99 and 55 Squadron. Although smoother than the previous day, the meeting of all three squadrons was still creating problems. However, they eventually headed north to cross the lines at Pont-à-Mousson with 104 Squadron leading and 99 Squadron in tow; 55 Squadron were also present but took up their position above the two DH9 formations as on previous combined raids.

Once over the lines the formation headed north-west towards Conflans hoping to avoid the anti-aircraft battery at Metz, however they strayed too near and came under fire, several bursts coming close. Prior to their arrival at Thionville, 104 Squadron lost 2Lt McConchie and his observer 2Lt Brie who dropped out of formation with engine trouble; they also had a damaged wing, both 'wounds' possibly the work of flak from Metz. The remaining five machines arrived over Thionville at 14,000ft dropping two 230lb and six 112lb bombs, bursts were seen east of the objective as attention turned to the arrival of Jasta 18 from Metz. The engagement was hard pressed with the rear Squadron, 99, losing a machine, 104 returning to Azelot unscathed to find McConchie and Brie safe; twelve photos of the target area were taken. Air Ministry records report that the Carlshutte works at Thionville were hit on the 27th, but no damage was done.

Target: Station and Sidings at Thionville

27th June			Take Off:	14.15
99 Squadron			Returned:	17.15
Formation 1				
Capt A.D.Taylor	Lt H.S.Notley	C6153		
Lt R.F.Freeland	Lt L.G.Claye	C1679	ret e/t 15.45	
Lt F.G.Thompson	2Lt S.C.Thornley	C6113		
2Lt J.Whattam	2Lt T.K.Ludgate	C6210		
Lt M.T.S.Papenfus	Lt A.L.Benjamin	D5568	photo machine	
Lt J.W.Richards	2Lt E.J.Munson	D7223		
Formation 2				
Capt V.Beecroft	Lt R.F.Connell	C6278		
Lt E.A.Chapin	2Lt T.W.Wiggins	D1669	K.I.A./K.I.A.	
Lt S.M.Black	2Lt E.Singleton	C2173		
Lt H.Sanders	2Lt W.B.Walker	C1670	W.I.A./photo m/c	
Lt C.A.Vick	2Lt E.Beale	C1668		
Lt K.D.Marshall	2Lt O.Bell	C6145		

Once again the daylight squadrons of the I.A.F. would attempt a combined raid in the hope of causing maximum damage or total destruction of a single target. Thionville lying approximately twenty-five miles over the lines, was the target with 104 the lead Squadron, followed by 99. 55 Squadron would fly above as on the previous day. Captain Taylor and the recovered Captain Beecroft would lead the two formations of 99 Squadron in the hope that their greater experience would help in keeping the formations together, and thereby reduce casualties.

Climbing over the field the two formations headed out north to cross the lines at Pont-à-Mousson, engine trouble forcing Lt Freeland and Lt Claye to return as they could not keep formation. The remaining eleven DH9s continued north where they encountered moderate archie over Metz. Thionville was finally reached where seven 230lb and eight 112lb bombs were dropped. Fifteen photos were taken of the target area, some bursts were observed south and east of the railway but more pressing on the minds of the observers was the arrival of Jasta 18 from their aerodrome at Montingen near Metz.

Heading for home, 99 Squadron being the tail end formation, received most of the attention from the hard pressing Jasta as they attempted to force aircraft out of formation. Lt Elliott Chapin and 2Lt Thomas Wiggins were seen to drop out of formation in flames, spinning down and eventually breaking up in the air. Both men were killed, the sixth victory of Lt Hans Müller of Jasta 18. The engagement was intense with 2Lt Walker firing eighty rounds at two hundred yards range into an enemy scout which was seen to trail smoke then catch fire and enter into a vertical dive. Another enemy scout was claimed by 2Lt Singleton who fired two hundred rounds at a scout to the right of the formation which glided away and then broke up in the air after about five seconds. Both observers were given victories for these claims, Lt Walker being awarded the Distinguished Flying Cross for this action as well as his work on other raids. Despite the intense pressure of Jasta 18 the formations stayed together and the remaining ten DH9s made it back to Azelot. Lt Sanders managed this despite a bullet wound below the knee. Three enemy scouts were claimed in this engagement, two by 99 Squadron and one by 55 Squadron. However Jasta 18 suffered no losses this day so the enemy scout seen breaking up was probably DH9 D1669 flown by Lt Chapin and 2Lt Wiggins. Chapin aged twenty-three, and Wiggins from the 17th Lancashire Fusiliers, were both buried at Chambières in France.

Beecroft's leadership was bitterly criticised by some who had been on this raid. He had mistook the target and took his flight on a wide turn to start another bomb run. However the other formations (including Captain Taylor's) continued onward to the correct target, leaving Beecroft's flight out on their own and easy prey. During the turn the formation had become disorganised, and Lt Marshall was firing green Very lights to draw his leader's attention to their plight. With the single formation broken, an enemy scout had slipped in and was firing at Chapin and Wiggins from nearly point-blank range. Jasta 18 were driven off by the diving DH4s of 55 Squadron, and the remnants of Beecroft's flight eventually joined the other DH9s. Beecroft recorded later that he was tapped on the shoulder by his observer Connell, and watched as Wiggins scrambled out of his burning cockpit and jumped to his death rather then burn.

ELLIOT ADAMS CHAPIN was born on 10th May 1895 at Somerville, Massachusetts, USA. He was educated at Newton High School, and later at Phillips Andover Academy graduating with the class of 1914. While studying at Harvard College he was a keen player of both football and baseball. At the end of his junior year he enlisted in the USNRF Coast Patrol, after having been declined the US Aviation Service due to a minor defect in one eye. Eager for action he obtained an honourable discharge from the USNRF and enlisted in the Royal Flying Corps on 26th August 1917. He reported at Toronto, Canada, and received his training at Deseronto and Long Branch receiving further training at Fort Worth, Texas. In December 1917 he was commissioned 2Lt. On 31st December he set sail from Halifax on the *Tunisian*. More training followed at Old Sarum, Salisbury, and he was commissioned Lt in April. In early May he was ordered to France where he joined 99 Squadron. Squadron colleagues claimed that after Chapin's machine caught fire at about thirteen thousand feet, he turned to his observer and shook hands as their machine started to plummet down.

Lt William Beresford Walker (Highland Light Infantry)
D.F.C. gazetted 21st September 1918
This officer has taken part in twenty-one bomb raids, and has rendered excellent and valuable service in photography and general observation. He has shown himself a brave and skilful officer in action, notably on one occasion when his formation was attacked by twelve hostile scouts which approached to within short range; he engaged one at 150 yards and drove it down in flames. In another engagement he attacked one enemy aeroplane at close range and drove it down; he then engaged several others with good effect.

Target: Railway Workshop east of Thionville

27th June			Take Off:	14.30
55 Squadron			Returned:	17.35
Formation 1				
Capt F.Williams	Sgt E.Clare/Price	B3957		
Lt A.S.Keep	2Lt W.R.Patey	A7781	photo machine	
Lt A.Clarke				
2Lt J.Cunliffe				
Lt D.J.Waterous				
Lt S.L.Dowswell				
Formation 2				
Lt E.F.Van der Reit				
Lt P.E.Welchman				
2Lt C.R.Whitelock				
Lt E.Blythe				
Lt C.A.Bridgland			photo machine	
Lt E.Young			e/t force-landed	

A three-squadron attack was again aimed at railway workshops, this time at Thionville. The lead squadron on this day was 104 Squadron, followed by 55 led by Captain F.Williams; 99 Squadron would also participate being the rear formation. The weather in the morning was overcast, but gaps in the clouds had appeared by the afternoon, giving the three squadrons a better chance of doing serious damage, to an important part of the railway network supplying Germany's armies on the Western Front.

The formations climbed over the airfield through cloud and headed out towards the lines. Lt E.Young dropped out of formation with engine trouble and force-landed at St Dizier, while the rest of 55 Squadron followed the lead Squadron, 104, crossing the lines at Pont-à-Mousson. The formation continued north over Metz where a moderate barrage of flak opened up, they then carried on towards Thionville where fourteen 112lb, two 230lb, and twenty-four 25lb bombs went down hopefully on the target which was obscured by light cloud.

The formation turned south-east and headed for the lines, and the rear Squadron, 99, was seen to come under attack by twelve enemy aircraft. Captain Williams turned back with his flight of five DH4s in an attempt to discourage the enemy aircraft from continuing their pursuit. Lt Dowswell joined with the second formation of 55 Squadron and headed towards the lines still following 104 Squadron.

The enemy aircraft were a mixed formation of two Fokker Triplanes, and ten Albatros DVs, all with red wings and white fuselages. Led by Ltn August Raben, Jasta 18 had moved into Montingen aerodrome near Metz on 14th June. The fighting was fierce with Jasta 18 trying to split the flights up, and so make it easier to single out aircraft for attack. One enemy aircraft attacked from under the lower left wing of the machine flown by Captain Williams, passing up to the tail, where Sergeant Ernest Clare fired a whole drum into it.

The enemy aircraft banked away down under the tail falling out of control and crashing into a wood. Captain Williams flying B3957, or 'Number Six' as he called it, was fortunate to make it home, one of his elevator controls having been shot through. Donald Waterous was to have an even narrower escape. After landing he noticed a bullet hole in the back of his seat, and assumed the round must have struck when he was leaning out of his seat. Despite the attention of Jasta 18, all eleven machines of 55 Squadron returned to Azelot.

Captain 'Billy' Williams was not in favour of these combined raids. He noted in his diary that 104 Squadron led very slowly and badly. Also they did not make use of a large cloud bank which stretched from Verdun to the target, which he would have used making it harder for the flak crews. Before leaving Azelot Williams was told: "Don't let the Hun bag the nines." He later wrote in his diary regarding this incident: "Good Lord, he'll bag the lot if we don't stop him." Undoubtedly Williams' action helped 99 Squadron, but different performance in aircraft and operating procedure was the real culprit on these mass raids. The reason for two observers shown in B3957 is that in Combat Reports at the Public Records Office at Kew, Sergeant Ernest Clare is reported as Captain Williams' observer, whereas in his diary Williams states a Sergeant Price as his observer on this raid.

Leutnant August Raben had previously served in Italy with Jasta 39 where he scored twice before being wounded by anti-aircraft fire on 17th November 1917. He was again injured in an accident on 20th March 1918, but he still took command of Jasta 18 three days later. From 20th August he was Commanding Officer of Jagdgruppe 'Raben' a post he held until the end of the war. He and his men would encounter I.A.F. bombers on several occasions.

Note: Operational records regarding this raid only list pilots; observers (as is often the case with 55) are not recorded.

Reconnaissance

27th June			Take Off:	15.10
55 Squadron			Returned:	18.25
Capt B.J.Silly	Lt J.Parke	A7942		

Crossed lines at 20,000ft at Nomeny and exposed plates over Bolchen, Hans-sur-Nied, Remilly, Fallenberg, St.Avold and Freibuss und Hilsprich. Re-crossed lines at 22,000ft at Arracourt with seventeen plates.

Target: Frescaty Aerodrome

28th June			Take Off:	18.15
104 Squadron			Returned:	20.20
Formation 1				
Capt J.B.Home-Hay	Lt C.C.Blizard			
2Lt R.J.Gammon	2Lt P.E.Appleby			
Lt E.Cartwright	2Lt A.G.Mullen			
2Lt C.L.Startup	2Lt K.C.B.Woodman			
Lt W.L.Deetjen	Lt F.P.Cobden		lost in cloud ret	

Formation 2
Capt E.A.McKay

A virtually overcast sky with bad visibility greeted the crews preparing for a raid on Frescaty aerodrome, situated just south-west of Metz. Also tasked with this target was 99 Squadron who aborted their raid, using the day instead to train new pilots in formation flying, and to service damaged machines. The formations took off, formated, and headed out north to cross the lines at Pont-à-Mousson. Most of the route was flown through thick cloud. Lt William Ludwig Deetjen became lost in cloud and returned to Azelot landing at 19.40, just as the rest of the Squadron were arriving over the target. Two 104 machines this time from the second formation also landed back at Azelot, possibly due to engine trouble or they too had become lost in cloud.

Frescaty was spotted through a gap in the clouds from 13,000ft and the remaining nine aircraft dropped thirteen 112lb and sixteen 25lb Cooper bombs on the airfield below. Bursts were unobserved owing to the bad visibility. No enemy aircraft were spotted and all nine aircraft returned safely, just, as one DH9 returned with a 112lb bomb which failed to release.

Note: Records are incomplete regarding crews for this raid.

Target: Badische Aniline Und Soda Fabrik Works at Ludwigshafen west of Mannheim

29th June			Take Off:	06.10
55 Squadron			**Returned:**	**10.20**

Formation 1

Capt B.J.Silly	Lt J.Parke	A9270
Lt A.Clarke	Lt J.M.Carroll	D9273
Lt P.E.Welchman	2Lt C.L.Rayment	B3967
2Lt J.Cunliffe		
Lt C.A.Bridgland	2Lt E.R.Stewart	D8413
2Lt J.R.Bell		

Formation 2

Lt A.S.Keep		photo machine
2Lt C.R.Whitelock		
Lt E.Blythe		
2Lt E.J.Whyte		ret e/t obs ill 6.50
Lt S.L.Dowswell	Sgt G.Howard	D9236

Because this mission would be a long flight, 55 could not afford to spend too much time gaining height over the airfield so headed straight for the lines. They were crossed at 12,000ft over Blâmont minus 2Lt E.J.Whyte who returned with engine trouble, as well as his observer being taken ill. Flying up the Vosges the formations encountered thick cloud banks south of Sarrebourg; Captain Silly flying by compass continued and headed north-west picking up Landau through a hole in the clouds. Now certain of his position he brought the formation up to 17,000ft and headed north-west towards clearer skies at Kaiserslautern. Upon reaching Kaiserslautern it was possible to fly west again, around the cloud bank to reach the assigned target.

Before bombs could be dropped however, a formation of Albatros DVs descended on the bombers in a diving attack. The lead Albatros, trailing streamers, singled out Captain Silly and his observer Lt Parke, and as this enemy aircraft came down Parke fired a long burst. The enemy aircraft dived under the machine and reappeared in front where Captain Silly fired twenty rounds from his Vickers. The enemy aircraft stalled and went down in a spinning nose dive for about 500ft. Lt Bridgland and 2Lt Stewart also fired at this particular aircraft as it dived, and reappeared, in front of the formation. The rest of the enemy aircraft were driven off before reaching the target where twelve 112lb, two 230lb, sixteen 25lb and four 40lb phosphorous bombs were dropped with good results despite considerable and accurate archie.

On the return journey attacks by the Albatrosses became more determined. One enemy aircraft dived on the formation from the front and Lt Welchman put his nose down and fired fifty rounds of Vickers at the German before it passed underneath and swung round towards the tail of their aircraft. Here his observer, Lt Rayment, fired a hundred rounds from close range. The enemy machine turned over appearing out of control, but then righted itself, and glided down at a steep angle, apparently under control. Lt Dowswell and Sergeant Howard also fired at this aircraft seeing it glide away under control. Sergeant Howard did well to drive off the enemy aircraft throughout the engagement after suffering two gun stoppages. The first was a broken cartridge guide spring and the second was a striker which broke on the return journey. Sporadic attacks continued all the way to the lines which were crossed at Raon-l'-Etape at 14,000ft. The return journey was flown mainly by compass headings, with very few references to the ground available, and despite the cloud cover, twenty-four photographic plates were exposed, some of Speyerdorf aerodrome home of No.2 Bavarian Military Flying School, situated south of Mannheim.

Air Ministry reports gathered after the war confirmed the reports of 55's observers. One bomb fell on the Palmin Factory of Schlink & Co, another hit the Neckar Coal Station. Four bombs fell in warehouse yards belonging to various companies while a single bomb fell on the old town hall. Three bombs hit two ships on the River Neckar, while a single bomb exploded on the Kammer sluice gate. Other bombs were reported exploding on private property. No German losses this day correspond to claims made for enemy aircraft by 55 Squadron.

Note: Observers' names given were found in Combat Reports, 55 at this time still did not record observers on bomb raid reports.

Target: Landau Chemical Works near Mannheim
Secondary Target: Aerodrome at Haguenau

30th June	**Take Off:**	**04.40**
55 Squadron	**Returned:**	**08.25**

Formation 1	
Capt F.Williams	
Lt A.S.Keep	ret obs ill 6.05
Lt A.Clarke	
Lt P.E.Welchmann	
Lt S.L.Dowswell	
2Lt E.J.Whyte	ret obs ill 06.05
Formation 2	
Capt H.S.P.Walmsley	
Lt E.Blythe	
2Lt C.R.Whitelock	
Lt C.A.Bridgland	
2Lt W.Beer	ret e/t 6.50
2Lt J.Cunliffe	ret obs ill

An early start for 55 as twelve DH4s headed out east to cross the lines at Badonviller, and then hopefully on to their target at Mannheim. Upon reaching 14,000ft 2Lt Whyte, Lt Keep and 2Lt Cunliffe all dived for Azelot with sick observers. Cunliffe did not make it and put his machine down at Bettoncourt aerodrome. 2Lt W.Beer also left formation before reaching the lines, returning with engine trouble.

Crossing at 14,500ft the two formations became one as they headed over the Vosges to pick up the Rhine. Having only eight aircraft out of twelve, Captain Williams decided to attack the secondary target, Haguenau aerodrome, dropping twelve 112lb, one 230lb, eight 25lb bombs and two 40lb phosphorous bombs. Climbing to 16,000ft for the return trip, the eight DH4s reported seeing 99 Squadron, before crossing the lines at Senones without encountering any German fighters. No photos were taken as both photo machines had returned early.

One half of an experienced crew, Captain Orlie Lennox Beater received news of his D.F.C on this day. The other half Captain Wyndham Brookes 'Fifi' Farrington had already left for Home Establishment on 26th June after a rather sombre leaving party at the Stanislaus restaurant in Nancy. Beater had first arrived in France on June 19th 1917 with the 9th Battalion Royal Dublin Fusiliers. He left for R.F.C. Headquarters at Hesdin on July 13th and arrived at No1 School of Aerial Gunnery at Hythe on the 30th of July to begin his training. He arrived at No1 Aircraft Depot on September 10th and reported to 55 Squadron at Boisdinghem on the 16th. He moved with the Squadron to Ochey on 13th October, and again to Tantonville on November 7th. On January 9th 1918 he returned to England for some much deserved leave. He returned on the 23rd and continually served until May 20th, when he again returned to England for leave. Arriving back at Tantonville via Paris he found 55 had moved to Azelot. Applying for pilot training he left for Paris on 3rd July. Good friends with William Russell Patey they often took long walks after dinner. His address during the war was 10 Westfield Street, Glasgow. The citation for Beater's D.F.C. read as follows:

Captain Orlie Lennox Beater
D.F.C. gazetted 3rd August 1918

Has proved himself on many occasion a most skilful and gallant observer on long-distance bombing raids, bringing back much valuable information and good photographs. He has taken part in twenty raids and eight photographic reconnaissances.

Target: Aerodrome at Haguenau

30th June			Take Off:	04.40
99 Squadron			**Returned:**	**08.30**

Formation 1

Capt W.D.Thom	Lt L.G.Claye	C6210	
Lt K.D.Marshall	2Lt O.Bell	C6145	
Lt H.D.West	2Lt W.B.Walker	C6092	ret e/t 18.05
Capt V.Beecroft	Lt R.F.Connell	C6278	photo machine
Lt F.G.Richards	2Lt E.J.Munson	C6202	ret vacuum control

Formation 2

Capt A.D.Taylor	Lt H.S.Notley	C6153	
Lt F.G.Thompson	2Lt S.C.Thornley	C6113	
Lt S.M.Black	2Lt E.Singleton	C2173	ret e/t 18.15
2Lt J.Whattam	2Lt T.K.Ludgate	D1668	ret e/t 18.05
Lt M.T.S.Papenfus			photo machine

The two previous days of bad weather had given 99 Squadron valuable time to bring on the new pilots and observers who had recently joined. Casualties due to enemy action on eleven raids amounted to five men missing, presumed killed and one wounded. These losses although heavy were not the main reason for the lack of experienced pilots and observers. Sickness was taking a heavy toll on men, several with bad cases of influenza. Also, replacements recently arrived like Lt W.C.Francis were found to be unsuitable for high altitude flying and sent back to Home Establishment, thus reducing the effective strength of the Squadron still further.

For the attack on Haguenau aerodrome all available crews were assigned making two formations of five aircraft, led by the experienced Captains William Thom and Captain Ashley Taylor. Crossing the lines north of Raon-l'-Etape under moderate archie, the two formations were soon down to three machines each as aircraft started to abort with engine trouble. Lt Richards returned with vacuum control problems, was also sick and was soon to come down with influenza. The remaining machines made up one formation and continued east over Sarrebourg towards Haguenau. Reaching Haguenau moderate archie was encountered as the single formation dropped six 112lb and three 230lb bombs. Several enemy aircraft were spotted on the landing field although none were hit, bursts being observed on the eastern part of the field.

On the return journey ten enemy scouts were engaged over Sarrebourg, where a fierce engagement took place with the six observers firing off nearly two thousand rounds between them. No enemy aircraft were claimed but more importantly no crews were lost with all six machines returning safely. The German unit was probably either Jasta 80 flying from Morsberg, or Jasta 78 from Buhl. Jasta 70 were also flying from Buhl at this time but they were busily engaging 104 Squadron well to the north near Landau. Fifty-five Squadron also hit Haguenau in the early morning after their aborted trip to Landau, whether before or after is not sure but their higher operating altitude might explain the lack of attention from enemy scouts on the return journey.

Note: DH9 C6153 was borrowed from 104 Squadron. The observer for Lt Papenfus is missing from records as well as the aircraft serial number.

Target: Barracks and Railway Station at Landau

30th June			Take Off:	04.55
104 Squadron			Returned:	09.00

Formation 1

Capt J.B.Home-Hay	Lt C.C.Blizard	D7225	
Lt E.Cartwright	2Lt A.G.Mullen	D5729	
Lt A.Moore	Lt F.P.Cobden	C6272	
2Lt C.L.Startup	2Lt K.C.B.Woodman		ret e/t force-landed
2Lt R.J.Gammon	2Lt P.E.Appleby		ret e/t 05.55
Lt W.L.Deetjen	2Lt M.H.Cole	C5720	K.I.A./K.I.A.

Formation 2

Capt E.A.McKay	Capt R.H.Wetherall	C6171	
Lt G.C.Body	2Lt W.G.Norden	C6262	
2Lt R.J.Searle	2Lt R.A.C.Brie	B9347	
2Lt F.H.Beaufort	2Lt C.G.V.Pickard	D1008	force-landed
2Lt O.J.Lange	Sgt V.G.McCabe 263228	D1729	W.I.A./W.I.A.

Landau, situated ten miles south-west of Mannheim on the western side of the Rhine, was a trip sure to attract enemy fighters giving them time to climb and engage the bombers on their eighty-mile legs, to and from the target. Captain Home-Hay led out eleven machines gaining height before they crossed the lines at Senones just north of St.Dié. However they were down to ten before they crossed, 2Lt Gammon returning with engine trouble. Once over, the formations were down to nine as 2Lt Startup jettisoned his 230lb bomb just over the lines and returned with engine trouble to a forced landing at Raon-l'-Etape. The remaining nine aircraft proceeded north over the Vosges until they reached Saverne, where they turned north-east towards Wissembourg.

Over Wissembourg at 07.30, two enemy two-seaters and three scouts stopped shadowing the formations, and started the attacks. The second formation of 'nines' was 1,000ft above the first giving Captain Wetherall a clear shot at an Albatros scout attacking the first formation. Lt Blizard was also firing at this Albatros scout only one hundred yards on his left flank; Blizard fired a burst while Wetherall fired a drum and a half. The Albatros was seen to side-slip then enter three spins from which the pilot recovered; it was last seen spinning several thousand feet below where it broke up. Lt Cobden also fired at an Albatros scout with other observers. The enemy aircraft side-slipped then started spinning out of control. Arriving over Landau the enemy fighters and two-seaters dropped back as the archie started, and the two formations dropped five 230lb and eight 112lb bombs.

Captain Home-Hay turned the formations around quickly as the enemy fighters were manoeuvring to re-engage. Once clear of the target a running fight ensued; however, the worst was yet to come. Jasta 70 joined the attack south-west of Molsheim with ten Fokkers, making in total, according to some observers, twenty enemy aircraft. The DH9 formations were now in real trouble; Captain Home-Hay not only had his tail shot about, but his engine was shot through and losing oil before they even reached the target, so it could now only be a matter of time before his engine stopped. 2Lt Beaufort was also in trouble soaked in oil from his damaged engine. The fight continued with the German fighters firing on the rear machines then diving away under their tails. Several observers reported seeing an enemy aircraft out of control, one in flames and another breaking up in the air. The aircraft on fire was probably that of Lt William Ludwig Deetjen of the U.S. Signal Corps (Aviation Section) and 2Lt Montague Henry Cole, 3rd South African Infantry. 2Lt Norden saw their DH9 drop out of formation on fire, but under control followed by an enemy fighter. Norden saw the DH9 crash and he also spotted 2Lt Oscar J.Lange, and Sgt V.G.McCabe dive away under control followed by an enemy scout. McCabe managed to drive the scout off while Lange was able to pancake their crippled machine on the allied side at Raon-l'-Etape, where both, slightly wounded, were taken to the French Hospital at St Dié. Their machine was wrecked. Also forced to land was 2Lt Frank Beaufort and Lt Cecil Pickard. Beaufort also had little luck with his forced landing and wrecked the machine borrowed from 99 Squadron. Both men returned to Azelot after dark. Photographs later revealed three bursts on the barracks to the south of the town, and five bursts just south of the barracks.

As the rest of the formations neared the lines, front-line anti-aircraft fire started. The fighters broke off their attack and the remaining seven DH9s made Azelot. Vizefeldwebel Heinrich Krüger of Jasta 70 was credited with Deetjen and Cole, who were killed, coming down at Schirmeck. Senior Unteroffizier Dörr of

Jasta 70 was credited with Lange and McCabe. Both men claimed DH4s, a common mistake even amongst experienced pilots. Three enemy aircraft were claimed out of control, two by 2Lt Norden at 07.35 the other by Captain Wetherall also at 07.35. Lt Blizard claimed a destroyed at 07.40 while 2Lt Norden claimed a destroyed at 08.20 on the return journey. Jasta 70 had no losses this day nor, as far as is known, did Kest 1a stationed at Mannheim or Kest 1b stationed at Karlsruhe, both likely candidates for the enemy aircraft on the inward journey.

William Deetjen was buried at Meuse-Argonne, Romagne in France, while Montague Cole from Elliot, Cape Province, was buried at Plaine, France; he was twenty-nine years of age. Further tragedy was to befall this family on 30th September, the day his brother, Reginald Herbert Cole, of 216 Squadron was killed. He was buried at Chambières in France aged twenty-seven years.

Reconnaissance

30th June			Take Off:	07.50
55 Squadron			Returned:	11.30
Capt B.J.Silly	Lt J.Parke	A7942		

Crossed lines at 18,000ft, exposed three plates over Frescaty and two over Dommary-Baroncourt when pilot had to return due to oxygen and engine trouble.

CHAPTER 3

OPERATIONS – JULY 1918

Target: Railway Sidings at Coblenz
Secondary Target: Railway Station at Treves & Karthaus

1st July		**Take Off:**	**04.40**
55 Squadron		**Returned:**	**09.00**
Formation 1			
Capt H.S.P.Walmsley			
Lt E.Blythe			
2Lt C.R.Whitelock			
2Lt W.Beer			
Lt A.S.Keep			
Lt S.L.Dowswell			
Formation 2			
Lt J.R.Bell			
Lt P.E.Welchman			
Lt C.Young			
2Lt E.J.Whyte		photo machine	
2Lt J.Cunliffe			
Lt A.Clarke		ret 6.05 e/t	

First day of the month and a two hundred and eighty-mile round trip to Coblenz greeted the crews. Losing Lt Clarke in the second formation to engine trouble, the remaining eleven gained height and headed for the lines. Crossing at Pont-à-Mousson, both formations received heavy anti-aircraft fire as they flew north towards Metz. Once over Metz however bigger problems lay in store, as nine enemy fighters were milling around and started to shadow the two formations of DH4s.

The wind was blowing stronger as the two formations headed north-east towards their distant target still shadowed by the fighters. The attention of the fighters and the strong wind convinced the leader that it would be foolish to continue to Coblenz so he opted to bomb the railway and workshops at Karthaus instead. Eleven 112lb bombs were dropped by the first formation with good results, but the second formation keeping watch on the enemy fighters failed to see the new target and over flew it. Treves soon appeared ahead and number two formation dropped two 230lb, four 112lb, eight 25lb and two 40lb phosphorous bombs. Both formations turned for home carrying fifteen photos, and as the enemy aircraft did not engage at any stage during the raid, all eleven DH4s returned safely.

Note: Only pilots' names are given in surviving operational records.

Target: Station and Sidings at Konz

1st July			**Take Off:**	**05.00**
99 Squadron			**Returned:**	**08.45**
Formation 1				
Capt W.D.Thom	Lt L.G.Claye	C1670		
Lt K.D.Marshall	2Lt O.Bell	C6145		
Lt S.M.Black	2Lt E.Singleton	C6196	ret e/t 06.00	
Capt A.D.Taylor	2Lt R.E.Sothcott	D1679	ret obs sick	
Lt F.G.Thompson	2Lt S.C.Thornley	C6113		

Formation 2

Capt V.Beecroft	Lt R.F.Connell	C6278	/W.I.A.
Lt M.T.S.Papenfus	Lt A.L.Benjamin	C1666	
Lt H.D.West	2Lt W.B.Walker	C6196	
2Lt J.Whattam	2Lt T.K.Ludgate	C6202	ret pilot sick
Sgt H.H.Wilson	2Lt B.S.W.Taylor	B7232	ret 06.55

The experienced Captain William Thom was leading the first raid of the month as he had in June, this time against the railway sidings and junction at Konz, just south of Treves. The Commanding Officer, Major Lawrence Arthur Pattinson, was leading all new pilots and observers on a practice flight, which left only ten pilots available for this raid so the two formations of five machines each took off, and headed off for the lines. Shortage of experienced pilots in 99 Squadron was severe, for with Major Pattinson included, the grand total in 99 Squadron of qualified pilots was only eleven.

Heading north to cross the lines at Château-Salins, Lt Black left formation and headed home with a faulty carburettor. Captain Taylor returned as his observer 2Lt Sothcott had fainted; 2Lt Whattam also returned feeling sick, and was admitted to hospital and eventually struck off strength, leaving seven machines in total. Sergeant Harry Holsten Wilson, on his first raid, was signalled away to return to Azelot resulting in a more manageable standard six formation. Once over the lines, the bombers were attacked and pursued by four enemy fighters for some distance before breaking off the attack. Following the Moselle river to Konz the six bombers were again attacked this time by five enemy fighters, however the formation stayed tight dropping two 230lb and eight 112lb bombs. Two good bursts were observed on the engine sheds as the DH9s turned for home still engaged by the five enemy fighters.

Heading south and straight for the lines, there was a short respite as the enemy fighters withdrew, but reaching Metz, the formation was again attacked by four enemy fighters. Possibly the same four from earlier. The attacks were hard pressed but all machines crossed the lines safely, although Lt Connell was wounded in the wrist and never returned to active service with 99 Squadron. Opponents of 99 Squadron as they crossed the lines could have been Jasta 18 from Metz, Jasta 65 at Mars-la-Tour or Jasta 80 stationed at Bensdorf. Oberleutnant Gottlieb Rassberger of Jasta 80 was slightly wounded on this day. Bensdorf aerodrome was situated near the bomber's route, but without German records of the engagement, his name is mentioned only as a possible victory of 99 Squadron. Kest 2 would have been the nearest home defence unit near the target. Kest 3 stationed at Morchingen airfield were also en route and could have intercepted the bombers as could any of the above.

Lieutenant Papenfus managed to take eight photos despite the near constant attention of enemy fighters to and from the target, a taste of what was to come perhaps.

Target: Railways at Karthaus
Secondary Target: Triangle of Railways at Metz-Sablon

1st July			**Take Off:**	**05.00**
104 Squadron			**Returned:**	**07.45**

Formation 1

Capt E.A.McKay	Capt R.H.Wetherall		/W.I.A.
2Lt F.H.Beaufort	2Lt C.G.Pickard	D5650	
Lt T.L.McConchie	2Lt K.C.B.Woodman	C6307	P.O.W./P.O.W.
Lt G.C.Body	Lt W.G.Norden	C6262	P.O.W./P.O.W.
2Lt R.J.Gammon	2Lt P.E.Appleby	C6264	
Lt E.Cartwright	2Lt A.G.L.Mullen	D5759	
Sgt W.R.Moore	2Lt J.E.Belford	C6171	crash landing

Led by Captain Evans Alexander McKay ten DH9s took off from Azelot to attack the railways and station at Karthaus, south of Treves. Taking off, the ten became nine as the pilot last in the formation could not start his engine; this number reduced further following aircraft nine crashing on take-off. The remaining eight aircraft climbed skyward within view of their sister Squadron, 99, which left at approximately the same time. 55 Squadron had left fifteen minutes before and were probably out of sight with the better performing DH4. 104 Squadron were further reduced as two machines dropped out of formation with engine trouble, Sgt Moore making a forced landing while the other machine is believed to have made it back to Azelot.

Crossing the lines at Verdun the six remaining machines were heavily archied as they pressed on northeast towards Thionville. However, the six soon became five as Lt Graham Campbell Body jettisoned his bombs and glided to earth, apparently under control. Over Conflans five Pfalz scouts engaged the formation forcing 2Lt Lloyd McConchie to glide away, followed by two Pfalz scouts. Six down with four to go, and still engaged by enemy aircraft, Captain McKay decided to bomb the large triangle of railways at Metz-Sablon instead. Over Ars at 07.05 2Lt Pickard claimed a Pfalz scout driven down while at 07.15 2Lt Mullen fired at a Pfalz scout which started to emit black smoke or oil, and this machine was seen to glide away near Metz. The formation of four was shadowed all the way to Metz where they dropped two 230lb and four 112lb bombs observing three bursting on the railway lines, and two on houses, north and south of the target.

Once out of the anti-aircraft barrage above Metz, five Albatros scouts, and four Pfalz scouts attacked the formation. 2Lt Appleby fired ninety rounds at an Albatros scout which then entered a spin, and was seen to crash. The enemy scouts continued to attack all the way to the lines at Pont-à-Mousson, only breaking off the attack because 104 Squadron came under front line anti-aircraft fire. These remaining four aircraft landed at Azelot.

Captain Robert Hodgson Wetherall formally of the 14th Northumberland Fusiliers was seriously wounded in the left leg. Who his pilot was on this day is unclear but an educated guess points at Captain McKay. This was Wetherall's last flight with the I.A.F., and he relinquished his commission on 17th December 1918, on the grounds of ill health from wounds. Pilots Body and McConchie both became prisoners of war, as did their observers, Keith Chatfield Barrington Woodman and Walter George Norden of the Royal Engineers. Graham Campbell Body was born on 5th May 1894 in Warana, Invernell, New Zealand. He joined 104 Squadron on 19th May 1918, and was repatriated on 13th December. A sheep farmer before the war, his father worked for the Bank of New South Wales in Threadneedle Street, in the City of London.

German victories point towards Ltn Erich Spindler of Jasta 18 who bought down a DH9 near Avning at 08.20 German time, which is twenty-five minutes before 104 Squadron survivors landed. The times do not really match, however time keeping in the midst of combat is rarely a priority and Spindler was the only claimant of a DH9 in that area. Two machines were lost so it looks like Body and Norden were hit by archie as they crossed the lines, and landed due to engine or structural failure. McConchie and Woodman looks to have fallen to Spindler although he may have been awarded the victory over others.

Reconnaissance

1st July			**Take Off:**	**7.20**
55 Squadron			**Returned:**	**12.00**
Lt C.A.Bridgland	2Lt E.R.Stewart	A7837		

Crossed the lines at 19,500ft over Fresnes and exposed plates over aerodromes at Duzey, Constantine, Bouveille, Longuyon, Villers, and the supposed aerodrome at Chatillon. Flew over the railways at Arlon but no plates were taken owing to clouds covering all to the east of Longwy. Two enemy two-seaters were seen near Verdun where the lines were re-crossed at 19,000ft. Twenty-four plates were exposed in all.

Target: Station and Sidings at Konz
Secondary Target: Station and Sidings at Treves

2nd July			**Take Off:**	**07.25**
99 Squadron			**Returned:**	**10.15**
Formation 1				
Capt W.D.Thom	Lt L.G.Claye	C6210		
Lt K.D.Marshall	2Lt O.Bell	C6145		
Lt G.Broadbent	2Lt E.Beale	D1019	ret e/t 07.30	
Lt H.D.West	2Lt W.B.Walker	D1679	ret e/t 08.30	
Formation 2				
Capt A.D.Taylor	2Lt B.J.Munson	C6153	ret obs sick	
Lt M.T.S.Papenfus	Lt A.L.Benjamin	C1666		
Lt S.M.Black	2Lt E.Singleton	C2173		
Capt V.Beecroft	Sgt F.L.Lee	C6196		
Sgt H.H.Wilson	2Lt B.S.W.Taylor	D7232		

All available pilots and observers were called upon for a return raid to the railway sidings at Konz. Nine crews were all that could be mustered amongst the ranks of 99 Squadron as the two formations took off and headed for the lines. A decoy Squadron made up of twelve machines, six from 99 and six from 104 Squadrons took off at five a.m. and headed out towards the lines at Pont-à-Mousson at bombing height. Hoping to fool both the enemy fighters and the German ground observers, it was thought this ruse would give the actual bombers an easy run to the target. Both squadrons also used this flight to give badly needed experience to the pilots and observers of both squadrons. Decoy or not, planes and crews still continued to suffer. Lt Broadbent returned five minutes after take-off with an overheating engine. Climbing into DH9 C6202 with his observer he took off but could not catch the formation, returning after an hour. Also returning at this time, again with a sick observer, was Captain Taylor, swiftly followed by Lt West whose petrol cut off due to a leaking petrol tap, forcing him to glide home to Azelot.

Crossing the lines again with only six machines, Captain Thom headed north towards Konz as yet with no sign of enemy fighters. Approaching Saarburg at 09.15, twelve enemy fighters appeared consisting of Pfalz, Fokker DVII and Fokker Triplanes. The Pfalz scouts had the same markings as the previous day, silver with black spots. Lt Claye fired his twin Lewis guns at two enemy aircraft 150 yards away on his left hand side, and both aircraft dived away apparently hit. One of these two scouts zoomed upwards and continued to fight as the other continued downwards, heading towards a large forest north of Saarburg where Claye said it must have crashed. Heavily engaged, Captain Thom led the formation past Konz and dropped on Treves station and sidings. Four 230lb and four 112lb bombs hit the town of Treves and six bursts were observed in the square one of which started a fire. Turning for home, the formation was still being attacked. The Pfalz fighters came in from the front, while the Fokker DVIIIs and tri-planes attacked from the rear. Combined fire from all the observers was seen to send one fighter down in flames. Not put off by this the enemy scouts continued to attack all the way to the lines. The formation of DH9 held firm again, and landed without any losses. If these tight formations could be held firm under combat, but with twelve instead of six, then maybe losses could be kept to a minimum. For his leadership on this raid and on previous raids Captain William Dorian Thom was awarded the D.F.C., the citation reading as follows:

Captain William Dorian Thom
D.F.C. gazetted 3rd August 1918

A gallant and capable leader in long-distance bombing raids, in eighteen of which he has taken part during a period of six weeks. During the last raid his formation was attacked by thirteen enemy machines, but he nevertheless managed to drop his bombs on his objective, direct hits being obtained, and he also succeeded in destroying an enemy aeroplane.

Note: Thom was awarded a Bar to his D.F.C., gazetted on 3rd June 1919.

Target: Railway Sidings at Coblenz

2nd July	**Take Off:**	**07.25**
55 Squadron	**Returned:**	**12.15**
Formation 1		
Capt B.J.Silly		
2Lt J.Cunliffe		
2Lt C.R.Whitelock		
Sgt A.W.Mepsted		
Lt A.S.Keep		
Lt S.L.Dowswell		
Formation 2		
Lt J.R.Bell		
Lt P.E.Welchman		
Lt E.Blythe		
Lt A.Clarke	ret e/t 09.20	
Lt C.Young	ret e/t 09.15	
2Lt E.J.Whyte	ret e/t 08.50	

Leaving Azelot to the north, both formations crossed the lines at 13,000ft at Nomeny. Once over the lines the formations headed north-west towards Coblenz flying mostly by compass heading. Once abeam Saarbrücken the 'fours' encountered heavy but inaccurate archie. Before reaching the target three machines left the second formation, returning to Azelot with their bombs. The remaining nine aircraft dropped one 230lb bomb, sixteen 112lb bombs, eight 25lb Cooper bombs and two 40lb phosphorous bombs.

Due to the distance of the target, the return journey would be a reciprocal heading directly back to the lines, which would give the German Kest and Jasta units plenty of time to climb up to the bombers' height and intercept. To try and avoid interception the formations climbed up to 17,000ft on the return journey, and no enemy aircraft were seen. The formations crossed the lines at Château-Salins at 17,000ft landing at Azelot with fifteen photographic plates of the target. These photographs later revealed two bursts on the railway sidings, two bursts on an engine shed, and one burst on a large barge.

Note: Neither pilots nor the observers were listed for this raid in the bomb raid report. However the pilots were eventually found but again no record was made of the observers.

Reconnaissance

2nd July			**Take Off:**	**08.00**
55 Squadron			**Returned:**	**12.30**
Capt H.S.P.Walmsley	2Lt C.L.Rayment	A7837		

Crossed lines at 19,000ft, flew south-west of Dieuze, then to Bolchen, Bettembourg, Petange, Merville, Audin and Longuyon, re-crossed the lines at 22,000ft at St.Mihiel. Fifteen plates were taken.

Target: Railway Sidings at Coblenz

5th July			**Take Off:**	**04.40**
55 Squadron			**Returned:**	**09.25**
Formation 1				
Capt F.Williams	Sgt H.Mahoney			
2Lt J.Cunliffe				
Lt S.L.Dowswell				
Lt A.S.Keep			photo machine	
Lt C.Young				
2Lt W.Beer				
Formation 2				
Lt C.A.Bridgland				
Lt A.Clarke				
Lt E.Blythe				
Sgt A.W.Mepsted				
2Lt E.J.Whyte				
Lt D.R.G.Mackay		D9236	e/t crash landed	

Coblenz lying fifty miles west of Frankfurt was to be the target again for 55 Squadron. Lt Mackay had engine trouble and managed to crash-land his machine at Chaumont, which lay between Bar-le-Duc and Dijon, quite a distance from Azelot. The formations crossed the lines at Verdun, giving more time to climb to a safer altitude of 14,5000ft. Three enemy aircraft were spotted to the east as the lines were crossed but they did not venture near. Flying north until reaching Arlon, the formations then headed north-west for the remaining eighty miles to reach Coblenz.

Flying over an overcast landscape on a compass heading from Arlon, Coblenz was reached but obscured by cloud so Captain Williams started to turn the formations around to bomb Karthaus instead. As the formations started to turn the Coblenz battery of twelve 9cm guns opened fire. Captain Williams turned the formations towards the inaccurate archie where he spotted the Rhine river, then the fort of Ehrenbreitstein which lay opposite Coblenz. The eleven 'fours' dropped three 230lb bombs, ten 112lb bombs, twenty-four 25lb Cooper bombs and five 40lb phosphorous bombs, but no bursts were seen due to the cloud.

The route home was direct passing between Treves and Saarbrücken, then crossing the lines at Nomeny at 16,500ft. Seventeen plates were exposed of various targets over the whole route to and from the target.

Captain Williams in his diary suggests that intelligence sources, as well as German newspapers, reported several German soldiers killed in the fort while awaiting transportation to the front. The Air Ministry reports made after the war stated that considerable damage was done to the Coblenzer Zeitung Printing Works, and the Wiener Hof Restaurant. Several other public buildings were hit with total casualties amounting to eight wounded.

Note: Neither pilots nor observers were listed for this raid in bomb raid reports. However the pilots were eventually found but again no record was made of the observers. It is not certain if Mackay's machine was DH4 D9236, but this aircraft is recorded as being wrecked on this day.

Target: Station and Sidings at Kaiserslautern
Secondary Target: Railway and Station at Saarbrücken

5th July			Take Off:	04.50
99 Squadron			Returned:	08.05
Formation 1				
Capt W.D.Thom	Lt C.G.Claye	C6202	W.I.A./K.I.A.	
Lt K.D.Marshall	2Lt C.Bell	C6145		
Capt V.Beecroft	2Lt B.S.W.Taylor	C6278		
Lt W.G.Stevenson	2Lt W.B.Walker	C6210		
Sgt H.H.Wilson	Sgt F.L.Lee	D7232		
Lt G.Broadbent	Sgt J.Jones	D7223		
Lt H.D.West	2Lt E.Beale	C6092	ret e/t	

After two days of bad weather, the cloud had lifted sufficiently to allow a combined raid with a formation of six DH9s from 104 Squadron. Seven crews would formate hopefully with 104 Squadron and proceed to Kaiserslautern, seventy miles over the lines between Saarbrücken and Mannheim. Taking off, the group headed north-east towards Château-Salins. Before crossing the lines Lt West dropped out of formation and returned home with ignition trouble. 104 Squadron formed up and crossed the lines with 99 Squadron. Once over the lines 104 Squadron dropped back due to engine trouble with the lead machine, as Kaiserslautern looked to be cloud covered; Captain Thom decided to bomb Saarbrücken instead.

Overhead Saarbrücken at 14,000ft, two 230lb, six 112lb and eight 25lb bombs were dropped as nine enemy Albatros scouts attacked from the front and rear of the formation. One enemy scout stalled at the same height as the bombers, 2Lt Brian Samuel Taylor firing a good burst at the Albatros. It fell away and the wings were seen to come off. Sergeant Lee also fired at this enemy aircraft at the same time and saw it go down between Saarbrücken and Homberg. Heading for home the scouts closed the range and pressed home their attacks. 2Lt Clive Bell fired a long burst from his double Lewis guns. The scout suddenly climbed, stalled right in front of their DH9, then slowly fell upside down into a vertical dive, until lost to sight. The fight was not one sided by any means; Lt C.G.Claye was killed by a bullet wound to the thigh; his pilot, Captain Thom escaped with severe bruising to his arm caused by a bullet which was too close for comfort. The lines were reached without losing a machine although Captain Thom's machine was so shot about it had to be rebuilt. On paper 99 Squadron had destroyed one enemy aircraft and sent down another out of control, but only two Jasta pilots were killed this day neither in the vicinity of this raid. The German casualties however could have been from Kest units. Twenty-two photos were taken on this raid but no bomb bursts were observed due to the attention of enemy fighters. Lt Charles Geoffrey Claye was buried in Charmes Cemetery. Coming from Nottingham he had joined the 5th Sherwood Foresters before joining the Royal Flying Corps; he was twenty-three.

Target: Railway Station at Kaiserslautern
Secondary Target: Village of Barbas

5th July			Take Off:	04.55
104 Squadron			Returned:	07.00
Formation 1				
Capt J.B.Home-Hay	2Lt C.C.Blizard			
Capt R.J.Gammon	2Lt P.E.Appleby		photo machine	
Lt M.J.Ducray	2Lt R.G.Gibbs			
Lt E.Cartwright	2Lt A.G.Mullen			

| 2Lt R.J.Searle | Sgt A.C.Wallace | ret e/t |
| 2Lt F.H.Beaufort | Lt C.G.Pickard | ret e/t |

Records on this raid are scarce but six machines of 104 Squadron led by Captain Home-Hay were detailed to bomb the railways at Kaiserslautern, with aircraft of 99 Squadron. The formation was soon down to four as Lt Searle and 2Lt Beaufort returned with engine trouble.

Crossing the lines south of Château-Salins with 99 Squadron in front, Captain Home-Hay had a big end run out, so he dropped his bombs on the village of Barbas just south of Blâmont. Unfortunately the other machines in his formation mistook this signal for all of them to release, and Barbas received two 230lb and four 112lb bombs. It appears that either 104 Squadron were already in a descent perhaps following their leader down, or were not yet at normal bombing height around 13,000ft as they fired four hundred rounds at ground targets near Barbas. Nineteen photos were taken and all returned safely.

Note: Aircraft serial numbers have so far eluded the author.

Target: Railway Triangle at Metz-Sablon

6th July			Take Off:	18:25
99 Squadron			Returned:	21:05
Formation 1				
Capt W.D.Thom	2Lt E.Singleton	C1670		
Capt V.Beecroft	2Lt B.S.W.Taylor	C6196		
Lt G.Broadbent	Sgt J.Jones	D1026		
Lt W.G.Stevenson	2Lt W.B.Walker	C6210	photo machine	
Lt H.D.West	2Lt E.Beale	C6092		
Sgt H.H.Wilson 7054	Sgt F.L.Lee	D7232		

After Sunday evening service, the weather had cleared to allow the squadrons to take off from Azelot. Captain Thom led six machines which gained height, and headed north towards the lines. Arriving over Metz the Squadron was confronted by heavy and accurate archie as well as eight enemy scouts. Quickly dropping three 230lb and six 112lb bombs, bursts were not observed on the ground due to cloud cover. Soon the formation of DH9s was involved in a running fight with the enemy scouts, south of Metz and heading for the lines. Sergeant Harry Holsten Wilson had his radiator holed. He put his nose down, dropped out of formation and headed for the lines; the remaining five machines maintained altitude and landed back at Azelot.

Sergeant Wilson was fair game at a lower altitude with a leaking radiator, so he fired Very lights in the hope of assistance and his prayers were answered. Captain Jeffrey Batters Home-Hay was leading 104 Squadron who were also attacking Metz-Sablon railway station. Seeing the plight of Wilson and Lee, Home-Hay led his formation of six aircraft down from 14,000ft to 9,000ft, and picked up the struggling Wilson into his formation. Crossing the lines at Morville, Wilson was unable to make Azelot and put his machine down in a rough grass field nearby. His undercarriage was broken but both occupants were alive and well. Lt Stevenson and 2Lt Walker managed to take four photos despite the archie and fighters.

Target: Railway Triangle at Metz-Sablon

6th July			Take Off:	18.30
104 Squadron			Returned:	21.05
Formation 1				
Capt J.B.Home-Hay	2Lt C.C.Blizard	C2960		
Capt R.J.Gammon	2Lt H.O.Bryant			
Lt E.Cartwright	2Lt A.G.Mullen			
Lt A.Moore	Lt F.P.Cobden			
Lt M.J.Ducray	2Lt N.H.Wildig			
2Lt R.J.Searle	Sgt A.C.Wallace			

Taking off after 99 Squadron, six machines led by Captain Home-Hay started to climb in amongst the cloud and make their way towards the lines at Regnéville. Crossing at 14,000ft, the six came under considerable anti-aircraft fire which was uncomfortably accurate. Pressing on, the formation flew over Jouaville, arriving over Metz at 20.45, where they dropped three 230lb and six 112lb bombs from 13,000ft, but no bursts were observed due to the darkness.

Over Metz, five Pfalz scouts and two Fokker Triplanes intercepted the bombers. One scout ventured to within one hundred yards. 2Lt Blizard fired thirty rounds, then watched as the scout entered a vertical sideslip pouring smoke; Sgt Wallace also fired at this particular fighter. Just south of Metz, Captain Home-Hay spotted a DH9 of 99 Squadron lower down over Verny, firing Very lights for assistance. Leading the formation down to 9,000ft they picked up the straggler and re-crossed the lines with it at Morville still at 9,000ft. The combat report doesn't state what type of enemy aircraft was shot down, and German air losses this day along the whole front amounted to just two casualties which were well away from this action. The enemy aircraft may well have been damaged, possibly written off, but over friendly territory, high up, with quite a few aerodromes and a lot of open space, there was a good chance of putting down an aircraft which was not in flames, and walking away unharmed. Blizard was awarded an out of control victory, but credit must go to all the observers who expended 1,368 rounds keeping the enemy at bay.

Note: Pilots and observers for this raid were eventually found, the only serial number comes from a combat report made by Captain Home-Hay and 2Lt Blizard.

Target: Explosive Factory at Düren
Secondary Target: Railways at Metz-Sablon

6th July		**Take Off:**	**19.00**
55 Squadron		**Returned:**	**21.10**
Formation 1			
Capt B.J.Silly			
2Lt W.J.Pace			
2Lt C.R.Whitelock		photo machine	
Lt E.Blythe			
2Lt J.R.Bell			
Lt P.E.Welchman			
Formation 2			
Capt H.S.P.Walmsley			
Lt C.A.Bridgland			
Lt A.Clarke			
2Lt J.Cunliffe			
Lt A.S.Keep			
Lt D.R.G.Mackay			

Not until early evening did the weather clear sufficiently to allow operations to begin. Captain Benjamin James Silly led as both formations crossed the lines at Pont-à-Mousson. Encountering heavy and accurate archie which holed his radiator letting out all the water, Silly decided to bomb Metz-Sablon instead. Dropping five 230lb, twelve 112lb, eight 25lb and two 40lb phosphorous bombs on the railway below, the formations spotted six enemy aircraft as they turned for home, which did not engage and all machines returned safely; twenty-four photos were taken.

The explosive factory at Düren was the target assigned to 55 in their orders. However this target would not have been reached at such a late time in the day.

Note: No record was made of observers, or aircraft serial numbers.

Target: Railway and Factories at Kaiserslautern

7th July		**Take Off:**	**12.50**
104 Squadron		**Returned:**	**17.10**
Formation 1			
Capt E.A.McKay	Lt R.A.C.Brie	D2812	
2Lt R.J.Searle	Sgt A.C.Wallace		
Lt E.Cartwright	2Lt A.G.Mullen	D7229	
Lt A.Moore	Lt F.P.Cobden	D2868	P.O.W./K.I.A.

| Lt M.J.Ducray | 2Lt N.H.Wildig | D2878 | P.O.W./K.I.A. |
| Lt G.H.B.Smith | Sgt A.H.Morgan 392770 | D5658 | crashed/W.I.A. |

Six machines from 104 Squadron, combined with six from 99 Squadron, were to bomb Kaiserslautern situated between the large towns of Mannheim and Saarbrücken. The two spare machines returned to Azelot as the formation of six crossed the lines in formation with 99 Squadron at 13,000ft over Blâmont, being severely archied as they did so. Once over the lines, Lt Smith experienced engine difficulties and left the formation gliding back over the lines, and crash landing at Veinsei. Smith was okay but Morgan broke several ribs. With 99 Squadron in the lead the bombers headed north-east towards Saarbrücken. Over Homburg three enemy two-seaters attacked the formation, and Lt Moore dropped down out of formation apparently under control followed by one enemy aircraft.

Over Kaiserslautern at 13.45, 104 Squadron dropped two 230lb and six 112lb bombs from 13,500ft recording hits just south of the railway, damaging a brewery and a furniture store. Turning for home the aircraft flew a reciprocal heading, and were intercepted by eight Pfalz scouts over Saarburg. It wasn't long before the scouts got in amongst the formation of 104 Squadron, splitting the bombers up and sending down Lts Ducray and Wildig near Rixingen. Followed by four scouts, Wildig in the rear cockpit was fighting all the way down and was seen to shoot one down. Lt Brie and 2Lt Mullen both fired at a Pfalz scout which came within one hundred yards. Brie fired sixty rounds, while Mullen fired twenty and the German was seen to spin for a thousand feet, then tail slide, finally falling to one side and spinning again. The fight continued until the lines were crossed with the three machines of 104 Squadron landing at Azelot and despite being badly shot up, they also managed to bring back five photos.

The two-seaters over Homburg were described as Halberstadts by McKay in his combat report, victors for Moore and Cobden therefore are more difficult to find due to poor records. Vizefeldwebel Hans Mittermayr of Kest 2 claimed a DH4 over Kaiserslautern for his second and last victory of the war. Several of the Kest units had two-seaters in their inventory, usually used as R/T machines for tracking and leading scouts to the bomber formations. Mittermayr could well have been flying one of these with or without an observer, this is of course pure speculation but he was credited with a DH4. 55 Squadron were not operating this day so as is often the case, a DH4 was mistaken for a DH9. Ltn Sauermann previously of Kest 2, now flying with Jasta 70, claimed a DH9 over Rixingen at 17.30 German time, clearly being the victor of Ducray and Wildig. As so often happened, especially in the DH9, the observers fared worse with both Cobden and Wildig killed in action; Moore and Ducray luckily went to sit it out as prisoners of war. Norman Hugh Wildig from Chester, in Cheshire, was only nineteen years old, and was buried at Réchicourt-le-Château in France. Frank Pargeter Cobden was from Farringdon in Berkshire, and had joined the Royal Berkshire Regiment. He transferred to the Royal Flying Corps and was buried at Niederzwehren; he was twenty-one.

Note: Aircraft serial numbers come from combat reports.

Target: Railway and Factories at Kaiserslautern

7th July			Take Off:	12:55
99 Squadron			Returned:	17:05
Formation 1				
Capt W.D.Thom	Lt O.Bell	C6110		
Capt V.Beecroft	2Lt B.S.W.Taylor	D7232		
Lt W.G.Stevenson	2Lt W.B.Walker	C6210		
Lt H.D.West	2Lt E.Beale	D5568		
Lt G.Broadbent	Sgt J.Jones	D1026		
Sgt H.H.Wilson	Sgt F.L.Lee	C1666		
Capt A.D.Taylor	Lt H.S.Notley	C6153	crashed t/off	

A combined raid with six machines from 104 Squadron was mounted to attack the railway and factories at Kaiserslautern, approximately seventy miles over the lines. Captain Thom led both formations, his fifth raid of the month in seven days. Captain Evans Alexander McKay would be leading 104 Squadron. Seven machines from 99 Squadron took off, one spare in case of engine failure. The spare machine was needed as Captain Taylor experienced an engine failure immediately after take-off. His machine crashed in a corn field just outside the aerodrome, sliding into a ditch and wrecking the machine, although both occupants were unscathed.

Climbing away, the two Squadrons joined together and headed out towards the lines at 13,000ft. Crossing the lines east of Lunéville at Blâmont, the formation of twelve became eleven when one of 104 Squadron's machines returned with engine trouble. Heading over Sarrebourg the bombers continued north-east; just north of Zweibrücken but over Homburg, the rear group (104) was attacked by three enemy two-seaters, and one DH9 was seen to drop out of formation.

Reaching Kaiserslautern 99 Squadron released three 230lb and six 112lb bombs. A direct hit was scored on the railway while four or five bursts were observed near the factories, next to the railway tracks. Anti-aircraft fire was active but was not very accurate as the two formations headed for home. Reaching Sarrebourg they were intercepted by eight Pfalz scouts of Kest 2. The fighters concentrated mainly on 104 Squadron and 99 Squadron witnessed one enemy scout go down under the guns of 104 Squadron. Lt William Gordon Stevenson showed excellent skill and steadiness in these recent raids which was reflected in his D.F.C. citation which read as follows:

Lt/Temp. Captain William Gordon Stevenson
D.F.C. gazetted 2nd November 1918

A fine leader, who has taken part in twenty-six successful raids, displaying marked skill and gallantry, notably on 7th July, when with five other machines, he carried out a successful raid. On the return journey the formation was engaged by ten hostile aircraft, who made repeated and determined attacks; that these attacks were repulsed without loss was largely due to the cool judgement and strong initiative shown by this officer.

Reconnaissance

7th July			**Take Off:**	**13.30**
55 Squadron			**Returned:**	**17.00**
Capt F.Williams	2Lt C.L.Rayment	A7837		

Crossed lines at Verdun at 19,000ft, exposed plates at Longuyon, Longwy, Athus, Bettembourg and Bolchen (two large enemy aircraft out). New aerodrome at Drogny, landing 'T' out and six large hangars. Re-crossed at 20,000ft at Château-Salins, forty-eight plates taken.

Target: Explosive Factory at Düren
Secondary Target: Railway triangle south of Luxembourg

8th July		**Take Off:**	**05.05**
55 Squadron		**Returned:**	**09.10**
Formation 1			
Capt F.Williams	Capt W.H.Mason-Springgay		
2Lt W.J.Pace			
Lt P.E.Welchman			
2Lt W.Beer			
2Lt C.R.Whitelock			
Lt S.L.Dowswell			

Formation 2
2Lt J.R.Bell
2Lt J.Cunliffe
Lt A.Clarke
Lt E.Young
2Lt E.J.Whyte
Lt D.R.G.Mackay

The formations joined up over the field and headed out north towards Verdun. Crossing the lines accurate archie was encountered as the formations continued north towards Bastogne. Once past Bastogne the formations turned north-west towards Düren, however their path was blocked by continuous overcast all across the Rhineland. Captain Williams was unsure of his location. He did not set course before losing sight of the ground, but then he spotted a clearing in the overcast approximately twenty miles from his position and made for it. Upon arrival he did not recognise the land below and made for another gap in the clouds not far away. A crescent-shaped wood was all that was visible in the clearing. His observer Mason-Springgay did not recognise the terrain either, so being worried about bombing neutral Dutch territory, Williams turned the formations south and headed for Luxembourg.

The collection of railway tracks south of the town of Luxembourg was easily visible as both formations dropped their mixed ordinance of four 230lb, twelve 112lb, sixteen 25lb and three 40lb phosphorous bombs from 15,000ft. Good bursts were observed as the formations turned south-east to pass east of Thionville and Metz and their considerable anti-aircraft batteries. As the formations crossed the lines at Château-Salins, four enemy aircraft were seen but did not attempt to engage. All twelve aircraft returned safely bringing with them twenty-two photographic plates.

Note: No observers were listed, Mason-Springgay being recorded in Williams's diary.

Target: Buhl Aerodrome

8th July		Take Off:	15.15
104 Squadron		**Returned:**	**17.20**
Formation 1			
Capt J.B.Home-Hay	2Lt C.C.Blizard		
2Lt A.Haines	2Lt R.G.Gibbs		
2Lt J.C.Uhlman	2Lt H.O.Bryant		
2Lt B.H.Stretton	Sgt R.F.Crockett 317127		
Capt R.J.Gammon	Lt R.A.C.Brie	ret rad leak	
2Lt F.H.Beaufort	Lt C.G.V.Pickard	ret e/t	

Another combined raid with 99 Squadron saw Captain Home-Hay leading a formation of six DH9s to attack Buhl aerodrome, home at this time to Jastas 70 and 78. Recent losses to German fighter aircraft may have been the reason for the attack, but it was more likely the weather which had been overcast across Germany for most of the day, and the limited number of experienced crews which both squadrons could muster.

This time 104 were the lead squadron climbing to 12,500ft to cross the lines at Reillon where they encountered moderate archie. The formation of six was down to four with two machines returning with engine trouble as the combined force headed further east towards Buhl. At 16.25 they were over Buhl, dropping two 112lb, and twenty-four 25lb bombs on the airfield. Two direct hits were seen on the large hangar on the northern side of the aerodrome next to the road, while another was observed to impact south-east of this large hangar on a smaller building. Other bursts were scattered east of the hangars which ran parallel to the road, while another fell on the landing ground in front of the hangars.

Heading back only two enemy aircraft were seen by 104 Squadron before they re-crossed the lines. These aircraft kept their distance and did not attack although the observers fired off 150 rounds, maybe as a warning.

Although no victories were claimed this day, Gefreiter Rudolf Lang of Jasta 78 was wounded during a bombing raid on his aerodrome at Buhl; small payback for recent losses but payback none the less.

Target: Buhl Aerodrome

8th July			Take Off:	15.50
99 Squadron			**Returned:**	**17.10**
Formation 1				
Capt A.D.Taylor	Lt H.S.Notley	D1679		
Lt E.L.Doidge	2Lt W.B.Walker	D1019		
Lt G.Broadbent	Sgt J.Jones	D1026		
Lt W.G.Stevenson	Sgt H.L.Bynon	C6210		
Lt W.J.Garrity	2Lt E.Beale	D1668		
Sgt H.H.Wilson	Sgt F.L.Lee	C6196		
Lt F.G.Thompson	2Lt S.C.Thornley	C6113	ret e/t	

The weather was again bad for most of the day, but cleared sufficiently in the afternoon for a raid to Buhl aerodrome, fifty miles over the lines. Home to both Jasta 70 and Jasta 78, this lay on the eastern side of the Rhine river between Strasbourg and Karlsruhe. Practice flights were again being held to bring on the new pilots and observers. Influenza and other illnesses were depleting squadron strength as well as casualties;

2Lt Whattam and Lt Underwood, both pilots, were struck off squadron strength and admitted to hospital this date.

Captain Taylor took the lead as the seven aircraft left Azelot and climbed eastward towards the lines. After a quarter of an hour Lt Thompson returned with engine trouble leaving a more manageable six formation, to cross the lines. Crossing the lines archie was active and fairly accurate but Buhl was reached without any interference from enemy fighters. Under slight anti-aircraft fire the formation dropped six 112lb and twenty-four 25lb bombs, and excellent results were observed. Two enemy aircraft were seen to take off while another three were parked outside, just in front of sheds. One 112lb bomb was seen to hit directly on one of the larger permanent hangars on the north-eastern side of the aerodrome, while another was seen to strike a smaller building on the southern side. Other hits were scattered on or near the airfield with quite a bit of smoke; photos later confirmed what the observers had reported.

Heading back towards the lines, three enemy aircraft were spotted trailing the formation, but they did not venture near and all machines crossed the lines safely. The I.A.F. were not having all their own way as Azelot was bombed for the first time that night. No aircraft were hit but some personnel were hurt in this attack and admitted to hospital.

Target: Railways at Offenburg

11th July		**Take Off:** 06.00
55 Squadron		**Returned:** 09.30
Formation 1		
Capt B.J.Silly	Sgt H.Mahoney	
Lt P.E.Welchman	Lt J.M.Carroll	
2Lt C.R.Whitelock	Lt G.Bryer-Ash	
Lt A.S.Keep	2Lt W.R.Patey	photo machine
Lt E.Blythe	2Lt W.H.Currie	
Lt C.Young	Lt R.H.Butler	
Formation 2		
Lt C.A.Bridgland	2Lt D.W.Stewart	
2Lt W.J.Pace	Sgt W.E.Baker	
Lt A.Clarke	2Lt J.G.Quinton	
Lt S.L.Dowswell	Sgt G.Howard	
Lt D.R.G.Mackay	2Lt H.C.T.Gompertz	
2Lt E.J.Whyte	Sgt E.Clare	photo machine

Offenburg railway junction, lying south-east of Strasbourg in the Rhine valley was the target for this early morning raid. Leaving Azelot to the south-east the formations crossed the lines at Senones at 12,500ft, and headed straight for the objective. As the two formations neared Strasbourg heavy but inaccurate archie opened up, so Captain Benjamin Silly led them up to 13,000ft as they neared Offenburg.

At 07.50 they let go three 230lb, fourteen 112lb, sixteen 25lb and three 40lb phosphorous bombs. Several were seen to land in the sidings, two bursts were observed in houses east of the sidings while two of the 40lb phosphorous bombs landed harmlessly in a field. The two photo machines were busy taking thirty-three plates and noting rail and road movements in the Strasbourg area. Returning via the same route, both formations received more accurate flak as they crossed the lines. Four enemy aircraft had been seen in different places but they did not venture near. Photographs later showed a direct hit on the electricity works and another on a building close by.

Note: 55's records are more complete regarding crews at this time. Aircraft however are not listed in their bomb raid reports.

Target: Bosch & Daimler Works at Stuttgart
Secondary Target: Railway Sidings East of Sarrebourg

12th July		**Take Off:** 09.00
55 Squadron		**Returned:** 12.10
Formation 1		
Capt H.S.P.Walmsley	Capt R.P.Ward	

2Lt W.J.Pace	2Lt D.W.Stewart	
Lt P.E.Welchman	Lt J.M.Carroll	
2Lt A.W.M.Bryant	Lt R.A.Butler	
Lt A.S.Keep	2Lt J.S.Pollock	photo machine
Lt G.T.Richardson	2Lt T.F.L.Myring	ret e/t 10.15

Formation 2

2Lt J.R.Bell	2Lt E.R.Beesley	
Lt S.L.Dowswell	Sgt G.Howard	ret e/t 09.30
2Lt J.Cunliffe	2Lt G.E.Little	
Lt E.Blythe	2Lt W.H.Currie	
2Lt E.J.Whyte	Sgt E.Clare	photo machine
Lt E.P.Critchley	Sgt G.E.Lewis	

Gaining height over the field the two formations headed out east to cross the lines at Badonviller at 14,000ft. As the formations went over Lt Dowswell left the formation with engine trouble, the remaining eleven aircraft heading towards the Rhine valley. Before reaching the Rhine it was obvious that due to complete cloud cover an attack on Stuttgart or Cologne was impossible. Lt Richardson was compelled to abort with engine trouble at this point, firing a green Very light and leaving the formation.

Captain Hugh Walmsley turned the formations north in the hope of finding another target but again everything was covered by cloud. High winds and huge cloud banks began to swell as Captain Walmsley turned them north-west, deciding to bomb the large railway sidings one mile east of Sarrebourg. The formations dropped at 10.50 their mixed load of three 230lb, twelve 112lb, eight 25lb and two 40lb phosphorous bombs with good bursts being observed on the tracks. Four enemy aircraft were seen while the formations were over the lines, yet only two Albatros scouts ventured near closing to within 300 yards, but quickly retreated after vigorous fire from the squadron observers who expended 2,100 rounds. Walmsley always told observers to fire at enemy aircraft, even at long distance, because they had noticed that tracers did not set planes alight from 100 yards out. This advice was the exact opposite of what they were taught in observer school before leaving for the front.

The lines were re-crossed at Blâmont at 15,000ft, and despite the weather the two photo machines managed to take twenty-four photographic plates. Anti-aircraft fire throughout the trip had been very slight, while road and rail movement seemed to be normal where it was spotted through the clouds.

HUGH SYDNEY PORTER WALMSLEY was born on 6th June 1898 at Windermere, and was educated at Old College, Windermere and Dover College. Commissioned as a 2Lt in the 3/4th Battalion Loyal North Lancashire Regiment he was transferred to the Royal Flying Corps in 1916. Serving with 55 Squadron between September 1917 and September 1918, he was awarded the Military Cross before leaving for Home Establishment. After several postings in the UK he again saw service with 55 Squadron in Iraq between 1921 and 1923. Based at Mosul in northern Iraq he was awarded the Distinguished Flying Cross in 1922. In 1933 he was made Commanding Officer of 33 Squadron and between 1935-37 he commanded 8 Squadron in Aden. During the Second World War he commanded 71st Wing Advanced Air Striking Force before moving to Bomber Command where he held various appointments before being made Senior Air Staff Officer at Command HQ. Post war he commanded 232 Group at Singapore before moving to India to become Air Officer C-in-C India in October 1946. On 1st March 1950 he was made Air Officer C-in-C Flying Training Command. He left this post and the Air Force for Air Services Training Limited on 1st August 1952. His last known address was Upwood, Tiptoe, Lymington in Hants. He passed away on 2nd September 1985.

Note: The two primary targets assigned to 55 Squadron were the Bosch & Daimler Works at Stuttgart or Cologne weather permitting. The secondary target was the railway sidings at Offenburg, but these were covered in cloud as well. Information concerning the main target eluded the author for some time. It is known that the priority target issued on 8th July was either Cologne or Coblenz. A new priority target wasn't issued to 55 Squadron until the evening of 12th July. Although priority targets were issued all the time, weather was usually the deciding factor governing targets.

Target: Buhl Aerodrome

15th July		**Take Off:**	**04.45**
99 Squadron		**Returned:**	**07.20**

Formation 1

Capt W.D.Thom	Lt H.T.Melville	D1679	
Lt K.D.Marshall	2Lt O.Bell	C6145	
Lt W.G.Stevenson	Sgt H.L.Bynon	C6210	
Lt H.D.West	2Lt M.A.Dunn	C6092	
Lt E.L.Doidge	2Lt W.B.Walker	D1019	photo machine
Lt G.Broadbent	Sgt J.Jones	D1026	

Formation 2

Capt V.Beecroft	Lt A.L.Benjamin	ret e/t
Sgt H.H.Wilson	Sgt F.L.Lee	ret e/t
Lt F.G.Thompson	2Lt S.C.Thornley	ret e/t
Lt W.J.Garritty	2Lt E.Beale	ret e/t
Lt L.V.Dennis	2Lt F.W.Wooley	ret e/t
Lt S.M.Black	2Lt E.Singleton	ret e/t
	2Lt R.E.Sothcott	ret obs sick

No offensive operations by 99 Squadron had taken place since the 8th of July due mainly to weather, but this allowed valuable time to train new pilots and observers. Lt R.F.Freeland, an experienced pilot, was admitted to hospital and struck off strength. However new crews were arriving all the time, several from the U.S.A. Aviation Section and these crews were being brought on as quickly as possible. A workers' strike in England at this time was stopping valuable supplies getting through, and this also curtailed operations for a few days but it was a useful time for 99 Squadron.

They were led by Captain Thom, this time with thirteen aircraft and crews on a return trip to Buhl, including one spare in case of illness or more likely engine trouble. In the event engine trouble was to wreck this raid. Even before crossing the lines the thirteen aircraft had been reduced to six! Engine trouble was the main culprit, and 2Lt Sothcott returning due to sickness. The remaining six aircraft crossed the lines heading east towards Buhl encountering only slight and inaccurate archie. Reaching Buhl they let loose three 230lb and six 112lb bombs, and most hits were observed south-east of the aerodrome behind the hangars. Only one scout at low level was seen the entire raid, and all six aircraft returned safely complete with eight photos.

Lt Sothcott was indeed ill being admitted to hospital for appendicitis. Fortunately casualties were slight at the moment but illness was doing as good a job as German machine-gun bullets.

Note: Records for this raid do not list the pilot for 2Lt Sothcott.

Target: Railways at Offenburg

15th July		**Take Off:**	**15.00**
55 Squadron		**Returned:**	**18.15**

Formation 1

Capt F.Williams	Capt W.H. Mason-Springgay	
Lt A.Clarke	2Lt J.G.Quinton	
Lt S.L.Dowswell	Sgt G.Howard	
Lt G.T.Richardson	2Lt T.F.L.Myring	
Lt P.E.Welchman	Lt J.M.Carroll	photo machine
Capt D.R.G. Mackay	2Lt H.C.T.Gompertz	

Formation 2

Lt C.A.Bridgland	Sgt H.Mahoney
Lt A.S.Keep	2Lt J.S.Pollock

2Lt J.Cunliffe	2Lt G.E.Little	
Lt C.Young	Lt R.A.Butler	
2Lt W.J.Pace	2Lt D.W.Stewart	photo machine
Lt E.Blythe	2Lt W.H.Currie	ret e/t 15.15

Stuttgart was the intended target for 55 this day, but weather conditions changed in the afternoon making it unfavourable for a long distance raid. Whilst climbing through gaps in the clouds over the airfield, the rear formation had Lt Blythe and 2Lt Currie abort due to engine trouble. The remaining eleven aircraft headed south-east to cross the lines at Raon-l'-Etape, crossing at 14,000ft. The formation headed east in a straight line towards Offenburg, covering most of the fifty-mile route by compass heading due to cloud cover.

Approaching Offenburg at 17.00 hours, sporadic archie was encountered as the bombers climbed to 15,000ft and released four 230lb, twelve 112lb, eight 25lb and one 40lb phosphorous bomb. Good bursts were observed on the sidings and railway sheds, while one burst was seen to hit the electric power station; several bursts were also seen in fields.

Turning south to follow the Rhine towards Freiburg, four enemy aircraft were observed but were driven off by the observers who fired 1,100 rounds. Turning west over Lahr the formation headed back towards the lines, a single enemy aircraft was spotted but it did not engage and the formations crossed the lines at 15,000ft over St.Dié. Twenty-six photographic plates were exposed, and train movement in the Strasbourg area was reported higher than usual.

Although the bomb raid report says targeting was accurate, Williams recorded in his diary "Bombing not very good, owing to Bridgland cutting across in front of us, but some good bursts on engine sheds". Intelligence reports suggest that a military camp was destroyed by aeroplanes, many soldiers being killed and injured.

Reconnaissance

15th July			**Take Off:**	**15.25**
55 Squadron			**Returned:**	**18.15**
2Lt C.R.Whitelock	Lt G.Brier-Ash	A7837		

Crossed lines at Fresnes at 19,000ft, and exposed plates over Frescaty, Metz, Metz-Sablon, Bolchen and Freisdorf, re-crossed at 19,500ft at Nomeny, twenty-five plates exposed.

Reconnaissance

16th July			**Take Off:**	**5.05**
55 Squadron			**Returned:**	**09.45**
2Lt W.J.Pace	Lt D.W.Stewart	A7942		

Crossed the lines south-west of Château-Salins and flew over Dieuze, Biersdorf, Lauterfingen, Bensdorf, Morhange, Remilly, Boulay and Freisdorf. The return leg was flown over Boulay, St.Avold, Morhange and north of Château-Salins where the lines were re-crossed. Six enemy aircraft were seen over Morhange at 10,000ft, and a single aircraft was seen over Destry at 20,000ft. In all thirty-six plates were taken.

Target: Thionville Station and Goods Yard

16th July			**Take Off:**	**11.25**
99 Squadron			**Returned:**	**13.50**
Formation 1				
Capt W.D.Thom	Lt H.T.Melville	C1670		
Lt K.D.Marshall	2Lt O.Bell	C1666		
Lt W.G.Stevenson	Sgt H.L.Bynon	C6210		
Lt E.L.Doidge	2Lt W.B.Walker	D1019		
Lt G.Broadbent	Sgt J.Jones	D1026		
Lt H.D.West	2Lt M.A.Dunn	C6092		
Formation 2				
Capt V.Beecroft	Lt H.S.Notley	C6149		

Lt W.J.Garrity	2Lt E.Beale	C1668	
Lt F.G.Thompson	2Lt S.C.Thornley	D1679	
Lt L.V.Dennis	2Lt F.W.Wooley	D7223	
Sgt H.H.Wilson	Sgt F.L.Lee	C6196	
Lt S.M.Black	2Lt E.Singleton	D7223	
Lt F.T.Cockburn	Sgt V.Foulsham	C2173	crashed t/off
Lt G.Martin	Sgt F.Coulson	C6191	ret spare machine

A joint raid with 55 Squadron against Thionville and its mass of railway tracks and goods sidings was the target on a very cloudy day, with strong westerly winds. Captain Silly would be leading 99 Squadron who this time would be taking fourteen aircraft aloft in the hope of getting at least twelve across the lines. Take-off was eventful with Lt Cockburn crashing his machine after his engine cut out; both he and his observer were unhurt. The remaining thirteen got away without incident, climbing into huge banks of clouds, a test of how far their formation flying had come along.

Crossing the lines near Verdun, the formations became two standard sixes as Lt Martin in the spare machine turned for home. Continuing north-east over Briey towards Thionville, both formations were looking good, the first time 99 Squadron had taken a full complement of bombers to a target. Approaching Thionville, Captain Duncan Mackay from 55 Squadron joined the rear group of 99 Squadron after becoming separated in cloud from his Squadron. The anti-aircraft fire increased as the bombers neared the objective. The heavy barrage was uncomfortably accurate but five 230lb and fourteen 112lb bombs sailed down towards the station below. Four bursts were observed near or on the nearby gas works, five on the railway starting a large fire and several secondary fires and explosions; smoke was seen to rise to 6,000ft. Turning south for the lines, they were intercepted by four enemy scouts. No aircraft were claimed and none lost as the formations re-crossed the lines and returned safely to Azelot, complete with nine photos.

It was clear to the pilots and observers that considerable damage had been done, how much damage was later recorded after the war by a commission to investigate bomb damage to German targets. They recorded as follows: *Two ammunition trains received direct hits, fifteen trucks exploded and caught fire causing secondary explosions, five additional trucks in sidings also exploded. Exploding shells then set fire to the Goods Shed and nearby trucks and burnt out the despatch buildings. West of the Goods Shed, on the other side of a road were two buildings containing shells, these exploded setting fire to two more buildings containing hand grenades. Sixty horses were killed in their wagons by the main munitions train, five engines which were unable to move were seriously damaged in the northern part of the station. The water mains was destroyed and telephone lines were cut, eighty-three soldiers and ten civilians were killed. In all approximately fifty trucks were destroyed and another fifty damaged, four hundred soldiers were drafted in to clear the mess. The railway tracks were down for two days forcing the Germans to divert their rolling stock via Longuyon, Audun-le-Roman and Metz.*

Reconnaissance

16th July			Take Off:	09.30
55 Squadron			Returned:	13.10
Lt C.A.Bridgland	2Lt C.L.Rayment	A7837		

Crossed lines at 19,500ft at Nomeny. Exposed plates over Boulay (three enemy aircraft out), flew from Bouzonville to Saarlouis and through gaps in the clouds over St.Avold. Re-crossed the lines at Château-Salins at 18,500ft, twenty-one plates exposed.

Target: Railway and Sidings at Thionville

16th July			Take Off:	11.30
55 Squadron			Returned:	14.00
Formation 1				
Capt B.J.Silly	Lt J.Parke		lost in cloud	
Capt D.R.G.Mackay	2Lt H.C.T.Gompertz			
Lt P.E.Welchman	Lt J.M.Carroll		lost in cloud	
2Lt W.Beer	Sgt W.E.Baker		ret obs sick	
2Lt C.R.Whitelock	Lt G.Bryer-Ash	D8373	crash t/off	
Lt C.L.Heater	Sgt A.S.Allan		lost in cloud	

Formation 2
2Lt J.R.Bell	2Lt E.R.Beesley		
Lt A.Clarke	2Lt J.G.Quinton		lost in cloud
Lt A.S.Keep	2Lt J.S.Pollock		
Lt E.Blythe	2Lt W.H.Currie	D8392	/D.O.W.
2Lt E.J.Whyte	Sgt E.Clare		photo machine
Lt E.P.Critchley	Sgt S.E.Lewis		

Both 55 and 99 Squadron were tasked to bomb Thionville station and sidings. The weather conditions for these raids were very bad with considerable banks of clouds and high winds. The two flights lined up and took off, but the photo machine in the first flight flown by 2Lt Whitelock failed to clear a parked DH9 on the aerodrome. The undercarriage was ripped from the DH4 as one of the 112lb bombs they were carrying fell away and exploded beneath their machine, Whitelock was killed, his observer Bryer-Ash was severely wounded. The two flights left Azelot heading north-west to cross the lines at Verdun at 13,500ft, but before reaching the lines the first formation lost another aircraft; 2Lt Beer returned with a sick observer.

Once over the lines the formations turned north-east flying over Etain towards Briey and Thionville. Between Etain and Briey dense cloud made formation flying difficult, and the remaining three aircraft in the first formation led by the experienced Captain Benjamin Silly became lost in cloud as did Lt Clarke from the second formation, so all returned to Azelot at 13.15. Detached from the first formation in cloud, Captain Duncan Mackay spotted 99 Squadron ahead and closing with them he joined the rear formation and successfully bombed Thionville, landing at Azelot at 13.45.

The second formation led by 2Lt John Bell managed to thread their way through the cloud and reached Thionville at 13.00. The five remaining machines climbed to 14,000ft and dropped one 230lb, six 112lb, eight 25lb bombs and two 40lb phosphorous bombs on to the already burning station, courtesy of 99 Squadron.

The single formation turned south heading for home when they encountered ten enemy aircraft east of Metz. A running fight ensued up to the lines where Lt E.Blythe, streaming petrol, and with a severely wounded observer due to machine-gun fire, put his nose down and left the formation. The remaining four aircraft fought off the enemy scouts and returned to Azelot after expending 2,200 rounds. The photo machine flown by 2Lt Whyte managed to take thirteen photographic plates. Lt Blythe landed his damaged aircraft on allied territory, but unfortunately his observer on probation, 2Lt Walter Howard Currie, died of his wounds. Currie was from Toronto in Canada and was twenty-eight years of age; he is buried in the I.A.F. Cemetery at Charmes. Also buried at Charmes was Charles Railton Whitelock, who came from Barnsley in Yorkshire, aged only twenty.

Reconnaissance

16th July			**Take Off:**	**11.50**
55 Squadron			**Returned:**	**14.45**
Capt H.S.P.Walmsley	Capt R.P.Ward	A7942		

Crossed lines west of Thiaucourt at 18,000ft, but owing to clouds from 15,000ft to 22,900ft reconnaissance abandoned, re-crossed at Château-Salins.

Reconnaissance

17th July			**Take Off:**	**09.30**
55 Squadron			**Returned:**	**13.10**
Lt P.E.Welchman	Lt J.M.Carroll	A7837		

Crossed lines at Château-Salins 18,500ft, flew to Baronville aerodrome, St.Avold, Porcelette, Felsberg, Bousonville aerodrome, Freisdorf aerodrome, Boulay aerodrome and re-crossed at Forêt-de-Besarge at 13,000ft, thirty plates taken.

Target: Thionville Station and Goods Yard

17th July			**Take Off:**	**09.35**
99 Squadron			**Returned:**	**12.40**
Formation 1				
Capt W.D.Thom	Lt H.T.Melville	C1670		

Lt W.G.Stevenson	Sgt H.L.Bynon	C6210	
Lt K.D.Marshall	2Lt O.Bell	C6113	ret e/t
Lt E.L.Doidge	2Lt W.B.Walker	D1019	
Lt G.Broadbent	Sgt J.Jones	D7233	ret e/t
2Lt F.T.Cockburn	Sgt V.Foulsham	C6092	ret e/t

Formation 2

Capt V.Beecroft	2Lt S.C.Thornley	C6278	
Sgt H.H.Wilson	Sgt F.L.Lee	C6196	
Lt G.Martin	Sgt F.Coulson	C6149	
Lt C.W.Hewson	2Lt H.W.Batty	C1666	left formation
Lt W.J.Garrity	2Lt E.Beale	C1668	ret e/t
Capt A.D.Taylor	Lt H.S.Notley	D1679	ret e/t

Another windy day, although somewhat clearer, greeted 99 and 55 Squadron for their return trip to Thionville, hoping to capitalise on their previous day's work. Despite the mass destruction of the previous day a repeat performance was unlikely, with the sun climbing higher and the temperature rising, engine overheating could be a real problem. Magneto trouble was the culprit with Captain Taylor returning after only twenty-five minutes, followed by Lt Marshall after one hour twenty-five minutes; Broadbent and Cockburn returned shortly after with magneto trouble too. Lt Garrity returned after an hour and a half; magneto trouble was not the problem this time, his engine was overheating. Crossing the lines Lt Hewson mistook a signal and also returned, leaving one formation of six machines to head for Thionville.

The wind was judged by Captain Thom to be about thirty-five miles per hour, making headway to the target rather slow, the other problem was anti-aircraft fire which was usually heavy, and accurate, near Metz and Thionville. Despite the heavy archie one 230lb and ten 112lb bombs fell towards Thionville, two bursts were observed north-west of the main station, while a good cluster of bursts were seen just over the river. Turning for home the formation was confronted by six enemy scouts and a fight ensued right to the lines but no victories were claimed by either side. One enemy scout was painted red, possibly Jasta 18 from nearby Montingen near Metz. 2Lt Walker had been busy with his camera, taking fifteen photos in the target area.

Major Pattinson had an eventful, if short flight with 2Lt Taylor on a photography and rigging test in DH9 D7223. After take-off he was forced to land just south of the aerodrome, but the aircraft was not damaged and Captain Beecroft returned the aircraft four hours later with Corporal Griffiths in the back. Although there were no fatalities in this incident, accidents like this were becoming more common and any squadron in the I.A.F. especially 99, could not afford to lose any crews, especially experienced ones.

Target: Railways at Thionville

17th July		Take Off:	09.50
55 Squadron		**Returned:**	**12.45**

Formation 1

Capt B.J.Silly	Lt J.Parke		
2Lt J.Cunliffe	2Lt G.E.Little		
Lt S.L.Dowswell	Sgt G.Howard		
Lt G.T.Richardson	2Lt T.F.L.Myring		photo machine
Lt C.A.Bridgland	Sgt H.Mahoney		
Lt G.C.Sherman	Sgt W.E.Baker		

Formation 2

2Lt E.J.Whyte	Sgt E.Clare		
2Lt W.J.Pace	2Lt D.W.Stewart		
Capt D.R.G.Mackay	2Lt H.C.T.Gompertz		
Lt C.Young	Lt R.A.Butler	D8386	e/t landing crashed
Lt E.P.Critchley	Sgt S.E.Lewis		
Lt C.L.Heater	Sgt A.S.Allan		

After the devastation of the previous day, both 55 and 99 Squadron were detailed to return to Thionville in the hope of shutting down the station for a considerable amount of time. While climbing over the field Lt

Young was forced into a quick landing because of engine trouble, crashing his machine, but both occupants escaped unharmed and were back in action two days later. The remaining eleven DH4s headed out to the north-west, the two formations crossing the lines at Fresnes at 12,500 feet coming under moderate but accurate fire.

Turning east the two formations flew over the railway station at Conflans, spotting a single enemy aircraft below; changing direction they then headed over Hagondange towards Thionville. While flying this route Captain Silly led the two formations up to 13,500 feet from where they bombed at 11.35 letting loose three 230lb, fourteen 112lb, eight 25lb bombs and two 40lb phosphorous bombs. Several bursts were observed west of the station, while others hit houses and railway tracks beside the River Moselle.

As the formations turned south-east, five enemy aircraft approached and a running fight ensued. The combined fire of the observers kept them at bay and the enemy aircraft did not close sufficiently to engage. The two formations flew over Boulay aerodrome which was unobserved due to cloud, then south re-crossing the lines at Nomeny. In all nineteen photographic plates were taken while train movement was reported to be well below normal.

Note: Although 55's records improve they still do not list aircraft serial numbers used on the raids.

Reconnaissance

19th July			**Take Off:**	**07.10**
55 Squadron			**Returned:**	**11.10**
Capt F.Williams	Capt W.H.Mason-Springgay	A7836		

Crossed lines at Verdun at 19,000ft and exposed plates over objective, railway movement normal, re-crossed at Pont-à-Mousson, thirty-four plates exposed.

Target: Mauser Munition Works at Oberndorf

19th July		**Take Off:**	**08.45**
55 Squadron		**Returned:**	**13.10**
Formation 1			
Capt H.S.P.Walmsley	Capt R.P.Ward		
2Lt W.J.Pace	Lt D.W.Stewart		
Lt C.L.Heater	Sgt A.S.Allan		
2Lt A.W.M.Bryant	Sgt W.E.Baker	ret e/t 10.30	
2Lt E.J.Whyte	Sgt E.Clare	photo machine	
Lt E.P.Critchley	Sgt S.E.Lewis	ret e/t 09.50	
Formation 2			
2Lt J.R.Bell	2Lt E.R.Beesley		
2Lt J.Cunliffe	2Lt G.E.Little		
Capt D.R.G.Mackay	2Lt H.C.T.Gompertz		
Lt G.T.Richardson	2Lt T.F.L.Myring	ret e/t 09.45	
Lt A.S.Keep	2Lt J.S.Pollock	ret e/t 10.46	
Lt C.Young	Lt R.A.Butler		

Oberndorf munitions works, one of the biggest in Germany, lay on the River Neckar in the Kingdom of Württemberg, thirty miles east of Strasbourg. After gaining height over the field the two formations flew south-east to cross the lines at St Dié at 14,000ft. The two formations were already down to five machines each, Lt Critchley returning with petrol problems, while Lt Richardson aborted with engine trouble.

Once over the lines slight flak was encountered as the two groups headed east over Schlettstadt, then north-east towards Lahr where two enemy aircraft were spotted. Before reaching Lahr however, Lt Whyte and Lt Keep both left their formations with engine trouble, both returning to Azelot. The enemy aircraft kept their distance as the two formations turned south-east towards Wolfach, then east towards Oberndorf. At 10.35 flying at 15,000ft the remaining eight 'fours' dropped two 230lb, eight 112lb, sixteen 25lb and four 40lb bombs. Only one burst was observed on a shed next to the munitions factory, the rest being obscured by cloud.

With only one photographic machine over the objective (due to the early return of Lt Keep), it was inevitable that the remaining camera, normally very reliable, in the aircraft of 2Lt Whyte and Sgt Clare would jam after only three shots. The camera most commonly used by observers on bombing missions was the Williamson L camera. It was housed in a bay behind the observer in a sponge and rubber frame to absorb the aircraft's vibrations, thus giving clearer pictures. The exposure mechanism was wind driven but prone to icing so often crews disconnected the wind vane, and operated the camera by hand.

Captain Walmsley turned the formations around and headed back towards Wolfach, then over Lahr and west towards Schlettstadt. Re-crossing the lines at St Dié, the formations received more attention from the front line archie batteries then they had earlier. However, all returned safely to report practically no rail movement, and no interception by hostile aircraft.

Reconnaissance

19th July			Take Off:	11.20
55 Squadron			**Returned:**	**15.10**
Capt J.B.Silly	Lt J.Parke	A7837		

Crossed lines at 20,000ft at Pont-à-Mousson and exposed plates over Fleury, Boulay and Saarbrücken (Burbach Works), re-crossed east Lunéville at 21,000ft, seventeen plates exposed.

Target: Mercedes Aero Engine Works at Untertürkheim
Secondary Target: Railway and Station at Offenburg

20th July			Take Off:	04.45
99 Squadron			**Returned:**	**08.05**
Formation 1				
Capt A.D.Taylor	Lt H.S.Notley	C1666		
Sgt H.H.Wilson	Sgt F.L.Lee	C6196		
Lt L.V.Dennis	2Lt F.W.Wooley	D1032		
Lt F.Smith	Sgt F.Coulson	C6113		
Lt G.Martin	2Lt T.K.Ludgate	C6149	/W.I.A.	
Lt F.G.Thompson	2Lt S.C.Thornley	D1679	P.O.W./ P.O.W.	
Formation 2				
Capt W.D.Thom	Lt H.T.Melville	C1670	ret e/t	
Lt W.J.Garrity	2Lt E.Beale	C1668		
Lt G.Broadbent	Sgt J.Jones	D1026		
Lt E.L.Doidge	2Lt W.B.Walker	C6145		
Lt W.G.Stevenson	2Lt O.Bell	C6219	ret e/t	
Lt C.W.Hewson	2Lt E.Singleton	C6278		
2Lt F.T.Cockburn	Sgt V.Foulsham	C6092	ret e/t	
Lt P.Dietz	Sgt H.S.Bynon	D3039	crashed t/off	
Lt P.Dietz	Sgt H.S.Bynon	D7223	ret obs sick	

The Mercedes Aero Engine Works at Untertürkheim near Stuttgart was the target for 99 and 55 Squadron, both having been on standby to hit this facility after two days of bad weather. Stuttgart and its aero engine plant was approximately one hundred and ten miles over the lines, so conditions would have to be perfect to reach it. Considerable time had been spent on repairing the engines after their poor performance on the raid to Thionville on 17th, so it was hoped that at least twelve machines would make Stuttgart out of the available fourteen which took off, led by Captain Taylor. Taking off was becoming more hazardous of late; Lt Phillip Dietz an American, who had recently arrived on 5th July from the United States Army Aviation Section swerved on take-off and struck a hangar. Both men were unhurt and quickly climbed into DH9 D7223 and took off. They soon returned however with Sgt Bynon feeling sick, not a good start for Dietz on his first raid. Dietz was on loan from 104 Squadron for two weeks.

Heading west towards St Dié, Lt Cockburn experienced ignition trouble and turned for home, shortly followed by Lt Stevenson also with ignition problems. With six in the first formation and five in the rear formation, both crossed the lines coming under heavy but inaccurate archie. Once over, five would soon become four, with Captain Thom following Stevenson turning for home with a broken petrol pump, so the rear formation of four machines was now led by Lt Doidge. Lack of aircraft was not the only problem as a strong wind was still blowing, therefore Captain Taylor decided to bomb Offenburg station instead. Just before reaching Offenburg two enemy two-seaters and approximately twenty Pfalz scouts attacked both groups as they dropped five 230lb and ten 112lb bombs. One burst was observed on the largest engine shed, while three hits were seen on the sidings and one on the track next to the engine shed; no other bursts were observed due to the large force of fighters closing for combat. Heading straight for the lines, the lead formation seemed to be getting more attention. Lt Thompson and 2Lt Thornley were hit in the radiator as they crossed the Rhine, and emitting steam they were last seen in a shallow descent over Molsheim, at about 6,000ft. Thompson when repatriated was still suffering from a gun shot wound to the leg. The fight continued but no more aircraft were lost with both formations holding tight. 2Lt Ludgate was wounded in the hand during this engagement, but the enemy aircraft did not have it all their own way, Lt Broadbent and 2Lt Beale claiming one scout driven down.

Jasta 78b operating out of Buhl near Offenburg look to be the likely victors over Thompson and Thornley. Offizierstellvertreter Eduard Prime claimed a DH9 at 08.10 German time at Blaesheim, both time and location fit as German time was one hour ahead of Allied time. Judging by the size of the force Jasta 78b were mixed in with Kest 4b who were engaging 55 Squadron nearby. Offizierstellvertreter Paul Felsmann of this unit was killed in action over Schwarzwald. A casualty of Broadbent and Sgt Jones is unlikely and his death was probably due to fire from 55 Squadron. Dropping by 99 had been good and sidings belonging to the Mauser works were hit. Extensions of the Mauser works were also hit.

Target: Mercedes Aero Engine Works at Untertürkheim
Secondary Target: Mauser Munitions Works at Oberndorf

20th July			Take Off:	05.05
55 Squadron			Returned:	09.12
Formation 1				
Capt F.Williams	Capt W.H.Mason-Springgay	B3957		
Lt C.A.Bridgland	Sgt G.Howard			
2Lt G.T.Richardson	2Lt T.F.L.Myring			
Sgt F.E.Nash	Sgt W.E.Baker	A7876	W.I.A./K.I.A.	
Lt A.S.Keep	2Lt J.S.Pollock	A7427	W.I.A./D.O.W.	
Lt C.Young	Lt R.A.Butler	D9275	K.I.A./K.I.A.	
Formation 2				
Lt P.E.Welchman	2Lt E.R.Beesley	B3967		
Lt E.P.Critchley	Sgt S.E.Lewis	A7546		
Lt C.L.Heater	Sgt A.S.Allan			
Lt P.J.Cunningham	2Lt H.C.T.Gompertz		ret e/t 06.30	
2Lt W.J.Pace	Lt D.W.Stewart	A7703	photo machine	
Lt G.C.Sherman	Lt G.C.Smith			

Located in the suburbs of Stuttgart was the Mercedes Aero Engine Works at Untertürkheim, the target for 55 Squadron on a day of good visibility and high cloud formations. Climbing over the field the formations headed out to cross the lines at St.Dié at 14,000ft, where Lt Cunningham left the rear formation returning with engine trouble. Crossing the lines they encountered heavy archie as they headed east towards Lahr. Heading north-east towards Stuttgart, Captain Williams noticed a strong wind developing in their face. Concerned about fuel he turned south-east over the Black Forest, and followed the River Neckar down towards the Mauser factory, visited by 55 only the day before.

Approaching Oberndorf at 7.15, the formations climbed to 14,500ft and dropped two 230lb, fourteen 112lb, sixteen 25lb bombs and three 40lb phosphorous bombs. Bursts were observed on railways, housing and the munitions factory where the formations whilst turning for home, noticed a small fire start in the factory. Alert observers also noticed the incoming mixed formation of five Albatros DIII and five Pfalz fighters of Kest 4b, from their airfield at Freiburg. Also in attendance were two Albatros CX powered by the 260hp Mercedes engine. These two-seaters were used in reconnaissance and artillery observation work but may well have been employed by Kest 4b as R/T machines, in contact with ground stations to update the location of the enemy. They could also be used to lead the fighters to the bomber formations.

The Kest pilots with their crucial height advantage attacked from above. Lt Christopher Young and his observer Lt R.A.Butler were flying No6 in the front formation, and quickly had an Albatros fighter behind them. Falling out of formation the DH4 was covered in flames as it fell to earth. Lt Butler jumped to save himself the horror of burning to death, his body being found two weeks later in a clump of fir trees. A tremendous dog fight ensued with the Albatros CX firing into the front formation from behind, while the enemy scouts dived in threes. Sergeant S.E.Lewis spotted three enemy aircraft diving from the left front of the rear formation; he fired three good bursts, and the leader of the three was seen to go down out of control. Seeing the Albatros CX 100ft below, Lt Patrick Eliot Welchman and 2Lt William John Pace dived on the two-seater, both firing good bursts from their Vickers before climbing back up to rejoin their formation; the Albatros CX turned over and was seen to crash.

Sergeant F.E.Nash and his observer Sergeant W.E.Baker were in the thick of the action when suddenly water and steam gushed over Nash's thighs as his radiator was holed. Looking over his shoulder he saw Baker's twin Lewis guns pointing skywards as the smell of petrol from the under seat tank filled his nostrils. Nash stayed with the formation until Spandau bullets ripped into his shoulder; fragments of the main petrol tank also penetrated his flying suit, lodging in his back. Falling unconscious the DH4 fell away in a vertical dive, but Nash came around at 7,000ft with the aircraft doing 180 mph. Managing to close the throttle he tried to level the aircraft but could not move the control column. Sergeant Baker in the rear seat was slumped against the emergency stick, but Nash was able to free the control column then look for a suitable field to land in. Given the solitary choice of one small field bordered by fir trees, he side-slipped to lose height but straightened out too late hitting a ridge and ripping off the undercarriage. Pancaking from fifteen feet the DH4 ground to a halt. Lifting himself from his shattered cockpit Nash tried to pull out Baker's dead weight so he could burn the aircraft. Hearing an aircraft overhead he looked up and saw an Albatros scout circling and coming in to land. The pilot of the Albatros walked over to Nash and offered him a "particularly nasty cigarette" as they waited for assistance. Nash was taken to the nearby village hall and shortly afterwards moved to the hospital at Oberndorf, where judging by the crowd around the hospital doors, he was not too popular. Nash attended the funerals of Lt Young and Sgt Baker who were buried with full military honours at Oberndorf cemetery. After spending two months in Tubingen hospital, Nash was sent to various camps until repatriated on December 8th 1918.

The remaining ten aircraft of 55 Squadron battled towards the lines. Before crossing north of Colmar, DH4 A7427 flown by Lt Keep left the formation and headed for the French hospital at Rambervillers. Upon landing he discovered his observer 2Lt Pollock had already died of his wounds. Keep himself had been wounded in the arm and promptly fainted. Vizefeldwebel Heppner and Offizierstellvertreter Pohlmann of Kest 4b were both credited with their only victories of the war. Offizierstellvertreter Paul Felsmann of Kest 4b was killed over Schwarzwald, most likely the victim of 55's observers.

The strain of high altitude flying and combat was beginning to take its toll on the men. Captain Mason-Springgay who was suffering from jaundice at this time mistook Lt Bridgland's DH4 for an enemy fighter as they crossed the lines. Captain Williams "banked sharply to put Springgay's aim off" and so prevented an accident on a day where 55 Squadron had lost six aircrew, four dead, one wounded and one taken prisoner. Despite the attention of enemy fighters, 2Lt Pace and Lt Stewart managed to take eighteen photographic plates of the target.

Lt Christopher Young, aged twenty-seven from Streatham, London, and Lt Reginald Arthur Butler, aged twenty-four from Egham in Surrey, were both buried at Niederzwehren in Germany. Also buried at Niederzwehren was Sergeant William Edward Baker from Heaton in Northumberland. 2Lt James Ferguson Pollock was buried in the I.A.F. Cemetery at Charmes.

Note: In the DH4 and DH9s observers had a control column in the event of pilots being knocked out; it was hoped that observers would be able to get the machine down and if lucky return to base. Often machines seen going down then stalling, then continuing down meant an observer desperately trying to save his own life, as well as his pilot's.

WILFRED HARRY MASON-SPRINGGAY was born on 20th November 1893 in Kent. He worked from 1910-1914 as a secretary at East Kent Railways, before joining the East Kent Regiment upon the outbreak of war. He was awarded the Military Cross on August 9th 1917, presumably while still with the East Kent Regiment, as he did not start at No1 School of Aerial Gunnery until 14th November 1917. From here he joined 55 Squadron on 22nd February 1918. Hospitalised on 23rd March 1918, he returned to 55 Squadron where he was commissioned Lt observer on 24th May 1918. Hospitalised with jaundice on 27th July, he was returned to Home Establishment where upon recovery he taught map reading. A well liked member of 55 Squadron, Mason-Springgay like many others at this time was avoiding the Medical Officer for fear of being taken off operations. Months of high altitude work was taking its toll on the longest serving members of 55 Squadron. His home address given while serving was 12 Belgrave Road, Dover.

Reconnaissance

20th July			Take Off:	08.20
55 Squadron			Returned:	12.15
Capt H.S.P.Walmsley	Capt R.P.Ward	A7942		

Crossed lines at Château-Salins at 19,000ft and proceeded to Morchingen aerodrome, Boulay aerodrome, Freisdorf aerodrome, Antilly, Metz and Fleury, re-crossed at 19,500ft at Nomeny. Twenty-six plates exposed.

Target: Mercedes Aero Engine Works at Untertürkheim
Secondary Target: Powder Factory at Rottweil

22nd July		Take Off:	07.30
55 Squadron		Returned:	11.35

Formation 1

Capt B.J.Silly	Lt J.Parke	
2Lt J.Cunliffe	2Lt G.E.Little	
Lt C.L.Heater	Sgt A.S.Allan	
Lt G.T.Richardson	2Lt T.F.L.Myring	
2Lt W.J.Pace	Lt D.W.Stewart	photo machine
Lt G.C.Sherman	Lt G.C.Smith	

Formation 2

2Lt E.J.Whyte	Sgt E.Clare	
2Lt J.B.McIntyre	2Lt H.C.T.Gompertz	ret e/t 09.20
Lt D.J.Waterous	2Lt C.L.Rayment	
Lt E.P.Critchley	Sgt S.E.Lewis	
Lt P.E.Welchman	2Lt E.R.Beesley	photo machine
Sgt A.W.Mepsted	Sgt G.Howard	ret e/t 09.15

Again 55 would try and reach the Mercedes Engine Works at Untertürkheim, the main target given to the daylight squadrons of the I.A.F. in July. Leaving Azelot to the south-east, the formations crossed the lines at Markirch, and headed towards Schlettstadt which lay south of Lahr. Once over the lines, 2Lt McIntyre and Sergeant Mepsted both returned to Azelot with engine trouble, leaving the remaining ten aircraft to fly on towards Stuttgart.

Reaching Schlettstadt high winds again discouraged the long haul to Stuttgart and Captain Silly decided to attack the powder works at Rottweil. Flying east over the Black Forest the squadron crossed over Triburg and approached Rottweil lying on the banks of the River Neckar, just south of Oberndorf. As the two formations approached the target, the Rottweil battery put up a considerable barrage but it was well below the formation as they climbed to 14,500ft and dropped one 230lb bomb, sixteen 112lb bombs, eight 25lb bombs and two 40lb phosphorous bombs. Numerous bursts were observed on the factory buildings, while in the north-east corner of the complex a huge fire started causing continuous explosions.

The formations turned south and headed for Villingen spotting four enemy aircraft approaching. A long-range running fight ensued, the enemy scouts keeping their distance as the formations turned west over Villingen towards Freiburg where Kest units 4 and 5 were stationed. As 55 Squadron passed overhead taking photographs they noticed five enemy machines nearby, which did not engage and 55 crossed the lines near Colmar. In all twenty photographic plates were taken while 4,500 rounds had been expended keeping the enemy at bay. Photographs later revealed a burst on the buildings of the powder factory, and a burst on the stores to the east of the powder factory. Intelligence sources stated a large fire had broken out and 200 tons of explosives were destroyed during the raid.

Note: Again 55's records do not list aircraft flown on this operation.

Reconnaissance

22nd July			Take Off:	09.05
55 Squadron			Returned:	13.15
Capt F.Williams	2Lt J.G.Quinton	A7942		

Crossed lines at Blâmont at 18,000ft, exposed plates over Sarrebourg and Neustadt, sixteen plates exposed over Mannheim. Re-crossed lines at 19,000ft, twenty plates exposed altogether.

Target: Mercedes Aero Engine Works at Untertürkheim
Secondary Target: Railway and Station at Offenburg

22nd July			Take Off:	14.20
99 Squadron			**Returned:**	**17.10**
Formation 1				
Capt W.D.Thom	Lt H.T.Melville	C1670		
Lt F.Smith	Sgt F.Coulson	C6113	force-landed	
Lt W.G.Stevenson	Lt H.S.Notley	C6210		
Lt E.L.Doidge	2Lt W.B.Walker	D1019		
Lt F.T.Cockburn	Sgt V.Foulsham	C6145		
Lt G.Broadbent	Sgt J.Jones	D1026	force-landed	
Lt H.D.West	2Lt M.A.Dunn	C6092		
Formation 2				
Capt V.Beecroft	2Lt B.S.W.Taylor	C6278		
Lt G.Martin	2Lt H.W.Batty	C6149		
Sgt H.H.Wilson	Sgt F.L.Lee	C6196		
2Lt L.V.Dennis	2Lt F.W.Wooley	D1032		
Lt T.M.Ritchie	Lt J.K.Speed	D3048		
Lt W.J.Garrity	2Lt E.Beale	C1668		
Lt C.W.Hewson	2Lt E.Singleton	D7223		

Strong winds would again determine whether 99 Squadron would reach Stuttgart on this day. 55 Squadron had tried earlier in the day but failed to reach the target. Early afternoon saw a drop in the wind speed and fourteen aircraft took off led by Captain Thom towards the lines. Once aloft it was clear the wind was still too strong for a realistic attempt on Stuttgart, and it was decided to bomb Offenburg again. Lt West and Lt Hewson piloting the spare machines returned to Azelot.

Crossing the lines the two formations of six machines each came under considerable archie crossing the Vosges mountains, then, as the bombers approached the Rhine enemy aircraft were spotted. Accurate anti-aircraft fire greeted 99 Squadron as they dropped six 230lb and twelve 112lb bombs on the station below. One burst was seen on the main station building, with another just east of it. There was another burst on the northern part of the town while a good cluster fell on the tracks near the station. Observers also noticed enemy aircraft taking off from the nearby airfield at Lahr.

Turning for home the observers readied themselves for the onslaught of enemy aircraft which totalled two two-seaters, and approximately sixteen scouts, some of which were Albatros DIIIs. Clear of the objective the scouts attacked, diving across the formation from right to left. Sgt Frederick Lee saw an Albatros scout firing from about sixty yards away almost in a stall. He swung his double Lewis gun around and emptied half a drum from each. The Albatros went into a vertical nose dive for 7,000ft and was seen to crash into a wood west of Molsheim; 2Lt Wooley also fired seventy rounds at this enemy aircraft. The situation was getting worse as the town of Schirmeck appeared. More enemy aircraft arrived in front of the two formations of DH9s circling to the rear and attacking at the top of the stall. Lt Smith and Lt Broadbent both dropped out of formation with holed radiators and were quickly fastened onto by some enemy scouts. Sgt Coulson was hit in the arm and things were looking bleak for the two DH9s losing height with the Vosges mountains looming ahead. Near the lines Captain Thom led the remaining ten aircraft down onto the enemy scouts attacking Smith and Broadbent, a light was fired by one of the scouts and they returned east leaving both Smith and Broadbent landing west of the lines near Raon-l'-Etape in the Vosges while the remaining ten DH9s returned to Azelot with fifteen photos, some of which were taken over the target. Smith managed to put his machine down on a steep hill among tall fir trees. Most of the fabric and parts of the machine were scattered in amongst the trees, but he finally came to a halt with the engine buried in the soft ground. Both were alive if a bit shaken and the engine was salvaged at a later date. Broadbent put down in a narrow valley among foot-hills with little damage to his machine. Unsure of their whereabouts they hid until they heard the sound of the voices of American soldiers looking for them. The local American unit helped salvage these machines and returned all four crews to the Squadron. Photographs revealed a burst on the western end of the main station, and three bursts on the railways to the south of the station. One burst was shown on the western end of a bridge over the railway.

Lt Kurt Seit of Jasta 80 claimed a DH9 on the 22nd of July at 17.00 German time which crashed into Celles Wood. The time fits well with German time still one hour ahead of British, and Jasta 80 could well have been in the area on patrol from their base at Bensdorf near Morsberg. Sgt Lee claimed his victory at 16.00 British time which also fits with Kurt Seit's time of combat. A combat report from Sgt Lee states that some enemy aircraft had red top planes, with red and white fuselages. Jasta 80 according to US intelligence, had black and white markings on lozenge fabric. Although the colours of the enemy aircraft differ there were up to sixteen enemy scouts, implying that there was more than just one Jasta, or Kest unit involved. This involvement by another Jasta is backed up by a claim for a DH9 at Celles Wood also at 17.00 German time by Offizierstellvertreter Eduard Prime of Jasta 78. Prime was not awarded this claim which wouldn't be the last time it would happen involving aircraft from the I.A.F. Both DH9s crash landed in amongst trees on the allied side, needing confirmation from another German source for Seit to be awarded the victory. He was awarded this victory which is why it has been referred to here. No German loss can be found to coincide with Sgt Lee's victory.

Target: Mercedes Aero Engine Works at Untertürkheim
Secondary Target: Railway at Lahr

30th July			Take Off:	05.05
99 Squadron			Returned:	08.20
Formation 1				
Capt V.Beecroft	2Lt B.S.W.Taylor	D7233		
Lt C.W.Hewson	Lt H.E.Alsford	C6278		
Sgt H.H.Wilson	Sgt F.L.Lee	C6196		
Lt W.J.Garrity	Lt H.T.Melville	C1668		
Lt T.M.Ritchie	Lt L.W.G.Stagg	C6149		
Lt S.M.Black	2Lt E.Singleton	D2916	ret e/t	
Lt L.V.Dennis	2Lt F.W.Wooley	D1032	ret e/t	
Formation 2				
Capt A.D.Taylor	Lt H.S.Notley	C1666		
Lt G.Martin	Lt S.G.Burton	C6210	W.I.A./K.I.A.	
Lt C.D.Clark	Lt A.T.Bowyer	D1019	left formation	
Lt P.Dietz	2Lt H.W.Batty	D7223	K.I.A./K.I.A.	
Lt F.Smith	2Lt K.H.Ashton	D3039	left formation	
Lt J.W.Richards	2Lt E.J.Munson	B9366	ret e/t	
Lt H.D.West	2Lt M.A.Dunn	C6092	ret e/t	

The recent thorn in the side of the I.A.F. – Stuttgart – beckoned once more for 99 Squadron and her stable mates 55 and 104. Taking off with two emergency machines, Captain Beecroft left Azelot climbing to the east towards the lines at Badonviller and the rendezvous. The previous eight days had been showery with low cloud, this day looked to be no exception with the land east of the Vosges almost completely covered in mist. A more pressing problem on the mind of Captain Beecroft was the rapidly depleting Squadron around him. The first to return was Lt Black with a faulty magneto, quickly followed by Lt Dennis with carburettor trouble and Lt Richards with an ignition problem. Three machines down left eleven, more than enough until Lt West in the other spare machine returned with an overheating engine. Ten would do but as the lines approached Lts Clark and Smith left the formation and started home. Clark was unable to keep formation and started for Azelot. However, in the worsening conditions he was unsure of his position and put his machine down at Dijon, quite a distance from Badonviller. Smith had a defective magneto and put his machine down at Epinal south of Nancy, returning to Azelot at 11.05.

Captain Beecroft did not hang about for the rendezvous and proceeded over the lines heading east hoping to pick-up the Rhine river. Crossing the Rhine the weather was becoming more overcast and it was decided to bomb the railway station at Lahr, twenty miles south-east of Strasbourg and east of the Rhine. The time was 07.20 as slight anti-aircraft fire greeted the eight DH9s as they dropped three 230lb and ten 112lb bombs; bursts were noted east and south-east of the station in the town. Prisoners of war stationed near the town later revealed that six bombs had partly destroyed a brewery.

Once past the objective seven enemy scouts were waiting, mostly Albatros scouts judging from combat reports, and these were below the formation, attacking using their stall technique. Four other enemy scouts arrived from Lahr which was behind the formation now, these also stayed below the formation and used the stall for their attack. When the DH9s reached Oberhat six more enemy scouts arrived from the west but these continued on, possibly the ones which attacked 55 Squadron at Offenburg. The battle was pretty even until six enemy scouts attacked from out of the sun. These scouts closed to about twenty yards in their attack, and one was sent down by Lt Notley in flames using his double Lewis gun while another was seen to dive away emitting steam. Lt Melville fired thirty rounds at twenty-five yards at an enemy scout which was seen to dive away sharply, possibly the scout mentioned above. The whole formation were banging away trying to keep the scouts at bay. Sgt Lee fired one hundred rounds claiming an Albatros scout where the pilot was seen to fall out; this was Lee's third victory this month. Lt Taylor also claimed an enemy aircraft. However, in the confusion it is hard to establish who got who, especially when all the observers could be firing at the nearest enemy aircraft which was naturally the biggest threat. The fighting was not all 99 Squadron's way, as Lt Phillip Dietz and his observer Horace Walter Batty were killed when their machine was seen to come apart and break up. Lt Martin's machine was badly shot up, had a hole punched in the radiator and with a badly wounded observer he headed earthwards, crash-landing allied side in a marsh near Jaeninime. A bullet wound to his foot did not stop him attending his stricken observer, but unfortunately Burton had already died from his wounds. The remaining six DH9s crossed the lines and landed safely back at Azelot. With unreliable engines resulting in a lack of numbers across the lines, and with increasingly hostile air activity, the future was looking bleak for 99 Squadron and the other units.

Vizefeldwebel Karl Kallmünzer of Jasta 78b received confirmation of his claim for a DH9 over Gross Rombach at 08.40 German time, this claim is believed to be Dietz and Batty, his second and last victory of the war. It is clear Jasta 78b were involved in the action especially being stationed nearby at Buhl aerodrome, but another Jasta unit to be involved was Jasta 18 with Lt Kurt Monnington receiving confirmation for Martin and Burton. Ltn Josef Filbig of Jasta 80 could be another claimant for either victory, claiming a two-seater over Parroy Wald on this day, his first kill of the war. There is no time recorded for this victory which makes it harder to match to the 99 Squadron losses, however it was awarded all the same as was Monnington's without a time so it has been included here as Jasta 80 could well have been in the area, and with the amount of enemy aircraft around there was more than just one unit involved. Ltn Robert Dycke of Jasta 78 was wounded in action against DH9s in Albatros DVa 7225/17 over Thannweiler. He may have been hit by any of the three daylight I.A.F. squadrons who were all in the area, but 99 Squadron look favourite. Ltn Hans Laurisch of Kest 4b was killed in action this day, flying out of Freiburg and he was well within range of the I.A.F. raids and has been included as a possible casualty of the I.A.F. Lt Stanley George Harold Edgar Burton of the 15th London Regiment, aged twenty-four, was buried at Charmes. He originated from Westcliff-on-Sea in Essex. The other observer killed this day was Horace Walter Batty who was from Chicago, Illinois. Aged eighteen, he was buried at Plaine in France along with his American pilot Lt Dietz.

Two observers were noted for decorations on this day, 2Lt Taylor, and Sgt Lee from Ockley; their citations read as follows:

2 Lt Bryan Samuel William Taylor
D.F.C. gazetted 2nd November 1918

A gallant and skilful observer who has been engaged in nineteen successful bombing raids during the past five months. During one of these raids eight of our machines were attacked by twenty enemy aircraft on the return journey, and during the course of the close fighting (which had become somewhat confused) Lieutenant Taylor destroyed an enemy aeroplane just at the moment when matters were critical for our formation, which resulted in affairs being straightened out immediately to our advantage. Lieutenant Taylor has always distinguished himself by the efficient manner in which he has carried out any operation allotted him, notably in the various long-distance raids.

Sgt Frederick Lee 7054
D.F.M. gazetted 21st September 1918

On a recent long-distance bombing raid, his machine was attacked over the objective by twenty enemy aircraft; he engaged one with his double Lewis, which caused the enemy aircraft to turn over and the pilot to fall out.

Target: Mercedes Aero Engine Works at Untertürkheim
Secondary Target: Railway Sidings at Offenburg

30th July			Take Off:	05.15
55 Squadron			Returned:	08.35

Formation 1

Capt F.Williams	2Lt E.R.Stewart	B3957	
Capt D.R.G.Mackay	2Lt H.C.T.Gompertz		
Lt G.T.Richardson	2Lt T.F.L.Myring		
2Lt W.Beer	2Lt A.S.Papworth		
Lt D.J.Waterous	Lt G.N.Tressider		photo machine
Lt P.M.Payson	Sgt A.S.Allan		

Formation 2

2Lt E.J.Whyte	Sgt E.Clare		
2Lt J.B.McIntyre	Sgt G.Howard		ret e/t 06.55
2Lt J.Cunliffe	2Lt G.E.Little		
Sgt A.W.Mepsted	Sgt R.R.S.Barker		/W.I.A.
Lt P.E.Welchman	2Lt E.R.Beesley		/W.I.A.
2Lt P.J.Cunningham	2Lt L.J.B.Ward		

The elusive Stuttgart was again the target for 55 Squadron but this was to be a combined raid with 99 and 104 Squadron. Taking off ten minutes later then the other two Squadrons, the rendezvous was a wash-out, as 99 Squadron were already well over the lines when 55 Squadron crossed at Badonviller at 14,000ft. Before crossing the lines 2Lt W.Beer and his observer 2Lt A.S.Papworth left the first formation, but had still not arrived at Azelot when the squadron returned. Once over the lines Captain Williams was confronted with thick fog and low cloud and with 2Lt McIntyre returning with engine trouble, he decided to make for Offenburg.

Crossing over the Rhine valley and approaching Offenburg from the east, the anti-aircraft batteries opened up as the formation climbed to 14,500ft and prepared to drop. On a white Very light fired by the leader two 230lb, twelve 112lb, sixteen 25lb and four 40lb phosphorus bombs fell towards the sidings and engine sheds below. Bursts were observed on the sheds and railways while several bombs fell in adjacent housing causing fires. Photographs revealed bursts near the repair shops and on a large amount of rolling stock.

As the two formations left the target area at 07.25, five Albatros scouts dived in on the first, singling out one De Havilland which was a bit low. Second Lieutenant Earle Richard Stewart fired a long burst at one of these which promptly put its nose down, and tried to pass the formation. Stewart stood on his seat and emptied a whole drum of ammunition into it seeing the enemy aircraft fall away out of control. Jubilation was short lived as ten Fokker DVIIs descended into the mêlée and added to the enemy firepower. The fight continued for some time but concentrated fire from the squadron observers drove the attacking scouts off. Lt Welchman's photographic machine was badly shot up, his observer 2Lt Beesley was shot in the leg, but he sat down and continued to fire, as and when opportunity allowed; Sergeant Barker was also wounded although not seriously. The two formations crossed the lines at St.Dié at 15,000ft after firing three thousand rounds and taking twenty-three pictures.

Reconnaissance

30th July			Take Off:	06.55
55 Squadron			Returned:	11.25
Capt B.J.Silly	Lt J.Parke	A7837		

Crossed lines at Château-Salins, flew over Morhange then Diefenburg, Vahl-Ebersing, Porcelette then Boulay, Freisdorf then by compass over clouds to Saarbrücken. Returned via Lunéville, thirty-seven plates exposed overall, most over new aerodromes at Hellimer and Lanningen.

Target: Cologne
Secondary Target: Factories, Station, Barracks at Coblenz

31st July			Take Off:	05.20
55 Squadron			Returned:	10.20

Formation 1

Capt B.J.Silly	2Lt W.R.Patey		

Lt G.C.Sherman	2Lt N.Wallace	
Lt C.L.Heater	Sgt A.S.Allan	
Lt E.P.Critchley	Sgt S.E.Lewis	
2Lt J.Cunliffe	2Lt G.E.Little	photo machine
Lt K.N.Cunningham	2Lt H.H.Bracher	ret e/t 08.55

Formation 2		
Lt P.E.Welchman	Sgt G.Howard	
2Lt J.B.McIntyre	2Lt L.J.B.Ward	
Lt D.J.Waterous	Lt G.N.Tressider	
Lt W.Beer	2Lt J.R.Fox	ret e/t 07.15
Capt D.R.G.Mackay	2Lt H.C.T.Gompertz	photo machine
Lt P.M.Payson	2Lt J.A.Lee	

Cologne, approximately one hundred and fifty-five miles from Azelot, was the target for 55 Squadron on a day of mixed cloud formations and high winds. Leaving Azelot to the north the two formations headed towards the lines crossing at Nomeny at 13,000ft.

Once over the lines, Lt W.Beer who had got lost the previous day, left the second group with engine trouble and returned to Azelot. The bombers continued north noticing considerable train movement to the east of Metz as they approached Boulay airfield, which was also very active. Lt Cunningham was experiencing engine trouble and now departed company with the first formation, landing back at Azelot at 08.55. Passing abeam Dillingen the DH4s carried on north towards Treves where they encountered cloud and very high winds. Captain Silly, realising that Cologne was impossible due to the strong wind, decided to make for Coblenz which could just be seen through small holes in the cloud. Over Coblenz at 08.10 the twelve flak guns of the town's battery put up a considerable but inaccurate barrage, as the bombers dropped one 230lb, fourteen 112lb, sixteen 25lb and four 40lb phosphorus bombs.

No bursts were observed due to cloud as the fours turned south and headed for home. Flying directly south to Pirmasens, the two formations climbed up to 17,000ft to make it harder for any enemy aircraft trying to intercept them; no enemy aircraft were seen and the bombers re-crossed the lines at Blâmont, carrying only six exposed photographic plates due to poor visibility.

Note: Again records give crews but do not record aircraft.

Target: Railways and Station at Mainz
Secondary Target: Railways and Station at Saarbrücken

31st July			Take Off:	05.30
99 Squadron			**Returned:**	**08.25**
Formation 1				
Capt A.D.Taylor	Lt H.S.Notley	C1666		
Lt J.W.Richards	2Lt E.J.Munson	B9366	ret e/t	
Lt C.W.Hewson	2Lt H.E.Alsford	D7233		
Lt M.T.S.Papenfus	Lt A.L.Benjamin	D3039	P.O.W./P.O.W.	
Lt S.M.Black	2Lt E.Singleton	C6278	P.O.W./P.O.W.	
Lt F.Smith	2Lt K.H.Ashton	D1029	P.O.W./P.O.W.	
Formation 2				
Lt E.L.Doidge	Lt H.T.Melville	C6145	K.I.A./K.I.A.	
Lt G.Broadbent	Sgt J.Jones	D1670	ret e/t	
Lt H.D.West	2Lt J.K.Speed	C6092	ret e/t	
Lt W.J.Garrity	2Lt G.H.Stephenson	C6196	P.O.W./P.O.W.	
2Lt T.M.Ritchie	2Lt L.W.G.Stagg	C6149	P.O.W./K.I.A.	
Lt L.V.Dennis	2Lt F.W.Wooley	D1032	K.I.A./K.I.A.	

Mainz, nearly one hundred and twenty miles over the lines, was the target for twelve DH9s led by Captain Taylor. This was a surprisingly long-distance target given the losses of the previous day, and the number of relatively inexperienced crews who would undoubtedly be meeting the growing number of enemy scouts, waiting the other side of the lines. Five minutes after take-off, Lt Broadbent returned with a cracked cylinder head, while the remaining eleven climbed away and headed north-east to cross the lines near Château-Salins. On such a long trip it is unlikely that much time would have been spent gaining height over the field. Before the lines were reached Lt Richards returned with magneto trouble while Lt West returned with an overheating engine.

Anti-aircraft fire was slight, and inaccurate, as the bombers crossed the lines heading north-east towards Saarbrücken. Doubts must have been forming in the mind of Captain Taylor whether to push on towards Mainz, or to bomb something closer, unfortunately his mind would shortly be made up for him. Near Sarralbe, just south of Saarbrücken, the formation of nine bombers were intercepted by five Albatros scouts, the first of a total of forty enemy aircraft they'd meet. One machine dropped out of formation and was seen to go down; this was probably Lt Papenfus whose petrol tank was shot through. He was last seen under control over Puttelange north-west of Sarralbe probably trying to land as soon as possible before his machine ignited. He did and both he and Benjamin became prisoners of war. Past Sarralbe twelve enemy scouts arrived from the north and attacked the rear formation of bombers, while another twelve arrived from the east and started to engage. At this point three DH9s dropped out of formation, which were probably Garrity, Ritchie and Dennis who were all last seen in combat near St.Avold. Lt Garrity and Stephenson's machine was hit in the radiator and they both, like Ritchie, became prisoners of war; Stagg, Dennis and Wooley were all killed in action.

Saarbrücken was now the target for the remaining five DH9s as more enemy aircraft arrived; two 230lb and six 112lb bombs fell on Saarbrücken from 13,000ft, and two bursts were seen in the centre of the town as the fight grew in momentum, and numbers. The combat report filed by Captain Taylor and his observer Notley described the enemy aircraft as six triplanes, fifteen Albatros scouts, fifteen Pfalz and three DVIIs. The five DH9s headed for home totally outnumbered, and Lt Doidge was last seen at 6,000ft near St.Avold under control. Also last seen near St.Avold were Lts Black and Smith. Doidge must have been pursued in his descent as both he and Lt Melville were killed in action; Lt Black and Singleton became prisoners of war. Smith and Ashton crash-landed half a mile south of Rohrbach, just west of the Rohrbach and Derfewbach road, both becoming prisoners of war.

Now over Dieuze, only Taylor and Hewson remained, still followed by up to fifteen enemy scouts. However, a saving sight greeted them as 104 Squadron, on their way to Saarbrücken, deflected the attention of the remaining enemy fighters, allowing Taylor and Hewson to return to Azelot. Both Notley and Hewson claimed an enemy aircraft, Notley's was out of control streaming smoke and side-slipping while Hewson's went down under control emitting steam. Both observers reported seeing two DH9s break up in the air, and these were probably Doidge and Dennis.

Fritz Salb of Jasta 80 was killed in his Albatros DIII over Grossblittersdorf by DH9s this day. Jasta 80 from Morsberg were in the fight and Salb almost certainly fell under the guns of 99 Squadron. 55 and 104 Squadron did not claim any enemy aircraft on this day. Fritz Salb was credited with a DH9 near Saargemünd, which one is not clear, but he was credited after his death none the less. Unteroffizier Ludwig Wittmann previously of Jasta 78 claimed a DH9 while flying with Jasta 80 over Willerwald, so it is obvious that Jasta 80 were in the thick of it. Vizefeldwebel Ludwig Reimann of Jasta 78 claimed a DH9 over Ruhlingen at 09.15 but it was not confirmed, while Vizefeldwebel Eduard Prime of Jasta 78 also claimed a DH9 but it was not confirmed either. Leutnant Kurt Monnington of Jasta 18 was above Grossblittersdorf and had his claim for a DH9 confirmed. Jasta 65 pilots were also in the fight with Offizierstellvertreter Tiedje and Vizefeldwebel J.Hohly both claiming DH4s. Why some victories were confirmed and some not is unclear, there were certainly enough DH9s on the German side for confirmation, so the best seven victors have been presented here as information allows; DH9s were often quoted as DH4s and vice versa in German combat reports.

General Trenchard visited the Squadron in the afternoon while General Newall and Lieutenant-Colonel Baldwin stayed for dinner spending time with the men. The time would have been better spent perhaps procuring better aircraft preferably without a radiator that stuck out like a target. The losses on this day and the previous would put 99 Squadron out action until mid August, by which time replacements would be trained sufficiently to keep formation, in what was becoming a very hostile environment.

Habadingen Cemetery near Sarralbe, was the resting place of 2Lt Leslie William Gilbert Stagg, aged eighteen from Woodford Green in Essex. Lt Leonard Victor Dennis and 2Lt Frederick William Wooley were buried in Sarralten Cemetery, also near Sarralbe. Wooley was twenty-one and came from Whaley Bridge in Derbyshire. Lt Ernest Lancelot Doidge and Lt Harry Taylor Melville were both buried near Sarralbe. Doidge came from Vancouver, British Columbia, and served previously with the Manitoba Regiment.

Marthinus Theunis Steyn Papenfus was born on 11th October 1893 and came from Standerton in South Africa. He studied aerial gunnery at Turnberry near Stonehenge. He was repatriated to England on 13th December 1918, and returned to South Africa on 18th October 1919. He was a farmer before the war and was fluent in Dutch.

HARRY TAYLOR MELVILLE was born on 23rd April 1892, near Ceres, near Fife, in Scotland. He attended the George Watson College between 1902 and 1906. After leaving here he started working for Lorner Fairburn & Lightbadge, as a Land & Building Surveyor. In 1912 he changed company to Scott Morton, again as a surveyor. Once war was declared, he joined the Royal Scots and proceeded to France in 1915. In 1916 he received a commission in the 7th Seaforth Highlanders, fighting with this regiment on the Somme, where he was wounded in August. In the battle of Arras in 1917, he was the only unwounded officer left in his company. Transferring to the Royal Flying Corps, he learnt his trade at the No1 School of Navigation and Bombing, and completed an aerial gunnery course at Hythe. He was posted to 99 Squadron on 18th May 1918. He was wounded by anti-aircraft fire while on a raid to Metz-Sablon on 1st June 1918. Melville was twenty-seven when killed. The family's address during the war was 1 Ruseborn Gardens, Edinburgh.

Target: Factories and Sidings at Saarbrücken

31st July		**Take Off:**	**05.40**
104 Squadron		**Returned:**	**09.20**

Formation 1

Capt E.A.McKay	Lt R.A.C.Brie	
Lt G.H.B.Smith	Sgt W.Harrop	
2Lt J.E.Parke	Lt C.Hitchcock	
2Lt R.J.Searle	Lt J.J.Redfield	
Lt G.H.Patman	2Lt T.Bailey	crash landed
Lt L.D.Merrill	Lt L.G.Best	

Formation 2

Capt J.B.Home-Hay	Sgt G.A.Smith	
Lt D.P.Pogson	2Lt W.E.Bottrill	
2Lt G.Pickup	2Lt B.Johnson	/W.I.A.
Lt W.H.Goodale	Lt L.C.Prentice	
2Lt E.C.Clarke	Capt J.L.C.Sutherland	
2Lt W.S.Greenwood	2Lt E.C.Black	

Leaving ten minutes after 99 Squadron, fourteen aircraft led by Captain McKay took of to bomb the Usine Electric Works which lay close to the railway sidings in the town of Saarbrücken. Among the ranks of 104 Squadron this day were three Americans, one South African and one Canadian. Lt Linn Daicy Merrill from Chicago joined the Royal Flying Corp on 2nd October 1917 graduating as a pilot nearly one month later on 1st November 1917. Other fellow Americans were Lt John J.Redfield, and 2Lt E.C.Black who would only fly on this one occasion with 104 Squadron, before transferring to 99 Squadron. Lt Searle was from South Africa, while William Eric Bottrill came from Ontario, Canada, although originally born in Burton-on-Trent.

One machine in the second formation returned with engine trouble and was replaced, while the second spare aircraft returned to Azelot. Crossing the lines at Blâmont, the twelve machines were at 13,000ft as they headed north-east towards Sarreguemines which lay south of Saarbrücken. Reaching Saarbrücken at 8.30, eight 230lb and six 112lb bombs were dropped, ten bursts were seen inside the factory perimeter and none outside; one machine failed to drop its 230lb bomb as the release gear jammed. The anti-aircraft fire was quite accurate as the formation of twelve left the target area heading south-west.

Overhead Sarreguemines before reaching the target, twenty-two enemy aircraft were counted 500ft below, of which only five tailed 104 Squadron while the rest presumably fell on 99 Squadron. The enemy aircraft kept their distance not venturing closer than 300 yards and firing from long range. 104 Squadron observers fired 1,399 rounds back and no serious engagement took place although 2Lt Benjamin Johnson was wounded by machine-gun fire. Re-crossing the lines at Embermenil, all machines returned safely except Lt Patman and 2Lt Thomas Bailey who crash landed at Azelot; Patman was okay but Bailey was slightly injured. Photos taken on the raid totalled nine although once in the target area a huge black cloud of smoke hung in the air as if trying to camouflage the town. The smoke worked as most of the town was obscured from view, the first time this counter measure had been used against the I.A.F.

Note: Although no aircraft were listed in the bomb raid report, DH9s D5598, C2220 and D3101 were wrecked this day while on the strength of 104 Squadron. Two of these aircraft may have been flown by Patman and Pickup.

Reconnaissance

31st July			**Take Off:**	**06.55**
55 Squadron			**Returned:**	**11.40**
2Lt W.J.Pace	2Lt D.W.Stewart	A7942		

Crossed lines at Château-Salins at 18,000ft and proceeded to Mannheim via Haguenau. Plates were exposed over aerodrome at Sarrebourg and Neustadt and whole of Mannheim. Returned via Zweibrücken and re-crossed lines at 21,000ft over Château-Salins, forty plates taken overall.

Reconnaissance

31st July			**Take Off:**	**11.05**
55 Squadron			**Returned:**	**14.00**
Capt F.Williams	2Lt E.R.Stewart	A7837		

Crossed lines at 18,000ft over Arracourt, then over Morhange, Diefenbach, Saarbrücken, Porcelette and aerodrome at Freibuss, re-crossed at 20,000ft at Forêt-de-Parroy with twenty plates.

CHAPTER 4

OPERATIONS – AUGUST 1918

Target: Workshops and Railways at Karthaus
Secondary Target: Railway Station at Treves

| 1st August | | | Take Off: | 05.15 |
| **104 Squadron** | | | **Returned:** | **09.10** |

Formation 1

Capt E.A.McKay	Lt R.A.C.Brie	D2812	
2Lt E.O.Clarke	Capt J.L.C.Sutherland	D3088	
Lt L.D.Merrill	Lt G.Best		
2Lt H.G.Leyden	Lt J.J.Redfield		landed at Neuf
2Lt G.H.B.Smith	Sgt W.Harrop	C2179	
2Lt J.E.Parke	Lt C.G.Hitchcock		
Spare aircraft			ret e/t 07.15

Formation 2

Capt R.J.Gammon	2Lt P.E.Appleby	C6264	
2Lt A.Haines	2Lt R.G.Gibbs	B7588	W.I.A./
2Lt B.H.Stretton	2Lt W.E.Jackson	E624	
Lt W.H.Goodale	Lt L.C.Prentice	D2960	K.I.A./K.I.A.
Lt P.C.Saxby	Lt W.Moorhouse	F5844	
2Lt F.H.Beaufort	Lt C.G.Pickard		ret e/t 07.10
Spare aircraft			ret e/t 07.10

Evans Alexander McKay led the first show for 104 Squadron this month, the target being railway sidings and workshops at Karthaus, near Treves, approximately seventy miles over the lines. The DH9s of 104 Squadron were no more reliable than those of 99 as fourteen aircraft took off, gained height and headed north for the lines at Nomeny. Lt Frank Beaufort returned at 07.10 with engine trouble while Lt Leydon lost the first formation, and landed at Neufchâteau. The two spare aircraft also returned, both with engine trouble, so McKay with only the remaining ten machines crossed the lines accompanied by moderate and inaccurate archie.

Continuing north the bombers flew over Boulay aerodrome, then Saarbrücken and onto Karthaus. Karthaus however was covered by mist so McKay decided to bomb nearby Treves instead. Over Treves at 08.00, seven 230lb and six 112lb bombs fell from 13,000ft scoring one direct hit on a workshop building, and several other hits in the vicinity of the railways. German official reports stated that several bombs fell in the Kuhnenstrasse district killing one person and injuring four. The building hit was in fact an electricity transformer, cutting off the town's electricity supply for a considerable time. Three bombs also fell in the Sudalle district, one blowing up a large house whilst the other two seriously damaged the Hofscheuer cabinet makers.

Albatros and Pfalz scouts had been shadowing the formations since Treves, and they now attacked. 2Lt Jackson fired fifty rounds at a blue scout which went into a spin and shed its left wing, then its right wing crumpled before it was seen to crash into a wood. Also at this time, Sgt Harrop fired a short burst at a red Albatros which tried to get under the tail of their DH9. The enemy scout then turned over on its back, and Harrop fired the remainder of the drum into it. The red Albatros entered a vertical spin and was seen to crash; this aircraft was also reported to be on fire minus both its wings. Lt Gibbs also stated seeing a Halberstadt two-seater going down as well. Percival Ewart Appleby was also firing at a red scout, his however was reported as a Pfalz which entered a spin after Appleby had fired a hundred rounds at it, it then shed its left wing and continued down crashing into a wood. He also stated in his combat report seeing another enemy aircraft going down in a spin. In all it was thought that twenty-four scouts attacked from between the target and Boulay aerodrome. The two-seater seen going down may well have been the Canadian Walter Goodale, and his American observer 2Lt Lee Prentice, who when abeam Metz left the second formation and dived for the lines.

The engagement was certainly fierce with 2Lt Alfred Haines being wounded, although he managed to stay in formation and crossed the lines with the remaining nine bombers who between them had fired 5,186 rounds. Walter Goodale of the 15th Reserve Canadian Battalion, and Lee Prentice of the United States Reserve Signal Corps were both killed and were buried in St.Imigen Cemetery. Investigations after the war found only that their aircraft had been hit in the petrol tank, and this may well have been the aircraft seen below the formations on fire without wings by several observers, but this is only speculation.

In total 104 Squadron claimed three destroyed and one driven down out of control, although German Jastas in the area (4, 18, 65, 67, 77 and 80) report no losses for this day, neither do the closest Kest units Kest 2 or Kest 3. German pilots in the area claimed two DH9s at 9.40 German time, still one hour ahead of British time. The combat reports from 104 Squadron observers say that combat started from about 08.15 and lasted until near the lines. Offizierstellvertreter Wilhelm Kühne of Jasta 18 had an unconfirmed DH9 while Leutnant Kurt Seit of Jasta 80 had a confirmed DH9 at Loveninghem for his second victory. Jasta 67 were also in action and claimed a DH9 this day. Unteroffizier Hans Heinrich Marwede, previously with Kest 2, shot down a DH9 at Wiegingen for his first victory. He later shot down four balloons before being brought down himself after attacking a balloon of the 6th US Balloon Company on the 3rd of October. He survived the resulting crash and spent the rest of the war as a prisoner. Of the three daylight I.A.F squadrons, only 55 and 104 were flying this day, and only one aircraft was lost as above. Leutnant Kurt Seit of Jasta 80, or Unteroffizier Hans Heinrich Marwede of Jasta 67 are the two most probable victors.

WALTER HENRY GOODALE was born on 14th August 1894, in Wadina, Saskachewan, Canada. He worked as a bank clerk for the Bank of Columbia (Canada) between February and August 1914. He joined up and went overseas with the Sask Regiment of the Canadian Expeditionary Force. He was seconded to the R.F.C. on 12th October 1917, and started training at No3 Training School on 18th February 1918. On 1st April he was made Lieutenant. On 3rd May he went to No4 Auxiliary School of Aerial Gunnery. From here he joined 104 Squadron on 24th May. His address during the war was White House, Glinton, Peterborough, England.

Note: DH4 D7312 was recorded as wrecked on this day according to 104 records. It was again back in service on 11th August. D7205 was also damaged this day but also returned to service. 2Lt Leyden was most probably the pilot of one of these aircraft in his forced landing at Neufchâteau. Records of aircraft serial numbers are not given with crews.

Target: Cologne
Secondary Target: Factories at Düren

1st August			Take Off:	05.20
55 Squadron			**Returned:**	**10.25**
Formation 1				
Capt F.Williams	2Lt E.R.Stewart	B3957		
Lt D.J.Waterous	Lt G.N.Tressider			
Lt P.M.Payson	2Lt J.A.Lee	e/t 07.50		
Lt K.M.Cunningham	2Lt H.H.Bracher			
2Lt J.B.McIntyre	Sgt G.Howard			
Sgt A.W.Mepsted	2Lt J.R.Fox			
Formation 2				
Capt D.R.G.Mackay	2Lt H.C.T.Gompertz			
Lt C.L.Heater	Sgt A.S.Allan			

Lt G.T.Richardson	2Lt T.F.L.Myring
2Lt W.J.Pace	Lt D.W.Stewart
Lt E.P.Critchley	Sgt S.E.Lewis
2Lt P.J.Cunningham	2Lt L.J.Ward

A new month and an early start as the crews rose for another go at Cologne, one of the furthest targets on the I.A.F. list. Captain Williams led the first formation, with Captain Mackay leading the rear one. All the machines got away as they gained height flying abeam Nancy and St.Mihiel crossing the lines near Verdun at 12,500ft. Over St. Mihiel the crews got an unexpected visitor as Major Alexander Gray, Commanding Officer of 55 Squadron flew alongside, inspecting his squadron. The early start had caught the anti-aircraft batteries off guard, and only moderate flak which was inaccurate greeted the eleven DH4s. Lt Payson returned to Azelot with engine trouble landing at 07.50.

Heading north over Arlon the formations were in a gradual climb to achieve their bombing altitude of 15,000ft. No opposition from enemy fighters was encountered as they proceeded north over Diekirch near the Our river towards Prüm. Euskirchen was passed next as the formations continued towards their prize. Resistance from Kest 6 stationed at Bonn was a possibility although there was still no sign of enemy aircraft. Arriving virtually above Cologne, the weather had vanquished 55 Squadron again as the ground below was covered in cloud. Turning for Düren situated south-west of Cologne, eleven DH4s became ten as Captain Mackay left his formation apparently with engine trouble. At 08.30 the remaining ten machines dropped one 230lb, fourteen 112lb, sixteen 25lb and four 40lb phosphorous bombs on Düren. All bombs were seen to impact on the town causing a large fire. Houses, the post office and two public schools were hit, while other bombs hit the Magistrate's office. Twelve people were killed while fourteen were seriously wounded, but according to German sources no factories or military targets were damaged. Intelligence reports and photographs however, revealed that one bomb had exploded on the Krafft und Sohn explosive factory.

The bombers headed back towards Verdun climbing to 16,000ft so making it harder for enemy aircraft to intercept them. None were seen despite the same route being flown back to the lines and all machines crossed safely. Fuel however was a major concern; 2Lt McIntyre and Sgt Mepsted both had to put their machines down at Ochey. Many machines ran out of fuel but were able to glide to Azelot. The leader, Captain Williams, glided in from 6,000ft as his fuel ran out. Captain Mackay must have been given up as lost with engine trouble so far over the front line, but he wasn't and managed to bring his machine back landing a mile behind the French lines at Verdun. This was a well executed raid resulting in fourteen photos and no interference from enemy fighters. However, weather again prevented bombs hitting the main target, a major frustration for the crews, especially to such a long-distance target.

This was the last raid flown by CAPTAIN FREDERICK WILLIAMS with 55 Squadron. It was also his last raid in DH4 B3957 with its distinctive white number 6 on the cowling, and the Union Jack pennant attached to a strut that Williams always flew with. Williams was born in the Maranoa district of Queensland, Australia. He contracted TB while on a troop ship in 1923, and passed away in 1963. An exceptional leader and already the holder of the Military Cross and the French Croix de Guerre, his D.F.C. citation read as follows:

Captain Frederick Williams M.C.
D.F.C. gazetted 21st September 1918

Since this officer was awarded the Military Cross for exceptional leadership of a long-distance bombing raid, he has taken part in twenty-seven successful operations over the lines, ten of which have been photographic reconnaissances. The information he has bought back has been of the greatest value. He is an excellent leader, and a most able instructor. Recently he led a formation to attack an important enemy town. Owing to thick mists and low clouds he was unable to locate his objective. Turning he succeeded in locating another town, which he bombed with excellent effect, despite heavy hostile anti-aircraft fire.

Note: Aircraft serial numbers are not given with crew records. DH4 B3957 was recorded in Williams' personal diary.

Target: Factories at Rombas (Rombach)

8th August		**Take Off:**	**10.03**
55 Squadron		**Returned:**	**13.30**

Formation 1

Capt B.J.Silly	2Lt W.R.Patey	
Lt C.L.Heater	Sgt A.S.Allan	
Lt G.C.Sherman	2Lt N.Wallace	
Lt K.M.Cunningham	2Lt H.H.Bracher	
Lt J.Cunliffe	2Lt G.E.Little	
Sgt A.W.Mepsted	2Lt J.R.Fox	

Formation 2

Lt E.J.Whyte	Sgt E.Clare	
Lt E.P.Critchley	Sgt S.E.Lewis	
Lt G.T.Richardson	2Lt T.F.L.Myring	photo machine
Lt P.M.Payson	2Lt J.A.Lee	
Lt J.B.McIntyre	Sgt G.Howard	
2Lt P.J.Cunningham	2Lt L.B.J.Ward	ret bracing wire

After several days of unsuitable weather, the cloud had lifted to allow a raid to the factories at Rombas. Situated between Thionville and Metz, the factories and railway sidings were on the southern banks of the River Orne. Next to the sidings was the town's gas works, so in all quite a tempting target. The twelve DH4s led by Captain Silly took of into patchy cloud, and headed towards Fresnes, below Verdun, to cross the lines. Not long after being airborne, 2Lt Cunningham was forced to return as his centre section cross bracing wire had snapped. He made it back to Azelot and the remaining eleven DH4 continued west following a formation of DH9s probably 99 Squadron. Although 55 Squadron were the only daylight I.A.F bomber squadron in action this day, both 104 and especially 99 Squadron were trying to train their new pilots whose preparation in England was felt below standard, especially in the increasingly hostile environment in which the I.A.F. now found itself to be.

Crossing the lines at 15,000ft, the two groups were accurately archied as they flew east over cloud, until they picked up the railway line at Conflans, which ran all the way to Rombas. The cloud formations varied with some starting at 2,000 and rising to 14,000ft. There were also banks of mist in places but Rombas was reached at 12.20 and two 230lb, twelve 112lb, sixteen 25lb and four 40lb phosphorous bombs went down, one 230lb failing to release owing to a jammed bomb rack. Two blast furnaces were damaged, though not seriously, with most bombs falling in the rolling mills, breaking pipes and circuits. All bombs landed within the factory area but the plant was only closed for eight hours according to German reports.

Heading south towards the lines, fourteen German scouts were spotted over Metz and a running fight ensued. Concentrated fire in the form of 3,000 rounds kept the scouts at bay and all eleven DH4s crossed the lines safely at Pont-à-Mousson. A successful raid with 2Lt Myring taking eleven photos despite the weather.

Leutnant Rudolf Neitzer of Jasta 65, was killed in action with DH4s near Metz on this day. Born in Krefeld on 28th July 1898, he had one victory to his name, a balloon brought down near Mandres on 22nd July. He had only recently joined Jasta 65 from Jastaschule II on 5th July.

Note: Crews are given but aircraft are not recorded.

Reconnaissance

10th August			**Take Off:**	**16.00**
55 Squadron			**Returned:**	**20.15**
Lt W.J.Pace	Lt D.W.Stewart	A7942		

Crossed the lines at Lunéville at 20,000ft, followed railway line to Sarrebourg and exposed plates over aerodromes south of Lorquin and one just west of Hatigny, re-crossed lines at 19,000ft east of Lunéville.

Reconnaissance

10th August			**Take Off:**	**16.10**
55 Squadron			**Returned:**	**19.45**
Capt B.J.Silly	2Lt T.F.L.Myring	A7837		

Crossed the lines at 19,500ft north of Munster, large clouds eventually cleared photos being taken of Schlettstadt, Ebersheim, Coxweiler and Meistratzheim. From Oberehnheim a compass course was steered over clouds coming out west of Moyenmouther, nineteen plates exposed.

Reconnaissance

11th August			**Take Off:**	**07.40**
55 Squadron			**Returned:**	**13.15**
Lt P.E.Welchman	2Lt W.R.Patey	A7837		

Crossed the lines east of Lunéville at 19,000ft, then over Sarrebourg, Sarralbe, Bitche, Saarbrücken, Boulay, St.Avold to Morhange. Plates exposed in between clouds, re-crossed at Arracourt at 18,000ft, train movement reported as normal.

Target: Benz Works at Mannheim
Secondary Target: Railway Station at Karlsruhe

11th August			**Take Off:**	**07.05**
104 Squadron			**Returned:**	**11.05**
Formation 1				
Maj J.C.Quinnell	2Lt C.Hitchcock			
Lt H.P.Wells	Lt J.T.Redfield	D2917		
Lt L.D.Merrill	Lt G.Best			
Lt E.Cartwright	2Lt P.E.Appleby	C6264	photo machine	
2Lt G.H.B.Smith	Sgt W.Harrop	C2179		
2Lt J.E.Parke	2Lt W.W.Bradford	D501	P.O.W./P.O.W.	
Formation 2				
Capt J.B.Home-Hay	Sgt W.T.Smith	D7225		
Lt D.P.Pogson	2Lt W.E.Bottrill			
2Lt E.O.Clarke	Capt J.L.C.Sutherland	D3088		
2Lt J.C.Uhlman	2Lt P.Sutherland			
2Lt H.G.Leyden	Sgt A.Windridge	D7312	photo machine	
2Lt O.F.Meyer	Sgt A.C.Wallace		ret lost formation	

Major John Charles Quinnell, Commanding Officer of 104 Squadron, led this raid against the Benz Aviation Factory at Mannheim. The only daylight Squadron in the I.A.F. operating on this day, 104 could expect plenty of attention from enemy scouts, especially hitting a target one hundred miles over the lines. Leading fourteen aircraft, and two spare, the two formations of seven gained height and headed east towards the lines. Major Quinnell, with the lines fast approaching, signalled the two spare aircraft to return to Azelot. Soon after the spare aircraft departed, 2Lt Meyer entered the slipstream of another aircraft in the rear formation and lost control of his machine. Recovering from the spin, Meyer was unable to catch up with the rear formation and decided to return to Azelot where he landed safely at 09.05. The remaining eleven machines crossed the lines over Allarmont at 12,000ft, with only a few puffs of archie to greet them.

Over Saverne at 09.10, Albatros and Pfalz scouts attacked, accompanied by Halberstadt two-seaters. If the attention of fighters wasn't enough, two aircraft in the rear group had dropped down to 9,000ft and were falling behind. Quinnell knew that these two bombers wouldn't last long, so he slowed down, and descended to 9,000ft, picking up the stragglers. Large banks of cloud were being met as the two formations headed north-east towards Landau, still followed by scouts which began pressing home their attacks more vigorously.

Mannheim was completely covered by cloud so a compass course was flown towards Karlsruhe. Through a small gap in the clouds Karlsruhe was spotted and the eleven DH9s dropped seven 230lb and eight 112lb bombs at 09.40 from 9,000ft. Quinnell was aiming for the railway station and one 230lb bomb was seen to hit the main building causing secondary explosions, while another three were observed to hit railway tracks. Despite picking up the two stragglers, the formations were at a lower height making it easier for the scouts to engage. 2Lt John Parke and 2Lt Wilfred Bradford headed down, followed by some of the scouts as the remaining ten bombers went for the lines.

Since Saverne the bombers had been under near constant attack. The fighting was heaviest over the target, borne out by the number of combat reports and claims made by the observers. Captain Sutherland fired fifty rounds at one scout which ventured too close, and it went into a vertical dive, stalled, and was lost to sight as it entered cloud; this scout had a red fuselage with a gold tail. Sergeant Smith also saw this scout fall away before firing half a drum of Lewis at a rapidly closing Pfalz. The Pfalz dived away and was seen to enter a spin four hundred feet from the ground. Sergeant Windridge fired nearly a whole drum of Lewis at another Pfalz and watched as it nose-dived towards a wood. Just above the wood the scout flattened out and departed the area. Percival Ewart Appleby, a Canadian from Port-la-Tour, Nova Scotia, fired fifty rounds at an Albatros scout which spun away then dived towards the ground. Sergeant Harrop upon landing, reported seeing a red and white Pfalz spinning down, and a blue and white Albatros also going down. Despite these apparent losses the scouts kept up their attack until the formations passed Saverne. The DH9s crossed the lines at Allarmont at 10,000ft, returning to Azelot with eighteen photos. The crews had expended 3,865 rounds defending themselves and did well not to take further losses, especially as they were operating at a much lower altitude then usual.

Lt John Edward Parke, born 23rd May 1891, was repatriated on 26th November 1918 from the hospital at Courbain where he had been since 19th November. Before the war he worked as a cashier at Capital & Counties Bank Ltd, in Threadneedle Street in the City of London. He was awarded the French Croix de Guerre on 8th February 1919; his home address during the war was given as 394 Clapham Road SW9.

Intelligence sources reported the station refreshment room was totally destroyed, killing twelve officers inside. Other bombs destroyed the 1st and 2nd class carriages as well as the luggage van. The stable stores near the station were burnt out and the driver of the train killed; also hit were the Eisenbain Haupt Werke, the local railway repair workshops. Some intelligence reports list three killed and ten injured, others give eighty civilians wounded, fourteen French wounded prisoners of war killed, and fifty-two travellers on the train killed. Major Quinnell received a telegram from Hugh Trenchard on this day, it read: "A great day for you and 104. It will help the battle up north. It showed determination, pluck, and good leadership. Well done all."[1]

Leutnant Sauerman of Jasta 70 received confirmation for Bradford and Parke, his second DH9 victory, and his last kill of the war. Previously with Jasta 27, he then flew with Kest 2, still without any victories, until joining Jasta 70 in July 1918. Leutnant Straube, also of Jasta 70, was wounded by DH9s near Haguenau but this seems to be the only loss to German units in the vicinity of the raid. Obviously Jasta 70 were in the middle of it, while the other enemy scouts may have been from Jasta 78b also from Buhl, or Kest 1b from Karlsruhe, or Kest 1a at Mannheim. The German lines of communication were excellent for the time, and the Halberstadt two-seaters were almost certainly fitted with W/T receivers and transmitters and the information gave the Jastas the location and heading of the raiders as they took off to intercept.

MAJOR JOHN CHARLES QUINNELL, aged twenty-seven, started the war as a 2Lt in the Royal Field Artillery. In February 1915 he transferred to the Royal Flying Corps, and graduated from Shoreham with his wings in April 1915. Sent to France in July, he was posted to 10 Squadron where he flew on Corps Reconnaissance missions in BE2cs. He was wounded and returned to Home Establishment in July 1916. On 1st January 1916 he was promoted to Flight Commander and transferred to 7 Squadron also on Corps Reconnaissance. After returning home again, he was promoted to Squadron Commander on 1st December 1916, and was in charge of the newly formed 83 Squadron. He was then transferred to 63 Squadron and took them out to Mesopotamia on RE8s in June 1917. He returned to England at the end of 1917 and was posted to Andover and put in charge of the newly forming 104 Squadron. He received the D.F.C. in the 1919 New Year's Honours List. After the war Quinnell stayed in the new Royal Air Force, and became a Wing Commander with 83 Squadron in 1925. At the start of WW2 he was an Air Commodore and AOC to 6 Bomber Group. He retired in 1945 and lived in Southampton.

Note: Records give crews but do not list aircraft taking part in this raid.

---

[1] The 'battle up north' was the Battle of Amiens, which began on the 8th.

Target: Factories and Railways at Frankfurt am Main
Secondary Target: Buhl Aerodrome

11th August		Take Off:	07.20
55 Squadron		Returned:	09.30/10.00

Formation 1

Capt J.R.Bell	Lt G.N.Tressider	
Lt C.A.Bridgland	2Lt E.R.Stewart	
Lt S.L.Dowswell	2Lt C.W.Clutsom	ret e/t
Lt K.M.Cunningham	2Lt H.H.Bracher	
Lt D.J.Waterous	2Lt J.R.Fox	
Lt G.T.Richardson	2Lt A.S.Papworth	

Formation 2

Capt D.R.G.Mackay	2Lt H.C.T.Gompertz	
Lt A.Clarke	2Lt A.C.Roberts	
Lt C.L.Heater	Sgt A.S.Allan	
Lt P.M.Payson	2Lt J.A.Lee	
Lt W.J.Pace	Lt D.W.Stewart	photo machine
2Lt P.J.Cunningham	2Lt L.J.Ward	

Leading for the first time, Captain John Ross Bell took twelve bombers to Frankfurt, a round trip of approximately two hundred and twenty miles. The second formation was led by the experienced Duncan 'Jock' Mackay as twelve DH4s climbed away from Azelot and headed straight for Badonviller, trying to gain as much height as they could on the way. Lt Dowswell couldn't maintain any height due to engine trouble and was back on the ground at Azelot one hour after take-off.

Crossing at 11,000ft, the archie was accurate but not good enough to trouble the two formations as they headed north towards Phalsbourg west of Saverne. Pressing on the bombers were intercepted over Sarrebourg by nine German fighters which first attacked head-on. Captain Bell was soaked in petrol as his tank was holed by bullets. He immediately left the formation followed by Lt K.Cunningham and 2Lt P.Cunningham, but the remaining DH4s pressed on now led by Captain Mackay.

Because he was soaked in petrol Bell couldn't fire a Very light, and his observer was also reluctant to use his Lewis gun. Bell was fortunate that two machines accompanied him out of formation, offering more protection against scouts that would have been more than interested in a lone bomber flying along streaming petrol. Bell however was not beaten and he and his two compatriots dropped one 230lb and four 112lb bombs on Buhl aerodrome on the way home from 10,000ft, seeing one detonate between two hangars. Captain Mackay and the other crews were still being harried and with the formation badly broken up he turned for home. Bell and his two wingmen re-crossed the lines at 8,000ft at Raon-l'-Etape and touched down at Azelot. Captain Mackay returned with the rest of the aircraft half an hour later at 10.00 all carrying their bombs. 4,000 rounds had been fired while Lt Stewart managed to take three photos. An eventful first raid with 55 Squadron for Captain Bell, one which could have so easily finished for him above Sarrebourg in flames.

Note: Records do not list aircraft on this raid.

Target: Factories and Railways at Frankfurt am Main

12th August		Take Off:	05.20
55 Squadron		Returned:	10.50

Formation 1

Capt B.J.Silly	2Lt W.R.Patey	A8020
Lt J.Cunliffe	2Lt G.E.Little	
Lt D.J.Waterous	2Lt J.R.Fox	photo machine
2Lt P.J.Cunningham	2Lt N.Wallace	
Lt P.E.Welchman	Sgt E.Clare	D8388/6
Lt E.P.Critchley	Sgt S.E.Lewis	A7972

Formation 2

Capt D.R.G.Mackay	2Lt H.C.T.Gompertz	B7812	
Lt G.T.Richardson	2Lt G.Madge		
Lt C.L.Heater	Sgt A.S.Allan	D8396	
Lt P.M.Payson	2Lt J.A.Lee	A7783	
Lt C.A.Bridgland	2Lt E.R.Stewart	B3957	/K.I.A.
Lt S.L.Dowswell	2Lt C.W.Clutsom	A7586	

Frankfurt was again the target with Captain Benjamin James Silly leading and Captain Mackay again heading the rear formation. Flying east, 55 Squadron had a full complement of twelve bombers as they crossed the lines at 11,000ft at Badonviller, with large amounts of archie but very inaccurate; possibly an unexpected early start for the front line flak crews.

Over Phalsbourg, fighters started to shadow the Squadron but did not press an aggressive attack and the two formations continued flying north-east. The five Pfalz scouts which had arrived from south-east of Bitche were joined by another five Pfalz and fired at the formations from long range. As the bombers reached Pirmasens, another eight Pfalz scouts arrived and they started to close the range. It was not until Mannheim that the scouts pressed their first serious attack with four of them diving on the rear formation. All the observers returned fire seeing one enemy aircraft drop a wing then spin away. It flattened out and then entered a slow spin till several thousand feet below the formations. All the time fighters, including Albatros scouts and two-seaters, were joining the fight until about forty were in the area. The scouts, although numerically superior in numbers, were not aggressive, preferring to keep their distance due to the tight formations being flown by 55 Squadron and the concentrated fire they gave out. Some Albatros scouts were said to have green and black wings with dark fuselages and white tails, while others were reported as having black wings and fuselages with white tails. One of these Albatros scouts ventured too near and was hit by fire from the rear formation. It was seen to dive steeply turning onto its back streaming petrol, and break up in the air. As the two formations reached Offenheim the scouts broke off their attack and left the bombers to fly over Gr.-Gerau south of Frankfurt, and then on the target. At 08.00 two 230lb, eighteen 112lb, eight 25lb and two 40lb phosphorous bombs fell from 14,000ft with hits being observed in the town east of the goods station. Most bombs fell on private property in the Bockenheimer Landstrasse district of the town demolishing two buildings, while another bomb fell on the town's Opera House. Sixteen people were killed and twenty-six injured although the evening performance at the Opera House went ahead as usual, despite the considerable damage. Photographs showed three bursts near the gasworks, two bursts near the Wilhelm Bridge and further solitary bursts near the quayside and a provision store near the artillery barracks. The offices of the Leopold Cassella Dye Works were also hit.

On the return journey the enemy two-seaters flew above the two formations of bombers, using their rearward-firing machine guns to rake the bombers. The enemy scouts however did not attack with much vigour, and all machines returned safely to Azelot. Lt Bridgland landed safely, but unfortunately his observer, Lt Earle Richard Stewart aged twenty, from British Columbia in Canada, had been killed by machine-gun fire, and was buried at Charmes. Jasta 70 and 78 operating out of Buhl both lost a pilot this day. Vizefeldwebel Heinrich Krüger of Jasta 70 was killed in combat over Grunstadt. 104 Squadron were attacking Mannheim but only got as far as the aerodrome at Haguenau far to the south of Grunstadt making Krüger with a DH4 and a DH9 to his credit, a scalp of 55 Squadron; the hunter had become the hunted. Vizefeldwebel Karl Kallmünzer of Jasta 78 was severely injured in a crash landing after combat with DH4s over Wasselinheim, and later died in hospital. He had two victories, one of which was a DH9 of 99 Squadron on 30th July 1918 crewed by Lt Dietz and Lt Batty who were both killed. An excellent raid largely helped by the weather conditions with hardly any wind. Lt Stewart was awarded the D.F.C. the citation of which read as follows:

Lt Earle Richard Stewart
D.F.C. gazetted 21st September 1918

For gallantry and skill as an observer on long-distance bombing raids. During a raid a few months back he was in the deputy-leader's machine (which usually has to bear the brunt of an attack), and in the course of repelling vigorous enemy attacks he had a breakage in his gun, with the result that he could only fire single shots. In these circumstances he would have been justified in causing his pilot to close up under the remainder of the formation, but with great coolness and sound judgement he maintained his place, and thus avoided the risk of impairing the Squadron's defensive efficiency. By his actions he rendered the most valuable assistance to his formation in holding off the enemy, and by the time the enemy had been dispersed he had fired two-hundred rounds by single shots with excellent effect. Lt Stewart has rendered further distinguished services during the past two months, displaying great ability and absolute fearlessness.

Note: DH4 for Welchman and Clare could be either D8388 or D8386 as the combat report from which it was taken was unclear.

Target: Benz Works at Mannheim
Secondary Target: Haguenau Aerodrome

12th August			Take Off:	05.30
104 Squadron			Returned:	09.05
Formation 1				
Capt J.B.Home-Hay	2Lt C.C.Blizard	D7225		
Lt D.P.Pogson	2Lt W.E.Bottrill	D3122		
2Lt J.C.Uhlman	2Lt P.Sutherland	F5844		
2Lt H.G.Leyden	Sgt A.Windridge	C6264		
2Lt G.Pickup	Lt A.B.Rattray	B7568		
2Lt E.O.Clarke	Capt J.L.C.Sutherland		ret e/t	
Formation 2				
Capt E.A.McKay	2Lt C.Hitchcock			
Lt H.P.Wells	Lt J.J.Redfield	D2917		
2Lt G.H.B.Smith	Sgt W.Harrop	C2179		
2Lt G.H.Patman	2Lt J.M.S.McPherson	D3084	P.O.W./P.O.W.	
2Lt O.F.Meyer	Sgt A.C.Wallace	D2931	P.O.W./P.O.W.	
Lt L.D.Merrill	Lt G.Best	D7210		

Captain Home-Hay led the Squadron for this return trip to Mannheim, the target again being the Benz Aero Works. So far this month 104 Squadron had lost five crew, two killed, two prisoners of war and one wounded in action. Not severe by 99 Squadron standards, but serious enough considering they had only been over the lines twice in twelve days. Home-Hay took the fourteen aircraft towards the lines at Allarmont; one of the spare machines returned with engine trouble while the other was signalled to return as both formations were complete as they approached the trenches. Engine trouble near the lines was to rob 104 Squadron again of a full complement of bombers, Lt Clarke dropping out to land back at Azelot at 07.30.

Crossing the lines over Allarmont at 12,000ft, the archie was more active then the previous day but was not particularly accurate. Only four miles over the lines at Schirmeck, the two formations were intercepted by up to twenty-three enemy scouts, mostly Albatros, Pfalz, Fokker DVIIs and the usual two-seaters. The formation were being heavily engaged and upon reaching Saverne, Captain Home-Hay decided to battle the scouts. Fighting spread was taken up with both formations making a semi-circle, one formation in front of the other, flying in large circuits. This tactic did not discourage the enemy and a ferocious air battle ensued. Markings recorded in some combat reports for the Germans describe them as having black wings, white fuselages, and black and white tails. This particular report was made by 2Lt Sutherland who also claimed a scout at which he fired four bursts from one hundred yards range. The scout then stalled, fell over on its back and nose-dived, rolling as it descended. Sergeant Harrop fired ninety rounds into a red Pfalz scout which went down in flames. Twenty minutes later he fired a whole drum at a blue and white Albatros which spun away and crashed in some buildings south of Saverne, witnessed by Sergeant Windridge.

Captain Home-Hay was definitely in fighting mood. He dived at a red Fokker DVII, which ended up in front of the lead bombing machine. Home-Hay fired fifty rounds at one hundred yards and watched as the Fokker entered left and right hand spins before finally breaking up. A Pfalz scout was seen to dive away then spin for several thousand feet after fire from Lt Rattray hit in the engine. Lt Redfield claimed a scout which he hit in the cockpit from three hundred and fifty yards. The scout entered a nose dive and crashed into a wood to the left of the formation. Redfield fired two bursts into the engine of another scout which stalled, entered a spin and was lost to sight. Both claims were witnessed by 2Lt William Eric Bottrill whose combat report is the most descriptive of the engagement: *". . . at 07.25 enemy aircraft appeared and attacked immediately in a series of dives on both flanks and the rear. One enemy aircraft painted with gold spangled upper planes and black crosses with silver edges dived at B Flight (second formation) and fired at machine on left rear. Whole formation fired their Lewis guns at it, did not see enemy aircraft re-appear. Later several enemy aircraft attacked from the right rear, and I saw Lt Redfield's tracers striking two separate enemy aircraft, these went down vertically out of control. One enemy aircraft attacked Redfield then came past myself where I fired a long burst as he made a turn, tracer hitting him in engine and fuselage, he then nose-dived, stalled and ended up spinning . . ."*

After forty minutes and two large circuits, Home-Hay decided to bomb the nearby aerodrome at Haguenau. All eleven machines made the target and dropped six 230lb and ten 112lb bombs at 07.45; it appears the aerodrome was attacked while flying the semi-circle defensive pattern. One 230lb bomb was seen to hit a large hut while another exploded between four machines which were parked close to a hangar. The two formations turned for home still heavily engaged but suffering no losses. The run for the lines may well have upset the fighting pattern of the bombers as the rear group lost two aircraft both hit in the petrol tanks. Covered in petrol, 2Lt Meyer and 2Lt Patman both tried to get down before being engulfed in flames, and both landed safely but on the wrong side of the lines. 2Lt McPherson was wounded, with a bullet through his right arm. All four men were prisoners of war. The scouts then withdrew and flew off towards Buhl. The remaining nine bombers re-crossed the lines and landed safely back at Azelot, complete with eleven photos.

Jasta 18 look the likely candidates for 104's losses this day with Leutnant Kurt Monnington and Offizierstellvertreter Richard Schleichardt both claiming DH9s, one at Maurmünster and the other at Buhl-St-Marie. Jasta 70 and 78 were flying out of Buhl but these were engaged further to the north with 55 Squadron and did not claim any aircraft shot down. Jasta 18 were approximately seventy miles from their home base at Metz when they shot down the two DH9s. On paper it looks unlikely that they could have intercepted the bombers so far away from their home base. R.A.F. photographic intelligence however, was locating fresh landing strips which enabled the scouts to operate away from home bases. Jasta 18 may have been on an offensive sweep of the front lines heading east, engaged the bombers and refuelled at Buhl before returning home. Other participants in this fight could have been Jasta 80, Kest 2, 3, 4, or 5. The participation of the now regular two-seaters points towards more RT machines being employed to lead scouts to the bomber formations once in the air.

In their initial bomb raid report, 104 Squadron claimed four enemy aircraft destroyed, six driven down out of control and two driven down, which was later changed to four destroyed and two driven down out of control. German losses in this part of the front (except for the two by 55 Squadron) do not correspond. So far this month 104 Squadron had claimed seven destroyed, nine out of control and two driven down, all on only three raids. Although not all these claims were awarded, many were, and by the end of the month 104 Squadron would claim a total of thirty aircraft. German losses are normally recorded where pilots were either killed, wounded or taken prisoner. Undoubtedly a number of aircraft crashed or force-landed where pilots survived unhurt.

GEORGE HERBERT PATMAN was born in Gillingham in Kent on 18th June 1897. He worked as a Bank Clerk at Ruffer & Sons, 39 Longhorn Street, between March and June 1917. His records show he had an aero accident on 18th March 1918, presumably while training. He joined 104 on 22nd June and was repatriated on 13th December 1918.

Target: Factories and Railways at Frankfurt am Main
Secondary Target: Buhl Aerodrome

13th August			Take Off:	11.20
55 Squadron			Returned:	13.50/14.20
Formation 1				
Capt J.R.Bell	Lt G.N.Tressider	A8388		
Lt W.J.Pace	Lt D.W.Stewart	A7703		
Lt C.A.Bridgland	Sgt E.Clare	A5020		
Lt E.P.Critchley	Sgt S.E.Lewis 22017	F5700	W.I.A./K.I.A.	
Lt J.B.McIntyre	Sgt H.Mahoney		ret pilot sick	
Lt G.T.Richardson	2Lt G.Madge	A7972		

Formation 2		
Capt D.R.G.Mackay	2Lt H.C.T.Gompertz	

Lt J.Cunliffe	2Lt G.E.Little		
Lt P.E.Welchman	2Lt C.W.Clutsom		
2Lt P.J.Cunningham	2Lt N.Wallace		ret e/t
Lt D.J.Waterous	2Lt J.R.Fox	F5703	photo machine
Lt P.M.Payson	2Lt J.A.Lee	A7586	

A cloudy day greeted the crews of 55 Squadron for a return trip to Frankfurt. Twelve DH4s led by Captain Bell headed east for Blâmont in order to cross the lines. Before reaching them 2Lt Cunningham left the formation and returned to Azelot with a defective petrol pump, followed by Lt McIntyre who was feeling sick.

Crossing the lines at 12,000ft, the two formations encountered inaccurate archie as they headed north-east towards Phalsbourg. Heading up the Vosges, thick banks of cloud greeted them some rising up to 14,000ft. Captain Bell, realising that Frankfurt was probably hidden by cloud, decided to bomb Buhl aerodrome which was visible to his right hand side through a big gap in the clouds. Crossing over the Rhine river two 230lb, fourteen 112lb, eight 25lb and two 40lb phosphorous bombs were dropped from 14,000ft at 12.45. Bursts were observed in fields around the aerodrome as the bombers turned for home.

Crossing back over the Rhine, they flew compass headings over solid cloud towards the lines at Blâmont. Abeam Phalsbourg, one enemy aircraft was seen to break out of the cloud shortly followed by nine others. Most were Pfalz and Albatros scouts but observers also reported seeing two Rumpler two-seaters as well. The Germans wasted no time with six attacking the first formation of bombers. Lt Critchley and Sgt Lewis were badly shot up as the fours continued towards Sarrebourg. A Pfalz scout came in close to the first formation; all the observers fired and the scout was seen to burst into flames. The enemy fighters withdrew to a safe distance until near the lines, but then a single scout closed with the first formation firing as it came. Sgt Clare fired a whole drum at this enemy aircraft which stalled; the pilot was seen to fall out, and the aircraft crashed on the allied side. The ten bombers crossed the lines near Blâmont. Lt Critchley had been wounded so put his machine down at Arches, south-west of Epinal. Unfortunately Sergeant S.E.Lewis (No. 22017) was dead from machine-gun fire. The fighting had been fierce with nearly 4,000 rounds fired; 2Lt Fox managed to take nine photos. Sidney Edward Lewis was buried at Charmes in the I.A.F. Cemetery.

Oberleutnant Reinhold Ritter von Benz, Commanding Officer of Jasta 78b, was killed in combat with DH4/DH9s this day in Fokker DVII 4461/18 at 14.00 German time falling at Mondon Wood. Combat reports timed by 55 Squadron note one of their combats at 13.00 British time which fits as German time was one hour ahead. Jasta 78 was stationed at Buhl and obviously could be in the area. 104 Squadron were attacking Thionville too far to the west, and not until 15.45, which puts them out of the equation. The fact the enemy aircraft was a Fokker DVII is quite confusing with only Pfalz, Albatros, and Rumpler two-seaters being mentioned in combat reports. German airmen, including some of the great aces, often mistook allied aircraft, and the same mistakes were also made by allied airmen. Although Fokker DVIIs were becoming common it may well have been a new type in the area or at least a new type in the inventory of Jasta 78, and if anyone was going to fly the new aircraft it was the C.O. Jasta 78 also previously flew Albatros scouts which goes some way to explain the mix of aircraft encountered by 55 Squadron.

Target: Railway Junction at Ehrang
Secondary Target: Railway Workshops at Thionville

13th August			Take Off:	13.10
104 Squadron			Returned:	16.30
Formation 1				
Capt E.A.McKay	2Lt C.Hitchcock	D2812		
2Lt G.H.B.Smith	Sgt W.Harrop	C2179		
Lt H.P.Wells	Lt J.J.Redfield	D2917		
2Lt O.F.Merrill	Lt G.Best			
2Lt G.Pickup	Lt A.B.Rattray	D5729		
2Lt H.P.G.Leyden	Sgt A.L.Windridge	D7229	K.I.A./K.I.A.	
Formation 2				
Capt J.B.Home-Hay	Sgt W.T.Smith	D7225		
2Lt E.C.Clarke	Capt J.L.C.Sutherland	D3088	K.I.A./D.O.W.	
2Lt F.H.Beaufort	2Lt H.O.Bryant	D2881	K.I.A./K.I.A.	
2Lt J.C.Uhlman	2Lt P.Sutherland	F5844	W.I.A./D.O.W.	

| Lt W.S.Greenwood | 2Lt R.G.Gibbs | D7205 |
| Lt E.Cartwright | 2Lt P.E.Appleby | | ret photo machine |

Ehrang railway junction lay just north of Treves on the banks of the River Moselle, approximately seventy miles over the lines. Roles were reversed for this raid with Captain McKay leading, and Captain Home-Hay taking the second formation. As on previous raids fourteen aircraft were led aloft into a sky filled with patchy cloud. As Verdun approached the two spare machines were signalled to leave, and the twelve machines crossed the lines. Once over, heavy and accurate archie started, which was usual at Verdun, but probably less dangerous than crossing at Nomeny with the heavy archie batteries at Metz, and the three Jastas stationed nearby. Shortly after crossing Lt Cartwright returned to Azelot with engine trouble landing at 15.30, leaving the remaining eleven to head over Conflans towards Thionville.

Over the lines the wind had picked up sufficiently to change the mind of Captain McKay, and the target was switched from Ehrang to Thionville which was appearing on the nose. Over Thionville at 15.45 the lead formation dropped their bombs which looked to be wide of the target. Home-Hay held back and sighted independently and watched as one bomb burst on the railway, while the roof of the railway workshop was reported to have big holes in it. Anti-aircraft fire over the target had punctured the radiator of 2Lt Clarke's machine, and he left the second formation and headed straight for the lines. It would seem that most of the six 230lb and ten 112lb bombs missed the target completely, as reports after the war suggest Thionville was not attacked at all this day.

Heading back for the lines, the ten bombers were intercepted by ten scouts between Thionville and Metz. The enemy aircraft were reported as having red wings with white tails and fuselages, the markings of Jasta 18. They arrived and set about the ten bombers. Sergeant Smith fired sixty rounds at a Pfalz which went down out of control and crashed at Corny. Another scout attacked, and Smith fired two short bursts and the scout went down in a vertical nose dive and crashed a mile south of Corny. Sergeant Harrop found a broken striker on his Lewis gun while testing it on the outward journey, but fortunately he was only attacked by one scout which he drove away by firing Very lights at it. John J.Redfield from America reported seeing a red scout being hit from either side of the formation. This scout dived underneath and entered a spin, recovered and went down under control. In the back seat for McKay was 2Lt Hitchcock who fired at a scout in a dive a thousand feet above the formation. He continued to fire at this scout until it passed underneath their machine. He thought his shots had caused the scout to sway from side to side, but after going down fast for two thousand feet it levelled off then entered a shallow dive under control.

Jasta 18 seemed to be having little effect until the two formations neared the lines. An anti-aircraft shell exploded directly under the machine flown by Frank H Beaufort. His aircraft instantly folded up and fell onto the machine flown by 2Lt Leyden from the first formation. Both craft were locked together and plummeted to earth with all four occupants being killed. Shortly after this German machine-gun fire forced 2Lt Uhlman and his American observer 2Lt Paul Sutherland out of formation. Uhlman managed to put his machine down at Treyen and both men were treated for their wounds. Sutherland was severely wounded, and died from his injuries on 19th August. The remaining seven bombers returned to Azelot and touched down waiting for news of their missing comrades. Clarke and Captain Sutherland did not return after being hit in the radiator over Thionville: Captain J.L.C.Sutherland of the 1st Royal West Kent Regiment became a prisoner of war while 2Lt Clarke died of his wounds. (Conflicting reports regarding J.L.C.Sutherland surfaced during research. One account stated that his DH9 exploded, while another stated that Sutherland became a prisoner of war with a gun shot wound to the right leg, just below the knee. This leg was amputated which may well have been what killed him. Both men were reported as being buried in Garrison Cemetery at Metz.) Frank Beaufort, another American, was believed to be buried in Arrich Cemetery, so it is probable all four occupants of the collision were buried there.

Leutnant Kurt Monnington of Jasta 18 had two DH9s confirmed, both crashing at Arrich-Arnaville just north of the lines at Pont-à-Mousson at 17.05 German time for his fifth and sixth victory. The times and obviously the location fit and he was awarded these kills despite one of them being hit by archie and colliding with the other. Clarke and Sutherland do not seem to be claimed by anyone, and Clarke may well have been killed trying to land his damaged bomber, or died from injuries received from the anti-aircraft fire that holed their radiator. Jasta 18 were having a field day claiming another four DH9s later in the day, from 205 and 206 Squadron. With two DH9s from 104 Squadron bought down the previous day, Jasta 18 were becoming the specialists in shooting down bombers, and suffered no casualties this day.

2Lts Herrick Peter Gladstone Leyden, and Alan Lacey Windridge, both twenty, were buried at Arry in France. Leyden was from Pontardawe, Glamorgan, while Windridge was from Notting Hill in London.

Edwin Cedric Clarke from Regina, Saskatchewan in Canada, joined 104 from 99 on 8th July 1918, and was buried at Antallin in France. Francis Henry Beaufort, aged twenty-seven from New York, and Harold Osborne Bryant, from Bristol in Gloucestershire, were both buried at Arry. Sources during the war suggested Leyden and Windridge were buried at Arrich Cemetery, while Uhlman and Sutherland were buried at Antallin Cemetery, although these reports were not confirmed. Arrich and Antallin may well have been the original burial places, with bodies moved after the war to Arry.

Reconnaissance

14th August			**Take Off:**	**13.50**
55 Squadron			**Returned:**	**17.10**
Capt J.R.Bell	2Lt W.R.Patey	A7837		

Crossed the lines at Raon-l'-Etape at 18,000ft, continued to Molsheim then north to Strasbourg and then to Offenburg and west to re-cross the lines at Raon-l'-Etape at 18,000ft. Plates taken over Altdorf, Molsheim, Ittenheim, Hansbergen, Strasbourg and Grafenstaden, thirty plates taken, rail and water traffic reported normal.

Reconnaissance

14th August			**Take Off:**	**13.50**
55 Squadron			**Returned:**	**19.00**
Lt W.J.Pace	Lt D.W.Stewart	A7942		

Crossed the lines at Lunéville at 18,000ft, flew over Sarrebourg, Phalsbourg, Bitche, Saarbrücken, Boulay, St.Avold and Morhange. Re-crossed lines at Lunéville at 18,000ft.

Target: Cologne
Secondary Target: Railway Sidings at Offenburg

14th August			**Take Off:**	**14.00**
55 Squadron			**Returned:**	**17.20**
Formation 1				
Capt D.R.G.Mackay	2Lt H.C.T.Gompertz	B7812		
Lt K.M.Cunningham	2Lt H.H.Bracher		ret pilot sick	
2Lt P.J.Cunningham	2Lt N.Wallace	A7783		
2Lt A.J.Robinson	2Lt C.W.Clutsom	A7703		
Lt J.Cunliffe	2Lt G.E.Little	A7589	photo machine	
2Lt J.Campbell	2Lt J.R.Fox		ret e/t	
Formation 2				
Lt D.J.Waterous	2Lt C.L.Rayment	F5703		
Lt P.M.Payson	2Lt J.A.Lee	A7781		
Lt C.L.Heater	Sgt A.S.Allan			
2Lt T.H.Laing	2Lt A.C.Roberts			
Lt G.T.Richardson	2Lt W.T.Madge		photo machine	
2Lt J.B.Dunn	2Lt A.S.Papworth	B3967		

Cologne with its factories and rail yards was the target for 55. The experienced Mackay was leading as the two formations headed east from Azelot towards the lines at Raon-l'-Etape.

A fair amount of accurate archie greeted them, as they crossed the lines at 13,000ft. Also there to greet them were eight enemy aircraft. If being intercepted at the lines wasn't enough, the twelve bombers soon became ten, when 2Lts Campbell and Cunningham returned with engine trouble and sickness respectively. The eight enemy scouts started to attack, but were driven off by concentrated fire from the observers. The two formations then set course for Strasbourg, from where they would hopefully head north towards Cologne[2]. Overhead Molsheim, four enemy scouts started to shadow the bombers and were joined by

---

[2] This route does not seem the most direct towards Cologne from Azelot, but opposition from Jastas in this sector was supposedly lighter. The other reason for choosing this route may be that Mackay had decided to select an alternative target due to the weather before they crossed the lines. However they crossed the lines at 13,000ft, which would indicate a long-distance target, as they would not have had enough fuel to climb to their normal operating altitude before crossing the lines.

another eight near Strasbourg. Arriving at Strasbourg thick cloud was encountered between 10,000 and 14,000ft, as far north as could be seen. Offenburg was spotted further east, and Mackay made for it. The presence of about twenty to twenty-five enemy scouts probably made up Mackay's mind as well. At 16.00 eighteen 112lb and one 230lb bomb headed towards the sidings at Offenburg. Observers noted several bursts around the sidings as the pilots turned for home.

Now pursued by up to twenty-five scouts, the formations held tight as repeated attacks commenced trying to split them up. 2Lt Wallace fired a whole drum of Lewis at a scout with black wings and tail, and a white fuselage. The scout entered a spin with smoke coming out, and was seen to crash in a wood north of Offenburg. 2Lt Little claimed two scouts near the target area. The first fastened onto their tail but was quickly dispatched by Little's twin Lewis guns. This scout appeared to break up in the air after it spun away. Another scout, a yellow Albatros, appeared on Little's left. After receiving hits this Albatros staggered and fell away into a spin. For six thousand feet below this scout was seen to spin, recover, and spin again. Little eventually lost sight while engaging other scouts. He stated in his combat report that the engagement with the scouts lasted until the lines were re-crossed. Another Albatros was claimed, this time by 2Lt Rayment and also near the target. The Albatros came in at forty-five degrees off Rayment's tail, and firing his twin Lewis guns he watched as it turned on its wingtip and spun away; he did not see it flatten out.

The running fight continued towards the lines where 2Lt Dunn was forced to land after his aircraft had been badly shot about. Climbing from the cockpit he was astonished to see the Albatros DV which had been chasing him prepare to land. The German pilot mis-judged his approach and stuck his aircraft into a large hedge. Helped from the cockpit by French soldiers, Unteroffizier Ludwig Wittmann of Jasta 80 became a prisoner of war[3]. The remaining nine bombers returned safely to Azelot.

Note: Records do not list aircraft on this raid.

Reconnaissance

15th August			Take Off:	12.20
55 Squadron			Returned:	17.05
Lt J.Cunliffe	2Lt G.E.Little	A7942		

Crossed the lines at Château-Salins, then flew over Morhange to Val Ebersing and then to Buhl. Re-crossed at Blâmont with eighteen plates.

Reconnaissance

15th August			Take Off:	12.35
55 Squadron			Returned:	15.55
Lt D.J.Waterous	Lt C.L.Rayment	A7837		

Crossed the lines at Badonviller, then flew onto Molsheim where eight plates were exposed. Engine revolutions dropped so re-crossed at Badonviller.

Target: Boulay Aerodrome

15th August			Take Off:	16.35
99 Squadron			Returned:	19.20
Formation 1				
Maj L.A.Pattinson	2Lt W.B.Walker	D1668		
2Lt W.T.Jones	Lt E.C.Black	D2860		
2Lt E.L.McCowen	2Lt W.Shaw	D3048	crashed on t/off	
2Lt W.Hodder	2Lt H.G.Ramsay	D1044	fuel problem	
Formation 2				
Capt A.D.Taylor	2Lt O.Bell	C1666	ret e/t	
Lt H.D.West	2Lt M.A.Dunn	C6092	broken oil pipe	
Lt F.K.Crosbie-Choppin	2Lt J.C.Barnes	C1675	ret e/t	
Lt G.Broadbent	Sgt J.Jones	2196		
Lt W.G.Stevenson	2Lt J.K.Speed	D7233	ret e/t	

---

[3] Wittmann was held by the French at Mandray. The report says he crashed at La Matacuelle, Saulcy-sur-Meurthe, Vosges. His aircraft was an Albatros DVa (OAW) 6831/17.

| Sgt H.H.Wilson | Sgt F.L.Lee | C6260 | |
| Lt C.W.Hewson | 2Lt H.E.Alsford | C6342 | ret e/t |

After the horrendous losses on 31st July, 99 Squadron spent most of their time training up new pilots and observers who had recently arrived on squadron strength. Formation flying was practised the most while new observers concentrated on map reading and local landmarks. Several days were overcast however allowing little practice to be done, but training for the more experienced pilots in cloud flying was accomplished on these days. Results were recorded as less then impressive, due mainly to lack of training received in England. New machines also started to arrive, but these needed a lot of work to be done to them, especially after the bad landings at Azelot by the more inexperienced pilots, which by now were becoming more common.

Squadron commanders were now allowed to cross the lines, but only on two occasions per month. Major Lawrence Arthur Pattinson led today's raid against Boulay aerodrome, home to some of the German Gotha bomber units which were operating at night.

Fourteen DH9s took off and headed north towards Nomeny, where a rendezvous with 104 Squadron had been arranged, in order to bomb Boulay together. First to return was 2Lt Hodder as no pressure from his petrol tank was causing his engine to stop. Captain Taylor was next to return with his engine overheating quickly followed by Lt Crosbie-Choppin with the same problem. Added to this 2Lt McCowen stalled his machine 200ft above the ground then impacted. McCowen received a broken leg and arm, while his observer received a deep cut on the instep of his foot, and injuries to one of his arms. Carburettor trouble forced Lt Hewson to return after an hour and forty minutes, followed by Lt West with a broken oil pipe; Lt Stevenson was unable to keep up with what was left of the two formations. Out of fourteen aircraft that started, only four crossed the lines at Nomeny following the eleven DH9s of 104 Squadron. The weather was hot but inexperience on the part of the newer pilots was largely to blame for the poor engine performance, and time wasted waiting for the aircraft to formate also added to the mess, causing the four serviceable aircraft to be some way behind 104 Squadron as the lines approached.

Receiving moderate archie as they crossed the lines, the formation of four headed north-east following 104 Squadron towards Boulay. Once over the target they dropped their bombs on the airfield below. Hits were unobserved as five Albatros and two Pfalz scouts arrived. Two of these scouts attacked from close range while the rest fired from between 300 and 500 yards, behind the four. The scouts kept up their attack until near the lines. This engagement had lasted approximately twenty minutes at about 11,000ft. Although lower than usual, no machines were lost but Lt Broadbent returned to Azelot with his machine badly shot about, while the other three machines all had several bullet holes through fuselages. Despite only four machines making the target, they flew a good tight formation and all returned safely, which is all that could be hoped for under the circumstances.

Note: The three missing crews from the first formation were unrecorded.

LAWRENCE ARTHUR PATTINSON was born in October 1890 in Beal, Northumberland. His parents were quite wealthy, and he was fortunate enough to be sent to one of the leading public schools, Rugby. After a time in Melbourne, Australia, he returned to England and studied History at Cambridge obtaining a Masters degree. When war broke out he joined the Durham Light Infantry but soon transferred to the Royal Flying Corps, joining 11 Squadron on BE2s. By June 1916 he was a Captain and the holder of a Military Cross. He was posted in December 1916 to command 57 Squadron which he led to France, and commanded, until November 1917. He was then transferred to 99 Squadron working up on DH9s at Old Sarum Airfield, (the airfield is still active today as are some of the old buildings). Pattinson led 99 Squadron to war in April 1918 as part of the 41st Wing. While serving in France, he was promoted to Lieutenant-Colonel and put in charge of the 41st Wing until after the Armistice when the I.A.F. was disbanded. In the new year he was put in command of the 89th Wing in northern France, receiving the Distinguished Service Order in June 1919. Released from the boredom of the Air Ministry in June 1920, he proceeded to a course at the Army Staff College until taking up a post as a Wing Commander in India between 1926 and 1929. Returning to England he was promoted to Group Captain, and then in 1933 he was Air ADC to King George V. He became an Air Commodore in charge of an Armament Group at Sheerness until promoted to Air Marshal serving his last four years in the R.A.F Expansion Programme. He retired in 1941 but was recalled in 1942 for a short period to lead an Air Training Mission to China. He retired again, and died on March 28th 1955, at Princess Mary's Hospital at R.A.F. Halton.

Target: Aerodrome at Buhl

| 15th August | | | Take Off: | 16.40 |
| 104 Squadron | | | Returned: | 19.25 |

Formation 1

Maj J.C.Quinnell	Lt A.B.Rattray		
Capt J.B.Home-Hay	Sgt W.T.Smith	D7225	
Lt E.Cartwright	2Lt P.E.Appleby		photo machine
2Lt G.H.B.Smith	Sgt W.Harrop	C2179	
Lt P.C.Saxby	2Lt W.Moorhouse		
Lt W.S.Greenwood	2Lt R.G.Gibbs		ret drift wire

Formation 2

Capt E.A.McKay	2Lt C.G.Hitchcock		
2Lt J.Valentine	Sgt F.M.J.Denney 99923		photo machine
Lt D.P.Pogson	2Lt W.E.Bottrill		
2Lt O.F.Merrill	Lt G.Best		
2Lt G.H.Knight	2Lt W.E.Jackson	D1729	
Lt H.P.Wells	Lt J.J.Redfield	D2917	

Major Quinnell led his second and last raid of the month, in a combined raid with 99 Squadron against Boulay aerodrome, home to some of the large German Gotha bombers. Boulay lay approximately thirty miles over the lines, and with a joint raid in numbers it was hoped to put the troublesome Gothas out of action for a while. All twelve bombers got away and headed north towards the lines at Nomeny for the rendezvous with 99 Squadron. 99 were experiencing difficulties, so 104 crossed the lines under moderate archie with 99 Squadron's four machines some way behind. Lt Greenwood left the formation and returned to Azelot landing at 18.15 with a broken drift wire; the remaining eleven continued north unopposed by enemy aircraft.

Arriving overhead Boulay at 16.40, six 230lb, eight 112lb and eight 25lb bombs were dropped from 11,000ft. One bomb exploded directly on a Gotha bomber, while ten bursts were seen in a line within ten yards of the hangars running east to west; another two burst in between two hangars while four exploded on the landing ground.

Leaving the objective eight enemy aircraft attacked, one seen to go down and crash near a wood after fire from 2Lt Jackson. Sergeant Harrop, Sergeant Smith and Lt John J.Redfield all shot down scouts out of control, all claims being for Pfalz scouts at Corny at 15.45. Captain Home-Hay received hits to his aircraft forcing him to leave the formation as it neared the lines. The remaining ten returned to Azelot with eighteen photos while Home-Hay landed safely at Serres. No German casualties this day match the location of units stationed near Boulay or the surrounding area.

* * *

How to put German airfields out of action had been pondered by Brigadier-General Cyril Newall, (later Marshal of the Royal Air Force) for some time and on 21st August 1918 he put forward this idea for an attack on Speyerdorf aerodrome just south of Mannheim:

Journey to objective

DH9s and DH4s to leave the ground as soon as there is sufficient light for a leader to be followed. I consider this course advisable, as if machines leave in the dark, a considerable number will never reach the objective. Lines to be crossed low. Journey to objective as low as possible, just over the tree tops would be safest. Course to be followed – Badonviller – Saverne – Line of the Vosges. If machines are really low and fly just west of the eastern boundary of the Vosges they should be hidden from the defences of the Rhine valley. No opposition from enemy aircraft is expected on the outward journey. Cameras to be carried by two DH4s for photographing the objective.

At the objective

DH9s as low as possible, also the DH4s engaging defences. Each observer to be ordered to retain a certain number of drums for the return journey. Protecting DH4s to be at about 3,000ft. All DH9s and DH4s attacking defences to use their guns freely, subject to their retaining a certain number of drums for the return

Top: The entrance to Azelot aerodrome.
Left: Captain John Bertram Fox.
Above: Lt Ernest Henry Van der Reit.

Top left: Lt Charles Edward Reynolds.

Top right: The inspirational Captain Patrick Eliot Welchman who rose through the ranks with 55 Squadron and went on to lead 99 Squadron.

Middle left: Col Christopher Lloyd Courtney.

Bottom: DH4 A8073 with 'A' on cowling shot down on 26th June 1918. 2Lt F.F.H. Bryan and Sgt A. Boocock both became P.O.W.

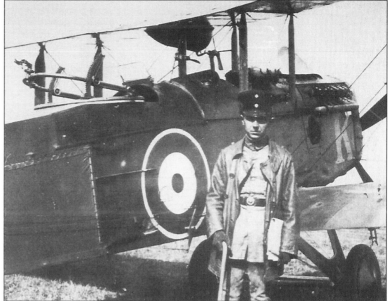

Top left: 2Lt James Bennett McIntyre.

Top right: August Raben, Commanding Officer of Jasta 18, with DH4 A7708, crewed by 2Lt H.H. Doehler and 2Lt A.S. Papworth on 30th August 1918.

Middle left: 2Lt Arthur James Robinson killed while on a reconnaissance on 25th September 1918.

Middle right: Left to right: Unknown, 'Pip' Rayment, Lt William John Pace, Captain Richard Percyvale Ward and Captain Wyndham Brookes Farrington.

Bottom left: 2Lt Herbert Roy Burnett killed with Robinson on 25th September 1918.

Top left: Standing from left to right: 2Lts A. J. Robinson and James Balfour Dunn. Both men were killed on the same day; officer seated unknown.

Top right: 2Lt William Russell Patey tries out the Vickers anti-aircraft defences at Azelot.

Bottom left: More anti-aircraft defences at Azelot of a higher calibre.

Bottom right: An accomplished pianist and apparently 55's mascot, 2Lt Earle Richard Stewart, killed on a raid to Frankfurt on 12th August.

Top left: Lt Günther von Büren of Jasta 18 who shot down a DH4 at Ennerchen, most probably 2Lts H.H. Doehler and A.S. Papworth.

Top right: Later to lead a flight in the American 166th Aero Squadron, Lt Phillips Merrill Payson.

Bottom: DH4 A7482 with left to right: Unknown, Captain O. L. Beater, Unknown, 2Lt D.W. Stewart and 2Lt K.M. Cunningham. This aircraft broke up in a dive near Metz on 1st June 1918. Lt L. de G. Godet and 2Lt A. Haley were both killed.

Top: Back row left to right: 2Lt O.E. Miller, 2Lt W.E. Johns, Captain D.R.G. Mackay, Unknown, Unknown, 2Lt K.M. Cunningham, Unknown. Middle row left to right: Unknown, Unknown, Captain J.R. Bell, 2Lt D.W. Stewart, Unknown, Lt D.J. Waterous, Unknown, Lt C.L. Heater. Front row left to right: Unknown, 2Lt A.E. Amey.

Bottom left: Lt Charles Louis Heater.

Bottom right: Captain Wyndham Brookes Farrington or 'Fifi' as he was known.

Top left: Captain William John Pace with one of the squadron's Crossley tenders.

Top right: Captain Benjamin James Silly with his pet fox cub in the orchard at Azelot.

Middle left: 2Lt Alfred Edward Amey.

Middle right: Left to right: Lt H.S.P. Walmsley, Captain 'Billy' Williams, Captain B.J. Silly, Captain W.B. Farrington and Captain W.H. Mason-Springgay.

Bottom right: Captain W.H. Mason-Springgay.

Top: Lt A.S. Keep and Lt Patey with DH4 A7781. This DH4 was shot down on 16th August with the loss of Lt J.B. McIntyre and 2Lt H.H. Brachner.

Bottom left: Left to right: 2Lt K.M. Cunningham, Lt D.J. Waterous, 2Lt W.R. Patey, 2Lt E.J. Whyte, 2Lt D.W. Stewart, Captain W.J. Pace and Captain P.E. Welchman.

Bottom right: 2Lt William Edward Johns whilst training with an RE8.

Top left: DH4 A7650 shot down while on an altitude test on 12th June by a German photo reconnaissance aircraft. Both Lt Max Greville Jones and 2Lt Thomas Elison Brewer were killed.

Top right: Lt H.S.H. Read of 99 Squadron.

Middle left: Aerial shot of Metz taken by either 2Lt M.E. Barlow or Sgt G. Howard on 15th September.

Middle right: CO of 99 Squadron Major Lawrence Arthur Pattinson.

Bottom right: Jasta 18 at Montingen near Metz. Left to right: Uffz Glatz, Offstv Wilhelm Kühne, Lt Hans Müller, Lt Kurt Monnington, Lt August Raben (CO), Lt Erich Spindler, Lt Kurt Baier, Lt Heinz Künster, Lt Kandt.

Top left: Captain William Dorian Thom.

Top right: The South African Lt Marthinus Theunis Steyn Papenfus, who became a P.O.W. on 31st July.

Bottom left: Leutnant Hugo Schäfer of Jasta 15, victor of 2Lt E.E. Crosby and C.P. Wogan-Browne on 13th September.

Bottom right: Major Claude Russell Cox previously served with 22 Squadron in 1916 flying FE2bs.

Top left: Captain Victor Beecroft.

Top right: Offizierstellvertreter Bernard Ultsch of Jasta 77 who claimed one of four DH9s of 99 Squadron lost in the Metz area on 26th September.

Middle: DH9 D3039 shot down on 31st July, Lts M.T.S. Papenfus and A.L. Benjamin becoming P.O.W.

Bottom left: Lt Harry Taylor Melville from Ceres near Fife in Scotland, K.I.A. on 31st July.

Bottom right: Harvard College graduate Lt Elliott Chapin from Somerville, Massachusetts. Shot down and killed by Lt Hans Müller of Jasta 18.

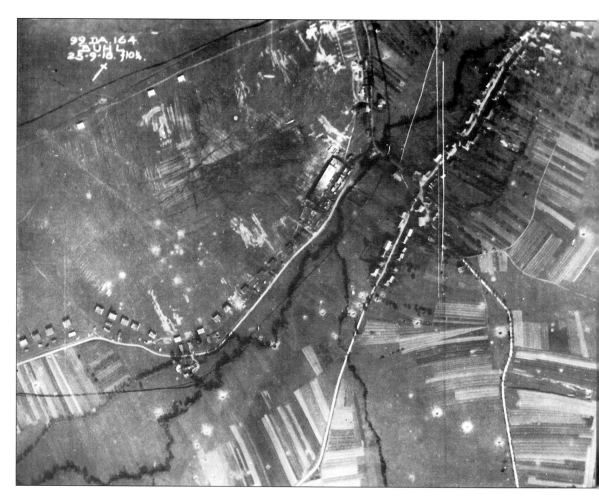

Top: Photo taken of Buhl aerodrome by 2Lt H. Crossley on 25th September. Several craters on the landing ground have been filled in. Note the many near misses.

Bottom left: Left to right: Lt H.S. Notley (W.I.A.), Captain Victor Beecroft and Captain Ashley Dudley Taylor (KIAcc) at Azelot.

Bottom right: 2Lt John Leslie McIntyre Oliphant.

Top: The aftermath, Thionville station and goods yard after an ammunition train was hit in the sidings. Probably the most successful raid by the daylight squadrons of the I.A.F.

Middle: DH9 D3213 shot down on 26th September, 2Lts W.H. Gillett and H. Crossley both becoming P.O.W.

Bottom: Leutnant Georg Weiner of Jasta 3 who would shoot down five aircraft from the I.A.F. daylight squadrons.

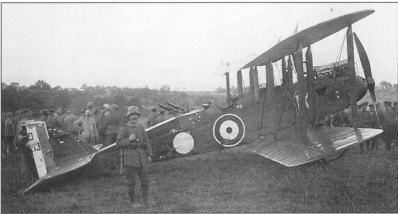

Top: 104 Squadron before leaving for France. Back row, left to right: Lt A. Moore (P.O.W.), Lt W.E. Jackson (D.O.W.), Lt R. K. Pollard (W.I.A.), Lt M.J. Ducray (P.O.W.), 2Lt C.G. Pickard (K.I.A.), 2Lt C.E. Bellord (K.I.A.), Lt S.C.M. Pontin (P.O.W.), Lt E. Cartwright (K.I.A.), 2Lt A.G. L. Mullen (K.I.A.), Capt R.J. Gammon, 2Lt P.E. Appleby, Lt W.J. Rivett-Carnac (W.I.A.), 2Lt M.H. Cole (K.I.A.). Middle row, left to right: Lt R.A.C. Brie (P.O.W.), R/O Robinson, E/O McMickle, Capt R.H. Weatherall, Lt W.G. Norden (P.O.W.), 2Lt R.L. Phillips, Lt F.W. Munday (P.O.W.), Lt C.G. Jenyns (P.O.W.), 2Lt K.C.B. Woodman (P.O.W.), 2Lt C.L. Startup, 2Lt H.C. Davis (P.O.W.), Lt C.C. Blizard. Front row, left to right: Lt W. Bruce (K.I.A.), Lt T. L. McConchie (P.O.W.), Lt G.C.Body (P.O.W.), Capt E.A. McKay (P.O.W.), R/O Wilson, Maj J.C. Quinnell, Capt J.B. Home-Hay (P.O.W.), Lt J. Valentine (P.O.W.), 2Lt F.H. Beaufort, 2Lt A.W. Robertson (W.I.A.), Kerrison.

Middle: Lt Walter Henry Goodale from Wadina, Sask, Canada. K.I.A. on 1st August on only his second raid, here he is seated in one of 104 Squadron's DH9s.

Bottom right: 2Lt Charles Edmund Bellord. A student at Balliol College Oxford studying History, he was shot down and killed on 15th September.

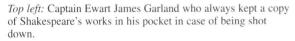

Top left: Captain Ewart James Garland who always kept a copy of Shakespeare's works in his pocket in case of being shot down.

Top right: Captain Evans Alexander McKay who previously served with 42 Squadron. Shot down on 22nd August to become a P.O.W.

Bottom left: Captain Home-Hay as a P.O.W. sporting a moustache. Shot down on 22nd August, 104 Squadron lost fifteen crew this day.

Bottom right: 2Lt William Eric Bottrill who rose to the rank of Colonel in the local Dundas Regiment in Canada in WW2.

Top: DH9 D2931 shot down on 12th August. 2Lt O.F. Meyer and Sgt A.C. Wallace became P.O.W.

Bottom: Kest 1b at Karlsruhe. Left to right: Ltn Legris, Ltn Glaeser, Ltn Willi Rosenstein, Ltn Rudolf Nebel, Hptm Willy Weber, Ltn Paul Blunck, Ltn Georg Klein.

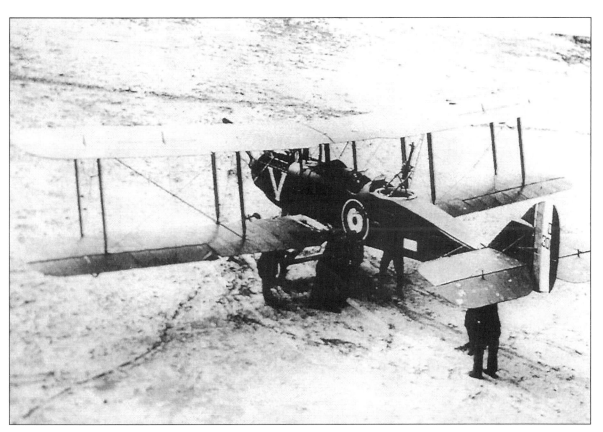

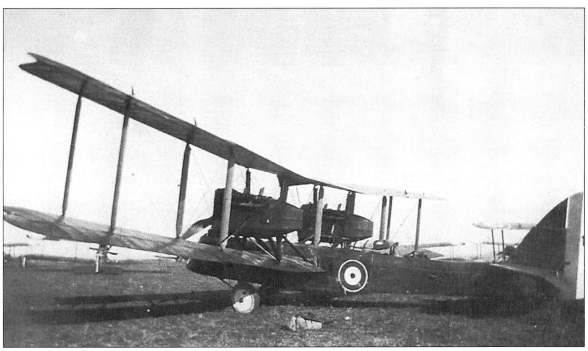

Top: DH9 D3084 shot down on 12th August probably by Jasta 18. 2Lts G.H. Patman and J.M.S. McPherson became P.O.W.

Bottom: DH10 F1867 flown by Ewart Garland on 10th November on a solo bombing raid.

Top: DH9a F1000 damaged on 25th September on a raid to Frankfurt. After repair this aircraft ended up with 99 Squadron in November 1918.

Bottom left: Lt Charles Bynon Ellis Lloyd shot down on 25th September.

Bottom middle: Leutnant Kurt Monnington of Jasta 18 who by war's end would have six I.A.F. aircraft to his credit.

Bottom right: Captain Arthur Lindley previously served with 55 Squadron in 1916. He was shot down on 25th September.

Top left: Major Louis George Stanley Reynolds who ran out of petrol on 21st October.

Top middle: Lt H.V. Brisbin brought down on 16th September by archie or Jasta 70.

Top right: 2Lt R.S. Lipsett who become a P.O.W. with his pilot Lt Brisbin.

Middle: Left to right: R. Robertson, 2Lt E. Bower, Lt H. Hinchcliff, Lt J.B. Wilkinson, 2Lt J.W. Sanderson and 2Lt B. Aitchison.

Bottom right: Lt K.B. Wilkinson while at the Royal Naval College Greenwich.

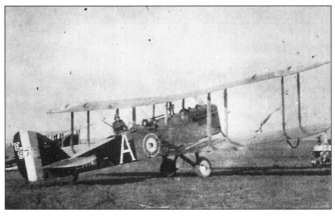

Top: Left to right: 2Lt F.H. Wilcockson, Unknown, Lt H. Hinchcliff, 2Lt J.W. Sanderson and Unknown.

Middle left: On the right 2Lt N.N. Wardlaw of 110 Squadron.

Middle right: DH9a E9711.

Bottom right: 110 Squadron at Bettoncourt, left to right: Lt R.P. Brailli, Lt W. Armstrong, 2Lt C.H.B. Stevenson, and Lt S.B. Bradley.

journey. I doubt the possibility of pilots being able to make much use of their guns. Bombs to be carried by DH9s, 25lb if possible and a certain number of incendiary bombs.

Return journey
DH9s as low as possible as on outward journey. All DH4s at about 3,000ft just behind them and on the flanks. I doubt if the enemy's system of communication will be equal to the occasion. Enemy scouts when they receive the warnings will probably proceed to the normal height at which our machines fly. Having once left the ground they cannot be told that our machines are flying low, and if these are really low they will probably never be seen by the main forces of the enemy aircraft. It is hoped the DH4s will be able to compete with any odd enemy aircraft encountered.

I am convinced that the secret of success will be found in flying really low.

In the field	C.A.Newall
21st August, 1918	Brigadier-General,
	G.O.C., 8th Brigade
	Royal Air Force.

With a round trip of approximately one hundred and eighty miles (if the route stated is followed) at low level, this was a recipe for disaster, and fortunately these suggestions were never carried out. Losses were severe enough amongst 99 and 104 Squadron, and a raid flown like this would have pushed the DH9s and probably the more reliable DH4s to the limit of their petrol, and if enemy aircraft could be redirected in the air by their accompanying RT machines, most of the DH9s would not have returned and a fair amount DH4s also. Also local units Kest 1a at Mannheim and Kest 1b at Karlsruhe would have been in easy reach as would Jasta 70 and 78 at Buhl. The 'Brass' must have realised by now that the DH9 was not suited for long-distance bombing, and neither were the in-experienced crews they were putting in them. Another point is that the Germans learnt quickly and if Newall's theory had been put into action, the surprise of low level raids would have been short lived.

Target: Railways at Köln (Cologne)
Secondary Target: Mannheim/Railway at Darmstadt

16th August			Take Off:	05.15
55 Squadron			Returned:	10.15
Formation 1				
Capt B.J.Silly	2Lt W.R.Patey	A8020		
Lt J.Cunliffe	2Lt G.E.Little	A7589		
Lt C.L.Heater	Sgt A.S.Allan	D8396	photo machine	
2Lt T.H.Laing	2Lt A.G.Roberts	F5703	/W.I.A.	
2Lt J.Campbell	2Lt J.R.Fox	A7813	P.O.W./ D.O.W.	
Formation 2				
Lt C.A.Bridgland	Sgt E.Clare			
Lt G.T.Richardson	2Lt N.Wallace	D8388	/W.I.A.	
Lt P.M.Payson	2Lt J.A.Lee		ret e/t	
2Lt A.J.Robinson	2Lt C.W.Clutsom	A2131		
Lt J.B.McIntyre	2Lt H.H.Bracher	A7781	K.I.A./K.I.A.	
2Lt E.A.Brownhill	2Lt W.T.Madge	D9273	K.I.A./K.I.A.	

A sky filled with large banks of clouds greeted the crews as they prepared for the long flight to Köln, one hundred and fifty-five miles over the lines. Once airborne Captain Silly decided to bomb the alternative target of Mannheim and its collection of targets, the biggest of which was the poison gas factories of Badische Anilin Soda Fabrik, and the Oppau Chemical Works.

Eleven DH4s took off from Azelot heading east to cross the lines at 13,000ft over Senones. Heavily archied as they crossed the lines, the machines flew north-east to Molsheim and on towards Haguenau. Lt Payson was forced to abort with engine trouble leaving two formations of five machines each. Overhead Haguenau, both groups were intercepted by German scouts, but the attack was half-hearted and the enemy machines soon withdrew. The Rhine valley was shrouded in haze as the bombers continued over the Vosges towards Landau, south-west of Mannheim. Captain Silly noted that the wind speed had not impaired the progress of the aircraft so he decided therefore to pass Mannheim and the heavy barrage of accurate anti-aircraft fire, and bomb the railway junction at Darmstadt instead. As the aircraft passed over Mannheim, Albatros scouts with red wings and grey fuselages attacked from out of the sun. William Russell Patey fired a whole drum from 200 yards range hitting a scout in the petrol tank. It did not catch fire and the clear fluid emitting from it as it dived towards Speyerdorf aerodrome may well have been water. Also claiming an enemy scout at this time was 2Lt G.E.Little who fired 200 rounds at an Albatros scout, and watched as it entered a spin which gained momentum until the aircraft was lost to sight. It seems the first formation was singled out for special attention as Sergeant Allan fired 75 rounds at an Albatros scout which dived at him from out of the sun. It then turned in a left bank and flew down towards Mannheim apparently under control until lost to sight in mist. In his combat report he stated that the Albatros had camouflaged wings with a dark body and white tail.

At 08.05 one 230lb and sixteen 112lb bombs were dropped from 13,500ft on Darmstadt, the only time this target would be attacked by the I.A.F. Most bombs fell in the civilian district of Woog, killing four people, while two bombs exploded in a coal depot but doing little damage. Reports from 55 Squadron say ten machines attacked the target, however only bombs from nine aircraft were reported dropped in the same report so one aircraft may have failed to release because of a jam although this is pure speculation. The error may well be just a mathematical one or typing error on the part of the adjutant or clerk.

Leaving the target area, enemy scouts started to appear from Kest 1a stationed at Mannheim. A running fight ensued with a DH4 falling under the guns of Vizefeldwebel Karl Bücher of Kest 1a; this machine was probably Campbell and Fox who both became prisoners of war, although Fox later died of his wounds.

Continuing towards Saverne, Kest 1a left the fight at Worms, but there was little respite as Kest 3 out of Morchingen attacked. Over Saverne the situation worsened as five scouts from the direction of Buhl joined the fray. These came from Jasta 70 and pressed home their attacks aggressively. The rear formation received most of the attention, and it wasn't long before two DH4s dropped out, apparently under control, but followed down by Germans. Vizefeldwebel Lemke of Jasta 70 claimed a DH4 at Dagsburg, while Offizierstellvertreter Grünwald of Kest 3 claimed a DH9 at Buchsweiler. These two claims were probably Lt McIntyre and 2Lt Bracher, 2Lts Brownhill and Madge who were all killed. However, Grünwald's claim was not upheld and his sole kill of the war remained the DH4 he had shot down the previous day at Courbesseaux.

The remaining seven bombers re-crossed the lines at Badonviller landing safely back at Azelot except 2Lt Laing who put his machine down at St. Clements, south-east of Lunéville, it being badly shot about and with a large hole in his petrol tank. His observer 2Lt Roberts was wounded but survived. 2Lt Wallace was also injured but not seriously, receiving bruising. Although set upon by two different Kest units, it wasn't until Jasta 70 intervened that things looked serious for 55 Squadron and within a short space of time the rear formation had lost two machines. Although one of these was lost to Kest 3, it was the Jasta units who were more experienced at splitting formations, and for even the most disciplined like 55 Squadron, with more Jastas arriving in September, the future looked bleak.

This was the worst day so far in regard to casualties for 55 Squadron since joining the I.A.F. Sergeant Allan managed to bring back eighteen photos, scant reward for their losses especially if you take into account actual damage done to the target. Ernest Albert Brownhill, aged twenty-five, from Sheffield in Yorkshire was buried at Niederzwehren in Germany. 2Lt William Thomas Madge, aged nineteen, was also buried at Niederzwehren. James Bennett McIntyre was buried at Sarralbe along with his observer Herbert Hector Bracher. Aged only eighteen, Bracher came from Lewisham in South London. John Robert Fox of the 10th Manchester Regiment was buried at Ingweiler Cemetery; aged twenty he came from Buxton in Derbyshire.

The only son of Scottish parents from Edinburgh, JAMES BENNETT MCINTYRE was born in Manitoba, Canada in 1894. He attended the George Watson College between 1904 and 1911 before returning to Canada. His first job was working on the surveying staff of the Canadian Northern Railway. He left this job and joined a bank in Ontario, from where he enlisted in the Canadian Dragoons in December 1915. From the Dragoons he joined the Royal Flying Corps and 55 Squadron with the rank of Lt. Although his machine was seen going down under control, it was later reported that it crashed in flames near Dagsburg.

CAPTAIN BENJAMIN SILLY was in Switzerland when war broke out. He managed to get home in three days and enlisted in the Public Schools Brigade on 3rd September 1914. He later transferred and served as a private in the 19th Battalion Royal Fusiliers, before being forced to take a commission in the Derry and Conscripts Army in September 1916. He was commissioned into the R.F.C. and trained at the School of Aeronautics at Oxford and with little formation flying experience he was shipped off to join 55 Squadron at Fienvillers in April 1917. Rising through the ranks, Silly would be promoted to acting Major on 20th September to take command of 55. At the end of October 1918 he went on a short course at Offordness with twelve pilots and observers, to study and practice long-distance raids, in formation in bad weather. After the war he again served with 55 when he was posted to Iraq on 23rd September 1923. After two years he was posted to H.Q. Middle East in Cairo for staff duties. While serving with 55 he was awarded the D.F.C. His citation read as follows:

Captain Benjamin James Silly
D.F.C. gazetted 21st September 1918

For exceptional skill and gallantry on long-distance raids, in 47 of which he has been engaged, and has been the leader on 22 occasions. Within the past month he led a formation of bombers which accomplished their object notwithstanding that the enemy scouts were encountered almost from the start, and at the destination they numbered 40 machines. Captain Silly's formation destroyed four enemy aircraft, and returned without losing a single machine.

Note: Records do not list aircraft on this raid.

Reconnaissance

16th August			Take Off:	09.00
55 Squadron			Returned:	14.05
Lt D.J.Waterous	Lt C.L.Rayment	A7837		

Crossed the lines at Arracourt at 18,500ft, flew onto Sarreguemines, Phalsbourg, Buchweiller, Haguenau, Bischweiller, Brumath, Saverne. Re-crossed lines at Arracourt at 19,000ft. Photos taken of Bensdorf aerodrome, Sarreguemines, Phalsbourg, sheds west of Dossenheim, Saverne and north of Brumath and Haguenau. In all thirty-two plates exposed.

Reconnaissance

16th August			Take Off:	15.30
55 Squadron			Returned:	17.40
LtCol J.E.A.Baldwin	Capt R.A.Ward	A7837		

Crossed the lines at Badonviller at 17,000ft, proceeded straight to Buhl and re-crossed at Badonviller. Baldwin and Ward were accurately archied as they crossed the lines; they took ten plates in all.

Target: Blast Furnaces at Dillingen

20th August			Take Off:	13.40
99 Squadron			Returned:	15.40
Formation 1				
Maj L.A.Pattinson	Lt W.B.Walker	C1668		

After the raid to Boulay aerodrome, the next three days were spent in practice, especially landings. The weather was suitable for operations but the practice was badly needed. On the morning of the 18th, Major Pattinson and Lt Walker attempted to reach the factories and blast furnaces at Dillingen, situated on the River Saar north-west of Saarbrücken. The entire route was planned to be flown over cloud until the target was reached, then fly above cloud for the return trip hopefully exposing themselves to minimal archie, and no enemy scouts. This type of bombing raid had been successfully tried before in 1916, by Captain Bourdillon of 27 Squadron, in a Martinsyde G100. So far it had not been tried by anyone in the I.A.F., but personal glory was not the reason. It was an experiment to see what could be achieved in bad weather, and the obvious reduction in casualties this type of operation could achieve. The weather on the 18th was unfortunately too clear and the idea was put off until the 20th.

The weather on the 20th was perfect with continuous cloud from a few hundred feet in the morning, which lifted to 2,000ft by midday. Taking off they headed north towards Pont-à-Mousson entering cloud which they broke through at 5,000ft. Not being seen or heard, they encountered no archie nor did they see any enemy aircraft as they flew north-east towards Dillingen. Flying for thirty-six minutes, on a heading of north-east, on his 5/17 Creagh-Osborne Compass (standard kit on an I.A.F. DH9), Pattinson descended and found himself four miles north-west of Dillingen. Flying towards Dillingen he attacked the southern end of the factory dropping two 112lb bombs fitted with fifteen-second delay fuses from 2,000ft. No anti-aircraft fire met the lone DH9 until the first bomb exploded near one of the blast furnaces causing lots of flames, while the other detonated on the perimeter railway track which enclosed the works. Pattinson did not wait around and quickly re-entered cloud flying a reciprocal heading back to the lines. After forty-five minutes, Pattinson popped out of the clouds and found himself over Ochey. Touching down at Azelot he must have felt elated for there had been a 25mph wind blowing west-north-west for the entire trip; his sums had been right and showed that it could be done.

A telegram of congratulation arrived from General Trenchard in the evening. However, reports made after the war conclude that one bomb hit the railway track, while the other fell outside the factory perimeter to the south-east, so blast furnaces were not hit during the entire war at Dillingen, either by day or by night. Lt Walker saw the flames, but these could well have been normal, considering the nature of the target. With a whole squadron the result may well have been different. If formation and climbing speeds could be kept constant while climbing through cloud, there was a good chance bombers could reach targets in bad weather not too far over the lines. But this was virtually impossible for any squadron in 1918. Twelve DH9s dropping twenty-four 112lb bombs from 2,000ft, could probably have inflicted considerable damage on many targets, but it would take an experienced and competent leader to get them there.

Reconnaissance

21st August			Take Off:	08.45
55 Squadron			Returned:	12.45
Capt B.J.Silly	Capt R.P.Ward	A7837		

Crossed the lines north of Verdun at 19,500ft and proceeded to the Rouvrois area, then to the Briey area. Over Conflans and Ayamont and re-crossed the lines at Fresnes, train movement reported normal and thirty-five plates taken.

Reconnaissance

21st August			Take Off:	10.10
55 Squadron			Returned:	14.35
Capt D.R.G.Mackay	2Lt H.C.T.Gompertz	A7942		

Crossed the lines at Blâmont at 18,000ft and proceeded by Saverne, north of Haguenau to Wissembourg. Then to Germersheim and Landau. Re-crossed the lines east of Lunéville, twenty-eight plates taken.

Reconnaissance

21st August			Take Off:	16.50
55 Squadron			Returned:	19.45
Lt W.J.Pace	Lt J.Parke	A7837		

Crossed the lines west of Château-Salins at 18,000ft and proceeded to Boulay, Vahl, Ebersing, Morchingen, Buhl and Lorquin. Re-crossed lines at Forêt-de-Parroy with eighteen plates.

Target: Badische Aniline Soda Fabrick Works, Mannheim

22nd August			Take Off:	05.10
104 Squadron			Returned:	09.30
Formation 1				
Capt J.B.Home-Hay	Sgt W.T.Smith	D1729	P.O.W./P.O.W.	

Lt E.Cartwright	2Lt A.G.L.Mullen	D5729	K.I.A./K.I.A.
Lt D.P.Pogson	2Lt W.E.Bottrill	D3122	
Lt P.C.Saxby	2Lt W.Moorhouse		/K.I.A.
2Lt G.H.Knight	2Lt W.E.Jackson	D3263	
2Lt J.W.Pope	Lt A.B.Rattray	D1050	
Spare aircraft			

Formation 2			
Capt E.A.McKay	Lt R.A.C.Brie	D2812	P.O.W./P.O.W.
2Lt R.Searle	2Lt C.G.Pickard	D1048	P.O.W./K.I.A.
2Lt G.H.B.Smith	Sgt W.Harrop	C2179	P.O.W./P.O.W.
Lt L.D.Merrill	Lt G.Best	D7210	
Lt J.Valentine	2Lt C.G.Hitchcock	C6202	P.O.W./P.O.W.
Lt H.P.Wells	Lt J.J.Redfield	D2917	P.O.W./P.O.W.

Mannheim was one hundred and fifteen miles over the lines, and both formation leaders knew they were up against it after recent attempts to reach nearer targets had been stopped purely due to attack by enemy aircraft. Owing to lack of aircraft and crew, only one spare aircraft was taken, thus only thirteen machines headed east to cross the line at Raon-l'-Etape.

Nearing the lines the spare aircraft was signalled away and the twelve machines crossed the lines coming under heavy and accurate archie. Both groups only got as far as Schirmeck when they were intercepted by eight enemy scouts which positioned themselves on the flanks, and exchanged fire from long range. Usually this tactic bought little reward but Lt James Valentine fired a green Very light and left, heading down under control, quickly followed by some of the scouts. Still followed by the remaining fighters, the bombers continued north-east where over Waldeck Wood, in the Vosges, Captain Evans Alexander McKay left the formation and went down apparently under control, with engine trouble. McKay and Lt Brie were taken prisoner by local peasants armed with scythes and pitchforks. Their radiator had been holed but both men were unscathed. Lt James Valentine from America, and his observer 2Lt Hitchcock also survived their forced landing which was due to engine trouble, and not enemy machine-gun fire. After McKay went down the enemy scouts dispersed, and the remaining ten bombers continued towards Mannheim as their comrades were led into captivity.

Captain Home-Hay pressed on despite these losses and the South African, 2Lt R.Searle, took control of the second formation. Nearing Mannheim, fifteen enemy aircraft appeared and engaged straight away, a mixture of Fokker DVII, Pfalz, Albatros and five Halberstadt two-seaters. Despite the attention of enemy aircraft the formation arrived over Mannheim at 08.05. Home-Hay sighted well and all bombs fell within the factory perimeter causing four fires; a further fire was caused on the east side of the river. The fighting was fierce with one of the Halberstadt two-seaters flying into the middle of the second formation for some minutes. Lt Best fired eighty rounds at this intruder in their formation with no effect; all observers from combat reports seem to have fired at this two-seater. Both formations must have been close for Lt Jackson in the first group fired several bursts which entered the cockpit. The Halberstadt rolled over and went down in a vertical dive which resulted in a crash in a field, just south of Mannheim. Other observers witnessed this crash too. Lt Rattray fired at a Pfalz scout with a yellow fuselage and white tail. Several bursts hit the scout and it headed down apparently to land, but as it approached a field it burst into flame. Rattray also fired at a Halberstadt with a black and white fuselage, which dived through the formation. The Halberstadt entered a series of stalls and spins before flattening out near the ground. Jackson also saw this Halberstadt go down and flatten out near the ground.

William Bottrill was at the mercy of the fighters shortly after leaving the target area. An extractor on his Lewis gun had broken and while trying to remedy it, he noticed a Pfalz scout close to within short range of the lead machine flown by Home-Hay. Sergeant Smith in the back seat also had a stoppage, and Bottrill watched as the German scout had a free shot from close range. Bottrill managed to get his Lewis going and immediately fired at this scout, which caught fire and went down in flames. Home-Hay and Smith were untouched but their machine was badly shot up and started to emit smoke and steam. Home-Hay immediately headed down but unfortunately was followed by the rest of the Squadron until their leader landed. Both formations, or what was left of them, were now at 6,000ft. Bottrill tied a large handkerchief to the scarf ring in the rear cockpit to symbolise taking the lead and his pilot, Desmond Phillip Pogson, tried to gather the remaining bombers into a group. The leader of the second formation, 2Lt Searle, had fallen, as had Lt Smith and the all-American crew of Horace Wells from Boulder, Colorado, and John J.Redfield from Montclair, New Jersey, who came down near Speyer. Wells and Redfield watched Searle spin away just before bullets thudded into their aircraft cutting wires and hitting the sand-filled seat Wells was sitting on. The radiator and the oil tank had been hit and their DH9 was shrouded in steam and smoke. Redfield in the back had been hit in the leg but was ready to fire the Pyrene extinguisher when the fire, which had started so quickly, burnt itself out. By now, down low, a warning shot was fired by the German pilot who indicated they should land. Wells put down on an airfield which was probably Speyerdorf, and was greeted by workmen brandishing spanners. Fortunately their victor, Offizierstellvertreter Eduard Prime of Jasta 78, also landed and saved the crew from a severe beating. Prime helped Wells put a tourniquet on Redfield's thigh. Wells was impressed by this and offered Prime a butterfly charm which he carried on his helmet. Both men were sent to Ratstatt then interrogated at Karlsruhe, then spent the rest of the war at Landshut prisoner of war camp. Cartwright and Mullen from the first formation were seen to spin down shortly after the target and were both killed in action.

The remaining five bombers crossed the lines at Raon-l'-Etape at 12,000ft and landed back at Azelot. The carnage however was not over for 104 Squadron. 2Lt Moorhouse had been hit by archie as they re-crossed the lines and was found dead in the back seat upon landing.

Leutnant Hanz Jungwirth of Jasta 78 was credited with a DH9 at Ingweiler; which one of the above is not clear but only three DH9s were claimed this day and the other was on the 17th German Army sector opposite the British part of the front. No German losses can be found but there may have been some within the Kest Units 1a and 1b which may well have been in action along with Jasta 78. Eduard Prime had Wells and Redfield's identity discs dropped over the lines with a "Quite well" note attached.[4]

With eleven men prisoners of war and three killed in action, 104 Squadron would be out of action for some time, the second DH9 squadron to be withdrawn since the I.A.F started its operations. The biggest loss was experience with both Captains Home-Hay and McKay out of the war for good. After the war investigators from the Air Ministry found that all bombs dropped on this raid missed the small fabric and dye factory and the larger factory nearby. Although the bomb raid report records a hit on buildings within the factory, it also states all twelve bombers made it to the target. Combat reports clearly state as does the second page of the bomb raid report that Valentine and Captain McKay were lost well before reaching Mannheim. Valentine was wounded in the left foot which was amputated at the Civilian Hospital in Saverne while he was a prisoner of war.

2Lts Edward Cartwright and Arnold George Leighton Mullen, were both buried at Roppenheim in France. Cartwright was nineteen and came from Sutton Coldfield near Birmingham. He was born on 19th June 1899, and attended Bishop Veseys Grammar School between 1914 and 1917. He was promoted to Lt on 1st April 1918 and was mentioned in despatches while with 104 Squadron. Mullen was previously with the 5th Durham Light Infantry, and came from Whitley Bay in Northumbria; he was twenty-two. 2Lt William Moorhouse from MacDuff, Banff, in Canada, served previously with the Royal West Kent Regiment. Buried in the I.A.F. Cemetery at Charmes, he was only eighteen. Another Canadian, Cecil Gerald Verity Pickard came from Exeter in Ontario, and was buried at Neiderzwehren in Germany, aged twenty-two.

JAMES VALENTINE was born on 24th January 1896. The family address during the war was 15 Douglas Road, Glen Ridge, New Jersey U.S.A. Valentine was a student of mechanical engineering at Stevens Institute of Technology, at Hoboken, New Jersey, from September 1914 to June 1917. He proceeded to England from Canada on 17th December 1917 and commenced his training at No.3 Flying School. He was made a 2Lt on 7th February 1918 and joined 104 Squadron on 18th May. Some reports say his aircraft was not shot up, but his records suggest that he was. He was known to have been in Charmes Hospital on 3rd December, listed as seriously ill. Here he had his leg amputated on 14th and his condition was reported as satisfactory. He was then sent back to England on 2nd January 1919, and put on the unemployed list in New York on 9th December 1920. It would appear with the amputation, that he received gun shot wounds, or damaged his leg while force landing.

---

[4] German casualties note two airmen near Darmstadt which might have been the crew of the Halberstadt.

EVANS ALEXANDER MCKAY was born on 3rd May 1896. A student at the James Collegiate Institute in Toronto before the war, he had already won a Military Cross while serving previously with 42 Squadron. A prisoner of war he was repatriated on 9th December 1918. His address in Canada was 12 Chicord Avenue, Ontario, Canada. While a prisoner of war, he was awarded a D.F.C. and his citation read as follows:

Capt Evans Alexander McKay M.C.
D.F.C. gazetted 21st September 1918

This officer led a raid on an important railway station; during this operation, which was most successful, 24 hostile aircraft attacked his formation. In the engagement he displayed fine leadership and skill. Three of the hostile machines were destroyed and one driven down. He is an exceptionally good formation leader, and his determination to reach his objective is only equalled by his coolness and courage when attacked.

Decorated for his actions this day was 2Lt Desmond Phillip Pogson. His citation read:

2Lt Desmond Phillip Pogson
D.F.C. gazetted 21st September 1918

In a recent long-distance bombing raid his petrol tank received a shot immediately after crossing the line, but he continued on his journey and bombed the distant objective. On the return journey very fierce fighting occurred, during which both leaders and deputy-leaders of our formations were shot down, and the remaining machines lost touch with each other. At this critical moment 2nd Lieutenant Pogson ordered his observer to tie his handkerchief to the gun-mounting to indicate that his was the leader's machine. He then circled over the area three times and picked up five of our machines, and in the face of very hostile opposition got them into formation and brought them all safely home. The prompt action of this officer was highly meritorious, and undoubtedly saved the remaining machines, which could not have coped with the greatly superior formations of the enemy.

Target: Railways at Köln (Cologne)
Secondary Target: Railway Sidings at Coblenz

22nd August		Take Off:	05.30
55 Squadron		Returned:	10.20
Formation 1			
Capt J.R.Bell	Lt G.N.Tressider		
Lt W.J.Pace	Lt D.W.Stewart		
Lt S.L.Dowswell	2Lt W.R.Patey		
Lt P.M.Payson	2Lt J.A.Lee		
Lt D.J.Waterous	2Lt C.L.Rayment		crash landing e/t
2Lt J.B.Dunn	2Lt A.S.Papworth	D8369	crash landing e/t
Formation 2			
Lt C.A.Bridgland	2Lt J.G.Quinton		
Lt G.T.Richardson	2Lt T.F.L.Myring		
Lt C.L.Heater	Sgt A.S.Allan		ret e/t
2Lt A.J.Robinson	2Lt C.W.Clutsom	A7979	
Lt J.Cunliffe	2Lt G.E.Little		
2Lt P.J.Cunningham	Sgt H.Mahoney		ret observer sick

Captain Bell led this raid to Cologne as the crews had again prepared for an early start, hoping to elude enemy aircraft, especially after their last encounter. The weather conditions looked favourable as the twelve machines climbed into a clear sky, and headed north towards the lines at Nomeny. Twelve soon became eleven, as 2Lt Dunn left with engine trouble wrecking his machine in a forced landing at Meuville-les-Champlette.

The early start had caught the flak crews seemingly unprepared. Scattered and inaccurate archie did little to trouble the two formations, illness did however, and 2Lt Cunningham returned to Azelot with his sick observer, Sgt Mahoney. Heading north the formations flew abeam Thionville as they pressed on towards

Treves. Engine trouble reduced the strength of the rear formation as Lt Chas Louis Heater from America turned for home. He made it, putting his machine down at Azelot at 07.15. Another American, 2Lt Donald Jayne Waterous also experienced engine trouble, and he dropped his two 112lb bombs on Wittlick before setting his machine down at Vadelaincourt. Over Treves, Captain Bell decided to attack the alternative target of Coblenz instead due to an increasingly strong wind; the two formations now totalled four machines each. Following the Moselle river, the bombers continued north-east towards Coblenz without seeing any enemy aircraft. At 08.05 Coblenz awoke to the sound of one 230lb and fourteen 112lb bombs raining down from 13,000ft. Bursts were observed on the town whilst three hits were seen in the Ehrenbreitstein Fort. An aqueduct was pierced by a bomb but most seemed to explode on private property killing two and injuring another two.

Heading for home, the two formations were expecting trouble being so far over the lines. Flying over Treves and Luxembourg towards Verdun, amazingly no enemy aircraft were seen and all eight machines landed back at Azelot. No photos had been taken as 2Lt Rayment and Sgt Allan, with their pilots, had returned earlier in the machines carrying the cameras.

Note: Aircraft serial numbers are not recorded in records for this raid.

Target: Factories and Railways at Mannheim
Secondary Target: Haguenau Aerodrome

22nd August			Take Off:	05.45
99 Squadron			**Returned:**	**08.35**
Formation 1				
Lt W.G.Stevenson	Lt J.K.Speed	D1668		
Lt H.D.West	2Lt M.A.Dunn	C6092		
Lt J.W.Richards	2Lt E.Smith	D1716	ret oil pressure	
Lt G.Broadbent	2Lt O.Bell	D2860		
Lt F.K.Crosbie-Choppin	2Lt A.T.Bower	D3215		
2Lt D.F.Brooks	2Lt R.Buckby	D3213	ret e/t	
Formation 2				
2Lt C.W.Hewson	2Lt E.Beale	C6342	ret abandoned	
2Lt W.T.Jones	2Lt E.C.Black	D7233	ret abandoned	
2Lt S.McKeever	2Lt H.A.Boniface	6366	ret e/t	
2Lt W.Hodder	2Lt H.G.Ramsay	C6272	ret abandoned	
Sgt H.H.Wilson	2Lt H.E.Alsford	C6260	ret fuel pressure	

A joint raid with 104 Squadron was detailed against Mannheim, more than one hundred miles over the lines, quite a distant target for such an in-experienced Squadron as 99 had become. Leading the two formations today would be Lt William Gordon Stevenson, and 2Lt C.W.Hewson. Captain Thom was suffering from influenza while on leave, Captain Beecroft was also on leave, and Major Pattinson had flown his two missions over the lines, leaving this long-distance raid in the hands of two untried leaders. The other problem was teaming up with 104 Squadron. Earlier attempts over recent months had proved on the whole disastrous, and these had been led by experienced leaders. On the whole Mannheim looked a bad choice of target with the aircraft and crews that were available.

Ten DH9s took off thirty-five minutes after 104 Squadron, and started to gain height as they headed towards the lines. Sergeant Wilson barely got off the ground before he was obliged to return with no pressure in his fuel system. Well ahead by now were 104 Squadron having started well before 99 Squadron. Meeting at the lines had obviously been abandoned before starting out, but Mannheim was still the objective for both Squadrons. Although a lot of time had been spent training new pilots and observers, replacements still had trouble handling their engines when trying to stay in formation. Engine trouble forced 2Lt McKeever to return as he couldn't keep up. After an hour and a half of trying to get his aircraft together, and with his formation now down to three, 2Lt Hewson returned to Azelot too and abandoned the raid.

Stevenson was also having difficulty with his group. Lt Richards returned with low oil pressure, followed shortly by 2Lt Brooks who was unable to keep up. The four remaining machines crossed the lines encountering little archie as they headed north-east towards Mannheim. Flying east towards the Rhine valley, fifteen enemy aircraft were seen north-west of Haguenau, while another eight were spotted north-east of it. The German aircraft were above the bombers at about 14,000ft, and with only four aircraft in the formation, Stevenson decided to bomb the Haguenau aerodrome below. Three 230lb and two 112lb bombs were dropped, bursts being observed on the north-western part of the aerodrome. The four bombers turned for home keeping an ever watchful eye on the enemy behind them. All four machines returned safely, and 2Lt Bell managed to take three photos over the target.

Of all the machines which returned early, only Sergeant Wilson's had a serious defect with a blocked fuel pipe. Inexperience was the culprit on this day; rough handling of unreliable engines was a recipe for disaster. It was fortunate that few machines crossed the lines. 99 Squadron were simply not ready for a serious encounter with a front line Jasta.

Reconnaissance

22nd August			Take Off:	07.35
55 Squadron			Returned:	11.25
Capt D.R.G.Mackay	2Lt H.C.T.Gompertz	A7837		

Crossed the lines at Cirey then via Lorquin and over Dieuze to Morhange and on to St.Avold and Boulay, forty-four plates exposed in all.

Target: Buhl Aerodrome

23rd August			Take Off:	05.15
99 Squadron			Returned:	07.25
Formation 1				
Lt W.G.Stevenson	Lt J.K.Speed	D1668		
Lt H.D.West	2Lt M.A.Dunn	C6092		
Lt D.F.Brooks	2Lt R.Buckby	D3213		
Lt G.Broadbent	Lt W.B.Walker	D2916	bomb release jam	
2Lt G.R.A.Dick	2Lt K.L.Turnbull	D3215		
2Lt S.McKeever	2Lt C.G.Russell	B9366		
Formation 2				
Sgt H.H.Wilson	Lt E.Beale	C6260		
2Lt H.E.King	2Lt J.L.M.Oliphant	D7233		
2Lt W.T.Jones	2Lt E.C.Black	D5573		
2Lt M.J.Poulton	2Lt S.Lane	D1666		
2Lt C.W.Hewson	2Lt H.E.Alsford	C6342		
2Lt J.L.Hunter	2Lt T.H.Swann	D1716	ret exhaust flames	

After the previous day's problems, and the decimation of 104 Squadron, a raid to Buhl aerodrome was detailed for 99 Squadron. Home to Jastas 70 and 78, Buhl lay approximately sixty miles over the lines and was a good test for the recent arrivals on the Squadron. Leaving early it was hoped enemy scout interference would be kept to a minimum, but maybe serious damage could be done to the victors of the previous day while still on the ground. Leading again was Lt Stevenson, with Sergeant Harry Holsten Wilson leading the second formation on his fifteenth raid with the Squadron. This raid would be a first for the following pilots: Dick, Brooks, King, McKeever and Poulton and a first for observers: Buckby, Turnbull, Oliphant, Russell and Lane.

Taking off, twelve machines started to gain height before heading east towards the lines at Blâmont in fair weather with some cloud. After fifteen minutes in the climb, 2Lt Hunter noticed flames emitting from his exhaust pipes, and quickly shutting down the engine he glided into land. Passing over the lines, only slight archie greeted the bombers as they steadily made their way east towards the Rhine valley. For the first timers, it must have seemed quite peaceful passing Strasbourg without enemy aircraft or archie to disturb them. Crossing the Rhine river, Buhl appeared on the nose, so did nine German fighters which fortunately were only at 9,000ft, well below the formations, as they dropped five 230lb, five 112lb, and nine 25lb bombs. A jam in the release gear of Lt Broadbent's machine forced him to take his bombs all the way home; his observer, however, managed to take eighteen photos. Lt Jones and 2Lt Black only had one 112lb bomb aboard their machine hence the odd number of five 112lb bombs. Sixteen bursts were seen on the aerodrome, most of which were on the landing ground, with some exploding in between hangars and buildings near the village.

The return trip was as uneventful as the outward one, all machines re-crossing the lines and landing safely back at Azelot. The new bloods had had their first taste of operational flying. Although tame compared to recent operations over the lines, it was however a good baptism.

Target: Barracks and Railways at Köln (Cologne)
Secondary Target: Central Station east of Treves

23rd August		**Take Off:**	**10.15**
55 Squadron		**Returned:**	**14.30/45**

Formation 1

Capt J.R.Bell	2Lt O.Bell (99 Squadron)	ret e/t
Lt C.A.Bridgland	2Lt J.G.Quinton	ret e/t
Lt S.L.Dowswell	2Lt W.R.Patey	
2Lt T.H.Laing	2Lt J.C.Barns (99 Squadron)	photo machine
Lt C.L.Heater	Sgt A.S.Allan	
2Lt P.M.Payson	2Lt J.A.Lee	

Formation 2

Capt D.R.G.Mackay	2Lt H.T.C.Gompertz		
Lt W.J.Pace	Lt D.W.Stewart	A7703	
Lt D.J.Waterous	2Lt C.L.Rayment		
2Lt P.J.Cunningham	2Lt E.Smith (99 Squadron)		
Lt G.T.Richardson	2Lt T.F.L.Myring	A7972	
2Lt A.J.Robinson	2Lt C.W.Clutsom	B3967	photo machine

Borrowing three observers from 99 Squadron, 55 set out again to attack the railways and barracks at Cologne. Captain Bell led the twelve DH4s as they headed north to cross the lines at Château-Salins at 13,500ft. The archie was active, but well below the formations as they headed north towards St.Avold. Captain Bell was forced to return with engine trouble, followed shortly by Lt Bridgland, also with engine trouble.

Captain Mackay took up the lead as the two groups continued north, flying over Saarlouis and onto Berncastel. Greeting them were huge banks of cloud rising from 10,000ft up to 18,000ft covering the area to the north-east as far as could be seen. Coblenz would be the new target and the formations continued over Treves towards his objective. Near Wittlich, north-east of Treves, Captain MacKay now had to give up the idea of Coblenz and turned the formations around, heading for the only sizeable gap which was back at Treves. Arriving overhead at 12.15, one 230lb and eighteen 112lb bombs were dropped from 15,000ft onto the central railway station east of Treves. Observers claimed three hits on station buildings, and several along the railway tracks with no hits being reported in the town itself. German official reports state one hit on the railway, and several hits on private property in the Kurenz suburbs although there were no civilian casualties.

Heading for the lines via the quickest route, the bombers made for Verdun, with still no sign of enemy scouts. Over Conflans between four and six German aircraft arrived from the east, reported as Pfalz scouts. One dived on the rear formation and was apparently hit by return fire from all the observers. The fighter side-slipped and went down in a steep glide, apparently under control. The remaining scouts shadowed the two formations to the lines which they crossed at Verdun at 16,000ft. Although a thousand feet higher than usual when re-crossing the lines, the two formations were still heavily archied but all returned safely to Azelot complete with twenty-one photos despite the cloud.

Flying in the first formation was one of many Americans serving with the I.A.F. CHARLES LOUIS HEATER, born on 5th August 1894 came from Mandon, North Dakota. He studied mechanical engineering at Purdue University, Lafayette, in Indiana from 1910. His early training took place at Chakis Hill where he did a course in wireless telegraphy. He went to Turnberry for aerial gunnery and Grantham for machine-gun training. He was made Lieutenant on 16th April 1918, and joined 55 Squadron once they had become part of the I.A.F. He was put in for a D.F.C. which was not granted, but General Fulois requested that Heater be moved on 24th August to command one of the new American bomber squadrons now arriving in France. Heater had flown thirteen raids with 55, and with the U.S.A.S commanded the 11th Bombardment Squadron till the Armistice with the rank of Captain.

Note: Aircraft serial numbers for this raid could not be located amongst records.

Reconnaissance

23rd August			Take Off:	10.50
55 Squadron			Returned:	14.50
Capt B.J.Silly	Lt J.Parke	A7837		

Crossed the lines at Blâmont at 18,500ft, flew over Sarralbe to Folpersweiler then onto Saarbrücken to Volklingen. From Volklingen where the hangars had been removed they flew to Thionville and Mars-la-Tour. Re-crossed the lines west of Pont-à-Mousson reporting lots of rolling stock in the Saar valley sidings, thirty-three plates were taken.

Target: Bettembourg Railway Sidings
Secondary Target: Railways at Arlon

25th August			Take Off:	11.50
99 Squadron			Returned:	15.35
Formation 1				
Lt W.G.Stevenson	Lt W.B.Walker	D1668		
2Lt W.Hodder	2Lt H.G.Ramsay	C6272		
Lt F.K.Crosbie-Choppin	2Lt A.T.Bower	D1670		
2Lt W.A.Warwick	Sgt H.L.Bynon	D3215		
2Lt D.F.Brooks	2Lt R.Buckby	C6092		
2Lt J.L.Hunter	2Lt T.H.Swann	D1716		
Formation 2				
Sgt H.H.Wilson	2Lt H.E.Alsford	C2192		
2Lt W.T.Jones	2Lt E.C.Black	D5573		
2Lt H.E.King	2Lt J.L.M.Oliphant	D7233		
2Lt M.J.Poulton	2Lt S.Lane	D2860		
2Lt G.R.A.Dick	2Lt K.L.Turnbull	B9366		
2Lt C.W.Hewson	2Lt H.A.Boniface	C6342		
Lt G.Broadbent	2Lt J.K.Speed	D2916	spare mc ret e/t	

An aborted raid on Buhl aerodrome on the 24th, cost 99 Squadron two officers who had come overseas with the Squadron and whose loss was felt by all who knew them. Captain Taylor with Lt Bell in the back had led a four-ship formation into increasingly bad weather over the lines. A thunderstorm erupted and forced the four machines to return to Azelot. At about 2,000ft, Captain Taylor's machine (DH9 D1695) entered a steep downward spiral until it impacted the ground; their bombs detonated and both men were killed instantly. It was believed Taylor had fainted due to the heat. Exhaustion and especially illness was rife, and a combination of all three was more likely to have caused him to faint. Both men were buried in the I.A.F. Cemetery at Charmes, south of Azelot on the banks of the Moselle river.

Led by Lt Stevenson, thirteen DH9s took off on a brighter day, but still with some cloud around obscuring a number of the more notable landmarks. The spare machine flown by Lt Broadbent returned after half an hour with an overheating engine leaving the main twelve heading west towards St.Mihiel. Bettembourg railway sidings lay just south of Luxembourg town. The twelve DH9s crossed the lines at Verdun being heavily archied as they did so. Sergeant Wilson was lucky to escape as an anti-aircraft shell smashed his propeller and wrecked his engine. Putting his nose down he managed to force-land at Bar-le-Duc near St.Dizier. The remaining eleven machines continued north with the pilots showing better handling of their engines at altitude. The formation flying could be improved further but at least eleven bombers were going to hit the target. The cloud was obscuring much of the landscape and Stevenson decided to bomb instead the railway at Arlon just east of Luxembourg town. As the triangle of railway tracks came into sight, four enemy scouts shadowed the formations but these were easily driven off. Arlon station received seven 230lb, and eight 112lb bombs, six bursts were seen on the tracks while two were observed on the station, and one was also seen to burst in the village west of the railway.

Leaving the target area seven enemy scouts arrived but these were also driven off. The eleven machines crossed the lines and headed back for Azelot complete with pictures of the target. One of the recent arrivals on the Squadron, Lt Brooks, became separated from the others, but managed to land at the American aerodrome at Colombey-les-Belles, unfortunately wrecking his machine in the process. With another successful raid behind them, 99 Squadron looked to be improving.

CAPTAIN ASHLEY DUDLEY TAYLOR was born in Essex on 25th April 1892. He started his ground school instruction on 12th August 1916 at Oxford. From here he joined 25 Reserve Squadron on 9th September 1916 before becoming a 2Lt observer on probation with 49 Reserve Squadron on 4th October 1916. Receiving his observer's wing on 6th March 1917, he was posted to 55 Squadron where he was wounded in the arm on 23rd April, on a bombing raid with seven other DH4s to an ammunition dump near Boue. His wound was not serious and he remained with the Squadron, returning to Home Establishment in October to commence pilot training. He joined 99 Squadron at Reading on 5th January 1918 becoming 'A' Flight Commander the following day. Major Pattinson put forward on Armistice day a recommendation for a D.F.C. for Taylor. It was very rare indeed that a D.F.C. was ever awarded posthumously and Taylor was no exception; his address given when he started service with R.F.C. was Saxonbury, New Wanstead in Essex. 2Lt Oliver Bell, from Desley, Cheshire, aged twenty, was buried at Charmes with his pilot.

Target: Barracks and Railways at Köln (Cologne)
Secondary Target: Railways at Luxembourg
Secondary Target: Morhange Aerodrome

25th August			Take Off:	11.40
55 Squadron			Returned:	15.30 For 1
			Returned:	13.50 For 2

Formation 1			
Capt J.R.Bell	2Lt A.J.C.Gormley	D8388	
Lt C.A.Bridgland	2Lt J.G.Quinton	F5711	
Lt D.J.Waterous	2Lt C.L.Rayment	D8396	
Lt P.M.Payson	2Lt J.A.Lee	A2131	/K.I.A.
Lt J.Cunliffe	2Lt G.E.Little		photo machine
2Lt J.B.Dunn	Sgt A.S.Allan	B3967	/D.O.W.

Formation 2			
Capt D.R.G.Mackay	2Lt H.C.T.Gompertz		ret e/t
Lt W.J.Pace	Lt D.W.Stewart		
Lt S.L.Dowswell	2Lt C.W.Clutsom		
2Lt P.J.Cunningham	2Lt C.E.Thorp		
Lt G.T.Richardson	2Lt T.F.L.Myring		ret e/t photo m/c
2Lt T.H.Laing	2Lt T.A.Jones		ret e/t

Cologne was about the furthest target that could be hit by the DH4s of the I.A.F. if the weather conditions were right, i.e. hardly any wind, and of course relatively clear skies. However, higher authority sent 55 Squadron against this distant target more in the hope of breaking the morale of the German populace, than of actually causing damage.

Captain Bell and his formation took off in good conditions and headed out for the lines at Nomeny hoping to rendezvous with the second formation led by Jock Mackay. As usual the secondary target was Coblenz if Cologne could not be reached. A more pressing problem however was the whereabouts of the second formation. Captain Mackay was having trouble with his engine, and while the rest of the DHs were trying to formate behind him, the distance between the two groups was growing. Bell could not afford to wait if Cologne or Coblenz was to be hit so crossed at 13,000ft over Nomeny, receiving heavy and accurate archie.

Mackay by now had given up with his broken engine and headed for home, and his deputy leader Lt Richardson also quit formation with engine trouble leaving Lt William John Pace from Edmonton, Canada, to take the lead. Crossing the lines at Château-Salins at 14,000ft, 2Lt Laing left the formation also with engine trouble. Pace continued on with his two wingmen and decided to head for Morhange aerodrome just north of Château-Salins. Overhead Morhange airfield at 13.15 six 25lb bombs fell earthward, two bursts were observed on the aerodrome while another was seen to explode just off the airfield. All three machines re-crossed at Château-Salins, untouched by the moderate and inaccurate archie put up at the lines and landed back at Azelot at 13.50. It must have seemed quite absurd for Pace to be sometimes bombing railways as part of the I.A.F. when his pre-war career as a civil engineer for Northern Railways in Canada had him planning their construction. Surviving the carnage of the First World War, he was killed in a motor accident on 26th April 1919, aged just twenty-seven.

Captain Bell decided against Cologne, due to lack of numbers and an increasingly strong wind, so Coblenz would be the new target as the formation of six headed over Boulay on the Moselle river towards Mettlach. Over Treves the wind was judged too strong even to reach Coblenz and the formation turned for Luxembourg. Arriving over here at 14.00, one 230lb and ten 112lb bombs were dropped from 13,000ft. Several bursts were seen on the southern end of the railway station, while others struck the triangle of railway lines. After leaving the target area, they were attacked by six Pfalz scouts from behind and to the left, although in the bomb raid report total enemy aircraft are stated as about fifteen. Whatever the number they attacked. Concentrated fire from 2Lts Quinton, Gormley and Rayment sent one down in a steep diving turn and then into a side-slip, apparently out of control. During this first attack however the formation had received injuries; Sgt Allan was wounded while 2Lt Lee had been killed. Lt Payson, now without an observer, slid his machine underneath that of Lt Waterous using his observer, 2Lt Rayment to keep the enemy aircraft off his back. The fight continued towards the lines which were crossed at Verdun at 13,000ft. The fight had been a tough one with 3,500 rounds fired. Eighteen photos had been taken but the plates were all smashed by machine-gun fire. All six machines made it back to Azelot with some badly shot about; Sgt A.S.Allan (No. 408711) was later to die of his wounds. From Perth in Scotland, this twenty-four-year old had won the Military Medal as well as the French Médaille Militaire.

The Commanding Officer of Jasta 65, Leutnant Otto Fitzner was slightly wounded this day flying out of Mars-la-Tour well within range of 55 Squadron, especially on their return trip. He had taken command of Jasta 65 on 19th March 1918 after scoring three victories with Jasta 17, returned to combat on 31st August 1918 finishing the war with nine victories. 2Lt John Alfred Lee, aged eighteen from Leighton Buzzard in Bedfordshire, was buried at Charmes Cemetery. Also buried at Charmes was Sergeant Alexander Stewart Allan.

Many sources indicate a 2Lt E.Wood and 2Lt G.S.Barber were injured in a crash landing after returning from a bombing raid to Luxembourg. This crash is probably from a training sortie as no evidence can be found of them on either of the raids mentioned. Such crashes were becoming more numerous as replacements pilots arrived, some with little experience. Details of them have been left out of this book purely because of their number which was nearly double that destroyed by enemy aircraft and archie.

PHILLIPS MERRILL PAYSON was born on 8th August 1892, in Portland U.S.A. He was educated at St.Paul's School Concord and Williams College. His first military experience was with the Ohio Cavalry at the Mexican Border, where he served for ten months. He first enlisted at Boston Massachusetts, in June 1917. Joining the R.F.C. on 17th October 1917, he completed his ground training at Oxford University, and his machine-gun course at Grantham. He received his wings in April 1918. He originally trained as a night pilot with 30 Squadron near Newcastle. He then transferred to Amesbury and later Turnberry before being sent to France. He served with 55 Squadron from 30th June 1918, to 30th September 1918, from where he joined the American 166th Aero Squadron as a Flight Leader. He made seven raids between October and November with the 166th Aero, and was recommended for promotion and the Distinguished Service Cross.

Reconnaissance

25th August			Take Off:	12.00
55 Squadron			Returned:	15.05
Capt B.J.Silly	Lt J.Parke	A7837		

Crossed the lines at Fresnes then flew over Mars-la-Tour and Conflans.

Target: Buhl Aerodrome

| **27th August** | | | **Take Off:** | **16.00** |
| **99 Squadron** | | | **Returned:** | **18.10** |

Formation 1

Lt K.D.Marshall			
2Lt M.J.Poulton	2Lt S.Lane	D2860	
2Lt G.R.A.Dick	2Lt E.Smith	D1008	
Lt G.Broadbent	2Lt T.H.Swann	C6342	forced landing
2Lt E.J.Kidder	Sgt H.L.Bynon	D1716	ret engine vibrating
2Lt W.Hodder	2Lt H.G.Ramsay	D3215	ret engine vibrating

Formation 2

Sgt H.H.Wilson	2Lt H.E.Alsford	C6260	ret carburettor
2Lt H.E.King	2Lt J.L.M.Oliphant	D7233	ret mistook signal
Lt F.K.Crosbie-Choppin	2Lt A.T.Bower	D1670	ret ignition trouble
2Lt L.S.Springett	2Lt C.G.Russell	D1675	ret mistook signal
2Lt W.T.Jones	2Lt E.C.Black	D5573	

Low cloud as on the previous day greeted 99 Squadron on what looked like another day of practice formation flying. On the previous day, Lt Keith Douglas Marshall from Tara, Ontario, Canada, recently returned from leave, attempted to bomb the aerodrome at Buhl with Lt Broadbent and Crosbie-Choppin over cloud, steering by compass alone. With a thirty-mile-an-hour wind at 2,000ft the raid was scrapped, and the remainder of the Squadron practised formation flying while other machines were worked on. The weather started to clear by early afternoon allowing eleven bombers (all that were available) to take off and head east towards the lines at Blâmont.

Although some of the machines were relatively new, accidents in and around the aerodrome had reduced the number that were air worthy, and some that were in the air would soon be returning. Lts Hodder and Kidder were the first to abort with engines vibrating, followed by Sgt Wilson with carburettor trouble and Crosbie-Choppin with ignition trouble. Wilson was the most experienced pilot by a long way. 2Lt Jones, however, made a signal to the remaining two that he was taking charge of the rear formation. The two pilots, 2Lt King and 2Lt Springett, mistook this signal and turned for home while Sgt Jones formed up with the first formation and headed over the lines.

Down to four machines, the bombers continued east towards Strasbourg where they were attacked by six enemy aircraft. Reaching Buhl three 230lb and two 112lb bombs were dropped with six bursts being observed on the southern part of the aerodrome. During the attack, Lt Broadbent received hits in his radiator, and it is not clear whether he dropped his bombs on Buhl or simply got rid of them in the hope of staying with the formation despite his predicament. The formation of four made it back to the lines where Lt Broadbent managed to put his machine down at Baccarat, just west of the lines.

Obviously wear and tear on machines had taken its toll, although the Siddeley Puma engines needed no encouragement. What was also evident was the inexperience of some crews especially regarding signals in the air. More work would have to be done and quickly, if most of the new pilots and observers were going to survive long enough to be an effective part of the campaign against the German war effort.

FREDERICK KEARTON CROSBIE-CHOPPIN was born on 21st February 1886. He was a student at King's School Canterbury from 1900 to 1903. Between 1913 and 1914, he worked for the London Telegraph Training School as a lecturer and demonstrator in electricity. His first posting during the war was at Reading in July 1916. He then moved on to Oxford, No.4 Reserve Squadron and then 58 Squadron. He was flying with 53 Squadron in 1917 when he was hospitalised on 19th February. After leaving hospital he went back to 58 Squadron where he was injured on 14th September as an assistant flying instructor. From No.1 Flying School he joined 99 Squadron on 14th July 1918. In January 1919 he returned to England. In May he teamed up with 99 Squadron again this time in India. On 26th July he was posted to Home Establishment and was finally de-mobbed on 9th October 1919. He was married with his wife living in Kensington.

Target: Railways at Bettembourg
Secondary Target: Sidings at Conflans

| 27th August | | Take Off: | 16.40 |
| 55 Squadron | | Returned: | 19.00 |

Formation 1

Capt D.R.G.Mackay	2Lt H.C.T.Gompertz	
Lt E.J.Whyte	2Lt A.J.C.Gormley	
Lt C.A.Bridgland	2Lt J.G.Quinton	
2Lt P.J.Cunningham	2Lt C.E.Thorp	
Lt G.T.Richardson	2Lt T.F.L.Myring	photo machine
Lt P.M.Payson	2Lt C.W.Clutsom	

Formation 2

Lt W.J.Pace	Lt D.W.Stewart	
Lt J.Cunliffe	2Lt G.E.Little	ret e/t
Lt D.J.Waterous	2Lt C.L.Rayment	
2Lt T.H.Laing	2Lt T.A.Jones	did not start e/t
Lt S.L.Dowswell	2Lt W.R.Patey	photo machine
2Lt J.B.Dunn	2Lt A.S.Papworth	

The weather in the morning was unfit for flying, but it was hoped that with the strong southerly wind conditions might improve in the afternoon to allow a short raid. Bettembourg, on the southern outskirts of Luxembourg, had the main railway line between Thionville and Luxembourg and was a vital link between the trenches and the rear lines of supply. Train movement on previous raids had been reported as normal, indicating a lack of disruption on the part of the I.A.F., something which Captain Mackay and eleven other DH4 pilots hoped to amend. The weather was still cloudy but with some clear patches as just ten DH4s climbed to gain height, before heading west to cross the lines at Verdun. The two machines which failed to start were those of 2Lt Laing, who remained on the aerodrome, and Lt Cunliffe who finally got his engine started and took off trying to catch the formations up; he failed to locate them and returned to land at 18.05.

Crossing at Verdun, the archie was heavy and very accurate as the machines headed north-east towards Luxembourg which was completely covered in cloud. The sidings at Conflans were on the nose and with only cloud before him Captain Mackay decided to bomb an objective which was at least visible. At 18.10, twenty 112lb bombs fell earthward despite the still heavy anti-aircraft fire. Unusually the two formations bombed from different heights, one from 10,000ft while the other dropped from 12,500ft. It may well have been the archie which put off their aim, but all bombs were seen to miss the railways completely and explode in the fields.

Turning for home, the two groups headed south-east to cross the lines at Pont-à-Mousson with all machines landing safely back at Azelot. Twenty-eight photos were taken by 2Lt Patey and 2Lt Myring, most probably of front line German defences, especially in the St.Mihiel sector which was always over-flown on the way to Verdun and which was soon to be the place of a major offensive by the Americans.

On his last bombing raid with 55 this day was CECIL ALCHIN BRIDGLAND born on 10th April 1896. Before the war Bridgland studied at King's School, Rochester, between 1907 and 1913. He was initially with the East Surrey Regiment before joining the R.F.C. Serving in Egypt in May 1917, he was up for posting in July and was made a 2Lieutenant on 28th August. He was eventually posted to 38 Training Squadron on 13th October. The following day he was posted to 62 Squadron flying Bristol fighters. By the end of the month however he was back with 38 Squadron. On 21st November he was sent to No.2 T.D.S. from where he joined 116 Squadron on 2nd December. 116 and their Handley Page 0/400s were not operational at this time, and Bridgland moved again on 9th February 1918 to 55 Squadron. Made a Lieutenant in May 1918, Bridgland saw extensive service with 55 and was awarded the Croix de Guerre with Palm on 17th August 1918. Posted to Home Establishment on 4th September, he returned to France on 8th October and found himself at No.14 T.D.S. on the 9th. Posted to 201 Squadron on 1st January 1919, he was awarded a D.F.C. which was gazetted on 3rd June 1919. The family address during the war was The Cedars, Darnley Road, Gravesend in Kent.

Note: Again 55 records lack aircraft serial numbers on this raid.

Target: Conflans Rail Junction/Doncourt Aerodrome

30th August   Take Off: 08.25
99 Squadron   Returned: 12.10

Formation 1

Lt K.D.Marshall	2Lt E.Beale	D1668	
2Lt W.T.Jones	2Lt E.C.Black	D5573	
Lt H.D.West	2Lt M.A.Dunn	C6260	
Lt G.Broadbent	2Lt J.K.Speed	D2916	photo machine
2Lt L.S.Springett	2Lt J.C.Barns	D1675	
Lt F.K.Crosbie-Choppin	2Lt A.T.Bowyer	D1670	
2Lt M.J.Poulton	2Lt S.Lane	B9347	

Formation 2

Lt W.G.Stevenson	Lt W.B.Walker	D3041	
2Lt W.A.Warwick	2Lt C.G.Russell	D3215	/K.I.A.
2Lt S.McKeever	2Lt H.A.Boniface	B9366	ret hit by flak
2Lt E.J.Kidder	Sgt H.S.Bynon	D3218	
2Lt G.R.A.Dick	2Lt E.Smith	D1008	
Sgt H.H.Wilson	2Lt H.E.Alsford	D7233	did not cross
2Lt W.Hodder	2Lt H.G.Ramsay	C6272	ret not keep up

Despite banks of cloud and strong winds, a raid was attempted on the 28th. Thirteen machines out of fourteen made two good formations but the weather worsened and the raid was scrapped. The weather on the 29th was worse with no flights in or out of Azelot, except one. A lone German Hannover two-seater buzzed the airfield without firing or dropping bombs, and was chased off by four French Spads which finally bought it down ten miles south of Azelot. The German crew survived and explained that they had become lost in cloud, and were expected in Metz, certainly not Azelot. Unfortunately one of the Spad pilots had been killed by a bullet through the head from the rear gunner.

On the 30th the weather was again cloudy with a strong south-westerly wind, but better then the previous day. It was decided to take off and bomb any targets that were visible. Fourteen machines went, two being spare, these soon became thirteen when Sgt Wilson landed his machine at the French aerodrome at Amanty with fuel problems. Lt Hodder in one of the spare machines could not keep up with the formation so he returned to Azelot. Crossing the lines near Verdun, Lt McKeever noticed he had a fuel leak. The accurate archie had pierced his fuel tank and while sorting the problem out he lost position and was so far behind he had no choice but to return. Once over the lines the eleven remaining machines were attacked by four Albatros scouts, which fired at the second formation from long range. One of these scouts managed to hit the DH9 flown by 2Lt Warwick, who was fine but his observer 2Lt Russell was killed by a bullet wound to the head. The first formation arrived over Conflans at 11.00 and dropped three 230lb, four 112lb and eight 25lb bombs observing one burst on the railway track and three just wide. The second formation spotted Doncourt aerodrome south-east of Conflans and dropped one 230lb and six 112lb bombs from 12,500ft scoring two direct hits on hangars. One also burst on the landing ground and another on a hut just off the aerodrome. Eight American Spads were seen near Conflans, and escorted the bombers for a short while. Records however do not say if it was before or after the target was hit.

The four scouts had now turned their attention to the first group but still continued to fire from long range. One of these scouts came in close and fired while in a stall at about fifty yards underneath the tail of Poulton and Lane. Once he had a clear shot, Lane fired a burst at this aircraft causing it to fall into a spin, it was seen to crash by two other observers. All eleven machines returned to Azelot complete with seven photos, a good display despite the difficult conditions. Both Jasta 18 and 65 lost a pilot this day but these were probably in combats with 55 Squadron.

Harry Holsten Wilson and his observer 2Lt Alsford had spent the night at the French aerodrome at Amanty near Toul. With their petrol problem rectified they took off for the return trip to Azelot. Unfortunately their DH9 stalled shortly after take-off and both men were killed. Wilson and Alsford, an experienced crew within 99, were buried in the I.A.F Cemetery at Charmes. Wilson learnt to fly at No.2 T.S.Northolt, a long way from his home at 2938 West Dauphin Street, Philadelphia, U.S.A. Wilson had also been a member of 110 Squadron, working up in England before he left for France to join 99 Squadron. Also buried at Charmes was 2Lt Cyril George Russell, aged eighteen, who came from West Kensington in London.

Target: Railways and Barracks at Köln (Cologne)
Secondary Target: Thionville Sidings
Secondary Target: Conflans Sidings

30th August			Take Off:	08.35
55 Squadron			Returned:	11.05 for 1
			Returned:	12.05 for 2

Formation 1			
Capt J.R.Bell	2Lt C.R.Rayment	D8388	
2Lt P.J.Cunningham	2Lt J.G.Quinton	A7783	K.I.A./D.O.W.
2Lt T.H.Laing	2Lt T.F.L.Myring	A7972	K.I.A./K.I.A.
2Lt H.H.Doehler	2Lt A.S.Papworth	A7708	P.O.W./P.O.W.
Lt S.L.Dowswell	2Lt H.C.T.Gompertz	A8069	/W.I.A.
Lt W.W.Tanney	2Lt A.J.C.Gormley	A7589	P.O.W/P.O.W.

Formation 2			
Lt E.J.Whyte	2Lt W.R.Patey	F5020 or D8020	
2Lt J.B.Dunn	Sgt A.J.Cousins		
2Lt W.G.Braid	2Lt L.J.B.Ward		
2Lt E.Wood	2Lt C.E.Thorp	F5711	/D.O.W.
Lt P.M.Payson	2Lt C.W.Clutsom		
2Lt R.I.A.Hickes	2Lt T.A.Jones	D8396	K.I.A./K.I.A.

The weather was again very cloudy with a strong south-westerly wind, but the target was still Cologne. With the weather as it was, Treves or Coblenz were more likely to be hit but even these must have been only hopeful targets as twelve DH4s led by Captain Bell took off and headed for the lines at Nomeny. The second formation led by Lt Whyte was unable to keep up with the first group, so headed west to cross the lines near Fresnes-en-Woëvre, south-east of Verdun.

The first formation headed north for Treves. Over Boulay, fighters attacked with two venturing close. 2Lt Rayment fired his double Lewis guns and watched the aircraft dive away under control. With more enemy aircraft starting to arrive and unfavourable weather conditions, Captain Bell turned north-west in an attempt to bomb the railways at Thionville.

The first enemy aircraft to arrive had been Pfalz scouts, now being joined by red Fokker DVIIs, probably Jasta 18 from Montingen near Metz. Lt Tanney and 2Lt Gormley were seen to drop out of formation hit by archie. Tanney became a straggler and was quickly latched onto by the fighters. Four Fokker DVIIs, two Triplanes and two Pfalz quickly set about this machine hoping to get a clear shot despite the return fire from the Irishman in the back, 2Lt Gormley from Dublin. Seconds later two bullets hit Tanney in the chest, one went in under his right shoulder blade while the other hit a rib and lodged in his diaphragm. Gliding down, his instrument panel was shattered by another burst of enemy fire. With his consciousness failing due to blood loss he managed to put his machine down. The German victor landed close by, and helped Gormley lift the now unconscious Tanney from his cockpit. Both men survived the war with William Tanney from Detroit, Michigan, carrying his two German souvenirs inside his body for the rest of his life.

The remaining five DH4s dropped ten 112lb bombs on Thionville. Bursts were unobserved due to the increasing number of enemy fighters. Combat reports suggest Pfalz, Triplanes, Albatros and Fokker DVIIs, but what also can be ascertained from these reports is that they were from Jasta units and they meant business. 2Lt Gompertz in his combat report said "single seaters, either Fokker DVII or Albatros, who dived in everywhere". Gompertz had a stoppage in his twin Lewis guns, but managed to clear one and fired at three enemy aircraft at 100 yards range. One of these aircraft spun quickly, then slowly, then erratically. He fired at another which went down in a side-slip and then onto its back. Gompertz however was not having it all his own way, for shortly after this, his ammunition ran out and his DH4 went temporarily out of control with the left aileron controls shot away. Followed by three German aircraft his pilot Lt Dowswell managed to cross the lines and crash-land at Pont St Vincent, south-west of Nancy. Gompertz was slightly wounded. Another American in trouble this day was 2Lt Doehler. He and his observer 2Lt Papworth were also shot down, fortunately both surviving to spend the rest of the war as prisoners of war.

The first formation was by now split. 2Lts Cunningham and Quinton were both wounded, but they managed to cross the lines crash landing near Toul. Cunningham died shortly after this heroic feat, his observer Quinton would later die of his wounds too. Another DH4 lost, crewed by 2Lt Laing and 2Lt Myring, who were both killed, went down on the German side, leaving Captain Bell to return to Azelot alone.

The second formation led by Lt Whyte crossed the lines and headed for Conflans, where they dropped twelve 112lb bombs, but results were unobserved as eight Pfalz scouts arrived. The fighting was aggressive with 2Lts Hickes and Jones heading down followed by the enemy, but apparently under control. Heading for the lines, Lt Whyte noticed a German 500ft below. He dived and fired one hundred rounds of Vickers in three bursts which seemed to pepper the enemy aircraft. Pulling out of his dive he watched as the enemy aircraft stalled and fell over on its side. As they passed it, William Patey in the back seat fired a full drum of Lewis at it, and the enemy aircraft continued down out of control. Although Hickes and Jones were last seen under control, they were both killed presumably by the pursuing fighters or the inevitable crash. The remaining five DH4s crossed the lines but only four landed at Azelot, 2Lt Wood putting his machine down at Pont St Vincent but to no avail; his observer 2Lt Thorp latter died of his wounds.

Known to be in the fight this day were Jasta 18. Leutnant August Raben, their Commanding Officer, brought down a DH4 at 12.00 German time (11.00 British time), near Amanweiler for his fourth and last victory of the war. Leutnant Günther Von Büren also scored for Jasta 18 claiming a DH4 down at Ennerchen. This was most probably Doehler and Papworth. Jasta 18 did not escape unscathed. Offizierstellvertreter Wilhelm Kühne was killed in combat. Also engaging 55 Squadron were Jasta 65. Leutnant Wilhelm Frickert, Commanding Officer, claimed a DH4 at Herméville for his ninth victory of the war. He was a much decorated pilot who would score another three victories before the war ended. Offizierstellvertreter Tiedje of Jasta 65 also claimed a DH4 shot down at Mars-la-Tour, but his claim was not upheld and he would finish the war with just three victories. Jasta 65 also lost a pilot with Unteroffizier Wilhelm Hofacker killed in combat with DH4s over Herméville, south of Etain, probably shot down by Whyte and Patey who had a credible claim in this area as they headed for the lines. Vizefeldwebel Christiansen of Jasta 67, flying out of Marville just west of Longuyon, claimed a DH4 west of Mars-la-Tour which was credited as his first victory.

As can be seen from the above, front line Jasta units could easily split open even the most disciplined formations, made easier this time by both DH4 formations being separated even before crossing the lines. Despite losing eleven crewmen on this raid alone, 55 Squadron would be back in action on the 2nd of September. The casualty list for this month made sombre reading with fifteen men dead due to enemy action, six as prisoners of war and four wounded. Although not as bad as other squadrons it must have been a shock to 55 who had only lost seventy-three men either killed in action or prisoners of war in the fourteen months before joining the I.A.F.

2Lts Patrick Joseph Cunningham and James George Quinton were both buried at Charmes. Quinton was from Southampton, Hants and was aged only eighteen. Cunningham was born 10th November 1898 at Blackrock, Co Dublin, Ireland. He was a dental student from August 1915, until he joined the R.F.C. on 7th August 1917. 2Lts Thomas Harry Laing and Thomas Frank Leslie Myring were both buried at Arnaville. Laing was twenty-one and came from Aberdeen, while Myring was only nineteen, and came from Ealing in Middlesex. Robert Ian Alexander Hickes, also aged nineteen, from Market Weighton in Yorkshire was buried along with his observer Thomas Alfred Jones at Labour-en-Woëvre in France. Jones came from Rainfall in Lancashire and was also only nineteen.

Note: The confusion regarding the machine flown by Whyte and Patey is due to the combat reports. Whyte signed his combat report with the aircraft serial number as F5020. Patey also signed his combat report but with the aircraft serial number as D8020. Neither aircraft can be found on the strength of 55 Squadron, or any other squadron for that matter.

CHAPTER 5

OPERATIONS – SEPTEMBER 1918

Target: Buhl Aerodrome

2nd September			**Take Off:** **09.00**
99 Squadron			**Returned:** **11.15**
Formation 1			
Lt W.G.Stevenson	2Lt J.K.Speed	D3264	
2Lt W.T.Jones	2Lt E.C.Black	D5573	
2Lt H.E.King	2Lt J.L.M.Oliphant	D1668	
Lt G.Broadbent	2Lt E.Beale	D2916	photo machine
2Lt D.F.Brooks	2Lt R.Buckby	D3213	
Lt F.K.Crosbie-Choppin	2Lt A.T.Bower	D1670	
Formation 2			
Lt K.D.Marshall	Lt H.S.Notley	D3218	
2Lt W.Hodder	2Lt H.G.Ramsay	C6272	
2Lt S.McKeever	2Lt H.A.Boniface	B9366	
2Lt W.A.Warwick	2Lt E.Smith	D3215	
2Lt G.R.A.Dick	2Lt S.Lane	D1008	ret obs sick
2Lt J.L.Hunter	2Lt T.H.Swann	B9347	photo machine
2Lt E.J.Kidder	Sgt H.L.Bynon	D2860	spare ret e/t

There were two aerodromes in the I.A.F. vicinity which were beginning to seriously hamper the daylight operations. Buhl, home to Jastas 39, 70 and 78 was the most serious threat, purely because they seemed to be doing most damage. Destroying this menace on the ground would take an around-the-clock offensive, which would also involve the night bomber squadrons under I.A.F. command.

Lt William Gordon Stevenson led this raid as twelve DH9s headed east for the one-hundred-mile round trip. Only one spare machine was available and this returned before crossing the lines with engine trouble. With only slight archie encountered as they crossed the lines the twelve soon became eleven as 2Lt Dick turned for home, his observer 2Lt Lane having fainted in the back seat. The remaining bombers continued over the Vosges towards the Rhine river expecting to meet enemy scouts at any moment. None were seen except on the ground as they crossed the Rhine and Buhl came into view and with it the dropping of six 230lb, six 112lb, and eighteen 25lb bombs. A burst was observed on a small shed behind the large Zeppelin hangar while another burst was seen to destroy one of the three aircraft parked in the open. All other bursts were reported near the hangars and the southern road causing two fires in two of the smaller hangars.

With no enemy opposition, thirty-four photos were taken by Lt Beale and 2Lt Swann and all eleven machines returned safely to Azelot. This proved to be a successful raid in so much as eleven bombers reached the target and no casualties were sustained. Target photos revealed little damage but 99 would be airborne again in the afternoon hopefully to reap more damage along with 55 and 104 Squadrons.

Reconnaissance

2nd September			**Take Off:** **11.00**
55 Squadron			**Returned:** **14.25**
Lt P.E.Welchman	Lt J.Parke	A7836	

Crossed the lines north-west of Château-Salins at 18,000ft. Proceeded by way of Wallersberg to Boulay, then to Dillingen and down the Saar valley to Bons. Although twenty-two plates were taken the reconnaissance was incomplete due to a broken shutter release.

Reconnaissance

2nd September			Take Off:	9.15
55 Squadron			Returned:	12.05
Lt W.J.Pace	Lt D.W.Stewart	A7942		

Crossed the lines at Blâmont at 18,000ft, flew over Lunéville, but as it took less then ten minutes to go from there to Phalsbourg the pilot returned. No train movement was reported but four enemy aircraft were seen over Buhl. Six plates were taken en route over aerodromes between Buhl and Phalsbourg.

Target: Buhl Aerodrome

2nd September			Take Off:	09.25
104 Squadron			Returned:	11.45
Formation 1				
Maj J.C.Quinnell	2Lt G.V.Harper			
Lt O.L.Malcolm	2Lt E.B.Smailes			
Lt E.A.Forbes	2Lt R.W.Lewin			
Lt L.D.Merrill	Lt G.Best		photo machine	
2Lt L.G.Hall	2Lt W.D.Evans			
2Lt A.Hemingway	2Lt L.W.Launchbury			
Formation 2				
Capt R.J.Gammon	2Lt P.E.Appleby			
2Lt A.D.MacKenzie	2Lt C.E.Bellord			
2LtB.H.Stretton	Sgt F.H.J.Denney			
Lt J.W.Richards	2Lt P.James			
2Lt W.S.Greenwood	2Lt F.W.Aldridge			
Lt P.C.Saxby	Sgt W.E.Reast		photo machine	

Taking off after 99 Squadron, 104 were also detailed to bomb Buhl aerodrome near the banks of the Rhine river. Many new faces were on their first operational raid and it would be a good test for the new crews against a target approximately sixty miles over the lines. While climbing for height two aircraft returned to Azelot. The first was Lt Hemingway who lost formation, the second was Lt Greenwood who also returned, both landing within five minutes of each other. The remaining ten bombers made for the lines and crossed near Blâmont where the archie was light.

Heading east towards the Rhine, no enemy aircraft were seen at the same height as the bombers but four or five were observed low down and received about a hundred rounds from some of the observers. Buhl was reached at 10.35 where six 230lb and six 112lb bombs were dropped from 13,500ft. Three bursts were observed on buildings near the road on the southern part of the aerodrome, while another three burst on three small sheds near the hangars; four other hits were seen between the hangars and the road. It seems from the number of bombs dropped that one aircraft returned with its ordnance due to a jam, but which aircraft it was is not clear .

The ten DH9s all returned to Azelot safely, Lt Best and Sgt Reast had taken twenty-nine photos between them, which would have been quickly developed for damage assessment before the next raid, again against Buhl.

Target: Buhl Aerodrome

2nd September			Take Off:	09.30
55 Squadron			Returned:	11.30
Formation 1				
Capt D.R.G.Mackay	2Lt W.R.Patey			
Lt G.T.Richardson	2Lt L.J.B.Ward			
Lt D.J.Waterous	2Lt C.L.Rayment		photo machine	
2Lt W.E.Johns	2Lt F.N.Coxhill			
2Lt A.J.Robinson	2Lt H.R.Burnett	F5705		

Formation 2
Capt J.R.Bell	2Lt S.Burbidge	
Lt E.J.Whyte	2Lt C.W.Clutsom	photo machine
Lt S.L.Dowswell	Sgt G.Howard	
2Lt W.G.Braid	2Lt G.S.Barber	ret e/t
2Lt J.B.Dunn	Sgt G.F.W.Adams 220131	

After the crippling losses of the previous month, 55 Squadron were detailed to bomb the active airfield at Buhl along with 99 and 104 Squadron. For many of the new faces on the Squadron this would be their first operational raid. By the end of the day they would have two raids under their belts as the plan was to hit the airfield in the morning and afternoon. Taking off, twelve DH4s led by Captain Mackay gained height and headed east towards the lines at Blâmont following half an hour behind 99 Squadron. It seems 55 Squadron were 'riding shotgun' for 104 Squadron on this raid, being 500ft lower and slightly behind 55. Before the lines were crossed two aircraft returned, number five in the first formation turning back with engine trouble, while number five in the second group went back after losing his position.

Crossing the lines at Leintrey, 55 Squadron came under moderate archie as they flew a straight line towards Buhl on the banks of the Rhine. Engine trouble forced 2Lt Braid to turn for home before reaching the target, but he landed safely back at Azelot at 10.50. Arriving over Buhl at 10.40, one 230lb and sixteen 112lb bombs were dropped from 14,000ft onto the already smoking aerodrome. One hangar received a direct hit, while three bursts were observed on the buildings on the southern part of the aerodrome. Four bombs also burst between the hangars and the road just off the aerodrome.

The only enemy aircraft spotted had been down very low and presented no threat to the bombers. This did not deter some eager observers who fired off one hundred rounds in their general direction. The remaining nine DH4s re-crossed the lines and landed safely back at Azelot complete with twenty-nine photos. This would be the penultimate raid for Cyril Lancelot Rayment. Due to be posted to Home Establishment on 25th September, Rayment would see his D.F.C. gazetted while at home. His citation read as follows:

2Lt Cyril Lancelot Rayment
D.F.C. gazetted 21st September 1918

This officer has taken part in thirty-five successful operations, and his work throughout has been distinguished by clearness, accuracy of observations and disregard of danger, notably on one occasion when he was observer to the leader of our first formation which was vigorously attacked by four hostile machines. In spite of this the formation was led over the target, which was effectively bombed. Subsequently the formation was attacked by five hostile machines, but owing to skilful leadership the fire of our observers was so well controlled and directed that the enemy were kept at a distance and the formation returned in safety.

Note: Aircraft serial numbers were not recorded for this raid.

Target: Buhl Aerodrome

2nd September		**Take Off:**	**15.20**
55 Squadron		**Returned:**	**17.30**

Formation 1
Capt D.R.G.Mackay	2Lt W.R.Patey	
Lt G.T.Richardson	2Lt L.J.B.Ward	
Lt D.J.Waterous	2Lt C.L.Rayment	photo machine
2Lt W.E.Johns	2Lt F.M.Coxhill	
2Lt A.J.Robinson	2Lt H.R.Burnett	F5705

Formation 2
Capt J.R.Bell	2Lt S.Burbidge	
Maj A.Gray	2Lt C.W.Clutsom	photo machine
Lt S.L.Dowswell	Sgt G.Howard	
2Lt E.Wood	2Lt J.D.Evans	
2Lt W.G.Braid	2Lt G.S.Barber	
2Lt J.B.Dunn	Sgt G.F.W.Adams 220131	

As in the morning, 55 Squadron hit Buhl aerodrome again with 104 and 99 Squadron. Getting away first, 55 led by 'Jock' Mackay gained height and headed east towards the lines at Blâmont followed by the two DH9 squadrons. Hardly any archie greeted the eleven bombers as they crossed the lines heading east towards Strasbourg and the Rhine beyond.

Arriving over Buhl at 16.40, one 230lb and nineteen 112lb bombs hit the airfield with many bursts observed on and near the hangars. No enemy aircraft were spotted in the air as the formations turned for home after taking thirty-six photos over the target. Once 99 and 104 had dropped their bombs, 55 Squadron flew above both Squadrons for the return journey re-crossing the lines at Cirey next to Blâmont. All machines landed safely back at Azelot despite one of the 112lb bombs failing to drop because of a broken release wire.

The bomb raid report for this attack says only eleven aircraft took off; there may well have been twelve but if this machine did not cross the lines it would have been discounted. The morning raid reported ten aircraft taking off when in fact it was twelve, one machine got lost and one returned with engine trouble. It is most probable that twelve aircraft took off and the recording officer didn't bother to mention the returning aircraft.

MAJOR ALEX GRAY was on his first and last operational bombing raid this month. He was posted to Home Establishment on 19th September to be replaced by Captain Benjamin James Silly. Gray remained in the Royal Air Force and was a Group Captain in 1936. In WW2 he commanded 224 Fighter Group based at Chittagong on the Arakan coast in India during 1943; he latter rose to the rank of Air Vice-Marshal. He was mentioned in dispatches while serving with 55 Squadron and also received the French Croix de Guerre. He retired in 1949, living in Ferndown, Dorset, having been made a CB.

Target: Buhl Aerodrome

2nd September			Take Off:	15.30
99 Squadron			Returned:	17.30
Formation 1				
Lt W.G.Stevenson	Lt W.B.Walker	D3041		
2Lt W.T.Jones	2Lt E.C.Black	D5573		
Lt H.D.West	2Lt M.A.Dunn	D3264		
Lt G.Broadbent	2Lt E.Beale	D2916	photo machine	
2Lt W.H.Gillett	2Lt R.Buckby	D3213		
2Lt H.E.King	2Lt J.L.M.Oliphant	D1670		
Formation 2				
Lt K.D.Marshall	Lt H.S.Notley	D3218		
2Lt W.Hodder	2Lt H.G.Ramsay	C6272		
2Lt S.McKeever	2Lt H.A.Boniface	B9366		
2Lt E.J.Kidder	Sgt H.L.Bynon	D3270		
2Lt M.J.Poulton	2Lt B.S.W.Taylor	D2860		
2Lt J.L.Hunter	2Lt T.H.Swann	D1668	photo machine	
2Lt L.S.Springett	2Lt J.C.Barns	3813	ret e/t & rigging	
2Lt W.A.Warwick	2Lt E.Smith	D3213	spare ret	

For the raid in the afternoon, 99 Squadron would be following 55 Squadron into the target in the hope of doing considerably more damage than in the morning raid. Again Lt Stevenson was heading with Lt Keith Douglas Marshall leading the second formation as the fourteen DH9s pointed east for the lines. After fifteen minutes in the air, 2Lt Springett was compelled to return with a badly vibrating engine and his rigging was becoming slack; he managed to land back at Azelot safely.

Leading twelve machines over the lines, 2Lt Warwick was signalled to leave in the spare machine as the two groups made their way once again over the Vosges. Again the archie had been slight and no enemy aircraft were spotted until near the target. As five 230lb, ten 112lb and eighteen 112lb bombs were dropped nine enemy aircraft were spotted. They didn't close and only fired at the two bomber formations from long distance. Hits were observed on three small hangars which were all set on fire while another two bursts were seen within fifty yards on another two smaller hangars. Three bombs exploded on the southern part of the aerodrome, while six burst east of the main road behind the hangars. One bomb also exploded seventy yards in front of the large Zeppelin hangar. Lt Beale and 2Lt Swann had again been busy with their cameras bringing back seventeen photos between them.

All twelve machines returned safely, and from post-strike photographs taken by the observers of all three squadrons, it was ascertained that one enemy scout had been destroyed on the ground, one aeroplane shed had been demolished, and a second destroyed by fire, and two other hangars were probably damaged or burnt. Considerable damage could well have been wrought amongst parked aircraft in the hangars or in the open, by bomb splinters.

Target: Buhl Aerodrome

| 2nd September | | Take Off: | 15.40 |
| 104 Squadron | | Returned: | 17.45 |

Formation 1

Capt R.J.Gammon	2Lt P.E.Appleby	
2Lt A.D.MacKenzie	2Lt C.E.Bellord	
Lt J.Wrighton	Sgt F.H.J.Denney	
Lt P.C.Saxby	Sgt W.E.Reast	ret pilot fainted
2Lt B.H.Stretton	2Lt R.W.Lewin	
Lt A.V.Goble	2Lt E.D.Barnes	

Formation 2

Capt E.J.Garland	2Lt D.R.Hoon	
Lt D.P.Pogson	2Lt G.V.Harper	
2Lt B.F.Ross	2Lt L.W.Launchbury	
Sgt E.Mellor	Sgt E.Bryden	
Lt J.H.Cuthbertson	2Lt A.B.Rattray	
2Lt W.E.L.Courtney	2Lt A.E.Sabey	photo machine

Last to take off for the evening raid against Buhl, 104 Squadron had two spare aircraft as they again headed east towards the lines. After fifteen minutes in the air, Lt Saxby in one of the photo machines fainted and his machine fell out of formation; fortunately he regained consciousness and landed safely back at Azelot. Engine trouble would claim another two machines before the lines were reached, leaving eleven machines to cross the lines at Leintrey where they encountered moderate archie.

Enemy aircraft appeared in the shape of four scouts, but once fired upon they dispersed, entering shallow descents. Over Buhl at 16.55, six 230lb and eight 112lb bombs were dropped from 12,500ft all exploding in the vicinity of the aerodrome. In all nine bursts were observed in and about the hangars but no direct hits were claimed. One 230lb bomb exploded near a large shed on the south-eastern part of the aerodrome while another 230lb bomb failed to release due to a jam, perhaps from the same aircraft as on the morning raid.

Heading home no enemy aircraft were encountered and all eleven returned safely to Azelot; 2Lt Sabey had taken seven photos over the target. In all it had been a successful day for 104 Squadron without any losses and many new faces had got their first operational raid out of the way.

CAPTAIN RICHARD JOHN GAMMON, born on 5th January 1897, was a student of engineering at Chiswick Polytechnic before the war started. He flew many types while training to be a pilot including the BE2, BE12, DH6 and the DH4 before flying the DH9. He spent time at No.4 Auxiliary School of Aerial Gunnery before joining 104 Squadron on 1st May 1918 as a 2Lt. His address before the war was given as 46 Beachcroft Avenue, Southall, Middlesex.

Reconnaissance

3rd September			Take Off:	15.45
55 Squadron			Returned:	19.20
Lt W.J.Pace	Lt D.W.Stewart	A7942		

Plates exposed over Buhl, Lorquin, Morhange, Boulay and Vatimont from 20,000ft.

Target: Morhange Aerodrome

3rd September			**Take Off:**	**15.55**
99 Squadron			**Returned:**	**17.50**

Formation 1

Lt W.G.Stevenson	Lt B.S.W.Taylor	D3041	
Lt W.T.Jones	Lt E.C.Black	D5573	
Lt H.D.West	2Lt M.A.Dunn	D3264	
Lt G.Broadbent	Lt J.K.Speed	D2916	
2Lt D.F.Brooks	2Lt R.Buckby	D3213	
2Lt W.Hodder	2Lt H.G.Ramsay	C6272	ret e/t
2Lt S.McKeever	2Lt H.A.Boniface	B9366	ret e/t

Formation 2

Lt K.D.Marshall	Lt H.S.Notley	D3218	
2Lt W.A.Warwick	2Lt E.Smith	D3215	
2Lt E.J.Kidder	Sgt H.L.Bynon	D1008	
2Lt L.S.Springett	2Lt J.C.Barns	D3242	ret e/t
2Lt M.J.Poulton	2Lt J.L.M.Oliphant	D2860	
2Lt J.L.Hunter	2Lt T.H.Swann	B9347	
Lt F.K.Crosbie-Choppin	2Lt A.T.Bower	D1670	

Morhange aerodrome would receive the attention of both 99 and 104 Squadrons this day. The weather had changed in the afternoon with a westerly wind blowing. Lt Stevenson led fourteen DH9s aloft for the short trip to Morhange approximately fifteen miles over the lines. While climbing for height it was apparent that newer members to the Squadron had still not managed to get the best performance from their engines. 2Lt Hodder, 2Lt McKeever and 2Lt Springett all returned with apparent engine trouble and were unable to keep up.

Crossing the lines near Château-Salins at 12,500ft, archie was slight but accurate as the bombers approached Morhange. No enemy scouts were spotted as five 230lb, eight 112lb bombs and eighteen 25lb Cooper bombs were dropped. The scatter of bombs was good with three hangars receiving direct hits, and two bursts on parked aircraft which were destroyed. Several bombs fell near the railway bridge and tracks adjacent to the airfield. Turning for home the bombers were still un-molested by fighters. They re-crossed the lines near Château-Salins and all eleven returned to Azelot.

Post-strike photos revealed ten or eleven close bursts in front of two hangars and on the road near the railway lines next to the aerodrome. However, the photos revealed no direct hits on the hangars. Tactical bombing was not much of a science even at this late point of the war but results obtained on this raid laid out the pattern to which all subsequent raids would follow, in regard to when and where to drop the ordnance. The conclusion was that the leader of the first formation should approach the target downwind with the second group quite close to his own. Shortly before he was to release his bombs his observer would fire a white Very light. As soon as the bombs left the lead machine all aircraft in the two formations were to release theirs. Up to this point both leaders would have sighted the target independently and released their bombs. This new approach by 99 would hopefully render better results as long as the leader sighted the target correctly.

Target: Morhange Aerodrome

3rd September			**Take Off:**	**16.05**
104 Squadron			**Returned:**	**18.00**

Formation 1

Capt I.W.Leiper	2Lt E.D.Barnes	
Lt A.V.Goble	Sgt F.H.J.Denney	
Lt O.L.Malcolm	2Lt E.B.Smailes	
Lt L.D.Merrill	Lt G.Best	photo machine
Lt E.A.Forbes	2Lt R.W.Lewin	
2Lt G.C.Edmond	2Lt F.W.Aldridge	

Formation 2

Capt E.J.Garland	2Lt D.R.Hoon

Lt D.P.Pogson	2Lt G.V.Harper	
Lt J.H.Cuthbertson	2Lt A.B.Rattray	
Sgt E.Mellor	Sgt J.Bryden	
2Lt B.W.Ross	2Lt L.W.Launchbury	
2Lt W.E.L.Courtney	2Lt A.E.Sabey	photo machine

Captain Leiper would be leading his first raid for 104 Squadron against the airfield at Morhange. Taking fourteen DH9s aloft he proceeded to gain height before heading north towards the lines. When the lines were reached at Nomeny the two spare aircraft were signalled away, and the two formations of six headed east straight towards Morhange.

Arriving over the airfield at 17.25 eight 230lb and eight 112lb bombs were dropped from 13,500ft. The grouping of bombs was good with two direct hits on hangars running from east to west, while another four bombs exploded close to them. Three bursts were also observed on the landing ground. Heading for home three enemy aircraft were seen well below the formation. The observers fired two hundred and seventeen rounds at them but the enemy scouts did not climb to intercept.

Reaching the lines at Parroy, the formation encountered only slight archie (as on the outward leg) as the twelve machines crossed over and returned safely to Azelot. Lt Best and 2Lt Sabey had both been busy taking thirty-six photos between them, in all a successful raid.

CAPTAIN ISSAC WYPER LEIPER was born on 26 January 1892 and came from Lanarkshire in Scotland. After being wounded he was taken to a hospital at Rouen, from where he returned to England on 2 December 1918. He was originally with 103 Squadron on DH9s and flew out with the Squadron on 7th May 1918. While with 103 Squadron he took part in fifty-three raids and fourteen reconnaissance missions, and flew another six photo reconnaissance missions. He joined 104 Squadron on 26 August 1918. After the war he lived at 137 Wensley Drive, in Leeds, from where he applied for the Royal Air Force Volunteer Reserve in World War Two on 17 October 1939 and 2 August 1940. Like many he was awarded a D.F.C. in the New Year's Honours list. Unfortunately with so many decorations gazetted on 1st January 1919, citations were not given.

Note: Crews were recorded but aircraft serial numbers were not.

Target: Railway Station at Karlsruhe
Secondary Target: Buhl Aerodrome

4th September		Take Off:	06.30
55 Squadron		**Returned:**	**09.10**
Formation 1			
Capt J.R.Bell	2Lt S.Burbidge		
Lt E.J.Whyte	2Lt C.W.Clutsom	photo machine	
Lt S.L.Dowswell	Sgt G.Howard		
2Lt E.Wood	2Lt J.D.Evans		
Lt G.T.Richardson	2Lt L.J.B.Ward		
Formation 2			
Lt P.E.Welchman	2Lt W.R.Patey		
Lt D.J.Waterous	2Lt C.L.Rayment	photo machine	
Lt P.M.Payson	Sgt G.F.W.Adams 220131		
Lt W.G.Braid	2Lt G.S.Barber		
2Lt A.J.Robinson	2Lt H.P.Burnett	F5713	ret force landing

Led by Captain John Ross Bell, ten DH4s took off from Azelot and gained height before heading east towards the lines. Karlsruhe station on the eastern bank of the River Rhine, was the vital link south for all the railway lines north of Karlsruhe on the eastern side of the river. If this bottleneck could be put out of action, re-routeing the trains would mean supplies taking up to two days longer to reach the front lines and nearby aerodromes.

Crossing the lines slightly north of Blâmont, the Squadron was down to nine machines as 2Lt Robinson left the formation and turned for home. Robinson had to put his machine down at St.Dizier due to all the water in his radiator boiling away. Archie was slight but accurate as the formations headed north-east towards Sarrebourg. Abeam Saverne, Captain Bell headed east towards the Rhine river and decided to bomb Buhl aerodrome due to the now increasing wind. As the two formations approached Buhl at 07.55, aircraft were seen trying to get off the aerodrome as one 230lb and sixteen 112lb bombs headed down from 14,500ft. Most bursts were reported between the hangars and the billets as the bombers turned for home noticing eight enemy aircraft in the distance.

The lines were re-crossed without interference from enemy aircraft and all machines returned to Azelot without incident. Robinson was not there to greet them but must have put his machine down safely as he and his observer returned to operations on 14th September. Rayment and Clutsom had been busy bringing home twenty-four photos between them. This was to be Bell's and Patey's last raids with 55, as they now went on leave, where they received news of their D.F.C.'s.

Lieutenant John Ross Bell
D.F.C. gazetted 21st September 1918

This officer is an exceptionally gallant and determined pilot, who has taken part in thirty-seven raids, five of which he has led. On a recent occasion, the formation of which he was leader was attacked by twelve aeroplanes. He fought his way to his objective and successfully bombed it. On the return journey continuous fighting took place, and three enemy aeroplanes were driven down.

WILLIAM RUSSELL PATEY was born in London on 25th May 1897. He spent most of his younger life aboard ship; his father was a Master Mariner with Iredale & Porter of Liverpool. Before the outbreak of war he was a student at Conner Civil Service Institute in Belfast. His address at the time was 5 Adelaide Street, Belfast. He joined the 15th Battalion of the Royal Irish Rifles after the outbreak of war. Wounded with this battalion on 7th June 1917, he recovered and was seconded to the Royal Flying Corps. After training he joined 55 Squadron on 12th March 1918, and was promoted to Lieutenant on 19th June. After the war he emigrated to New Zealand, and then again to Canada. He settled in Vancouver, British Columbia, and worked for the *Canada Post*. On 22nd February 1987 he passed away at the age of ninety. His citation for his D.F.C. read as follows:

2Lt William Russell Patey (Royal Irish Rifles)
D.F.C. gazetted 21st September 1918

For consistent good work, gallantry, and skill as an observer on long-distance bombing raids and photographic reconnaissances. During a raid three months ago, his machine was heavily engaged by hostile aircraft. By very judicious management he remained master of the situation, and eventually destroyed one of the enemy machines. During the past month he has again displayed notable qualities of airmanship whilst encountering large numbers of enemy aircraft. Lieutenant Patey is always prepared to carry out any kind of operation entrusted to him, and the spirit he has shown when attacked has been of inestimable value to the squadron.

Note: As with most 55 Squadron records, aircraft serial numbers were not recorded for this raid.

Target: Morhange Aerodrome

4th September		Take Off:	06.45
104 Squadron		**Returned:**	**08.50**
Formation 1			
Capt R.J.Gammon	2Lt P.E.Appleby		
2Lt B.H.Stretton	2Lt D.R.Hoon		
2Lt W.S.Greenwood	2Lt F.W.Aldridge		
Lt J.W.Richards	Sgt W.E.Reast		
Lt J.Wrighton	Sgt F.H.J.Denney	B9355	/W.I.A.
Lt R.Rose	2Lt A.E.Sabey		

Formation 2

Capt I.W.Leiper	2Lt E.D.Barnes
Lt O.L.Malcolm	2Lt E.B.Smailes
2Lt L.C.Pitts	2Lt R.W.Lewin
Lt A.V.Goble	Sgt J.Bryden
Lt L.D.Merrill	Lt G.Best
2Lt L.G.Hall	2Lt W.D.Evans
2Lt A.Hemingway	2Lt L.W.Launchbury

Captain Gammon led this early morning raid against the now familiar airfield at Morhange. Taking off with one spare aircraft in the first formation, the thirteen machines climbed for height then headed out north towards the lines at Leintrey. There were no mechanical failures amongst the bombers but the spare aircraft crossed the lines along with the two formations of six.

Although only encountering moderate archie as they crossed over, the German gunners had got the range right and the formation was heavily shelled. In all seven machines were damaged by archie and one was written-off upon landing. Maybe this was the reason the spare aircraft continued in case of engine failure to one of the other machines due to this archie fire. The thirteen machines arrived over Morhange at 08.15 and dropped eight 230lb and ten 112lb bombs from 13,000ft. A cluster of bombs numbering six or seven were seen to explode all around a line of hangars which ran east to west across the airfield. One direct hit was reported on one hangar while another bomb exploded on the railway line next to them. As the bombers turned for home five enemy aircraft were seen taking off from Morhange. However, these aircraft had no chance of reaching the bombers before they re-crossed the lines. Nine other enemy aircraft were close enough to engage the bombers but preferred to keep their distance and fire from long range. The observers returned fire in the form of one thousand and seventy rounds but no claims were made by any of them.

All thirteen machines landed back at Azelot despite the archie and fighters. The only casualty due to an exploding anti-aircraft shell was Sergeant Francis Howard James Denney (No.99923). Fortunately he survived but saw no further action with 104 Squadron. It was this machine which was written off after a very heavy landing probably due to the anti-aircraft damage. In all twenty-three photos had been taken by Sgt Reast and Lt Best.

Note: 104 records do not list aircraft flown on this raid.

FRANCIS HOWARD JAMES DENNEY came from Bethnal Green in London. He enlisted in the Royal Flying Corps for the duration of the war on the 2nd of October 1917 giving up his job as a clerk. On 4th April 1918 in the newly formed R.A.F., he was promoted to Sergeant, then Sergeant Mechanic on 2nd August 1918. On 21st August 1918 he joined 104 Squadron. At 8th Canadian Stationery Hospital, he was treated for a gun shot wound to the thigh, before heading back for England on 12th September 1918.

Reconnaissance				
4th September			**Take Off:**	**09.10**
55 Squadron			**Returned:**	**14.20**
Lt W.J.Pace	Lt D.W.Stewart	A7842		

Crossed lines at Lunéville, exposed plates over Bitche, Speyerdorf, Mannheim, Speyer, Germersheim and over a new aerodrome north-west of Sarrebourg. Thirty-one plates were taken from 20,000ft.

Reconnaissance				
4th September			**Take Off:**	**14.35**
55 Squadron			**Returned:**	**17.20**
Maj A.Gray	Lt J.Parke	A7836		

Crossed lines at Château-Salins and exposed ten plates over aerodrome north of Gros-Tenquin from 18,500ft. Avoided three enemy aircraft, but clouds covering the ground towards Boulay forced the abandonment of the rest of the mission.

Target: Morhange Aerodrome

| 4th September | | | Take Off: | 18.55 |
| 99 Squadron | | | Returned: | 20.55 |

Formation 1

Lt K.D.Marshall	2Lt J.K.Speed	D3264	
2Lt W.T.Jones	2Lt E.C.Black	D5573	
Lt F.K.Crosbie-Choppin	2Lt A.T.Bower	D1670	ret e/t
2Lt J.L.Hunter	2Lt T.H.Swann	B9347	photo machine
2Lt L.S.Springett	2Lt J.C.Barns	D3243	
2Lt W.H.Gillett	2Lt H.Crossley	D3270	

Formation 2

Lt G.Broadbent	2Lt M.A.Dunn	D2916	
2Lt W.Hodder	2Lt H.G.Ramsay	C6272	
2Lt S.McKeever	2Lt H.A.Boniface	D2860	
2Lt E.J.Kidder	Sgt H.L.Bynon	D804	
2Lt D.F.Brooks	2Lt R.Buckby	D3213	ret hit by A.A.
Capt T.C.Creaghan	Lt H.S.Notley	D3218	photo machine
2Lt G.R.A.Dick	Lt E.Beale	D1668	ret pilot sick
2Lt H.E.King	2Lt J.L.M.Oliphant	C6260	spare ret e/t

Morhange was again the target as early evening approached and fourteen DH9s took off for the short trip over the lines. While climbing for height 2Lt King was forced to return with engine trouble. After climbing for an hour, 2Lt Dick in the other spare machine also returned after feeling sick. He was soon followed by Lt Crosbie-Choppin whose engine was misfiring, due to spark plug trouble. The remaining eleven bombers continued on towards the lines near Château-Salins.

While crossing over only sporadic anti-aircraft fire greeted the bombers, but some fighters appeared and began to fire from long range. One shell burst too close to the machine flown by 2Lt Brooks. Fortunately the aircraft was not severely damaged and Brooks managed to land safely back at Azelot. Now leading ten, Lt Marshall lined up on Morhange aerodrome and gave the signal to drop. Ten 230lb, eight 112lb and eight 25lb bombs fell towards the southern part of the aerodrome. One bomb exploded on the railway line next to the airfield while another burst on a hangar. Five bursts were observed on the landing ground while another three exploded near hangars, and seven small explosions were also seen on trenches near the railway lines

The ten DH9s turned for home keeping a watchful eye on the six fighters which had been firing from long range ever since they crossed the lines. The gap was never closed sufficiently by the Germans to worry the DH9s and they all returned to Azelot safely. During the raid eighteen photos were taken. Once developed they revealed less damage than on the previous day's raid, but the grouping of bombs was again well concentrated.

Lt Stevenson was promoted to temporary captain to fill the vacancy left by Captain Thom, who was taken ill whilst on leave. Lt Sanders who had been wounded below the knee on 27th June returned to the Squadron after convalescence in England. Also to arrive at the Squadron was another welcome addition in the shape of the new DH9As with their 400h.p. Liberty engines. Unfortunately there were not enough to be flown in squadron strength operationally, and they were only used in practice flights by the more experienced pilots, who welcomed their increased performance despite being heavier to handle then the DH9.

Target: Badische Anilin Soda Fabrik Works at Mannheim/Ludwigshafen

| 7th September | | | Take Off: | 11.00 |
| 99 Squadron | | | Returned: | 15.00 |

Formation 1

Maj L.A.Pattinson	2Lt B.S.W.Taylor	D1668	
Lt H.Sanders	2Lt E.Beale	C6260	
2Lt S.McKeever	2Lt H.A.Boniface	B9366	
Capt T.C.Creaghan	Lt H.S.Notley	D3264	
2Lt J.L.Hunter	2Lt T.H.Swann	B9347	
2Lt M.J.Poulton	Sgt F.L.Lee	D2860	

2Lt H.E.King	2Lt J.L.M.Oliphant	D3270	spare ret

Formation 2

Capt W.G.Stevenson	Lt W.B.Walker	D3041	
Lt K.D.Marshall	Lt J.K.Speed	D3213	
2Lt W.T.Jones	Lt E.C.Black	D5573	
2Lt L.S.Springett	2Lt J.C.Barns	D3228	
Lt F.K.Crosbie-Choppin	2Lt A.T.Bower	D1670	
Lt G.Broadbent	2Lt M.A.Dunn	D2916	P.O.W./P.O.W.
2Lt W.H.Gillett	Sgt H.L.Bynon	D1008	spare ret

Major Pattinson led this combined raid with 104 Squadron to the large chemical factory situated on the banks of the Rhine at Ludwigshafen, near Mannheim. Pattinson had given serious consideration to the tactics he wished to employ on this raid and gave Captains Stevenson, Gammon, and Garland from 104 Squadron a lengthy briefing. Mannheim was more than one hundred miles over the lines. If time was allowed for gaining height, it was doubtful, especially if any wind was blowing, that the target would be reached. Being so far over the lines it was easy for enemy scouts to climb to whatever altitude the bombers chose, particularly on the predictable return route which was easy to guess on long-distance targets. The other reason was that 75% of engine trouble was experienced above 10,000 feet; it was also easier to keep formation if engines were throttled back, instead of running at full rpm to maintain height at a higher altitude. If the formations could be kept together losses might be kept to a minimum.

The two previous days had been un-flyable with low cloud and some rain. The morning of the 7th found Azelot shrouded in heavy ground mist. By 10.00 the sun had started to work its magic and the mist began to lift, so the go ahead was given and fourteen 99 Squadron machines left the ground followed by twelve from 104 Squadron. The rendezvous for 99 Squadron went smoothly with both formations overhead the airfield at 10,000ft, forty minutes after take-off. Combining with 104 Squadron was more difficult then on previous occasions and after eighty minutes of trying, 99 Squadron headed for the lines at Raon-l'-Etape with 104 Squadron a mile behind, and a thousand feet higher.

The two spare aircraft were signalled away to return to Azelot despite 104 Squadron being two aircraft short due to engine trouble. A moderate amount of archie greeted the formations as they pressed on towards Saverne, the waiting enemy scouts beginning to appear in the distance. The scouts turned out to be Fokker DVIIs and they fired mainly at 104 Squadron and the rear formation of 99. Lt Broadbent was hit by machine-gun fire as was his aircraft and he was forced to leave the formation. Despite being wounded this officer managed to get his crippled machine and his observer down safely, and both men became prisoners of war. When Wissembourg was reached, 104 Squadron had caught up with 99 Squadron, and the enemy scouts retired to give both Squadrons an unmolested flight over Neustadt, and on towards Ludwigshafen. Arriving over the target, Pattinson found both Mannheim and Ludwigshafen shrouded in a thick black smog, which made target identification and observation difficult until directly overhead. The other problem was in the form of fifteen enemy scouts milling about above the target at 11,000ft. Pattinson slowed his formation to allow Stevenson to close to within sixty yards and all bombs were dropped simultaneously once the leader's had left. Pattinson had taken care to line the target up and all five 230lb, six 112lb and twenty-four 25lb bombs were thought to have impacted in or close to the Badische Anilin Soda Fabrik Factory.

Turning for home Pattinson noticed six enemy scouts preparing to re-attack from his right flank. He swung both Squadrons into a turn so all the observers could bring their guns to bear on these enemy scouts. This turn and the amount of fire bought to bear forced them to scatter. 104 Squadron, however, had been more heavily engaged and lost one aircraft over the target. Shortly after clearing the area, one of 104 Squadron's machines was seen by Pattinson at about 8,000ft. Pattinson brought both Squadrons down to formate with this straggler and the running fight was continued, mostly at long range, with several Germans who followed to Saverne. By the time the lines were in reach the formations were down to 7,000ft but trouble in the form of six Fokker DVIIs with scarlet wings and white fuselages meant the fight was still not over. The Fokkers, undoubtedly Jasta 18, attacked 104 Squadron up to the lines where they dispersed allowing eleven DH9s from 99 Squadron, and six from 104 Squadron to land at Azelot.

Photos taken on the raid showed little due to the defensive smoke screen put up over the target. Investigations after the war though revealed that one bomb exploded on workmen's dwellings near the Badische factory, while the others hit residential buildings and fields in the suburb of Friesenheim. One bomb exploded on railway lines in the factory harbour causing damage to the track.

Lt Broadbent managed to land his crippled aircraft despite a bullet wound to the right foot, but as a prisoner of war he caught pneumonia. Dunn was also hit with a bullet wound to his right arm. Broadbent and Dunn were most probably shot down by Leutnant Schulte-Schlutius of Jasta 3 who claimed a DH9 at 14.00 at Buchsweiler which was un-confirmed. Leutnant Georg Weiner of Jasta 3 also claimed two DH9s which were confirmed, but with no time of combat it is hard to ascertain if they were shot down before or after the target was reached.

Major Pattinson was rewarded for his leadership not only on bombing raids, but also for the general running of the Squadron, with the award of the Distinguished Flying Cross on the 12th September, the citation reading as follows:

Major Lawrence Arthur Pattinson M.C. (Royal Fusiliers)
D.F.C. gazetted 2nd November 1918

This officer is not only a capable and most efficient Squadron Commander, but also an exceptionally fine leader of bombing formations. On 7th September he led a combined formation of twenty-two machines; they were attacked by thirty aircraft, who made the most determined effort to prevent our formation reaching their objective. By skilful leadership and manoeuvring Major Pattinson repulsed the attack and dispersed the enemy formation. Leading well over the target, excellent results were obtained.

Target: Badische Aniline Soda Fabrick Works at Mannheim

7th September			Take Off:	11.00
104 Squadron			**Returned:**	**15.00**
Formation 1				
Capt R.J.Gammon	2Lt P.E.Appleby	C6264		
2Lt W.S.Greenwood	2Lt F.W.Aldridge	D7205		
Lt R.Rose	2Lt R.G.Gibbs	D1050	force-landed	
Lt J.W.Richards	Sgt W.E.Reast 16397	D7318	/D.O.W.	
Lt J.Wrighton	2Lt W.D.Evans		ret e/t	
2Lt A.D.MacKenzie	2Lt C.E.Bellord	D3263		
Formation 2				
Capt E.J.Garland	2Lt D.R.Hoon	D5568		
Sgt E.Mellor 99882	Sgt J.Bryden 242102	D3268	K.I.A./K.I.A.	
2Lt B.F.Ross	2Lt E.D.Barnes			
2Lt J.E.Kemp	2Lt E.B.Smailes	B7653	P.O.W./D.O.W.	
2Lt A.Hemingway	2Lt G.V.Harper		ret e/t	
2Lt W.E.L.Courtney	2Lt A.R.Sabey	D7210	P.O.W./D.O.W.	

After a lengthy briefing with Major Pattinson of 99 Squadron, Captains Gammon and Garland led two formations of seven DH9s each south-east to cross the lines near Raon-l'-Etape. Before the lines were reached, however, four machines returned, two with engine trouble, one with a radiator leak and another with an overheating engine. The remaining ten crossed the lines a thousand feet higher, and a mile behind 99 Squadron.

Moderate archie was encountered as they headed north-east towards Saverne. At Saverne fifteen enemy scouts attacked according to the bomb raid report. Combat reports made out by 104 and 99 Squadron note only six aircraft attacked over Saverne and nearby Sarrebourg. Although engaged by the same aircraft, 104 said they were Hannovers and Pfalz while 99 Squadron gave them as Fokker DVIIs. Whatever they were 2Lt Appleby claimed one over Saverne on the way to the target. The enemy scouts kept up a relentless attack all the way to Wissembourg where they exited the fight. 104 Squadron by this time had managed to close the gap between themselves and 99 Squadron. Lt Richards, despite a badly running engine, stayed with the formation all the way to the target, even though he was two thousand feet below the others and an easy target for enemy scouts. Disregarding the attention of the enemy, 104 arrived over the target with all ten machines and dropped five 230lb and ten 112lb bombs from 11,000ft on what they hoped was the Badische Aniline Soda Fabrick Works. The greatest worry, however, was the attacking German fighters.

Despite a steep turn to maximise the combined firepower of all the observers' Lewis guns, the Germans kept on coming and two DH9s were lost (Kemp and Smailes, Courtney and Sabey). In the face of such ferocious attention, Major Pattinson led the formations down to protect Lt Richards and his observer Sgt

Reast. With a rough running engine, wounded observer and still miles over the lines, Richards had every reason to put his nose down and try and save himself and his observer. He didn't and stayed with the formation hoping to reach the lines. The fighters were taking casualties as well with two scouts being claimed as driven down by 2Lt Appleby. Between Wissembourg and Saverne on the return trip Sgt Mellor and Sgt Bryden were seen to go down under control with a shot radiator. Once Saverne was reached on the return leg, the enemy scouts dispersed leaving a single formation of seven badly shot up bombers to follow 99 Squadron to the lines. The seven now down to 7,000ft were attacked by six Fokker DVIIs as they neared the lines. Lt Rose put his nose down and made the lines, force-landing at St.Clement, while the remaining six managed to make Azelot. Garland and Hoon had their machine written off due to machine-gun fire.

Of the four crew lost near the target, both pilots survived. 2Lt Sabey died of his wounds on the 11th of September, while 2Lt Smailes succumbed to his on the 13th of September. Mellor and Bryden were both killed that day. Lt Richards lost his observer Sgt Reast who had been hit in the head and the neck by enemy machine-gun fire and died two days later. Neither Richards nor Reast received any award for an outstanding piece of bravery, in flying for most of the mission on their own, with a faulty engine. They not only made the lines but Richards managed to reach Azelot where his machine was written-off due to battle damage. Richards claimed Reast had shot down three enemy scouts, however none were recognised. What is even more remarkable is that eighteen photos were taken by one machine as, according to the records, Richards and Reast were the only photographic machine to make Azelot since Courtney and Sabey in the other photo machine were shot down. The fighting was heavy and prolonged with 4,050 rounds of ammunition fired during the various engagements.

Attributing these losses to German pilots is quite difficult due to the number of casualties and the length of time spent over the German side. Several interceptions by different German units also adds to the confusion. Leutnant Kurt Seit of Jasta 80 claimed a DH9 which he saw force-land on the allied side of the lines, unfortunately the only time given is p.m. but Jasta 80 were stationed at Bensdorf aerodrome near Morsberg which is just north of where the bombers would have re-crossed the lines if flying the shortest route home (which considering the circumstances they probably were). Kurt Seit was probably in one of the six Fokker DVIIs which engaged the returning bombers at the lines and was awarded his third and last victory of the war. This DH9 is often quoted as being that of Richards and Reast. However, according to the bomb raid report Richards managed to land at Azelot, so the machine which came down just on the allied side was almost certainly that of Lts Rose and Gibbs at St.Clement. Kemp and Smailes, Courtney and Sabey were most probably shot down by Oberleutnant Rudolf Nebel or Unteroffizier Heinrich Forstmann both of Kest 1a. Rudolf Nebel, Commanding Officer of Kest 1a, was flying a Fokker DVII equipped with a wireless telegraphy set. He was directed onto the large formation of bombers and attacked with at least nine others. Nebel was immediately hit three times in the propeller as well as having his hand pump smashed by a bullet. Fragments of this pump hit him in the face and he descended below the bomber formations to assess the damage. Returning to the fray he attacked the last DH9 being forced to turn away nine times due to the volume of fire met every time. Nebel saw 'his' bomber leave formation and was sure it would crash. He did not witness this crash however, due to severe engine vibration which forced him to close his throttle and make an emergency landing. Nebel's machine had been hit twenty-nine times in and around his propeller and engine; one bullet had also shaved his shoe. He reported his claim and was told his adversary had come down near Buchweiler.

Forstmann entered the fight along with Leutnant Körner and Unteroffizier Sonnabend, firing one hundred rounds before his radiator was shot up. He saw the bomber he fired at leave formation and head down followed by a Fokker and then a Roland, but he failed to see the result due to hot radiator water being splashed in his face. These attacks took place at 14.26 and 14.15 which coincides with the formations leaving the target as German time was one hour ahead until the 16th of September. Nebel claimed his second and last victory of the war while Forstmann claimed his one and only. He was later killed in action on the 10th of October. Leutnant Georg Weiner of Jasta 3 claimed two DH9s at Dassberg and Burscheid for his fifth and sixth victories. These were awarded which makes a strong claim on machines already mentioned, however times for these victories are listed only as p.m. making it difficult to match losses. It is the author's opinion that Kest 1a shot down Kemp, Smailes, Courtney and Sabey.

Feldwebel-Leutnant Schiller of Kest 1a was severely wounded by DH9s this day most probably by 104 Squadron who received the most attention. Georg Weiner may well have shot down Sgt Mellor and Sgt Bryden but without times this is only an educated guess and these two sergeants could have fallen to any of the Germans mentioned above except Kurt Seit whose opponent made allied lines. Mellor and Bryden came down between Wissembourg and Saverne on the return leg of the journey. Sergeants Ernest Mellor and James Bryden were both buried at Schaeferhof, but after the war their bodies were moved to Sarralbe Cemetery. Mellor was nineteen and came from Bridehouse in Yorkshire, while Bryden came from Dumfries in Scotland. The other Sergeant killed on this day was Walter Ernest Reast; from Eastbourne in Sussex he was buried at Charmes in the I.A.F. Cemetery. Eric Bramall Smailes aged eighteen was buried at Niederzwehren in Germany. Another eighteen-year-old, 2Lt Sabey, from Brondesbury in Middlesex, was buried at Sarralbe Cemetery too.

Regardless of who got who this raid was a disaster for 104 Squadron who lost seven crew either dead, wounded, or prisoners of war. Engine trouble was also evident with four machines returning before crossing the lines. Although Richards and Reast received no award for this raid, Captain Richard John Gammon and 2Lt Percival Ewart Appleby both received the Distinguished Flying Cross on the 12th of September, their citations reading as follows:

Captain Richard John Gammon
2nd Lt Percival Ewart Appleby
D.F.C.s gazetted 2nd November 1918

Captain Gammon, with 2nd Lieutenant Appleby as observer, was the leader of two formations (ten machines in all) on a recent raid. En-route the formation was attacked by fifteen hostile aircraft; having driven these off, they reached the objective, which was successfully bombed. While thus engaged the formation was fiercely attacked by fifteen enemy machines, which continued the attack for some distance on the return journey, until they were driven off. Upon nearing our lines the formation was again assailed by seven machines; in the engagement that ensued one of these was destroyed and two driven down by Captain Gammon and his observer, and, in addition, three others were destroyed by our other machines. The officer who led the whole of the combined formations of this raid speaks in the highest terms of Captain Gammon's leadership and skilful co-operation. 2nd Lieutenant Appleby was of the greatest assistance to Captain Gammon throughout, keeping him informed of the movements and manoeuvres of the hostile machines. This officer has taken part in numerous raids, displaying on all occasions great keenness and determination.

JOSEPH WILLIAM RICHARDS was born on 25th June 1898. Before war broke out he worked for His Majesty's Customs and Excise at Customs House, Lower Thames Street, London. Records also indicate that on 29th April 1939 he was serving with the Royal Artillery with the rank of Major.

Target: Cologne
Secondary Target: Railways at Ehrang

7th September		Take Off:	11.35
55 Squadron		Returned:	15.05

Formation 1

Capt D.R.G.Mackay	2Lt C.W.Clutsom
Lt E.J.Whyte	2Lt L.J.B.Ward
Lt S.L.Dowswell	Sgt G.Howard
Lt W.G.Braid	2Lt J.D.Evans
Lt W.J.Pace	Lt D.W.Stewart
Lt P.M.Payson	Sgt G.F.W.Adams 220131

Cologne was the target for 55 Squadron on a day that started with heavy ground mist enveloping Azelot and the surrounding countryside. By 10.00 the mist had started to lift and by 11.00 Azelot was a hive of activity as all the squadrons attempted to get off. Mackay took off after 99 and 104 Squadron which were on a combined raid to Mannheim, and headed west to cross the lines near Verdun.

Crossing at 16,000ft, the archie was moderate as the six machines headed north-east towards Longuyon which was next door to the home of Jasta 67 at Marville. Heading north, Captain Mackay made the decision not to bomb Cologne and headed instead north-east towards Ehrang railway station. The reason for this change in target, despite the clear skies, was the south-westerly wind which was now blowing up to twenty-five knots. Cologne would have been reached with the wind behind them, but it is doubtful that the machines could have re-crossed the lines before running out of petrol, even if they managed to avoid enemy aircraft. Passing over Luxembourg, the formation of six continued towards Ehrang which they reached at 13.40. Dropping from 16,500 ft, three 230lb and six 112lb bombs fell in close proximity to the railway with some bursts directly on the tracks and others nearby.

Leaving the target area, Mackay led the formation in a gradual climb up to 17,500ft as they headed south and straight for the lines. Over Saarlouis, six enemy aircraft attempted to intercept the bombers but failed to close, probably due to the height of the formation, and all six re-crossed the lines at Arracourt near Château-Salins. Between the observers, 1,500 rounds of Lewis was fired at the enemy aircraft; which was perhaps the other reason they failed to close. 2Lt Evans had been busy with his camera taking twelve photos.

A raid by six aircraft to a target approximately one hundred and fifty-five miles away, was unlikely to inflict any great damage upon the German war effort. Material damage to the enemy was what would help end the war, and a raid to Cologne with six aircraft could have been better employed hitting an aerodrome containing one of the Jasta units which were taking a heavy toll on allied aircraft.

Note: Aircraft serial numbers are not listed for this raid.

Reconnaissance

55 Squadron			**Take Off:**	**12.20**
7th September			**Returned:**	**15.00**
Lt D.J.Waterous	2Lt C.L.Rayment	A7942		

Crossed lines at Blâmont at 19,000ft, exposed plates over Buhl and two aerodromes near Sarrebourg. Waterous and Rayment were taking photos of an aerodrome between Phalsbourg and Sarrebourg, then noticed three enemy aircraft 300ft above them. All three attacked and were joined by four more from 500ft below. Six of these enemy aircraft were Fokker DVIIs which were able to fire while literally hanging on their propellers; the other aircraft was described as a Hannover. Rayment fired at one scout which went down out of control. Trying to distance themselves from their attackers one enemy scout stayed with them for speed and climb, but when Rayment ran out of ammunition the scout closed and shot up the DH4 badly. Waterous had only one option which was to stuff the nose down and hope the machine stayed together and in fact they managed to cross the lines at 6,000ft. DH4 A7942 was patched together and flew again on a reconnaissance on 16th September.

Reconnaissance

7th September			**Take Off:**	**12.40**
55 Squadron			**Returned:**	**16.55**
Lt P.E.Welchman	2Lt W.R.Patey	A7749		

Crossed lines at Château-Salins at 19,500ft, flew over Gros-Tenquin, Boulay, Saar valley and Ehrang. Re-crossed the lines at Château-Salins with seventy-two plates exposed.

Reconnaissance

12th September			**Take Off:**	**08.10**
55 Squadron			**Returned:**	**10.45**
Lt P.E.Welchman	2Lt W.R.Patey	A7749		

Flew up and down the line several times, could see heavy shelling at Thiaucourt and Montsec. Large fire at Thiaucourt, many Spads above and over the lines, but few enemy aircraft seen.

Target: Triangle of Railways at Metz-Sablon
Secondary Target: Champey

12th September		**Take Off:**	**08.25**
104 Squadron		**Returned:**	**11.45**
Formation 1			
Capt I.W.Leiper	2Lt G.V.Harper		
Lt A.V.Goble	2Lt G.A.Faulkner	crash landed	
Lt O.L.Malcolm	2Lt H.Alexander	crash landed	

Lt L.D.Merrill	2Lt P.Davey		photo machine
2Lt B.F.Ross	2Lt L.W.Launchbury		
2Lt L.G.Hall	2Lt W.D.Evans	D3245	missing/returned

Formation 2

Capt E.J.Garland	2Lt W.E.Bottrill	
Lt J.H.Cuthbertson	Sgt D.Steward	ret e/t
Lt A.Hemingway	2Lt E.D.Barnes	crash landed
Lt A.C.D.Anderson	2Lt D.R.Hoon	ret e/t
2Lt R.F.Lynch	Lt L.R.Chandler	ret e/t
2Lt G.C.Edmond	Lt C.E.Bellord	ret pilot fainted

After 99 Squadron's aborted attempt, 104 Squadron took off at 08.25 into thick cloud banks. Captain Leiper must have had reservations when he broke cloud at about 3,000ft, finding another huge cloud bank above him. First to return with engine trouble was Lt Cuthbertson who landed safely back at Azelot thirty-five minutes after take-off. Fainting in the air could be disastrous, especially if you were the pilot, fortunately Lt Edmond who did so, regained consciousness and landed back at Azelot at 09.30 in one of the photo machines. Engine trouble was to claim two more machines both landing safely back at Azelot at 09.40 and 09.45, flown by Lts Anderson and Lynch both on their first operational raid, as was Lt Edmond.

After an hour and a half Captain Leiper with a single formation of eight bombers reached what looked like Pont-à-Mousson below and they headed north over solid cloud towards Metz without seeing or hearing any archie or enemy scouts. Continuing for another half an hour and reaching just north of Champey, Lt Malcolm jettisoned his eight 25lb bombs and turned for home with engine trouble. Lt Rose followed dropping his 230lb bomb before starting back. Captain Leiper then realised that the weather conditions were against them and signalled a wash-out for the raid.

The flight home would be a memorable one for many of the crews trying to find Azelot in amongst the overcast and the surrounding hills. Lt Linn Daicy Merrill, an American, was first to land with Lts Ross and Malcolm just behind, although Malcolm crashed on the aerodrome. Next to land was Captain Leiper and Captain Garland five minutes later. Lt Goble crash-landed at Lebenville while Lt Hemingway did the same at Bettoncourt. Both pilots had become lost while following the leaders down through the clouds. Another American, 2Lt Hall, was missing along with his observer 2Lt Evans, although they were believed to be down on the allied side; both men did return to operations next day.

It is interesting to note how inaccurate records can sometimes be. Hall in the first page of the bomb raid report, is given the initials G.J. while on the second page of the same report he is given the initials G.L., a simple typing error. However if you peruse a file containing the particulars of American officers serving with the I.A.F you will see his initials are Lt A.G.Hall, even his rank is different as he was a 2Lt. Various other references including his casualty card give his initials as L.G. as used above. His real name as stated on his casualty card was Lyle G.Hall. Rank is also hard to establish as different administrative officers used different methods, some always listing officers as Lt whether they are 2Lt or full Lt. This throws up the question of whether officers have been promoted, or it is just a different recording officer giving different information. With the amount of casualties and quick turn around of officers in the I.A.F it is therefore hard to be completely accurate.

Note: Aircraft serial numbers were not listed in the bomb raid report. However, DH9s D2945, D5785, C2201 and C6268 were recorded as wrecked in aircraft records for this day for 104. These aircraft were most probably the ones flown by either Goble, Malcolm or Hemingway. Which aircraft is attributed to which crew is unclear; the fourth aircraft wrecked this day was most probably involved in a training accident. DH9 D5843 was given over to 99 Squadron on this day.

Target: Courcelles Railway Junction

12th September			**Take Off:**	**12.00**
99 Squadron			**Returned:**	**13.15**
Formation 1				
Capt W.G.Stevenson	Lt W.B.Walker	D3041		
2Lt L.S.Springett	2Lt J.C.Barns	D1670		

After several days of bad weather which hindered operations, orders were received to bomb the railway junction at Courcelles just east of Metz on the evening of the 11th. This attack was designed to hinder the re-supply of men and munitions to the St.Mihiel salient, once the upcoming American and French offensive started. The preliminary bombardment could be heard at Azelot but help from the I.A.F. was curtailed by the weather which comprised rain, low clouds and strong winds at dawn. However, an attempt was made by two formations at 07.50 to carry out the attack. Beaten by the low cloud and rain they were forced to return. After waiting several hours for a change in the weather, orders were given for pairs of aircraft to attack the target independently. The first pair were an experienced crew, the second less experienced, who, flying on the wing, would hopefully make the target and return despite the conditions. Captain Stevenson and his wing-man 2Lt Springett were the first to leave. Crossing the lines near Nomeny the pair were heavily archied but continued north, and dropped four 112lb bombs from 5,000ft on the railway junction at Courcelles. Two bombs exploded on tracks in the sidings while another exploded within fifty yards of a train. Heavily archied on the return the pair landed back at Azelot and made their reports.

Target: Courcelles Railway Junction
Secondary Target: Orny Village/Sidings at Verny

12th September			Take Off:	14.55
99 Squadron			Returned:	16.00
Formation 2				
Capt V.Beecroft	2Lt B.S.W.Taylor	D1668		
2Lt W.H.Gillett	2Lt H.Crossley	D3270		
Lt K.D.Marshall	Lt J.K.Speed	D3213		
Lt F.K.Crosbie-Choppin	2Lt A.T.Bower	D1670		

Captain Victor Beecroft, recently returned from leave, led the second pair of the day, closely followed by Lt Marshall and his wingman Lt Crosbie-Choppin. All four aircraft took off and entered low cloud as they made their way towards the lines and Courcelles beyond. Once over the lines and free from the considerable front line archie, Beecroft searched for Courcelles but was unable to find it through the low cloud. Flying over Orny village south-east of Metz, German transport was spotted below and Beecroft dropped his bombs followed by 2Lt Gillett and either Marshall or Crosbie-Choppin. From the solitary 230lb and four 112lb bombs dropped a direct hit was observed amongst the transport. Two other 112lb bombs were dropped on the sidings at Verny nearby but no results were seen. All bombs had been released from 3,000ft through gaps in the clouds and all four machines had been under near constant anti-aircraft fire since crossing the lines. All four machines returned to Azelot just in time, as the weather worsened and operations for the rest of the day were scrapped.

Target: Railway Station and Sidings at Metz
Secondary Target: Ars/Orny/Verny/Arnaville

13th September			Take Off: 11.00/16.30	
99 Squadron			Returned: 12.55/17.45	
Wash Out Raid				
Lt H.Sanders		C6260	Bombed Orny	
2Lt W.H.Gillett		D3228	Bombed Verny	
Individual Raids				
2Lt F.A.Wood	2Lt C.Bridgett	D3218	K.I.A./K.I.A.	
Lt W.E.Oglivy	2Lt G.A.Shipton	D3228		
Capt V.Beecroft	Lt H.S.Notley	D1668	/W.I.A.	
Lt H.Sanders	2Lt E.Beale	C6260		
2Lt M.J.Poulton	Sgt F.L.Lee	C2197		
2Lt W.H.Gillett	2Lt H.Crossley	D5573		
2Lt G.R.A.Dick	2Lt E.Smith	D1006		
2Lt S.McKeever	2Lt H.A.Boniface	B9366		
Capt W.G.Stevenson	Lt W.B.Walker	D3041		
2Lt L.S.Springett	2Lt J.C.Barns	E632		

Lt K.D.Marshall	2Lt J.K.Speed	D3213	
2Lt W.T.Jones	2Lt E.C.Black	C6260	
2Lt J.L.Hunter	2Lt T.H.Swann	B9347	W.I.A./
2Lt E.E.Crosby	2Lt C.P.Wogan-Browne	D1670	K.I.A./K.I.A.
2Lt J.G.Dennis	2Lt H.G.Ramsay	D3213	
2Lt E.A.Bowyer	2Lt J.W.Howard	D3243	ret eng vibrating

Tasked with supporting the on-going St.Mihiel offensive, 99 Squadron were ordered to bomb the railway station and sidings at Metz, and the busy railway junction at Ars. While checking their aircraft the signs did not look good, with a strong northerly wind and dense cloud banks at 2,000 and 3,000 feet. Captain Beecroft led fourteen DH9s up to gain height before setting out north towards the lines. While climbing to operational height, two aircraft returned with engine trouble. Encountering further cloud banks at 5,000 and 8,000ft, Beecroft fired a Very light to wash out the raid and he started his descent towards Azelot. Descending through the clouds aircraft became separate and it was every man for himself in finding base. DH9 8370, flown by 2Lt King force-landed at Rosières being unable to find the aerodrome. Another machine, DH9 D1670, flown by the American 2Lt Kidder also became lost. After two hours and twenty minutes, his wheels finally touched down on Azelot. He was not alone however, and almost all the crews had trouble finding the aerodrome in amongst the hills around Nancy. Beecroft must have been anxious when three of his aircraft had still not landed half an hour after he touched down himself. King was down at Rosières while Kidder had been trying to avoid the hills around Nancy. Lt Sanders in DH9 C6260, and 2Lt Gillett, in DH9 D3228, were also missing; far from lost they had set a compass course for Metz while descending after the wash out, and were planning to drop out of cloud and attack any targets seen. However, they emerged only two hundred feet above the ground near Verny. Sanders dropped his two 112lb bombs watching one of them impact alongside a railway line south of Verny. Gillett released his two 112lb bombs on German transport near the village of Orny. All four bombs were fitted with fifteen-second delayed action fuses. Both machines returned low level to Azelot and had been in the air only one hour and ten minutes.

With the weather unlikely to improve, it was decided that individual aircraft would attempt to find and attack Metz flying low level to and from the target. With a low cloud base and heavy rain, it was unlikely any enemy scouts would be airborne, and if they were, it was hoped that a bomber at low level would be a hard target to locate. The first DH9 airborne was piloted by the American Francis Appleton Wood, which took off at 11.00. Wood and Bridgett reached Metz but they were shot down by ground fire near Ars-sur-Moselle on their return towards the lines, and both men were killed. Claude Bridgett was only eighteen and came from Putney in London; he is buried at Chambières in France.

Taking-off at midday Lt Oglivy and 2Lt Shipton headed north towards the lines and Metz. Once over they were unable to locate Metz and dropped their two 112lb bombs on the goods yard north of Ars station. Shipton upon landing reported silencing a machine-gun emplacement with his Lewis gun within the Moselle valley. This sortie had only taken fifty-five minutes.

Captain Beecroft was airborne at the front of six DH9s at 14.30, again heading out north with a slight improvement in the weather. Captain Stevenson and 2Lt Springett were airborne soon after Beecroft but took a different route. Beecroft led his formation along the Moselle valley. Low cloud obscured the target and Beecroft made for the station and sidings at nearby Ars. Climbing to 1,000ft the formation dropped two 230lb, four 112lb, and eight 25lb bombs on the station and sidings. Ground targets were attacked by the observers with their Lewis guns as they watched their bombs explode in amongst the sidings and transport around the station; four bombs exploded in the village amongst horse drawn transport. Anti-aircraft fire was intense and Lt Notley received a flesh wound in his leg from a piece of shrapnel. Despite the efforts of the German gunners, all six machines returned to Azelot after fifty minutes in the air. Captain Stevenson was trying to locate Metz amongst the cloud, when he spotted a transport camp packed with lorries and supplies, near the Verny-Chérisey road. Releasing his two 112lb bombs he watched them explode in amongst huts alongside the transport camp. Springett had also dropped his 230lb bomb, which scored a direct hit amongst the lorries. Heading home they spotted two formations of enemy scouts which they successfully evaded using cloud cover to reach the lines and safety. Both landed back at Azelot after one and a half hours in the air.

Another formation of six took off at 16.30, led by Lt Marshall and they headed north towards the lines in the hope of bombing targets near Ars. The formation was soon down to five as recently arrived 2Lt Bowyer returned with a badly vibrating engine. The others headed towards Arnaville just south of Ars. The decision was made very quickly to drop their two 230lb, and six 112lb bombs on Arnaville junction below. The reason for this was the appearance of seven Fokker DVIIs. The fighting was fierce and continued towards the lines which were not far away. These German pilots were professionals, however, and one DH9 soon dropped out of formation, closely followed by two scouts which continued to fire at the stricken bomber. Both 2Lt Crosby, and 2Lt Wogan-Browne were killed when their aircraft broke up in the air, and crashed near Pont-à-Mousson in the American front line trenches. The fighting wasn't over yet and 2Lt Hunter, a Canadian, was slightly wounded in the foot before the four bombers reached the lines and the scouts dispersed. The engagement wasn't totally one sided, as 2Lt Black, an American, claimed an enemy aircraft destroyed after it entered a spin and was seen to crash into a wood just east of the Moselle river, in German lines. The four bombers landed back at Azelot at 17.45 after an hour and a quarter in the air. Edward Eno Crosby was nineteen and came from Peterborough, in Lincs, both Crosby and Wogan-Browne were buried in the I.A.F. Cemetery at Charmes.

Leutnant Hugo Schäfer of Jasta 15 claimed a DH9 south-east of Pont-à-Mousson at 18.40 German time for his seventh victory. The time and place fit, with German time still one hour ahead, and Jasta 15 were obviously in the immediate area flying out of Tichemont, near Conflans. Another candidate for Crosby and Wogan-Browne is Unteroffizier Seidel of Jasta 3. He may well have been the other enemy scout firing at the stricken bomber. However, Schäfer was awarded the victory and he would soon come up against the I.A.F. again. Leutnant Siebert of Jasta 15 was injured this day after a crash landing; his injuries however were not serious and he stayed with his Jasta. He may well have been in the Fokker DVII that 2Lt Black claimed.

CHARLES PATRICK WOGAN-BROWNE was born on 10th June 1899. He was educated at Colfe's Grammar School at Lewisham Hill, Blackheath, from September 1911 until July 1915. He enlisted on 10th June 1917, but to which unit or regiment is not known. He initially went to the No.5 School of Aeronautics, followed by a spell at the No.1 School of Aeronautics. Upon leaving here he moved to Eastchurch on 11th May 1918 where he was awarded his observer wings on 21st July. Posted overseas he joined the I.A.F. on 1st September. Killed on his first raid he survived just twelve days.

Reconnaissance

13th September			Take Off:	11.40
55 Squadron			Returned:	13.20
Lt P.E.Welchman	Sgt E.Clare	A7749		

Flew over Conflans, Mars-la-Tour, Chambley, Ars and back to Pont-à-Mousson, rain storms made it impossible to reach Metz. This reconnaissance was flown at 2,000ft, most probably for American and French Intelligence regarding the St.Mihiel offensive.

Target: Triangle of Railways at Metz-Sablon
Secondary Target: Ars/Orly/Arnaville/Metz (Gare Central)

13th September			Take Off: 12.10/16.00
104 Squadron			Returned: 13.25/17.20
Formation 1			
Capt R.J.Gammon	2Lt P.E.Appleby		
2Lt A.D.MacKenzie	2Lt C.E.Bellord	D3263	
2Lt G.H.Knight	2Lt F.F.Bates		
Capt E.J.Garland	2Lt W.E.Bottrill		photo machine
Lt J.H.Cuthbertson	Sgt W.G.Steward		
2Lt B.F.Ross	2Lt L.W.Launchbury		
Capt I.W.Leiper	2Lt G.V.Harper		
2Lt E.A.Forbes	2Lt R.W.Lewin		
2Lt L.C.Pitts	2Lt P.Davey		
Lt J.Wrighton	Lt W.E.Jackson		
Lt O.L.Malcolm	2Lt H.Alexander	D5843	force-landed
Lt A.V.Goble	2Lt P.W.Scott		
2Lt L.G.Hall	2Lt W.D.Evans		

Lt R.Rose   2Lt T.J.Bond   D1050   /D.O.W.

With high winds and dense cloud banks, operations would be difficult. 104 Squadron watched as several aircraft from 99 Squadron took off on one or two-machine raids against the station and sidings at Metz. Captain Gammon would lead two other DH9s in the hope of finding Metz in amongst the clouds, or any target of opportunity they came across. Once over the lines the three machines became separated in their search. Captain Gammon dropped his two 112lb bombs on Ars railway station from 4,000ft, one burst being observed on the north-western corner of the station as they turned for home. The two other aircraft flown by 2Lts MacKenzie and Knight reached Metz and dropped two 112lb and one 230lb on the station. MacKenzie saw both of his 112lb bombs explode on the triangle of railways. Knight however, did not see the fall of his 230lb bomb due to cloud cover. Knight had dropped his bomb from 6,000ft while MacKenzie had dropped from 4,000ft. This may be the reason that Knight, on spotting six enemy aircraft climbing to intercept, escaped into cloud. MacKenzie at 4,000ft was involved in a running fight with four Pfalz scouts. Bellord in the back seat fired half a drum of Lewis at the nearest attacker sending it down in an inverted spin. MacKenzie escaped by flying into cloud and safely re-crossed the lines. Captain Gammon was first to land at 13.25 followed by MacKenzie at 13.30. Knight may well have had trouble finding Azelot in amongst the clouds but finally landed at 14.15.

   Next to take off were Captain Garland, Lt Cuthbertson and Lt Ross who all left Azelot at 13.15 again to bomb the railways at Metz. Unable to find the town all three machines dropped their ordnance on the railway junction at Arnaville. Garland released eight 25lb bombs from 1,500ft, observing hits on the railway and adjacent buildings as well as nearby roads. Cuthbertson also dropped his eight 25lb bombs from 1,500ft but saw no explosions. Ross dropped his 230lb bomb from 1,500ft, watching it explode near the railway. All three machines left the area and arrived back at Azelot at 15.15.

   Captain Leiper was to lead the next sortie with Lt Forbes and Lt Pitts taking off at 14.15 again to hit Metz. Captain Leiper led all three aircraft to the target, dropped his two 112lb bombs from 5,000ft on the Gare Central station observing two explosions on rolling stock. Lt Forbes dropped his eight 25lb bombs from 5,000ft on the triangle of railways observing numerous explosions within the area. He also saw four Fokker DVIIs which were trying to intercept him and Captain Leiper. Both machines slipped into cloud and shook off the enemy scouts. Lt Pitts dropped his two 112lb bombs from 5,000ft on the junction of the main roads leading into Metz from the north-east, near the Moselle river. The two bombs exploded on houses near the road as they were attacked by six enemy scouts. Lt Davey fired at them as Pitts flew into cloud and lost them. Captain Leiper landed at 15.20 followed by Forbes five minutes later, and Pitts ten minutes after that.

   Next to leave was Lt Wrighton who took off at 15.40 and made his way north towards the lines. Once over the lines Wrighton looked for troop concentrations on the Chambley-Conflans Road but could find none. While still searching for troops four enemy scouts in formation and two Halberstadt two-seaters started to climb to attack. Wrighton dropped his 230lb bomb from 2,500ft onto an anti-aircraft position at Villecey. Landing back at Azelot at 16.45 Wrighton reported a direct hit on this anti-aircraft battery.

   Lt Malcolm took off five minutes after Wrighton with eight 25lb bombs and headed north to find Metz-Sablon and its station whereupon he dropped his ordnance on the sidings then headed for home. Home unfortunately was harder to find than the target and they put their machine down at Champagneuf. Both men may well have been injured in this force-landing as Malcolm did not return to operations until the end of the month, and Alexander did not fly operationally again until the end of October.

   Lt Goble, 2Lt Hall and Lt Rose all left at virtually the same time although Hall's is the only aircraft with a recorded take-off time of 16.00. It seems as though the weather got slightly better in the early evening, as operations moved to a higher altitude. Hall was flying at 6,000ft when he spotted ten enemy aircraft heading his way. Dropping his two 112lb bombs on Mars station below, Hall headed for cloud to escape the fighters which were now engaging him. Losing his pursuers he landed safely at Azelot at 17.20. Lt Rose may well have had sight of Hall when he dropped his 230lb bomb on the triangle of railways at Metz-Sablon. Six fighters immediately attacked him raking his machine with bullets. Trying to run for home, the engine on the DH9 was badly shot about. 2Lt Bond in the back seat was badly wounded in the head and neck and there seemed little hope for him. Rose did make the lines, crash landing his machine between Faulx St.Pierre and Eulmont near Nancy. Bond was taken to the French Hospital at Agincourt where he unfortunately died the next day, and was buried at Charmes. Lt Goble had decided to climb higher then the other two aircraft and found himself over Orly aerodrome at 10,000ft. After dropping two 112lb bombs, the crew noticed a lone enemy aircraft climbing to intercept. Goble headed for the clouds and the German was shaken off. Goble returned to Azelot safely.

Reconnaissance

13th September			Take Off:	17.20
55 Squadron			Returned:	18.55
Lt W.J.Pace	2Lt M.E.Barlow	A7427		

Crossed at Nomeny at 13,000ft, flew to Bensdorf, nothing on railways at Delme, large fire north of Pont-à-Mousson.

Target Formation 1: Railway and Station at Metz
Target Formation 2: Aerodrome at Buhl

14th September			Take Off:	07.25 – 45
99 Squadron			Returned:	09.30 – 40
Formation 1				
Capt W.G.Stevenson	Sgt J.Jones	D3041		
2Lt L.S.Springett	2Lt J.C.Barns	E632	ret eng misfiring	
Lt W.E.Ogilvy	2Lt G.A.Shipton	D3264	P.O.W./P.O.W.	
2Lt J.G.Dennis	2Lt H.G.Ramsay	D3215	W.I.A./W.I.A.	
2Lt G.R.A.Dick	2Lt E.Smith	D1008	ret rod broken	
2Lt S.McKeever	2Lt H.A.Boniface	B9366		
Formation 2				
Capt V.Beecroft	Sgt F.L.Lee	D1668		
2Lt W.T.Jones	2Lt R.Buckby	D5573		
2Lt W.H.Gillett	2Lt H.Crossley	D3228		
Lt H.Sanders	2Lt E.Beale	C6260	photo machine	
2Lt M.J.Poulton	2Lt J.W.Howard	C2197	ret overheating	
2Lt E.J.Kidder	Sgt H.L.Bynon	B9347		

Although the weather had improved on the previous day, the sky was still overcast but with a much higher cloud base allowing operations to be flown at a higher altitude. The rain had also stopped which obviously improved visibility. Metz and its network of tracks and sidings was the target for the first formation led by Captain Stevenson. Metz would also be targeted again in the afternoon, but this time with a formation of twelve, hopefully. Buhl aerodrome was the target for the second formation led by Captain Beecroft, which took off twenty minutes after the first. While climbing for height before crossing over the lines, the first formation of six, soon became four, as 2Lt Dick returned after forty-five minutes with a broken connecting rod. Lt Springett was the second to return after an hour and fifty minutes in the air with a badly misfiring engine; both pilots managed to get their machines back to base. Beecroft was having slightly better luck. Only 2Lt Poulton returned after an hour with an overheating engine leaving the remaining five to continue east towards the lines.

Crossing the lines, the formation of four was accurately archied as they headed north. Archie was the least of their worries however as eighteen to twenty enemy scouts, mostly Pfalz, descended on them. Despite the odds the four bombers continued towards Metz where they dropped two 230lb and two 112lb bombs from 12,000ft. Bursts were not observed due to the fighting. Lt Ogilvy and his observer Shipton were seen to go down near the target emitting steam from a punctured radiator. Ogilvy managed to get his machine down safely and both men became prisoners of war. One enemy scout was seen to roll over after stalling, and enter a flat spin for at least a thousand feet. This enemy machine was hit by the fire of Sergeant Jones. Unbeknown to the rest of the formation until landing back at Azelot, 2Lt Dennis had been hit in the back by a bullet which perforated his intestines in several places. Despite intense pain he maintained formation and flew all the way back to Azelot. When pulled from the cockpit he was in a critical condition and was rushed to the 8th Canadian Stationery Hospital near Charmes. He was awarded the Distinguished Flying Cross while lying in his hospital bed on the 16th by General Trenchard, still in a critical condition. But for the skilful treatment received from the Canadian doctors and nurses, Dennis would have died. Fortunately he didn't and was off the danger list within a few days. Ramsay was also wounded with a bullet in the leg, but it was not too serious although this would be his last operational raid of the war.

Ogilvy and Shipton were most probably shot down by the Commanding Officer of Jasta 80, Oberleutnant Gottlieb Rassberger, who shot down a DH9 at 09.00 German time, near Polter, for his second victory of an eventual four.

Beecroft and his formation had crossed the lines and were preparing to drop when the air above Buhl erupted with bursts of accurate archie. Archie wasn't normally encountered over Buhl, and new anti-aircraft guns may have been bought in after the heavy raids at the beginning of the month. Despite the archie two 230lb, and six 112lb bombs were dropped from the unusually low bombing height of 10,000ft. One burst was observed on a large hangar while a second exploded close to another; two bursts were also seen on the road south-east of the aerodrome. The formation of five turned for home and landed back at Azelot at 09.40. The only enemy aircraft encountered on the entire trip were over Lorquin, at 10,000ft, and although numbering seven they did not venture near the bombers.

The citation for 2 Lt Dennis read as follows:

2 Lt James Gordon Dennis
D.F.C. gazetted 2nd November 1918

On a recent bombing raid this officer was engaged in a formation which was attacked by twenty of the enemy, and in the ensuing fight he was severely wounded. He at once signalled to his observer to take charge of the machine, but the observer had also been wounded, and was unable to comply. Lt Dennis decided that his duty demanded that he should remain with his formation to the end of the battle, and this he did, notwithstanding the loss of blood from his wounds. He succeeded in bringing his machine back to our Lines – a distance of over forty miles – a feat which surprised his Commanding Officer.

Target: Triangle of Railways at Metz-Sablon

14th September			Take Off:	07.30
104 Squadron			**Returned:**	**09.30**
Formation 1				
Capt I.W.Leiper	2Lt G.V.Harper	D7232		
2Lt A.A.Baker	2Lt P.W.Scott		ret e/t	
2Lt L.G.Hall	2Lt W.D.Evans	D3245		
2Lt L.C.Pitts	Lt P.Davey	D3248	photo machine	
Lt A.V.Goble	2Lt G.A.Faulkner	D3263		
Lt E.A.Forbes	2Lt R.W.Lewin			
Spare aircraft	Lt		collided 2,000ft	
Formation 2				
Capt E.J.Garland	2Lt W.E.Bottrill	D3035	photo machine	
Lt J.Wrighton	2Lt W.E.Jackson	D3211		
2Lt G.H.Knight	2Lt F.F.Bates	D5581	W.I.A.	
2Lt A.Hemingway	2Lt E.D.Barnes			
Lt J.K.Cuthbertson	Sgt W.G.Steward	D5786		
2Lt C.Workman	Lt L.R.Chandler		ret e/t	
Spare aircraft			collided 2,000ft	

More work was detailed against main line railway stations behind the St.Mihiel Salient in support of the American and French offensive. The rain and low cloud had improved from the previous day and 104 Squadron took off after a single formation of 99 Squadron which were also tasked with bombing Metz. While gaining height two aircraft collided at 2,000ft, one coming down at Tonnoy while the other returned to Azelot, all four crew were uninjured. With two spare aircraft it looked like a full complement of twelve would cross the lines until Lt Workman returned at 08.10, followed by Lt Baker at 08.55, both with engine trouble. The ten remaining bombers crossed at Pont-à-Mousson where they encountered moderate archie.

Heading north to the objective eight enemy aircraft attacked the formations, seven were Fokker DVIIs and the other a Halberstadt 2-seater. These aircraft attacked all the way to Metz where five 230lb, eight 112lb and eight 25lb bombs were dropped from 10,500ft. Eight bursts were observed on the railway lines at the south-eastern corner of the triangle while a 230lb bomb appeared to hit the railway bridge destroying one of the lines. While over the target 2Lt Knight was hit in the thigh by a large piece of shrapnel. Despite the severity of his wound he remained in formation. Once they had left the target the Fokkers attacked again but the formations held and the Germans broke off the engagement at Mailly. The fight, however, was not over as six Pfalz scouts attacked. A straggler from 99 Squadron (possibly Dennis) was attacked by a Pfalz and William Bottrill fired one of his Lewis guns which seemed to have no effect. Bottrill then fired both his

Lewis guns, the other having armour piercing rounds in it, and the enemy aircraft turned over on its back and fell like a leaf before nose diving into a field south of Metz.

All ten bombers landed safely back at Azelot including Knight who made an excellent landing. In all thirty-six photos were taken between Bottrill and Lt Davey. Garland mentions Bottrill's victory in his diary, he also states that their machine was written off upon landing. He also notes the collision, and that both machines managed to land safely at Azelot.

WILLIAM ERIC BOTTRILL was born in 1893 in Burton on Trent, thence moving to Canada as a young man with his family settling in Ontario. A successful salesman with the International Silver Combine of America, he also worked as a stock-keeper hoping to strike it rich in the mining area of northern Ontario. He worked for this company from 1911 until he enlisted at Hamilton, in the 36th Battalion Canadian Expeditionary Force on 20th April 1915 as a sergeant, and then an officer. He served in France with the 4th Battalion until posted to England on 12th March 1918. Volunteering for a course as an observer with the Royal Flying Corps, he was posted to 104 Squadron on 9th July. He was Mentioned in Despatches and received his Distinguished Flying Cross from King George V at Buckingham Palace, gazetted 10th October 1919. He left the Royal Air Force on 13th January 1919, and served on various army medical boards that expedited the return of Canadian servicemen from overseas. Serving with the Canadian Army in World War Two, he retired as a colonel in the local Dundas Regiment and died of a stroke on 6th October 1971 in Dundas, Ontario.

Reconnaissance

14th September			Take Off:	09.20
55 Squadron			Returned:	13.30
Lt S.L.Dowswell	Sgt G.Howard	A7973		

Crossed lines at Verdun at 19,000ft, could not see Thionville due to clouds. Plates exposed over Metz, no road or rail activity seen, twenty-two plates exposed.

Target: Railways at Ehrang

14th September			Take Off:	10.55
55 Squadron			Returned:	14.45
Formation 1				
Capt D.R.G.Mackay	2Lt C.W.Clutsom			
Lt W.G.Braid	2Lt G.S.Barber			
2Lt A.J.Robinson	2Lt H.R.Burnett	A7427		
2Lt C.Turner	2Lt M.E.Barlow			
2Lt E.Wood	2Lt J.D.Evans		photo machine	
2Lt G.P.Dymond	2Lt A.C.Heyes	D8384	force-landed	
Formation 2				
Lt E.J.Whyte	Sgt E.Clare			
Lt W.J.Pace	2Lt J.T.L.Attwood			
2Lt J.B.Dunn	Sgt G.F.W.Adams 220131	A7936	photo machine	
2Lt R.C.Pretty	2Lt G.R.Bartlett			
2Lt W.E.Johns	2Lt A.E.Amey			
Lt G.Gorrill	2Lt F.N.Coxhill			

After four days of heavy rain and no flying, things were hotting up on this part of the front. The American and French St.Mihiel offensive was already two days old, and with the great influx of aircraft over this part of the front, German high command had moved Jasta 15 and 19 into Tichemont near Metz, and Jasta 39 into Buhl. Ehrang was a bottleneck for train movement to the front, and this attack was part of a wider policy of shutting down supply routes and offensive airfields.

Heading west after gaining height, twelve DH4s soon became eleven as 2Lt Dymond left the formation and headed towards Toul apparently with engine trouble. The remaining eleven crossed the lines at 15,500ft over Fresnes just south of Verdun, receiving little attention from the archie batteries. A direct route was flown to Ehrang passing abeam Thionville and arriving over the target at 12.55. From 16,500ft ten 230lb and two 112lb bombs were dropped onto the railways below, three direct hits were spotted on the lines themselves and the rest in close proximity to the tracks.

The two formations turned for home and headed south over Saarlouis, St.Avold and re-crossed the lines near Delme. Observers reported seeing considerable movement on the railways around Luxembourg and Treves, while conditions over the battle area were reported as cloudy. No enemy aircraft were seen but 55 Squadron had two aircraft damaged this day. A crash on landing by 2Lt Dunn in the second photo machine damaged their aircraft; both men however were unscathed and back in action two days later. Dymond and Heyes, last seen heading towards Toul, had still not arrived when the Squadron returned, but they eventually contacted the Squadron having had to land near Neufchâteau. Both men may well have been hurt as Dymond did not return to operations until the 26th, and Heyes never flew with the Squadron again.

Note: Serial numbers for the two damaged aircraft come from aircraft records. Robinson's serial number is from his logbook. As usual 55 did not record aircraft on this raid.

Target: Boulay Aerodrome

| **14th September** | | | Take Off: 14.45/15.50 |
| **110 Squadron** | | | Returned: 16.55/17.20 |

Formation 1

Capt A.Lindley	Lt C.R.Gross	F997
Lt H.J.Cockman	2Lt C.H.B.Stevenson	F1000
Lt R.P.Brailli	Lt R.F.Casey	F993
Lt L.S.Brooke	2Lt A.Provan	F992
Lt J.W.L.McLaren-Pearson	2Lt H.Bell	F977
2Lt A.Brandrick	Sgt T.W.Harman	F980

Formation 2

Capt A.C.H.Groom	Capt G.E.Lange	F1005
Maj L.G.S.Reynolds	Capt J.D.Thomson	F983
Sgt A.Haigh	Sgt J.West	E8410
Lt C.B.E.Lloyd	2Lt H.J.C.Elwig	E9660
Capt A.G.Inglis	2Lt W.G.L.Bodley	F1010
Lt M.L.T.Leroy	2Lt G.Parker	F978

Formed at Rendcombe in Gloucestershire as a Nucleus Flight on 1st November 1917, 110 Squadron was sent to Dover and then to Sedgeford, where it was made up to strength. Intended to go overseas on 31st March 1918 equipped with DH4s or DH9s, it was kept at Sedgeford in the 7th Wing and used as a Training Squadron. After completing a course of cloud flying at Stonehenge aerodrome at the end of June 1918, the Squadron moved to Kenley for mobilisation and was equipped with the DH9A, each inscribed with the words "Presented by His Highness The Nizam of Hyderabad". Fully equipped the Squadron proceeded overseas on 31st August 1918. The whole Squadron landed at Lympne and from there were to proceed to Bettoncourt direct. Owing to some delay in restarting at Lympne, one flight had to land at Le Bourget for the night while the other two flights landed at Courban, No.3 Air Depot. One flight led by Captain Lindley did this journey of 309 miles in two hours fifty minutes, quite a feat. Next day all three flights landed at Bettoncourt. At their new base, 110 became part of the 88th Wing under Lieutenant-Colonel W.D.Beatty. Commanding Officer of 110 was Major Hazelton Nicholl (later an Air Vice-Marshal). The aerodrome came as a bit of a shock to pilots and observers who were used to the larger training aerodromes at home. Bettoncourt had a slope which went against the prevailing wind, making take-off hazardous, especially as the hangars had been placed at the end of the take-off run. Another problem was the ground which had been heavily ploughed before it became an airfield. When it rained the soil became heavy which also tended to make the take-off run longer. Accommodation at Bettoncourt was good with substantial living quarters. These quarters however had been camouflaged by Chinese coolies to prevent prying German eyes from seeing them. Crews from 110 Squadron, however, said they were in fact, from the air, the most conspicuous sight for miles!

After two weeks of preparation, Bettoncourt aerodrome heard the roar of twelve Liberty-engined DH9as take off for their first operational raid of the War. The DH9a would hopefully be able to fly to targets much further into Germany, as the DH4s of 55 Squadron were doing. The "Brass" had realised for a long time that the DH9 was unsuited for long-range flights at high altitude, and hopes for the DH9a were high, especially following climbing tests carried out with full bomb and fuel loads. The strategy drawn up was that 99 and 104 Squadrons would hit targets not too far over the lines, and 55 and 104 Squadron with better range and engines in their machines would hit the long-distance targets. It looks as though 99 and 104 may have had the easier option, but with the number of front line Jastas in the immediate area, even short raids over the lines were extremely hazardous. That is not to say once over the lines that 110 and 55 would have it that much easier. Operating at higher altitude, interception was harder but with the amount of time spent over the lines the enemy scout pilots had plenty of time to find them and would often engage on the way to the target, and again on the way back. How the inexperienced 110 Squadron would shape up against this formidable opposition would be keenly watched by those at Headquarters.

Captain Arthur Lindley led the first formation of six off at 16.55 to attack the aerodrome at Boulay, north-east of Metz. Once at sufficient height the single formation flew east over Charmes, and then north over the forests of Crémelly and Rémilly, arriving over Boulay at 16.05. From 15,500ft two 230lb and fourteen 112lb bombs were dropped as the archie came up to greet them. Turning for home, no enemy aircraft were seen and the only trouble was from archie east of Metz and at Bazoncourt, although no aircraft were badly hit. Flying directly south for the lines, they crossed near Château-Salins and continued south towards Lunéville where they flew west and home to Bettoncourt.

The second formation had taken off at 15.50 led by Captain Groom also to bomb Boulay. Flying east over Charmes, Captain Groom flew north-east on a compass heading over thick cloud. By calculation he knew he was over the lines but with only glimpses of the ground he was unable to locate the target, so he led his formation home where all aircraft landed safely with their ordnance.

The day had seen a mixed result concerning their objective. The engines proved to be more reliable and six aircraft had managed to get a lot of ordnance on the target. Usually the DH4 or DH9 would carry a single 230lb or two 112lb bombs. The bombs on the DH9a were the same except a single 230lb bomb was hung with a 112lb bomb. The DH9a was capable of more and tests carried out by 99 Squadron showed that a DH9a with two 230lb bombs could reach 15,000ft after forty-seven minutes. A DH9 with two 112lb bombs could only reach 12,000ft in forty-seven minutes. The DH9a was to be a far more reliable and powerful machine than the DH9, but close formation flying and concentrated defensive fire is what would keep the inexperienced crews alive.

Born in Sheffield on 29th April 1891, CAPTAIN ARTHUR LINDLEY was an experienced pilot having joined 55 Squadron on 13th September 1916. He was wounded in action on 10th April 1917, and returned to Home Establishment on 24th July 1917. Before the war, Lindley had worked at Vickers Ltd, in Sheffield, from 1904 to 1914. Married, Lindley would again cheat death, being made a prisoner of war on 10th October 1918, and repatriated on 29th November 1918. His address at this time was 460 Stamforth Road, Sheffield.

Reconnaissance

14th September			Take Off:	15.45
55 Squadron			Returned:	19.00
Lt D.J.Waterous	2Lt W.R.Patey	B7940		

Took eleven plates over Frescaty aerodrome from 19,000ft, but Bensdorf aerodrome was completely covered in cloud. Frescaty was reported as being active with between thirty-five and forty machines seen on the ground.

Target: Triangle of Railways at Metz-Sablon

14th September		Take Off:	15.40
104 Squadron		Returned:	18.00
Formation 1			
Capt I.W.Leiper	2Lt G.V.Harper		

Lt E.A.Forbes	2Lt R.W.Lewin	
2Lt L.G.Hall	2Lt W.D.Evans	ret e/t
Lt C.Workman	2Lt R.D.Vaughn	photo machine
Lt A.V.Goble	2Lt G.A.Faulkner	
2Lt L.C.Pitts	2Lt P.Davey	

Formation 2

Capt R.J.Gammon	2Lt P.E.Appleby	lost formation
Lt J.Wrighton	2Lt F.W.Aldridge	leaking radiator
2Lt A.D.MacKenzie	2Lt C.E.Bellord	ret e/t
Lt R.Rose	Lt E.T.Baddeley	ret e/t
Lt A.A.Baker	Sgt H.E.Tonge	

A second raid against the railways at Metz was scheduled for both 104 and 99 Squadrons. Captain Leiper led the Squadron as they took off and gained height over Azelot, but engine trouble would rob Leiper of four of his machines. Lt Rose was first to return forty-five minutes after take-off, followed by Lt Wrighton ten minutes later with a leaking radiator. Next to return with engine trouble was 2Lt Hall followed by 2Lt MacKenzie at 17.20. Captain Gammon, without a formation, returned to Azelot at 17.35 and Lt Baker joined the first formation. Now with a single group of six bombers, Leiper made his way north to the lines.

The archie put up at the lines was insignificant and all eyes were looking out for German scouts as both 104 and 99 Squadrons had been engaged in their morning raids. As the formation drew closer to Metz fighters were spotted over the objective. Arriving over Metz at 17.20, three 230lb, four 112lb and eight 25lb bombs were dropped from 11,500ft. Despite the attention of the now attacking scouts, three direct hits were observed on the railway lines, while another three bursts were seen within the triangle of railways. A single burst was spotted on the gasworks and another on the town's barracks. Leaving the target with the scouts in pursuit the single formation headed south towards the lines where a few miles south of Metz the Germans gave up the chase.

Returning to Azelot all six machines landed safely. Lt Vaughn had taken six photos, three over the objective.

Note: Aircraft serial numbers were not recorded on this raid.

Target: Triangle of Railways and Station at Metz-Sablon

| **14th September** | | | **Take Off:** | **15.50** |
| **99 Squadron** | | | **Returned:** | **18.00** |

Formation 1

Capt V.Beecroft	2Lt B.S.W.Taylor	D1668	
2Lt J.Jones	2Lt R.Buckby	D5573	
2Lt H.E.King	2Lt J.L.M.Oliphant	D3270	
Lt H.Sanders	2Lt E.Beale	C6260	ret eng vibrating
2Lt M.J.Poulton	Sgt J.Jones	B9347	
2Lt W.H.Gillett	2Lt H.Crossley	D3228	

Formation 2

Capt W.G.Stevenson	2Lt A.T.Bowyer	D3041	
2Lt L.G.Stern	2Lt J.Potter	D3215	
2Lt S.McKeever	2Lt H.A.Boniface	B9366	
2Lt E.J.Kidder	2Lt T.H.Swann	2196	force-landed
2Lt E.A.Bowyer	2Lt J.W.Howard	E632	ret e/t
2Lt L.S.Springett	2Lt J.C.Barns	D3243	
2Lt G.R.A.Dick	2Lt E.Smith	D7272	ret eng vibrating

Although taking off ten minutes after 104 Squadron, this was not a joint operation and 99 Squadron gained height and made their own way to the lines led by Captain Beecroft. Engine vibration was a problem for both Lt Sanders and 2Lt Dick who both returned to Azelot. DH9 632 had been misfiring on the morning raid, and it would return its crew back to base, again without reaching the target, and again with engine trouble.

Down to ten machines the two formations crossed the lines and headed north towards Metz. Arriving over the target six 230lb and eight 112lb bombs were dropped at 17.30. The grouping of bombs was good with six bursts observed within the triangle of railways. One exploded on the goods station, and two on the railway works. Archie was accurate as the formations turned for home, and headed straight for the lines. Just south of Metz, the bombers were attacked by five enemy scouts from long range. While passing over Frescaty aerodrome, also south of Metz, between thirty-five and forty fighters were spotted on the ground. Whether it was a lucky long-range shot or engine trouble is unclear, but whatever the cause, 2Lt Kidder was forced to land his machine at Faulx, just north of Pont-à-Mousson. Both men were unharmed and back on operations the next day.

On the whole it was a very successful day for 99 Squadron, and morale at this time was reported to be at one of its highest points during the war. Captain Patrick Eliot Welchman of 55 Squadron, was transferred to 99 Squadron on this day to take over from Captain Creaghan, who had broken his collar bone.

Flying his last bombing raid this day for 99 was the experienced VICTOR BEECROFT. Born on 18th September 1895, his address during the war was given as Airedale House, Horsforth, Leeds. He started work on 1st August 1912 as an engineer at the family run business, Beecroft Co, in Leeds. He served briefly with 88 Squadron flying Bristol F2bs between 5th April, and 16th April 1918. One of the original members of 99 who proceeded overseas, Beecroft was struck down by the influenza epidemic, and invalided back to England on 24th September 1918 and fortunately survived. He was awarded a D.F.C. after the war which was gazetted on 3rd June 1919 (no citation).

Target: Daimler Works at Stuttgart

15th September			Take Off:	07.20
55 Squadron			Returned:	11.50
Formation 1				
Capt B.J.Silly	Lt J.Parke	F5701		
Lt W.G.Braid	2Lt G.S.Barber			
2Lt R.C.Pretty	2Lt G.R.Bartlett	F5710	force-landed	
2Lt O.E.Miller	2Lt B.H.Du Feu			
Lt D.J.Waterous	2Lt M.E.Barlow		photo machine	
2Lt G.Gorrill	2Lt F.N.Coxhill	F5714	force-landed	
Formation 2				
Lt W.J.Pace	Sgt G.F.W.Adams 220131			
2Lt C.Turner	2Lt J.T.L.Attwood	A7427		
2Lt E.Wood	2Lt J.D.Evans		ret e/t	
2Lt W.E.Johns	2Lt A.E.Amey			
Lt S.L.Dowswell	Sgt G.Howard		photo machine	
2Lt A.J.Robinson	2Lt H.R.Burnett	F5712		

The Daimler Aero Engine Works at Stuttgart lay nearly one hundred miles behind the lines, and at this point it had not been attacked by any daylight squadrons of the I.A.F. Although not the furthest target, it gave the home defence aircraft plenty of time to gain altitude to try and intercept the bombers on their return route, a route predictable due to the limited endurance of the bombers which forced them to fly a reciprocal heading back to the lines.

Captain Silly led twelve DH4s aloft and headed east to cross the lines near St.Dié south of Raon-l'-Etape. With the size of opposition now facing the bombers attacking long-distance targets, a full comple-ment of aircraft was paramount if any serious damage was to be inflicted, but more importantly, it often made the difference between returning safely or becoming another alarming statistic at I.A.F Headquarters. Captain Silly lost 2Lt Wood first with engine trouble, followed by 2Lt Pretty also with engine trouble, then 2Lt Gorrill also left the first formation with a fuel pressure problem. Wood managed to reach Azelot while Gorrill force-landed at Epinal. Pretty on the other hand crash-landed on or near Bettoncourt aerodrome.

Crossing at 15,000ft, the remaining nine DH4s were heavily archied although the gunners got the bombers' height wrong, and both formations were untroubled. Heading towards Strasbourg, the crews must have expected to fight their way to the target with three Jastas stationed at Buhl, but so far there was no interference from enemy aircraft. The formations flew over Strasbourg then Baden, next to Buhl, taking photos of the aerodrome which had been attacked eight times so far this month. Arriving over the target at 09.40, seven 230lb and four 112lb bombs were dropped from 17,000ft, and hits were observed on houses next to the Daimler works as the formations turned for home. To the south of the town was the aerodrome at Böblingen where several aircraft were seen taking off. These aircraft apparently followed the two formations but never caught up. However trouble was soon to arrive south-east of Strasbourg as Fokker DVIIs intercepted the two groups. One of these DVIIs managed to get under the tail of 2Lt Turner's machine. Turner went into a climbing turn and his observer, Attwood, opened up, and the Fokker spun away and crashed into a wood. Captain Silly claimed a Fokker DVII in flames after firing at it, but this may well have been the same aircraft that attacked Turner and Attwood. The fight wasn't prolonged and the enemy aircraft were kept away by 2,000 rounds of Lewis allowing the nine to re-cross the lines near St.Dié with thirty-six photos of Buhl and the Daimler works.

Investigations after the war confirmed the observer's reports of bombs hitting housing next to the Daimler buildings. One bomb penetrated a house and exploded in the cellar which was being used as a large air-raid shelter, while other bombs fell on surrounding housing destroying part of the street. Reports state eight people were killed and another twelve injured with no bombs hitting the Works. The raid was significant in that the civil population protested about the lack of warning, but Daimler production was unlikely to have suffered. No German losses for units in this area can be found from the available records to match the aircraft claimed by 55 Squadron.

Note: DH4s F5710 and F5714 were recorded as wrecked, and missing, respectively, on 15 September 1918 by 55. These were probably the two aircraft flown by Pretty and Gorrill, but which crew flew which aircraft is not certain. The serial number for Robinson comes from his log-book, other serial numbers are not recorded.

Reconnaissance

15th September			**Take Off:**	**09.40**
55 Squadron			**Returned:**	**14.25**
Lt E.J.Whyte	Sgt E.Clare	D9233		

Crossed the lines over Dieuze and exposed plates over Zweibrücken, Kaiserslautern, Neustadt, Speyerdorf, Germersheim and objectives in special areas, including Karlsruhe sidings. Weather conditions good, re-crossed lines over Baccarat. Forty-five plates taken in all.

Target: Triangle of Railways and Station at Metz-Sablon

15th September			**Take Off:**	**09.45**
99 Squadron			**Returned:**	**11.45**
Formation 1				
Capt P.E.Welchman	2Lt T.H.Swann	B9347		
Lt K.D.Marshall	Sgt J.Jones	D3213		
2Lt S.McKeever	2Lt H.A.Boniface	B9366		
Lt F.K.Crosbie-Choppin	2Lt A.T.Bowyer	D544	photo machine	
2Lt L.S.Springett	2Lt J.C.Barns	E632		
2Lt G.R.A.Dick	2Lt E.Smith	C6272		
2Lt E.A.Bowyer	2Lt J.W.Howard	D3243		
Formation 2				
Lt H.Sanders	Lt B.S.W.Taylor	C6260		
2Lt J.Jones	2Lt R.Buckby	D5573		
2Lt H.E.King	2Lt J.L.M.Oliphant	D3270		
2Lt M.J.Poulton	2Lt J.Potter	D3033		
2Lt W.H.Gillett	2Lt H.Crossley	D3228		
2Lt L.G.Stern	2Lt R.Henderson	D1668		
2Lt E.J.Kidder	Sgt S.Beswick	D3041	spare returned	

The weather was fine as Captain Welchman led out 99 Squadron for the first time, Metz and its network of railways being the target. A joint operation with 104 Squadron was the plan, and 99 Squadron took off ten minutes after their sister squadron. The climb to altitude in formation went smoothly for 99 and they headed north towards the lines to formate with 104. Although 104 Squadron took off first, it is not clear if they should have been the lead squadron or not. However, 99 crossed first, followed by 104, and they were both heavily archied.

With both formations complete at the lines, the spare aircraft should have returned. 2Lt Kidder did but 2Lt E.A.Bowyer did not, and accompanied the two formations to the target. At eleven o'clock 99 Squadron dropped seven 230lb, ten 112lb and eight 25lb bombs on the railways below at Metz. Despite the intense archie, Welchman had lined the bombers up well. Four bursts were observed amongst the engine sheds, three exploded in the sidings, and four others just outside the triangle of railway lines. Enemy aircraft numbered eight but did not venture near 99 Squadron as they turned for home very sharply, followed by 104 Squadron.

All thirteen machines returned to Azelot safely, and photos taken by 2Lt A.T.Bowyer confirmed several hits on the railways and surrounding buildings. A successful first raid by Welchman had again lifted the morale in 99 Squadron despite four killed in action, four wounded, and four taken prisoner of war in the month so far. The casualties look bad on paper but four of the personnel killed, and two wounded, were casualties on the 13th, the day low level single operations were flown due to the weather. Despite the American St.Mihiel offensive drawing to a close on this day, the objective for 99 Squadron was still the vital railway junctions feeding the German war machine, and several of the large airfields. The German Jastas had been increased in number since the American offensive, and from Verdun to Blâmont there were now eight stationed near the lines. This formidable gauntlet would have to be run twice on every raid, and despite the growing confidence amongst the inexperienced crews of 99 Squadron, a big showdown with the German Jastas was inevitable.

Target: Triangle of Railways at Metz-Sablon

15th September			Take Off:	09.35
104 Squadron			Returned:	11.40
Formation 1				
Capt E.J.Garland	2Lt W.E.Bottrill		force-landed	
2Lt B.F.Ross	2Lt L.W.Launchbury			
Lt J.R.Tansey	2Lt P.W.Scott			
2Lt C.Workman	Lt L.W.Chandler			
Lt J.K.Cuthbertson	Sgt W.G.Steward			
2Lt L.G.Hall	2Lt W.D.Evans	D3245	D.O.W./P.O.W.	
Formation 2				
Capt R.J.Gammon	2Lt P.E.Appleby	C6264	force-landed	
2Lt A.A.Baker	Sgt H.E.Tonge 9020	D532	W.I.A./W.I.A.	
2Lt A.D.MacKenzie	2Lt C.E.Bellord	D3263	K.I.A./K.I.A.	
Lt J.Wrighton	2Lt W.E.Jackson	D3211	/D.O.W.	
2Lt F.Barker	2Lt F.F.Bates	D5581	crash-landed	
Lt R.H.Rose	2Lt E.L.Baddeley	D7205	P.O.W./P.O.W.	

If Metz-Sablon station and shunting yards could be put out of action, delivery of supplies to the German troops fighting in the St.Mihiel Salient would be severely hampered. Raids on the previous day, as well as night raids had mixed results. Daylight raids on the 14th had shut down the line running from Peltre to Metz for three hours, while the line from Metz to Augny was closed for fifteen hours. Three engines had been damaged at the Sablon shunting station, and considerable damage was done to private property. Night raids had caused several fires and cut off the electricity supply as well as damaging several engines and trucks, and some of the goods sheds were also slightly damaged. Despite this catalogue of mayhem supplies were still getting through and it was hoped a combined raid would cause enough damage to shut down the station.

While climbing to gain height, the spare aircraft in the second formation entered the slipstream of another and stalled. Losing too much height this machine returned to Azelot with the other spare. The twelve remaining machines headed towards the lines behind 99 Squadron completely.

Heavily archied as they crossed the lines the two groups continued behind 99 Squadron towards Metz. Near Laumont nine enemy aircraft met the bombers but did not attack. They climbed for more height into the sun and shadowed the squadrons to Metz. Arriving over the town at 11.05, the first formation dropped their bombs and executed a steep turn behind 99 Squadron led by Captain Welchman. The second formation of 104 Squadron released their ordnance but were now separated by quite a distance from the two groups of 99 Squadron, and the formation led by Captain Garland. Welchman may well have seen eleven more enemy aircraft join the nine already shadowing them, hence his quick turn to get back to the lines as soon as possible. Captain Gammon and his formation were left sitting ducks and the Germans rarely wasted an opportunity like this.

First to go down out of control was the aircraft of 2Lts MacKenzie and Bellord, and both men were killed. The enemy aircraft dived in at the formation closing to minimal range, and the inevitable happened – the formation split. Lt Rose and 2Lt Baddeley were seen going down under control, both men becoming prisoners of war. The fighting was not concentrated solely on the rear formation, as both Captain Garland and 2Lt Bottrill were shot up badly with Garland force-landing at a French aerodrome near Nancy with a holed radiator. Hall and Evans were not so lucky. Hall managed to get his damaged machine down, but both men were taken prisoner. Hall unfortunately later died of his wounds. Baker and Tonge were both wounded but were able to crash-land near Sivry north of Nancy; their radiator had also been holed. Lt Wrighton managed to get his wounded observer, Jackson, back to base. Jackson however died of his wounds. Captain Gammon was followed by six German aircraft all the way to the lines. Banking, stalling and trying every trick in the book, Gammon succeeded in spoiling the aim of the German pilots. Hits had scored however, and Gammon force-landed with a seized engine at Brette, north of Nancy. During this prolonged fight Appleby fired seventy-five rounds at a Pfalz scout which crashed near Verny. He also fired fifty rounds at another enemy aircraft which headed down under control. Of the original twelve bombers which made the target, only five landed back at Azelot. On their approach to Azelot, badly shot up with hardly any control over flying surfaces on their aircraft, Barker and Bates crashed near the aerodrome. The flying controls had finally given up and both men were injured, neither of them seeing active service with the Squadron again.

Once reports had been made it was ascertained that the seven 230lb, eight 112lb and eight 25lb bombs had all hit the target. Eight bursts were seen on railway tracks within the triangle while two exploded on the railway lines near the workshops, also within in the triangle. Official reports after the war confirmed the damage with the Sablon shunting station receiving fourteen hits. The roof of the Commissariat was damaged and several private houses were also hit.

This decimation of 104 Squadron was down to the skilfully led Jasta 15. Commanding Officer at this time was the high scoring Leutnant Josef Veltjens, who was also acting leader of Jagdgeschwader Nr.II. Leutnant Hugo Schäfer, Leutnant Georg Von Hantelmann and Vizefeldwebel Theodor Weischer all of Jasta 15 claimed DH9s south of Metz at 12.10, and two at 12.15. The times and locations all match but it is not certain who got who. MacKenzie apparently went down first according to R.A.F. records, but with all three going down within five minutes of each other, and up to forty aircraft together in a small piece of sky, one guess is as good as another. Leutnant Johannes Klein also of Jasta 15 was wounded this day but remained with the Jasta. If he was wounded by 104 he would get his revenge before the month was out. All that is certain is that Jasta 15 put nine aircrew of 104 Squadron out of the war. Two of the three aircraft which force-landed on the allied side were probably written-off as well. The experienced Flight Leaders, Garland and Gammon, were both nearly lost; one wonders if there were a few words exchanged between Gammon and Welchman in the Mess about quick turns over the target. Garland, when interviewed after the war about his experiences, commented that while serving with the I.A.F. he did not expect to survive the war.

Alec Dudley MacKenzie, aged nineteen, from Wallington in Surrey was buried with his observer Charles Edmund Bellord, at Chambières in France. Wilfred Edmund Jackson was from Dingle, near Liverpool. Born in March 1899, he had worked as a clerk from September 1913 to May 1917, when he became old enough to join the R.F.C.

CHARLES EDMUND BELLORD was born on 6th January 1900, and came from Hampstead in London. He studied at Downside School as a member of Caverel House, from September 1910 until 1917. He then went to Balliol College, Oxford, to study History. Reaching the age of eighteen, he volunteered for the Air Force, and arrived in France after six months training in August 1918. His brother served with 72 Squadron in Mesopotamia flying Bristol monoplanes. While listed as missing, reports first indicated that he was wounded and in hospital. Reports later surfaced that he was killed in action on the 15th of September. The family's home address was 40 Belsize Grove, London.

The Canadian PERCIVAL EWART APPLEBY scored his sixth and last claim of the war on this day. Born on 27th June 1894, he came from Port-la-Tour, Nova Scotia. Joining No.1 Field Ambulance in 1914, he served in France in February 1915 and also in Salonika. Returning to Britain, he was commissioned into the King's Royal Rifles on 26th April 1917 until January 1918, when he was attached to the Royal Flying Corps. He started as an observer with No.10 Kite Balloon Section until transferring to aircraft and joining 104 Squadron on the 17th of May. He returned to England on 21st October 1918 and left the service after the war settling down to become a farmer, then a small businessman; he also taught music. During World War Two he became a Recruiting Officer with the Royal Canadian Air Force. He died from a stroke in May 1968.

Note: Aircraft serial numbers were not recorded for this raid. DH9s D1026, D3122, C6264 were all noted as wrecked this day, one of which may have been the badly shot up aircraft flown by Captain Garland. This is further backed up by an extract in Garland's diary, claiming he was shot down this day, allied side. A holed radiator, and the resulting seized engine, forced him down. He landed on rough ground near Nancy and was entertained by French Artillery officers, until he was picked up by Major Quinnell in his staff car. This was certainly turning out to be a black September for Garland. Three machines written of in three days, and another on the 7th, and still only half way through the month!

Target: Buhl Aerodrome

| 15th September | | Take Off: 11.15/11.30 |
| 110 Squadron | | Returned: 13.20/14.00 |

Formation 1

Maj L.G.S.Reynolds	Capt J.D.Thomson
2Lt A.Brandrick	Sgt T.W.Harman
Lt R.P.Brailli	Lt R.F.Casey
Lt L.S.Brooke	2Lt A.Provan
Lt H.J.Cockman	2Lt C.H.B.Stevenson
Lt J.W.L.McLaren-Pearson	2Lt H.Bell

Formation 2

Capt A.C.H.Groom	Capt G.E.Lange	F1005
Lt S.B.Bradley	Sgt A.H.Banks 253777	F978
Capt A.Inglis	2Lt W.G.L.Bodley	F1010
Lt C.B.E.Lloyd	2Lt H.J.C.Elwig	E9660

Major Louis Reynolds led the first formation against Buhl aerodrome, and enemy scouts were expected to be met by the Squadron for the first time. Although only fifteen minutes elapsed between take-offs, it looks as if both formations attacked Buhl individually. All that can be made out from the bomb raid report is that all machines reached the target, dropping one 230lb and twenty-five 112lb bombs. The first formation's bombs burst on the aerodrome with three hitting hangars on the eastern side. The second group observed four or five bursts on the aerodrome, and one near a hangar on the north-west side of the airfield. In the event the only hostile aircraft seen were four on the ground and one low over the airfield.

MAJOR LOUIS GEORGE STANLEY REYNOLDS was born on 23rd December 1883. A student at Balliol College, Oxford, from 1901 to 1906 he joined the War Office as a civil servant. He was a Captain in the 8th London Regiment of the Territorial Army from 1909. While working at the War Office he transferred to the Air Ministry where he was made a Chevalier de la Légion d'Honneur in March 1916. After injuring himself playing football on 15th December 1917, he stopped instructing and returned to the Air Ministry. When he returned to active flying, he joined 110 Squadron on 29th August 1918, with fifty hours instructing and one hundred and fifty hours solo. Shot down on 21st October he was repatriated on 13th December 1918. He became an Officer of the Order of the British Empire on 3rd June 1919. The family address during the war was 29 Warwick Gardens, Worthing.

Reconnaissance

15th September			Take Off:	13.30
55 Squadron			Returned:	16.25
Capt D.R.G.Mackay	2Lt C.W.Clutsom	A8060		

Crossed lines at 18,000ft over Pont-à-Mousson and exposed plates over Frescaty and at railways round Metz. Owing to engine trouble the machine gradually lost height and the pilot had to return. Eighteen plates were exposed and one enemy aircraft seen over the lines. The engine trouble turned out to be a broken valve spring.

Reconnaissance

16th September			Take Off:	05.05
55 Squadron			Returned:	09.45
Lt W.J.Pace	Lt D.W.Stewart	A7942		

Crossed lines at Château-Salins, flew over aerodromes at Dieuze, Biedesdorf, Bensdorf, Morhange, Destry, Rémilly, Boulay and Freisdorf.

Target: Lanz Aero Works at Mannheim

16th September			Take Off:	12.20
55 Squadron			Returned:	16.40
Formation 1				
Capt D.R.G.Mackay	2Lt C.W.Clutsom			
2Lt E.Wood	2Lt J.D.Evans			
Lt W.G.Braid	2Lt G.S.Barber			
2Lt G.Gorrill	2Lt F.N.Coxhill		photo machine	
2Lt W.E.Johns	2Lt A.E.Amey	F5712	P.O.W./K.I.A.	
2Lt R.C.Pretty	2Lt G.R.Bartlett			
Formation 2				
Capt J.B.Fox	Sgt G.Howard		climbing ret e/t	
2Lt J.B.Dunn	2Lt H.S.Orange		ret with leader	
2Lt O.E.Miller	2Lt B.H.Du Feu		ret with leader	
2Lt C.Turner	2Lt J.H.Adams		ret with leader	
2Lt R.V.Gordon	2Lt S.Burbidge		airfield crash	
Lt J.Cunliffe	Sgt G.F.W.Adams 220131		ret with leader	

'Jock' Mackay and Captain J.B.Fox would be leading this raid against the Lanz Aero Works situated near Mannheim. Relative newcomers to the fray, 110 Squadron would also be hitting Mannheim. Although stationed nearby at Bettoncourt, this was not to be a joint raid despite 110 Squadron using the improved DH9a. All aircraft left the aerodrome and joined into their formations while gaining height on a warm but hazy day. Captain Fox was having trouble with his engine and his machine refused to climb any more, which caused enough delay for the second formation to miss the first. A Very light was fired to signal a "wash out" and the second formation returned to Azelot where 2Lt Gordon crashed his machine upon landing; both occupants were unscathed and would return to action the next day.

Mackay and his group crossed the lines at Raon-l'-Etape receiving moderate but accurate archie as they headed towards Saverne. This archie had indeed been accurate as 2Lt William Earl Johns found out, once he righted his aircraft after a particularly close burst. The cockpit was soon awash with petrol which was rapidly running down the length of the aircraft. Looking at his fuel gauge, he found the main tank was nearly empty and his observer 2Lt Amey reluctantly but carefully fired a green Very light to signal their departure from the formation. Running for home, Johns noticed seven Fokker DVIIs which had been following the formation in a steady climb. Unable to outrun them due to his lack of petrol, Johns still had a height advantage over the Fokkers of about 4,000ft and he was much lighter after his bombs had been jettisoned. With luck he might make the lines before the Fokkers got near enough to set alight the stream of petrol still emitting from his aircraft. The remaining five DH4s continued north-east flying over Haguenau, Landau, and on to Mannheim.

Johns was soon overtaken by the Fokkers which closed in on him and Amey. He was now flying with full on rudder to give Amey a better shot. One Fokker DVII, painted black, closed to point blank and Amey fell to the bottom of his cockpit badly wounded. Things in the front were no better and Johns was lucky to escape with only a glancing bullet wound to the hip. With his instruments shattered and a dead engine at 6,000ft, Johns entered a spin in the hope of at least getting down alive before their aircraft burst into flames or broke up. The DH4 was now virtually uncontrollable and impacted slightly nose up in trees at the edge of a field. Johns came to with a broken nose and cuts to his face from the butt of his Vickers gun; Amey from Wimbledon in South London was dead.

The remaining five bombers arrived over Mannheim at 14.35 and dropped three 230lb and four 112lb bombs from 16,000ft. Leaving the target, six enemy aircraft were spotted but reports suggest no engagement took place as the bombers headed towards Neustadt after observing explosions within the aero works and near the station. Eighteen photos of the raid, and eyewitness reports after the war, confirmed one hit on a railway line just south-east of the main railway station, and this was reported to have derailed two carriages. Mannheim slaughter house received two hits which killed some German soldiers working there. Other bombs destroyed a tobacco factory and housing nearby, but no bursts were reported in the vicinity of the aero works. The formation re-crossed the lines at Badonviller, and reported on landing that the train movements were normal, but river traffic was very active. A safer way of transporting war supplies perhaps, but considerably slower.

Johns had crash-landed near the village of Ettendorf near Saverne and was locked in a room at the local schoolhouse. Local emotions were running high after a recent bombing raid had caused casualties at a local sunday school. Amey who had defended his pilot so gallantly despite impossible odds was dumped unceremoniously onto the floor beside the other 'terrorflieger'. Leutnant Georg Weiner, Commanding Officer of Jasta 3, received credit for Johns and Amey for his seventh victory. Previously with Kest 3, Weiner was leading Jasta 3 from the airfield at Morchingen (which was shared with Kest 3) and was probably climbing up to operational height as 55 Squadron were spotted crossing the lines. Offizierstellvertreter Edward Prime of Jasta 78 also claimed a DH9 over Alt-Eckendorf at 13.30 German time, which was now the same as British time. Both time and location match but the victory was awarded to Weiner, not the first time Prime had had a victory quashed or lost in arbitration. German pilots did not share kills. Alfred Edward Amey was born on 22nd July 1899. He worked for Hayes Candy & Co of Friday Street, London, as a wholesale silk salesman. In March 1918 he tried to enlist, but was classed temporarily unfit. Undaunted Amey applied again and received his training at R.A.F. Eastchurch graduating on 16th July 1918. He joined 55 Squadron on 28th August and is buried at Sarralbe Military Cemetery in France. The family's address during the war was 129 Florence Hill, Wimbledon.

Johns tried to escape while awaiting transfer from Strasbourg to a prisoner of war camp, but he was caught and sent to Karlsruhe, then onto Landshut where he attempted to escape again. Arriving at Ingolstadt punishment camp on 7th November, he was soon released after the Armistice, and arrived back in England on Christmas Eve. He was reunited with his wife Maude and their son Jack on Christmas Day. Johns decided to stay in the R.A.F. and was posted to 59 Training Squadron as a flying instructor at R.A.F. Cranwell. However, by April he was unemployed due to cut-backs and returned to Little Dunham in Norfolk. Re-enlisting as a Recruiting Officer at Covent Garden in London, the Johns family followed and moved into a flat at Lancaster Gate. After several postings Johns left the service in October 1927 and moved to Lingfield in Surrey with his new partner Doris Leigh. Here he settled down seriously to aviation writing and painting which he had put on the back burner for many years. Johns wrote several articles for *The Modern Boy* magazine before introducing his most famous character, Captain James Bigglesworth, or 'Biggles' as he is more popularly known, while editor of the famous *Popular Flying Magazine* between 1932-1939. Johns died at his home near Hampton Court on 21st June 1958, aged 75.

Note: DH4s B7940 and D8365 were both wrecked while on the strength of 55 this day. Either of these two machines could have been flown by 2Lt Gordon.

Target: Badische Aniline Und Soda Fabrik Works at Ludwigshafen, west of Mannheim

16th September		**Take Off: 12.50/13.50**
110 Squadron		**Returned:**
Formation 1		
Maj L.G.S.Reynolds	Capt J.D.Thomson	ret e/t
2Lt N.N.Wardlaw	Sgt W.H.Neighbour	

Lt K.B.Wilkinson	2Lt H.Kettener	E8434	/W.I.A.
Lt C.B.E.Lloyd	2Lt H.J.C.Elwig	E9660	
Sgt A.Haigh	Sgt J.West	E8410	K.I.A./K.I.A.
Lt H.V.Brisbin	2Lt R.S.Lipsett	F997	P.O.W./P.O.W.

Formation 2

Capt R.C.H.Groom	Capt G.E.Lange
Lt H.J.Cockman	2Lt C.H.B.Stevenson
Lt R.P.Brailli	Lt R.F.Casey
2Lt A.Brandrick	Sgt T.W.Harman
Lt L.S.Brooke	2Lt D.P.Pogson
Lt J.W.L.McLaren-Pearson	2Lt H.Bell

The two hundred-mile round trip to Mannheim was given to 110 Squadron. 55 Squadron would also be going to Mannheim but to the Lanz Aero Works, although the DH9a would have easily kept pace with 55's DH4s. Again the two formations would fly to the target independently of each other and the first formation led by Major Reynolds left Bettoncourt at 12.50 and headed east towards the lines.

Conditions were hazy with a strong wind, but the single formation continued north-east over Saverne. Near Haguenau, Major Reynolds turned for home with engine trouble. The lead was taken rather surprisingly by the number six machine, Lt Brisbin who led the formation over Rinnthall, then over Schifferstadt south of Ludwigshafen. Just north of Schifferstadt enemy scouts were spotted in the distance, and a moderate amount of archie started coming up. The scouts were already in the air to intercept 55 Squadron, who had taken off half an hour earlier, and as they got closer there seemed to be between twenty-five and thirty of them. Dropping their bombs from 13,000ft, the Germans started to attack. Why this single formation were so low is not clear, but apparently Lt Brisbin lost altitude and the remaining DH9as followed. Whatever the reason it certainly made it easier for the scouts and anti-aircraft crews.

Just south of Neustadt, Sgts Haigh and West were seen going down with their tail shot off; both were killed. Lt Brisbin and 2Lt Lipsett also went down just south of Neustadt emitting smoke. Just before touching down DH9a F997 was hit by ground fire. Fortunately both men survived to become prisoners of war although Lipsett was hit in the foot and jaw.

Lt Wilkinson and 2Lt Kettner seem to have made the only claim for an enemy aircraft. Two Fokker DVIIs closed and exchanged fire with Kettner, who was wounded, but he saw his shots score hits on the fuselage on one of the Fokkers which was painted black. The formation of four continued over Bitche, Lorquin and the Forêt-De-Monson and passed over Charmes before landing back at Bettoncourt.

The second formation led by Captain Groom took off at 13.50 and crossed the lines near Blâmont. Heavy but inaccurate archie greeted them as they crossed and then headed north-east towards Saverne. No enemy aircraft were encountered as they flew over Haguenau and on towards Schwetzingen just north of Speyer, but fifteen enemy scouts were seen near the target. This second group of 110 Squadron had chosen height as their best defence and were bombing from 17,400ft despite haze and strong winds. No German aircraft reached the formation and after following the same track home, all returned safely.

Bomb damage was the same as recorded for 55 Squadron; though it is unclear as to which Squadron actually caused the damage. According to bomb raid reports only eleven aircraft reached the target despite three 230lb and twenty-three 112lb bombs being dropped. There are too many bombs for only eleven aircraft and looking at the report it seems the two aircraft lost came down after the target was bombed. Victors look almost certainly to be Jasta 70 with both Leutnant Anton Stephen, and Vizefeldwebel Metzger claiming DH9s at Germersheim and Landau. Events over the target are sketchy and some claim archie forced the two lost machines to crash. Bomb raid reports show the archie to be moderate to heavy but inaccurate. Jasta 70 did not escape unscathed with their Commanding Officer, Oberleutnant Hans Schlieter being slightly wounded.

Sergeant Arthur Haigh (No.99729) from Huddersfield, Yorks was buried at Niederzwehren in Germany with his observer John West from Birmingham.

Lt Harold Vincent Brisbin was born on 14th August 1893 in Coburg, Ontario. He operated a small garage in Coburg due to his passion for fast automobiles. However his official papers at the Public Records Office Kew, say he worked as a motor engineer for the Cadillac Motor Car Company, in Detroit, Michigan, between 1910 and 1914. Upon the outbreak of war he joined the 19th Battalion of the Canadian Expeditionary Force. Whilst serving on the Somme in 1916 as a Corporal, he was awarded the Military Medal. Brisbin joined the Royal Flying Corps on 13th August 1917 and trained at 19 TS at Hounslow where he had a serious crash in a BE2e on 23rd April 1918. 'Bris' as he was known, was a bit of a wild card, the accident report stating that the airframe had been "subjected to stresses far beyond the aircraft's designed limitations". However he received his wings while with A Squadron at Stonehenge, and joined 110 Squadron. Shot down on his first raid, he was wounded and moved to a Red Cross hospital in Germany. Word reached home that he was a prisoner of war on 30th October 1918. After the Armistice he was transported to Dover on 11th December 1918. From Dover he went to the Prince of Wales Hospital for further treatment. He relinquished his commission on 24th April 1919 and moved back to America with his English bride. When war broke out again in 1939 he returned to Canada. Commissioned as an officer in the Royal Canadian Air Force, he was put in charge of cadet training in Regina, Saskatchewan. In 1946 he returned to America where he died. His home address given while serving with 110 Squadron was 'Cromwell', 109 Herne Hill Road, Herne Hill, London.

Target: Railways at Karlsruhe
Secondary Target: Aerodrome at Haguenau

16th September			Take Off:	12.50
99 Squadron			Returned:	16.20
Formation 1				
Capt P.E.Welchman	2Lt T.H.Swann	D3041		
Lt K.D.Marshall	Sgt J.Jones	D3213		
2Lt S.McKeever	2Lt H.A.Boniface	B9366		
Lt F.K.Crosbie-Choppin	2Lt A.T.Bowyer	D544	photo machine	
2Lt L.S.Springett	2Lt J.C.Barns	E632	ret observer sick	
2Lt E.J.Kidder	Sgt S.Beswick	D7343		
2Lt G.R.A.Dick	2Lt E.Smith	C6272	spare returned e/t	
Formation 2				
Capt H.Sanders	2Lt E.Beale	D1668		
2Lt J.Jones	2Lt R.Buckby	5373		
2Lt H.E.King	2Lt J.L.M.Oliphant	D3270		
2Lt M.J.Poulton	2Lt J.Potter	D3032		
2Lt W.H.Gillett	2Lt H.Crossley	D3228		
2Lt L.G.Stern	2Lt R.Henderson	C2197	bomb jammed	
2Lt E.A.Bowyer	2Lt J.W.Howard	C6260	ret not needed	

Captain Welchman again led 99 Squadron, this time against a target further over the lines, the railways and sidings at Karlsruhe. The weather was fine as fourteen DH9s climbed to gain height before heading out. First to return after forty minutes was 2Lt Dick with an engine which kept cutting out. As the remaining thirteen approached the lines, 2Lt Bowyer turned towards Azelot as a full complement of bombers came under accurate archie, as they crossed the lines near Blâmont.

Welchman noticed that the wind speed was increasing and guessed it was blowing up to thirty-five mph, in a southerly direction. Making very little headway towards Karlsruhe, he decided to bomb the aerodrome at Haguenau instead. The twelve however soon became eleven as 2Lt Springett was forced to re-cross the lines with a sick observer. Haguenau was reached at 15.00 and four 230lb, and twelve 112lb bombs were dropped from the unusually low altitude of 10,000ft. Although 2Lt Stern reached the target his ordnance failed to release and he was forced to carry it home. Again Welchman had lined up well with three direct hits on hangars, three bursts just in front of them, and explosions near several parked aircraft.

Turning for home the eleven headed straight for the lines but encountered no enemy aircraft the entire time they were airborne. Six photos were taken which showed the accuracy of the bombing was very good, explosions had caused a fire on one of the large wooden hangars, and a small building behind the hangars had also been hit.

Patrick Eliot Welchman of the King's Own Scottish Borderers was awarded the D.F.C., his citation reading as follows:

Lt Patrick Eliot Welchman (K.O.S.B.)
D.F.C. gazetted 21st September 1918
A gallant, capable and determined leader of long-distance bombing raids. Within the past month he has rendered as deputy leader very valuable services by resolute co-operation with his leader, and the success attained was in no small degree attributable to the presence of mind and grasp of the situation which this officer displayed. Lieutenant Welchman has taken part in eighteen bombing raids, showing marked ability on all occasions.

Reconnaissance

16th September			Take Off:	15.00
55 Squadron			**Returned:**	**18.00**
Capt B.J.Silly	Lt J.Parke	F5701		

Crossed lines at Pont-à-Mousson at 18,000ft, flew over Frescaty aerodrome which was active, then Metz-Sablon. Boulay aerodrome and Morhange aerodrome were also active; flew over Lorquin and Aspach to re-cross the lines at Blâmont.

Reconnaissance

16th September			Take Off:	15.30
55 Squadron			**Returned:**	**17.40**
Lt Col J.E.A.Baldwin	Capt R.P.Ward	A7837		

Took ten plates over Buhl from 17,000ft, re-crossed lines at Badonviller.

Reconnaissance

17th September			Take Off:	15.00
55 Squadron			**Returned:**	**18.15**
Lt W.J.Pace	2Lt M.E.Barlow	A7352		

Crossed lines at Fresnes at 20,000ft, exposed plates over six northern aerodromes, re-crossed at Thiaucourt at 14,000ft.

Target: Buhl Aerodrome

25th September			Take Off:	08.10
104 Squadron			**Returned:**	**10.30**
Formation 1				
Capt R.J.Gammon	2Lt P.E.Appleby			
Lt J.Wrighton	2Lt C.E.Mason			
2Lt H.L.Wren	2Lt J.T.White			
2Lt B.H.Stretton	2Lt H.Grieve			
2Lt S.T.Crowe	2Lt L.L.Penstone			
2Lt I.L.R.Large	Sgt W.H.Ball			
Formation 2				
Lt O.L.Malcolm	2Lt G.V.Harper	wires broke		
Lt E.A.Forbes	2Lt R.W.Lewin			
Lt J.R.Tansey	2Lt J.M.Scott	followed leader		
Lt C.Workman	Lt L.R.Chandler	followed leader		
2Lt L.C.Pitts	2Lt I.Davey	ret e/t		
2Lt P.Hopkinson	2Lt H.Bridger	ret e/t		

With many new faces and the inexperience that goes with them, Captain Gammon led thirteen aircraft aloft to attack Buhl aerodrome. Despite the severe losses of the 15th, 104 had missed little of the action due to the very bad weather since their encounter at Metz with Jasta 15. Lt Malcolm leading the second formation was forced to return as some of his flying wires broke. Firing a green Very light to signal his departure from the formation, Malcolm was unfortunately followed by Lts Tansey and Workman who mistook the signal. Malcolm fired two more green lights but Tansey and Workman landed alongside their leader much to his annoyance. The remaining four aircraft in the second formation became one as Lts Pitts and Hopkinson returned with engine troubles followed by the spare aircraft. Forbes carried on and joined the first formation.

Crossing the lines at Leintrey the single group received little in the way of archie as they flew a direct line towards Buhl. Arriving overhead at 09.50 two 230lb, six 112lb and sixteen 25lb bombs were dropped from 12,000ft all impacting within the airfield. A good grouping was seen near the hangars on the south-eastern side of the aerodrome. One hangar received a direct hit while four bombs exploded in front of a line of hangars; one burst was seen on the road and another near a large shed. Enemy aircraft numbered five but were some way off and did not try to engage the bombers.

Re-crossing the lines over the Forest of Parroy all seven returned safely to Azelot at 10.30. No photos were taken as Lt Malcolm's was the only aircraft with a camera onboard. From the bomb raid report made out by Major John Charles Quinnell, the CO, it looks like Tansey and Workman may well have got quite a talking to despite being relative newcomers to the Squadron. Quinnell may have been angry, but with the quick turn around of crews due to casualties it was understandable that signals could be mis-interpreted, as Welchman, the new Commanding Officer of 99 Squadron, would find out later that morning.

Note: Aircraft serial numbers were not recorded in the bomb raid report.

Target: Railways at Frankfurt
Secondary Target: Munitions Works at Kaiserslautern

25th September			Take Off:	08.15
55 Squadron			Returned:	12.30
Formation 1				
Capt J.B.Fox	2Lt M.E.Barlow			
2Lt G.Gorrill	2Lt F.N.Coxhill			
2Lt J.B.Dunn	2Lt H.S.Orange	D8356	K.I.A./K.I.A.	
2Lt O.E.Miller	2Lt B.H.Du Feu			
Lt S.L.Dowswell	Sgt G.Howard			
2Lt R.V.Gordon	2Lt S.Burbidge	D8365	D.O.W./	
Formation 2				
Lt J.Cunliffe	2Lt G.E.Little	F5701		
Lt W.G.Braid	2Lt G.S.Barber	D8386	/K.I.A.	
2Lt E.Wood	2Lt J.D.Evans	D8392	W.I.A./	
2Lt C.Turner	2Lt J.T.L.Attwood		/K.I.A.	
2Lt G.B.Dunlop	2Lt A.C.Heyes	F5714	P.O.W./P.O.W.	
2Lt R.C.Pretty	2Lt G.R.Bartlett	D8388	P.O.W./P.O.W.	

The weather had improved after seven days of low cloud and rain, and strong winds which had all hindered any chance of operational flying. Again 55 Squadron would be hitting the same target as 110 Squadron. As before, they would be separate raids and both Squadrons would be on their own for the long trip to Frankfurt and its extensive rail system, which included three large goods yards. Losses so far this month for 55 Squadron had been light, but then so had the amount of opposition if compared to the previous month. With eleven Jastas now in the immediate area, major air engagements were more ominous, especially on long-distance targets such as Frankfurt where fighting to and from the target would be almost inevitable.

The two formations led by Captain Fox headed east from Azelot, and crossed the lines at Blâmont at 14,500ft. Archie at the lines was pretty much inactive as the two groups headed north-east towards Bitche and on towards Pirmasens. Continuing north-east, strong winds blowing west-south-west put an end to Frankfurt being reached, and the munitions works at Kaiserslautern was targeted instead. Arriving over the target at 10.10, nine 230lb and six 112lb bombs were dropped from 15,000 ft scoring hits on the eastern and south-eastern parts of the town despite the bombers coming under heavy and accurate archie.

The two formations were now running for home as twelve enemy aircraft started to close on the bombers. The first twelve enemy aircraft were kept at bay with one falling to the guns of 2Lt Evans. Evans fired at this aircraft to the right of the bombers, which was under the tail of a parallel DH4. His tracers seemed to enter the cockpit and the enemy aircraft spun away out of control. These machines were identified as Fokker DVIIs and Triplanes. What is also certain is that as they continued towards the lines, the numbers of enemy aircraft increased to about thirty in total at one time or another.

Among these aircraft were Jasta 70 flying out of Buhl and they started to get in amongst the two bomber formations and split them up. Vizefeldwebel Lemke shot down one of the DH4s at Bergzabern east of Pirmasens for his second and last victory. The wind was having an effect as the de Havillands were pushed further east as they tried to reach the lines. The second DH4 was to fall to Vizefeldwebel Krist going down near Brumath just north of Strasbourg. The bombers were battling both the wind as well as the increasing number of hostile aircraft. Evans fired several bursts at a scout which came across the tail of his aircraft, it spun away and crashed near Le Petit Pierre. Lt Braid and Lt Cunliffe both fired at enemy aircraft which overtook them to attack the first formation. Braid fired fifty rounds of Vickers at his target which went to the right of the formation and broke up, while Cunliffe fired one hundred rounds in bursts of twenty, his victim going down absolutely out of control according to his combat report. Despite these victories the formations were hopelessly split up east of Sarrebourg, and it was everyone for themselves. Leutnant Anton Stephen of Jasta 70 shot down a third DH4 south of Alberschweiler for his second and last victory of the war. He had already shot down a DH9a of 110 Squadron on the 16th of September. As they neared the lines, the remaining bombers which were riddled by machine-gun fire were subjected to more archie. The fighters were relentless in their pursuit following all the way to the lines according to Evans's combat report.

Of the original twelve, Captain Fox led six DH4s in to land at Azelot; 2Lt Gordon crashed on landing and was injured, eventually dying of his wounds. Burbidge his observer, was unscathed. Of the three crews shot down, Dunn and Orange were killed while Dunlop, Heyes, Pretty and Bartlett were all prisoners of war. Lt Braid landed at Azelot to find his observer Lt Barber dead in the rear cockpit, which was the same for 2Lt Turner who force-landed at Serres to his find his observer 2Lt Attwood also dead. Out of the second formation Lt Cunliffe was the only machine to make Azelot. 2Lt Wood crash-landed his badly damaged machine at Vitrimont after being hit in the leg, his observer Evans was lucky to be alive.

The observers' reports had been accurate as investigations after the war concluded that only houses had been hit in the eastern part of the town but with no casualties amongst the civil population. Again a long-distance raid had resulted in severe casualties for the Squadron with no effect upon the German war machine. German scout units lost only two pilots this day, one on the 7th Army sector, and one on the 18th Army sector, both well to the north. If 'the Brass' still hadn't realised the implications of un-escorted bombers penetrating long distances, they soon would when the remnants of the newly arrived 110 Squadron returned from their long-distance raid to Frankfurt.

James Balfour Dunn aged nineteen from Dundee, Scotland, and Harold Starling Orange, aged eighteen from Hackney in London, were both buried at Niederzwehren in Germany. Dunn had been a student at the Morgan Academy in Dundee, and left to enlist in April 1917 aged eighteen. Attwood from Old Hill, Staffordshire was buried at Charmes in the I.A.F. Cemetery along with 2Lt Barber.

Reconnaissance

25th September			Take Off:	Unknown
55 Squadron			Returned:	
2Lt A.J.Robinson	2Lt H.R.Burnett	D8413	K.I.A./K.I.A.	

According to some casualty lists, 2Lt A.J.Robinson and 2Lt H.R.Burnett were killed in action on this raid in DH4 D8413. All bomb raid reports list the twelve crews as above, and no mention is made in the narratives of these two Officers. In fact Arthur James Robinson aged twenty-one, and Herbert Roy Burnett, both died while on a reconnaissance mission. Burnett was a holder of the Military Medal. They were buried at Chambières Cemetery. This was the only aircraft lost on a reconnaissance mission while 55 Squadron were operating as part of the newly formed R.A.F. Robinson called his aircraft 'Khaki Lizzie'.

ARTHUR JAMES ROBINSON from Wood Lea, Hetton-le-Hole in County Durham, started the war as a motorcycle despatch rider and mechanic at Farnborough in November 1915. From Farnborough he moved to Roth Camp in Ireland in December. He seems to have stayed as a despatch rider until joining B Flight No. 1 Cadet Wing probably in 1917 before going onto 6 Squadron R.F.C. at St. Leonards-on-Sea. From here he went to 46 Training Squadron where he had his first flight on 25th February 1918. On 26th June he left 46 and went to No.1 Fighting School at Turnberry. From here he reported to the Air Ministry on 24th July with 2Lt Dunn (also killed on the 25th) and sailed from Southampton on the *Archimedes* which was loaded with American troops and aircraft. Arriving at I.A.F. Headquarters on 28th July, he was sent back to R.A.F. Headquarters in Paris. On 31st July he arrived back at I.A.F. Headquarters and was sent to Azelot. Upon arriving he hoped he would get 55 Squadron, as he had heard chances of survival would be better and they seemed to have had all the luck. He and Dunn joined 55, where Robinson shared a room with 2Lt Ernest Albert Brownhill who was killed two days later, a sobering thought for a new arrival.

HERBERT ROY BURNETT was born on 13th July 1895 in London. He joined the Royal Air Force as a cadet, but was turned down for pilot training on 4th May 1918. Applying for observer training he was successful and received his wing on 23rd August 1918 at Eastchurch. Two days later he arrived at Azelot to join 55. His address given at the time was 'Fairmead', Beaulieu Villas, Finsbury Park, London.

Target: Aerodrome at Buhl

25th September			Take Off:	08.20
99 Squadron			Returned:	10.35
Formation 1				
Capt H.Sanders	2Lt R.Buckby	D1668		
2Lt M.J.Poulton	Sgt F.L.Lee	C2197	W.I.A. crash-landed	
2Lt H.E.King	2Lt J.L.M.Oliphant	D3270	/W.I.A.	
2Lt W.H.Gillett	2Lt H.Crossley	C6260	photo machine	
2Lt E.A.Bowyer	2Lt J.W.Howard	D544		
2Lt L.G.Stern	2Lt F.O.Cook	D5573		
Formation 2				
Lt K.D.Marshall	Sgt J.Jones	3313	ret e/t	
2Lt E.J.Kidder	Sgt S.Beswick	D7343	mistook signal	
2Lt S.McKeever	2Lt H.A.Boniface	B9366	ret no formation	
2Lt L.S.Springett	2Lt J.C.Barns	E632	mistook signal	
2Lt L.B.Duggan	2Lt W.J.Tremellen	D3215	mistook signal	
2Lt G.R.A.Dick	2Lt E.Smith	D1008	mistook signal	
2Lt C.R.G.Abrahams	2Lt C.M.Sharp	C6272	mistook signal	

After several days of bad weather, 99 Squadron were detailed to bomb Buhl aerodrome along with 104 Squadron although not as a combined raid. Captain Sanders led thirteen DH9s aloft and gained height before setting out east towards the lines. Lt Marshall leading the second raid began experiencing engine trouble and was forced to return to Azelot. His deputy leader, 2Lt McKeever, tried to gather the rest of the second formation around him. Unfortunately inexperience showed and the second formation turned for home, landing after their formation leader. The remaining six aircraft in the first formation continued east towards the lines.

Crossing was accompanied by accurate archie as they made their way east towards the River Rhine. No hostiles were encountered as the formation approached Buhl at 11,000ft. At 09.45 three 230lb and six 112lb bombs were dropped on the airfield below, but no results were observed as the formation turned for home. The archie had been accurate over Buhl and a piece of shrapnel pierced the shoulder of 2Lt Oliphant. Once clear of the objective the formation was attacked by four Pfalz scouts, one painted in black and white stripes, and a two-seater. A running fight ensued which continued to the lines. 2Lt Poulton crash-landed two miles north-east of Azelot after having his aileron controls shot away, and he was slightly injured. The remaining five bombers landed back at Azelot safely. Fourteen photos had been taken by 2Lt Crossley. Oliphant although wounded stayed with the Squadron.

JOHN LESLIE MCINTYRE OLIPHANT was born on the 3rd of July 1899, in Hackney, East London. Shortly after the birth, the family moved to Southend-on Sea in Essex, where John lived until he enlisted in the 8th Battalion the Gordon Highlanders in 1915. Coming from a proud Scottish family, John served for two years in the trenches before transferring to the Royal Flying Corps. He started his training as a probationary observer 2Lt on the 5th of January 1918, and was posted to France on 6th August completing his training only two days previously. He joined 99 Squadron on the 9th of August, and survived a crash landing while on a practice formation flight with 2Lt Gillett. On the 20th of December 1918, he was transferred to 49 Squadron, also equipped with the DH9 until being put on the unemployment list in April 1919. Working as a clerk for a shipping company, he met and married his wife Violet Warr. When World War Two broke out, he became a Flight Lieutenant in the R.A.F. Regiment at Hurn, Dorset, while his wife served in the W.A.A.F. Returning to the shipping company after the war, he retired and died of a heart attack on 12th August 1985 having served his country well in both world wars.

Target: Railways and Factories at Frankfurt

25th September			Take Off: 09.55/10.05
110 Squadron			Returned: Unknown
Formation 1			
Capt A.Lindley	Lt C.R.Gross	F1030	P.O.W./P.O.W.
Lt J.W.L.McLaren-Pearson	2Lt H.Bell		
Lt H.J.Cockman	2Lt C.H.B.Stevenson	F1000	W.I.A./
2Lt A.Brandrick	Sgt T.W.Harman	F980	
Lt L.S.Brooke	2Lt A.Provan	F992	K.I.A./K.I.A.
Lt R.P.Brailli	Lt R.F.Casey	F993	/W.I.A.
2Lt N.N.Wardlaw	Sgt W.H.Neighbour	E8420	/K.I.A.
Formation 2			
Capt A.C.H.Groom	Capt G.E.Lange	F1005	
Lt C.B.E.Lloyd	2Lt H.J.C.Elwig	E9660	P.O.W./P.O.W.
Lt W.Armstrong	Sgt E.Ambler		
Sgt H.W.Tozer 57318	Sgt W.Platt 212033	E8422	K.I.A./K.I.A.
Capt A.G.Inglis	2Lt W.G.L.Bodley	F1010	
Lt R.C.Ripley	2Lt F.S.Towsler		

Bad weather had kept 110 Squadron out of the game since the losses on the 16th. Now back in action the target given was the factories and workshops at one of the main train stations in Frankfurt. Frankfurt had three main shunting stations. One was on the western edge of the town while the other two were on the eastern side. All three lay just north of a large canal which was fed from the River Rhine. Roughly a three hundred-mile round trip, this raid would push 110 Squadron all the way, that's if they were able to reach Frankfurt.

The weather was fine except for some haze and strong winds, as Captain Lindley led twelve DH9as over Lunéville, east of Nancy, before crossing the lines west of Blâmont. Once over the lines the formations were engaged west of Saverne at 11.15 at 16,500ft. Sergeant Harman fired two bursts at a Pfalz scout attacking from the left rear of the formation. This entered a spin and fell away out of control. Another claim was made near Saverne by 2Lt Bodley who fired at a Fokker DVII which also went down out of control. This Fokker had a black and white fuselage and a white rudder. The confusing point is that Bodley claimed the combat at 12.30 while Sgt Harman claimed his combat at 11.15, but what is consistent in the two combat reports is the altitude of 16,500ft. From reports it is hard to determine whether one DH9a went down during this engagement. Gefreiter Meyer claimed a DH9 at 11.15 south-east of Sarralbe which is just west of Saverne, obviously the time and location fit, as German time was now the same as British time. This claim was awarded and was his first victory of a final two.

The bombers continued on towards Kaiserslautern being continuously engaged the whole way. Reaching Oppenheim south of Frankfurt, the enemy aircraft were growing in number, and there were aircraft from both Kest 1b and Kest 9.

Over Frankfurt at 12.40, three 230lb and twenty-four 112lb bombs were dropped from 17,000ft. Four bursts were seen on the northern bank of the River Rhine, while three were seen to land in the river itself; two bursts were seen alongside the canal next to a bridge. Turning for home the Germans were still arriving and a running fight ensued. Lt Casey claimed two aircraft on the outward leg at Mannheim. The first was seen to go down out of control after three bursts from 150 yards, while the second fell vertically after a long burst, also from 150 yards. He was wounded over the target but sent an enemy scout diving down after a solitary burst, before claiming another aircraft which went spinning down for about 4,000ft. Sgt Harman claimed a Pfalz scout at Mannheim at 13.00, which went down in a vertical dive after three bursts were seen to hit its engine. These combat claims aside, 110 Squadron were in trouble with a strong wind blowing, pushing them eastwards. Leutnant Keisze of Kest 1b was awarded a DH4 near Mannheim at 14.30, while Vizefeldwebel Gott was awarded a DH4 at Darmstadt at 14.30 also. These two victories were most probably scored against 110 Squadron because no other DH Squadron went past Mannheim. 55 Squadron were the closest but only went as far as Kaiserslautern.

The wind seemed to be blowing the returning Squadron almost south along the Rhine. The remaining nine aircraft had a wounded pilot and observer amongst their number, while 2Lt Wardlaw had a dying if not already dead Sgt Neighbour in the back. Fuel was now becoming critical, especially for Lt Charles Bynon Ellis Lloyd who suddenly heard his engine cut out. Lloyd tried to land his machine in the northern Vosges, but crashed-landed as his badly shot up aileron controls finally gave way. (Lloyd later said that he got left behind when his engine started misfiring. He was pursued by five scouts, and after shooting one down, the rest flew off.) With a bruised forehead, cut lip and bleeding nose he tried to set fire to his machine with his observer 2Lt Elwig. With their machine only half burnt both men headed for the nearest woods and hid until dark. Once night had fallen both men drank, bathed their wounds in a brook, then walked for about three miles, still badly shaken from their ordeal. Sleeping until midday on the 26th, they set out to try and reach the lines. Hearing field guns and machine-gun fire, they hid and later crossed a valley at night divided by two roads and a single railway line. On the 27th, both totally exhausted, they surrendered to two German soldiers seen walking along a road. Taken to a nearby village they were given beer, coffee and food, then questioned. Travelling in an open cart, they were taken in the rain to Donon and then onto Sarrebourg. Here they were questioned by the Commanding Officer of Buhl aerodrome and told that Haigh and West had been killed, but that Brisbin and Lipsett were prisoners too. Moved to Strasbourg on the 28th, they were then taken to Karlsruhe on the 3rd of October, but there was no room. Both men were thus sent to Rastatt Fort where they remained until the Armistice. Lloyd, apart from the above, stated in his diary that they lost one machine on the way to the target, and that his engine started to run badly over the objective. He dropped his bombs and got left behind and was attacked by five 'Huns'. He claimed one enemy aircraft shot down and said the rest flew away before he crashed.

The likely victor of Lloyd and Elwig was Offizierstellvertreter Eduard Prime of Jasta 78b who claimed a DH4 at Bühl at 15.00 which was not confirmed. Other claims are those of Jasta 70. Vizefeldwebel Lemke at Bergzabern, east of Pirmasens for his second and last victory, and Vizefeldwebel Krist who also claimed a DH4 near Brumath just north of Strasbourg. Leutnant Anton Stephen of Jasta 70 shot down a third DH4 south of Alberschweiler which is near the lines at Blâmont.

Damage assessment after the war concluded that the observer reports were correct in that several bombs exploded by the canal causing damage to the Lock while one bomb caused slight damage to housing by the Wilhelms Bridge nearby. Other bombs damaged housing in the main thoroughfare the Kaiserstrasse, one person was killed and five injured. Morale amongst the middle classes of the town was severely shaken and calls were made to seek an agreement with the Allies about bombing towns.

No time is given for the remnants of 110 Squadron landing back at Azelot, but with a maximum endurance of five and three quarter hours, it must have been roughly 15.30. Lt Brailli landed at a French aerodrome, as did other aircraft which returned the following day. Whatever the time, 110 Squadron had had their baptism of fire with five killed, two wounded and four prisoners of war. Germany's Army may have been in retreat, but her Air Service was still second to none, and 110 Squadron would pay a still higher price in October.

Leonard Stopford Brooke, aged twenty-three from St. Johns Wood in London, was buried at Bergzabern in Germany. Brooke was on attachment from the K.R.R.C. Army Cyclist Corps. Alexander Yorker Provan, aged nineteen from Glasgow, in Lanarkshire, was buried alongside him. Sergeant Walter Herbert Neighbour from Finsbury Park in North London, was buried at the I.A.F. Cemetery at Charmes. Sergeant Herman William Tozer aged twenty-two from Bedminster, Bristol was buried at Sarralbe along with Sergeant Wilfred Platt, from Swinton, in Manchester. Three D.F.C.s were awarded for actions on this day. The citations read as follows:

Lt Robert Francis Casey (Royal Inniskilling Fusiliers)
D.F.C. gazetted 3rd December 1918

On 25th September the machine in which this officer was an observer on a long-distance bombing raid was attacked by a number of enemy aeroplanes. In the engagement Lieutenant Casey, having shot down two enemy scouts, was wounded in the thigh; he, however, continued the action until he fainted. At this time four enemy machines were firing at close range. The pilot roused Lieutenant Casey, who, with fine determination, brought his gun into action and shot down two of the attacking aeroplanes out of control; the remaining two then broke off the engagement. Exhausted by the effort, Lieutenant Casey again fainted, and landed in a French aerodrome. A very fine example of skill, courage and devotion to duty on the part of the Lieutenant.

Lt Herbert James Cockman
D.F.C. gazetted 3rd December 1918

On 25th September, when on a long-distance bombing raid, this officer performed very gallant service. Heavily attacked on the return journey, he was severely wounded, his left arm being shattered and his right leg hit. Owing to his wounds and loss of blood he was unable to control his machine, but by instructing his observer he was able to keep his formation until he crossed the lines. Owing to his condition he had the greatest difficulty in landing, and it was only due to his determined courage that he succeeded in doing so.

Capt Arthur Cecil Haywood Groom
D.F.C. gazetted 3rd December 1918

This officer led a formation in a successful long-distance bombing raid against an enemy town on 25th September; during the operation the leader of another formation was shot down, and this formation was broken up. Captain Groom rallied these machines and kept them together, displaying marked initiative and daring, for both on the outward and return journey, he was subject to incessant attacks by enemy formations. The skill and determination shown by this officer on this occasion calls for the highest praise, for it was largely due to his efforts that the objective was successfully bombed and that his formation and the remaining machines of the other returned safely in face of the hostile attacks.

Target: Triangle of Railways at Metz-Sablon

26th September				
104 Squadron			**Take Off:**	**14.20**
			Returned:	**16.40**
Formation 1				
Capt E.J.Garland	2Lt D.R.Hoon			
Lt A.C.D.Anderson	2Lt L.W.Launchbury			
2Lt C.Workman	Lt L.W.Chandler			
2Lt J.H.Cuthbertson	Sgt W.G.Steward		photo machine	
2Lt P.Hopkinson	2Lt E.D.Barnes		ret e/t	
2Lt H.L.Wren	2Lt J.T.White			
Formation 2				
Lt O.L.Malcolm	2Lt G.V.Harper	D7232	K.I.A./K.I.A.	
Lt E.A.Forbes	2Lt R.W.Lewin			
2Lt L.Hart	2Lt T.Bailey			
Lt J.R.Tansey	2Lt J.M.Scott			
2Lt S.T.Crowe	2Lt L.L.Penstone			
2Lt L.C.Pitts	2Lt P.Davey		ret e/t	
Spare aircraft			ret e/t	

Captain Ewart Garland would again lead with Lt Malcolm heading the second formation for a second time. It looks as if Malcolm was being groomed for promotion to become a flight leader. Fourteen DH9s took off and started to gain height. Engine trouble would claim three aircraft with Lt Hopkinson returning at 16.10 and 2Lt Pitts who also returned at 16.10. The two spare aircraft whose crews are not recorded as usual, both returned. One of these spare aircraft had engine trouble, while the other, according to Major Quinnell, landed back at Azelot its pilot thinking that his formation was complete. Whatever the reason 104 would cross the lines at Pont-à-Mousson with only ten aircraft for the short but hazardous route to Metz.

More archie was encountered than on more recent crossings but all eyes were on three enemy scouts who shadowed the formation to the target. Over Metz at 16.00 three 230lb, five 112lb and sixteen 25lb bombs were dropped from 11,000ft. The eastern side of the railway triangle was hit seven times while another bomb exploded inside the triangle. Three bursts were also seen on houses near the railway.

The three German scouts which had been stalking the formations were joined by two others, and all five started to attack. According to squadron reports, three of these were very persistent in their attacks, and it wasn't long before one DH9 was seen spinning down to crash near Verny. On board the spinning DH9 was Lt Malcolm and his observer 2Lt Harper who were both killed. The fight lasted until the lines which were re-crossed at Pont-à-Mousson. The remaining nine bombers landed back at Azelot after firing just over two thousand rounds at the Germans. No photos were taken although according to the report 2Lt Cuthbertson had a camera on his machine; 2Lt Pitts had the other photo machine.

Jasta 15 had again inflicted casualties on 104 Squadron with Malcolm and Harper falling under the guns of Leutnant Johannes Klein for his 16th and last victory of the war. Klein had claimed a Spad XIII also south of Metz but was not awarded this victory. Harper and Malcolm were contested by another Jasta 15 pilot, Leutnant Joachim Von Ziegesar. Ziegesar claimed his victory at Pont-à-Mousson, but this was unconfirmed. (Klein claimed his went down at Verny.) Ziegesar may not have been awarded the DH9, but he was awarded a Spad XIII at 15.40, at Pont-à-Mousson for his second of three victories. It looks as if Klein and Ziegesar were hunting together and were given one each.

George Victor Harper of New Bolsover, Chesterfield, was buried at Chambières in France. Orley Landon Malcolm was born on 2nd September 1895. Originally with the 5th Canadian Division, he transferred to the Royal Naval Air Service as a Probationary Flying Officer Mechanic. He was buried at Pullingen Cemetery. His home address during the war was given as 629 Christie Street, Toronto, Ontario, Canada.

Target: Railways at Audun-les-Romans

26th September			Take Off:	14.30
55 Squadron			Returned:	17.20
Formation 1				
Capt J.B.Fox	2Lt M.E.Barlow		photo machine	
2Lt G.Gorrill	2Lt F.N.Coxhill			
2Lt G.P.Dymonds	Sgt A.J.Cousins 220452			
Lt R.F.H.Norman	Sgt E.Clare		ret e/t	
Lt J.Cunliffe	2Lt W.H.S.Kingsland			
2Lt P.W.Scott	2Lt W.Ward		force-landed	
Formation 2				
Lt W.J.Pace	Sgt G.F.W.Adams 220131			
2Lt W.F.Smith	2Lt R.Dunn	A8060	crashed e/t	
Lt G.T.Richardson	2Lt J.H.Adams		ret e/t	
2Lt O.E.Miller	2Lt B.H.Du Feu			
Lt S.L.Dowswell	Sgt G.Howard		ret broken wire	
2Lt C.W.Trimnell	2Lt H.C.Allen		force-landed	

In support of the French 2nd and 4th Armies, and the American 1st Army, air attacks were ordered against vital rail links at very short notice. Both 99 and 104 Squadrons were assigned Metz, while 55 Squadron were ordered to attack Audun-les-Romans which was north-west of Metz and abeam Thionville.

Climbing away, Captain Fox led twelve DH4s west to cross the lines near Verdun. Engine trouble was to bring the twelve down to six within a very short time. Lt Dowswell was first to return with a broken wire shortly followed by Lt Norman with engine trouble; both made it back to Azelot. Engine trouble also forced 2Lt Smith out of formation and he crashed his machine at Mirecourt, but both men survived. Bettoncourt, home of 110 Squadron, was to receive two machines flown by 2Lt Scott and Trimnell who both landed on the aerodrome. Trimnell landed quite hard and damaged his undercarriage, his reason for landing being that his observer Allen was sick. There is no explanation given for Scott's return but the cause was probably engine trouble. The remaining seven continued on towards Verdun now in one formation. Lt Richardson soon left the formation with engine trouble and landed back at Azelot at 16.00.

The six remaining bombers crossed the lines at Vigneulles at 15,000ft, and immediately came under heavy and accurate archie. The single formation continued north-west and dropped five 230lb and two 112lb bombs from 15,000ft at 16.30, where five hits were observed on the western edge of the sidings. Heading south the bombers noticed six enemy aircraft taking off from Briey as they flew over Conflans and Thiaucourt and re-crossed the lines west of Pont-à-Mousson. All six landed back at Azelot. 2Lt Barlow had managed to take twelve photos despite the hazy conditions.

Note: Aircraft serial numbers were not recorded for this raid. DH4 A8060 was recorded as wrecked this day which makes it a strong choice for the aircraft crashed by Smith.

Target: Railways at Thionville
Secondary Target: Railways at Metz-Sablon

26th September			Take Off:	15.05
99 Squadron			Returned:	17.40
Formation 1				
Capt P.E.Welchman	2Lt T.H.Swann	B9347	D.O.W./P.O.W.	
2Lt S.McKeever	2Lt H.A.Boniface	B9366	W.I.A./Crash ldg	
Lt H.D.West	2Lt J.W.Howard	D544	/K.I.A.	
2Lt G.R.A.Dick	2Lt E.Smith	D7343	ret alt control	
2Lt C.R.G.Abrahams	2Lt C.H.Sharp	C6272	K.I.A./K.I.A.	
Formation 2				
Capt H.Sanders	2Lt G.M.Power	D1668	ret con rod broke	
2Lt L.G.Stern	2Lt F.O.Cook	D5573	K.I.A./K.I.A.	
2Lt H.E.King	Sgt S.Beswick	D3270	ret lost position	
Lt S.C.Gilbert	2Lt R.Buckby	E632	K.I.A./K.I.A.	
2Lt W.H.Gillett	2Lt H.Crossley	D3213	P.O.W./P.O.W.	

With short notice, 99 Squadron received orders to bomb the railways and bridges at Thionville, in support of the continuing land operations of the French and American armies near Verdun. Due to losses and accidents, there were only ten serviceable DH9s on Squadron strength. While there were an increasing number of DH9as there were still not enough to equip the whole Squadron for a raid. In amongst the two formations of five were some very inexperienced pilots and observers. Without twelve aircraft let alone the usual two spares, the formations could be in trouble if met by a sizeable hostile force, that's if engine trouble didn't beat the Germans to it. While climbing for height, Captain Sanders was forced to land with a broken connecting rod. The rest of the bombers formated with the first, while still climbing. Next to return was 2Lt King who was having trouble staying in formation, while 2Lt Dick followed shortly with a broken altimeter. The single formation of seven continued to climb before heading north to the lines at Pont-à-Mousson where they were accurately archied at 11,000ft.

The German Army may have been on the retreat but the German Air Service certainly wasn't as enemy scouts started to arrive in large numbers. Metz hadn't been reached before fifteen fighters attacked from underneath, while about ten to fifteen more attacked from the bomber formation's left flank. One DH9 fell, and Welchman decided it was impossible to reach Thionville, so dropped his ordnance on Metz followed by the other five. According to the combat report of 2Lt West, his observer 2Lt Howard shot down one enemy aircraft in flames and another out of control which dived for about 5,000ft. Howard was hit by machine-gun fire as the aircraft around him was literally shot to pieces. West reported seeing three DH9s with about thirty fighters around them, still with about six miles to run to the lines. West flew the only aircraft to make Azelot, but Howard unfortunately had been badly hit and died. Another badly shot up aircraft was that flown by 2Lt McKeever, who only just made the lines, landing his machine at Bratte near Pont-à-Mousson; his observer was okay but McKeever had been wounded in the foot. The rest of the formation had been lost with Abrahams, Sharp, Stern, Cook, Gilbert and Buckby all killed. Crossley had been slightly wounded and was sent to a prisoner of war camp along with his pilot 2Lt Gillett. Captain Welchman had been severely wounded in the lungs and was taken to the Lazarette Saint Clement Hospital at Metz. Shortly after the Armistice, Swann suffering from a severe leg wound, and Welchman, were both moved to the hospital at Charmes where Welchman later died. In all the Squadron lost five aircraft.

German claims for the downed bombers fell largely into two camps. Four to Jasta 77 and the other three to Jasta 4. Oberleutnant Ernst Udet, Commanding Officer of Jasta 4, claimed two DH9s near Metz, one at 17.10 and another at 17.20. The other claim made by Jasta 4 was by Leutnant Richard Kraut near Buch at 17.15. Jasta 77 claimed four DH9s in the Metz area between 17.25 and 17.30. These were by Leutnant Max Gossner, Offizierstellvertreter Bernard Ultsch, Vizefeldwebel Otto Agne and Vizefeldwebel Schäflein. Who actually got whom is hard to decipher, and the most likely claims have been listed here bearing in mind 104 Squadron also lost one. Jasta 77 received a casualty in Vizefeldwebel Robert Mossbacher who was wounded in action. What is certain is that one of 99 Squadron's observers hit Udet in the thigh, putting the highest scoring German ace still alive with sixty-two victories out of the war. Also out of the war until the 9th of October was 99 Squadron who had suffered seven men killed in action, five wounded in action, and eight men taken prisoner of war in the month of September, a black September indeed.

James William Howard, aged twenty-two from Southampton, was buried in the I.A.F. Cemetery at Charmes. Cecil Robert George Abrahams, aged twenty-three from Sandy, in Bedfordshire, was buried at Chambières. Alongside him was his observer Christopher Harold Sharp, aged twenty-seven of the 3rd Norfolk Regiment. Leopold Grahame Stern, from Henfield, in Sussex was only eighteen when buried alongside his observer Frederick Oliver Cook, aged twenty-three, from Long Eaton near Nottingham. Both men were buried at Chambières with Abrahams and Sharp. Stanley Claude Gilbert was buried at Raffin Cemetery in France along with his observer, Ralph Buckby. William Henry Charles Gillett was born 8th October 1898. He became a 2Lt on 23rd February 1918 and joined 99 Squadron straight from No.3 Flight School on 16th August 1918. He was repatriated on 13th December 1918 and demobilised on 24th February 1919. Between October 1912 and February 1917 he worked as a clerk at Curtis & Son, an estate agents. The family address during the war was Hillsboro Street, Clement Road, Bournemouth.

PATRICK ELIOT WELCHMAN was born on 17th March 1895, to Eliot and Caroline Welchman at Appleton Cottage, Ickenham, Middlesex. Educated at King's School Canterbury, he joined the King's Own Scottish Borderers. He was awarded the Military Cross on 13th October 1915, and was Mentioned in Despatches a month later. As a 2nd Lieutenant in January 1916, he was again Mentioned in Despatches. Joining the Royal Flying Corps he became an observer with 8 Squadron flying during the battles of the Somme and Ancre. He was wounded on 26th September 1916 but stayed with his Squadron, and returned to Home Establishment on 4th June 1917. On 1st April 1918 he was promoted to Lieutenant and with his two wings now on his chest, joined 55 Squadron on 3rd June 1918 as a pilot. He was promoted to Captain on 13th September 1918 and moved hangars to 99 Squadron on the same day. Awarded the Distinguished Flying Cross on 21st September 1918, he died of his wounds on 29th November 1918. His address during the war was given as 61 Primrose Hill Mansions, Battersea Park, London.

HAROLD CROSSLEY was born on 5th March 1898. He was an electrical engineer at Drakes Ltd in Halifax, before the war started. Joining as a cadet, he commenced his training at No.1 School of Aeronautics on 10th May 1918. From here he went to Eastchurch on 18th June, and then to No. 1 School of Aerial Gunnery on 22nd July; he also received his solitary wing this day. He joined 99 on 4th August and when shot down, was imprisoned at Karlsruhe. He was repatriated on 20th November. His address while serving was 3 Falcon Street, Halifax.

Whilst researching this book the author found a transcript of an interview between Welchman, and Major W.Wood-Shorten of the R.A.M.C. Major Wood-Shorten was a Surgical Specialist with No.42 Stationery Hospital I.F. at Charmes. The letter reads word for word as Welchman told his story on the 19th of November when he was first admitted.

Whilst flying over the German lines 26th September 1918 I was wounded and brought down. Taken to the German Hospital at Metz, where I was put in a ward with a number of dying other Ranks. For four days I received no attention, during which time blood from my wound was soaking through the bed and on to the floor. On the fifth day they found me still alive and removed me to the Officer's ward. This transfer was carried out by two Russian Orderlies one of whom dropped his end of the stretcher, causing me agonising pain and then he burst into laughter. On admission to the Officer's Ward a German surgeon put a tube into the wound in my left armpit. With the exception of being dressed more or less daily, nothing more was done for me, from that date until about 9th November 1918, beyond doping me with morphia to keep me quiet and to save them the trouble of operating on me. My dressings were done in a separate room away from the ward. Whilst being taken there and especially during the dressing I used to get exceedingly cold. From the date of admission I kept worrying them to X-ray me and to operate on me, but the only success I met with was of getting doped with morphia. Eventually after more persuasion they X-rayed me and shortly afterwards somewhere about the 9th November they operated on me, removing portions of two ribs low down on the left side of my chest without the use of any anaesthetics. During this operation they drained away pints of pus which I felt had been there for some considerable time. The pain during the operation nearly drove me mad. The food supplied me consisted mainly of black bread and of this I complained bitterly but with no avail.

Welchman died on 29th November from septic poisoning following prolonged absorption of pus. The wound was made from an explosive bullet entering in the left chest. From the interview he gave, it would seem better care early on may have saved his life. He was laid to rest with many of his colleagues in the I.A.F. Cemetery at Charmes.

CHAPTER 6

OPERATIONS – OCTOBER 1918

Target: Railways at Köln (Cologne)
Secondary Target: Railways at Treves

1st October			Take Off:	10.15/15
110 Squadron			Returned:	Unknown

Formation 1

Capt E.Windover	2Lt A.R.Wylde	F1023
Lt J.W.L.McLaren-Pearson	2Lt H.Bell	F1029
Lt W.Armstrong	Sgt E.Ambler	F1011
Lt R.C.Ripley	2Lt F.S.Towsler	E5421
Lt A.R.Macdonald	Lt A.R.Tarras	F1028
2Lt A.Brandrick	Sgt F.Quilter	F980

Formation 2

Maj L.G.S.Reynolds	Capt J.D.Thomson	F983
Capt A.G.Inglis	2Lt W.G.L.Bodley	F1010
Lt K.B.Wilkinson	2Lt B.Troth	E8434
Lt G.T.Griffith	2Lt A.G.Braham	F978
2Lt R.D.V.Howard	2Lt G.Parker	F985
Lt S.B.Bradley	Sgt A.H.Banks 233777	F995

Despite their decimation on 25th September, 110 Squadron were back in action and tasked with bombing long-range targets again. Railway junctions of importance like those at Ehrang, and Coblenz, if attacked, would do more damage to the German war effort. Cologne also possessed railway targets, but was attacked more to hit German morale. If Cologne could not be reached however, one of these vital rail junctions would be used as a secondary target. Captain Windover led the first formation of six away at 10.10 followed by Major Reynolds five minutes later. The weather on this part of the front was fine except for large banks of clouds between 8-10,000 feet. Both groups gained the necessary height before heading out for the lines.

Crossing over, archie was quiet as the pilots looked for their targets while heading north over the clouds. It looks as if both formations were working independently in finding their targets. The first formation returned without dropping their bombs, being unable to find a target through the clouds. The second formation spotted Treves through a gap in the clouds, and dropped one 230lb and thirteen 112lb bombs at 12.30, but no observations were reported due to the cloud cover. All machines returned to Bettoncourt, some however had to land outside the aerodrome to locate themselves, before taking off again and landing at the airfield.

JAMES DAVIDSON THOMSON was born on 5th October 1892 to Scottish parents, whose address during the war was 235 Great Western Road, Aberdeen, Scotland. His home address was 380 Mountain Avenue, Winnipeg, Canada. He was working as an accountant in Winnipeg between 1912 and 1914, so it looks like he joined up on the outbreak of war. This was his last raid for 110 Squadron as he was admitted to the 8th Canadian Hospital on 3rd October 1918. He then transferred to Home Establishment on 7th November, probably due to illness. Records state he was a Captain in the Canadian Army Service Corps, Canadian Expeditionary Force before joining the R.A.F.

Target: Triangle of Railways at Metz-Sablon

5th October		Take Off:	07.45
104 Squadron		**Returned:**	**09.55**

Formation 1

Capt R.J.Gammon	Lt P.E.Appleby
2Lt W.S.Greenwood	2Lt F.W.Aldridge
Lt J.W.Richards	2Lt A.M.Mitchell
Lt H.L.Wren	2Lt J.T.White
2Lt I.L.R.Large	Sgt W.H.Ball
2Lt S.T.Crowe	2Lt A.H.Penstone

Formation 2

Capt E.J.Garland	2Lt W.E.Bottrill
2Lt B.F.Ross	Lt L.W.Launchbury
2Lt P.Hopkinson	2Lt E.D.Barnes
2Lt J.N.Ogilvie	Sgt W.G.Steward
2Lt C.Workman	Lt L.R.Chandler
2Lt L.Hart	2Lt P.Davey

With good conditions in the morning, 104 took off fourteen strong for their first raid of the month to the large triangle of railways at Metz. Captains Gammon and Garland led the two formations as they climbed over Azelot and then headed out for the lines at Nomeny. As the lines approached the two spare machines were signalled to leave as both groups remained complete.

A moderate amount of archie greeted the bombers as they crossed over to the west of Nomeny at 12,000ft. A direct course was flown to Metz where the bombers arrived overhead at 09.25. Five 230lb and fourteen 112lb bombs headed down as the crews waited for any enemy aircraft to arrive. None were seen but two bombs were observed exploding in the centre of the triangle, two at the northern apex of the triangle and one in the south-eastern corner. Two further explosions were seen to the west of the triangle on double tracks. There were five trains below, a couple on the move, but from the position of the bursts on the lines it looked impossible now for the trains to leave. A moderate amount of archie kept on around them as the twelve bombers turned for home.

Heading south towards the lines, four enemy aircraft were seen very low near Ars, but no interception was made and they all returned safely to Azelot. No photos were taken on this raid as the photographic machine was deemed unflyable at the last minute and another without a camera was used. The hits reported by the observers of 104 rang true. Investigations after the war revealed that several tracks and goods wagons were badly damaged, and that rail traffic was suspended for twenty-four hours; the local water supply was also damaged and had to be turned off for four hours. A single bomb had exploded on the western coal depot, and some in civilians areas. Twelve people were killed and twenty-four injured.

Target: Factories at Köln (Cologne)
Secondary Target: Kaiserslautern

5th October			Take Off:	11.15/25
110 Squadron			**Returned:**	**Unknown**

Formation 1

Capt E.Windover	2Lt A.R.Wylde	F1023	
Lt J.W.L.McLaren-Pearson	2Lt H.Bell	F1029	
2Lt N.N.Wardlaw	2Lt C.J.H.May	F1036	/W.I.A.
Lt R.P.Brailli	2Lt C.H.B.Stevenson	F993	
2Lt D.P.Davies	2Lt H.M.Speagell	E8439	P.O.W./P.O.W.
2Lt A.Brandrick	2Lt H.C.Eyre	F980	P.O.W./K.I.A.
2Lt A.R.S.Proctor	Sgt F.Quilter	F1027	

Formation 2

Capt A.C.H.Groom	Capt G.E.Lange	F1005	
Lt W.Armstrong	Sgt W.G.Ambler	F1011	
Capt A.G.Inglis	2Lt W.G.L.Bodley	F1010	P.O.W./P.O.W.

2Lt D.P.Jones	Lt G.H.Tarras	F1028	
2Lt P.King	2Lt R.G.Vernon	F1021	
Lt R.C.P.Ripley	2Lt F.S.Towler	E8421	K.I.A./K.I.A.

Cologne (or Köln) was the target, with the railways at Coblenz or Ehrang as alternatives. The weather was very hazy giving poor visibility as the thirteen aircraft took off, and gained height before heading for the lines.

Captain Windover led the two formations over the lines north of Nancy, and headed north towards Treves. The weather conditions were worsening all the time, and landmarks were hard to spot as the thirteen bombers continued northwards keeping to the west of Treves. Being unable to see any noticeable landmarks Captain Windover turned the two formations east and headed towards Kaiserslautern. Another reason for the alternative target was the presence of enemy aircraft despite 110 operating at 17,000ft.

The aircraft were Fokker DVIIs, mostly painted shades of grey with white tails according to the observers who would soon stop looking, and start firing, as they started to engage. Aerial combat is confusing at the best of times, especially to those involved. Working out who was firing at what is just as confusing for any researcher. The first big engagement took place just as the formations left Treves or there about and headed east for Kaiserslautern. The number of fighters is not recorded, but from combat reports it seems to be three around Treves, and growing in number the further west the two formations ventured. Sergeant Quilter fired two bursts from 200 yards, at one of these which was attacking from his right hand side. He saw his tracers hit the engine of this scout, and watched as it started to emit black smoke. Another scout was claimed between Treves and Kaiserslautern by 2Lt Vernon, who fired a long burst at a dark grey Fokker and watched as it glided away to below three thousand feet, where it was lost to view. Captain Groom claimed a white-tailed Fokker DVII at 13.30 which was trying to attack the first formation. Groom lined up behind the scout and fired twenty-five rounds of Vickers from 150 yards. The Fokker dropped out of the fight according to Groom, and it was apparently leading the German formation.

While these combats were taking place the two formations were nearing Kaiserslautern which they finally reached about 14.00. From 17,000ft one 230lb and seventeen 112lb bombs were dropped but no observations were observed due to more fighters arriving. Looking at the amount of ordnance dropped it would seem that the four aircraft lost were shot down before Kaiserslautern was reached. Overhead the target, Sergeant Ambler fired four, eight-round bursts at an enemy scout which was flying towards a DH9a. This was apparently hit in the engine and descended in a left hand spin for three thousand feet and was lost to sight; this combat was timed at 14.00. Another scout was claimed five minutes later by 2Lt Bell who fired a long burst from 100 yards, the enemy machine dropped its nose and entered a spin emitting smoke and was lost to sight approximately a thousand feet below the engagement. Also claiming a Fokker at 14.15 was 2Lt Wylde. This was painted grey with a white tail, and was firing at the formation from the left and below. Wylde fired seventy-five rounds from 150 yards and saw them enter the machine between the cockpit and the engine, and he watched for one minute as it spun away below.

The formations then headed south from Kaiserslautern and flew over Pirmasens, From here according to bomb raid reports, they flew over Buhl aerodrome, before again heading west over Saverne and re-crossing the lines at Badonviller. The flight over Buhl may have been for reconnaissance purposes.

Apart from the four aircraft lost, 2Lt May was wounded and saw no further action with 110 Squadron. This was also the last raid with 110 for Captain Lange. His home address was given as Port of Spain, Trinidad, and he proceeded overseas with the British West Indian Regiment. He was hospitalised twice on the 16th and 22nd of October.

The most likely victors over the four bombers are Jasta 3, and Kest 3, both operating out of the airfield at Morchingen. Leutnant Georg Weiner claimed a DH9a at Heimbach for his ninth and last victory of the war. Weiner who was the Commanding Officer of Jasta 3 at this time now had five I.A.F. daylight bombers to his credit. He had previously served with Kest 3 where he shot down two Spads, and before that Jasta 20, with whom he shot down a Nieuport. Another bomber fell to Leutnant Franz Bacher who claimed a DH9a down at Leitweiler for his third and last victory of the war. The third member of Jasta 3 to make a kill was Vizefeldwebel Rudolf Kühne who shot down a DH9 at Ekenbach for his one and only victory. Senior Unteroffizier Hoffmann of Kest 3 claimed a DH9a at Trippstadt for his second and last victory of the war. Hugh Clement Eyre, aged nineteen from Sidcup in Kent, was buried in Cologne. Ripley and Towler were both buried at Niederzwehren in Germany. Towler was only eighteen, and came from Cathays, near Cardiff, in Glamorgan.

In six operations over the lines, 110 Squadron had suffered eight men killed in action, four wounded and thirteen as prisoners of war, twenty-five casualties in all and the worst was yet to come. As good an aircraft as the DH9a was, this just wasn't enough, and new inexperienced crews would soon fill the cockpits of replacement aircraft, and unfortunately suffer the same fate as their predecessors.

CAPTAIN ANDREW GLOVER INGLIS was born on 7th October 1894. The family address during the war was 16 Sefton Drive, Liverpool. Before the war, Inglis worked as an apprentice at the East India Company, Tower Buildings, Haley Street, Liverpool. Records appear to suggest he signed up on October 11th 1914 but no record of his aviation career can be found until he joined the No 1 School of Aerial Gunnery. He was repatriated on 13th December 1918.

Target: Triangle of Railways at Metz-Sablon

9th October		Take Off:	07.55
104 Squadron		**Returned:**	**09.45**

Formation 1

Capt R.J.Gammon	Lt P.E.Appleby	
2Lt I.L.R.Large	Sgt W.H.Ball	
Lt H.L.Wren	2Lt J.T.White	
2Lt S.T.Crowe	2Lt A.H.Penstone	photo machine
Lt W.S.Greenwood	2Lt F.W.Aldridge	
Lt J.W.Richards	2Lt A.M.Mitchell	
Lt J.R.Tansey	2Lt J.M.Scott	

Formation 2

Lt B.H.Stretton	2Lt H.Grieve	
2Lt L.Hart	2Lt R.D.Vaughn	
2Lt R.F.Lynch	2Lt H.Bridger	
2Lt H.D.Arnott	2Lt H.Alexander	
2Lt L.C.Pitts	2Lt E.G.Stevens	
Lt E.A.Forbes	2Lt L.G.Best	photo machine

Azelot was alive with two squadrons of DH9s being prepared for a large raid on Metz. Although both squadrons were hitting the same target it was not a combined raid which was probably a good idea due to the difficulties in the past. Captain Gammon would again have the lead with Lt Stretton leading the second bunch. Fourteen aircraft took off with two spares in two groups of seven, gained height and headed for the lines at Cheminot. The spare aircraft were signalled away but Lt Tansey stayed with the first formation and crossed the lines, which received moderate archie from below.

Enemy aircraft were not encountered until over the target. The five fighters were seen below them but climbing steeply. Despite their efforts the fighters could only watch as 104 dropped five 230lb, and sixteen 112lb bombs from 11,500ft at 09.25. Sighting by Captain Gammon was again superb with fourteen bursts seen in and around the triangle. One 230lb bomb was observed to hit two trains in the south-eastern corner, while six exploded in the sidings. A solitary burst was recorded on the railway workshops while another was seen on the railway lines leading west from the triangle. Five other bursts were scattered within the triangle.

The two formations left the target area keeping an eye on the five fighters still climbing up to their altitude. As the lines were reached the five scouts started an exchange of fire from long range, and 104 replied with a thousand rounds of Lewis but neither side claimed any hits. All thirteen aircraft landed back at Azelot complete with twenty-four photos. Reports were also made to the Intelligence Officer regarding large train movements at Verny. German reports are not quite as enthusiastic recording a railway line near the goods station damaged, as well as some private property.

Target: Triangle of Railways at Metz-Sablon

9th October		Take Off:	07.55
99 Squadron		**Returned:**	**09.45**

Formation 1

Capt W.G.Stevenson	Sgt J.Jones	
Lt H.S.H.Read	2Lt W.Glew	force-landed e/t

2Lt V.C.Varcoe	2Lt V.J.Fontannaz
2Lt D.F.Brooks	2Lt R.Henderson
2Lt E.A.Bowyer	Sgt P.A.Cuka
2Lt L.B.Duggan	2Lt W.J.Tremellen

Formation 2

Capt H.Sanders	2Lt G.M.Power
2Lt E.J.Kidder	2Lt C.D.Clarke
2Lt W.Hodder	2Lt J.K.Hall
2Lt E.C.Brown	Lt T.Llewellyn
2Lt A.R.Collis	2Lt C.B.Fairhurst
2Lt G.R.A.Dick	Sgt S.Beswick

After several days of bad weather, 99 Squadron were back in action after the disastrous losses of 26th September. Captain Thom had taken command of the Squadron on the 27th after recovering from influenza, as Major Pattinson was still in charge of the 41st Wing in the absence of Colonel Baldwin who had been transferred to Home Establishment. The Squadron had taken delivery of more DH9s as replacements, but the new DH9a which they longed for was still in short supply. This was to be a short hop over the lines to Metz-Sablon for 99 Squadron and their inexperienced crews, many of whom were on their first operational raid.

All twelve machines took off and started to gain height. Lt Read experienced an engine failure and was immediately forced to land. The remaining eleven bombers headed north to the lines were they crossed under heavy and accurate archie. Following the River Moselle's eastern bank they arrived over Metz at 09.25. From 11,500ft, six 230lb and ten 112lb bombs fell towards the triangle of railways below. The archie over Metz was heavy and observers reported seeing a smoke screen over the target. The smoke screen may well have been caused by 104 Squadron who were also hitting this target at approximately 09.25. Who actually got there first is not certain but observers claimed four bursts on the triangle, with three others south-east and four south-west of it.

Seven enemy aircraft appeared well below the formation as they turned for home, and despite the bad visibility twenty-eight photos were taken to and from the target area. All eleven machines returned to Azelot, with the new crews having been 'blooded'.

Note: During October, 99 Squadron changed from using a squadron record book, and instead filled out the bomb raid report forms as used by 55, 104 and 110. On these forms serial numbers of aircraft were not recorded next to the relevant crew. Serial numbers were only listed on a second page if an aircraft was missing.

Reconnaissance

10th October			Take Off:	12.10
55 Squadron			Returned:	16.35
Lt W.G.Braid	2Lt J.D.Evans	D8386		

Crossed lines at Tahure, flew over Vouzières to Mezières, where twenty-four photos plates were taken. Returned east of outward course and re-crossed lines at Grand-Pré. Forty-six plates taken in all. This reconnaissance was done at 19,000ft.

Reconnaissance

10th October			Take Off:	12.10
55 Squadron			Returned:	16.40
Capt W.J.Pace	2Lt C.W.Clutsom	A7750		

Crossed lines at Pont-à-Mousson and followed the Moselle river to Metz and Thionville. Then flew west over haze towards Longuyon which could not be located, steered south-west and re-crossed the lines at Etain. Plates were exposed over Frescaty and Metz, train movement was reported as normal. This reconnaissance was carried out at 20,000ft and eight plates were taken.

Reconnaissance

10th October			Take Off:	12.20
55 Squadron			Returned:	16.15
Lt D.J.Waterous	Sgt G.Howard	A7933		

Crossed lines at Thiaucourt, and flew over Puzieux, Mars-la-Tour to Conflans and then on to Briey aerodrome, north-west of Briey covered in thick haze. No train movement reported and sidings were said to be empty. This reconnaissance was carried out at 21,000ft and twenty-four plates were taken.

Target: Triangle of Railways at Metz-Sablon

10th October		Take Off:	12.45
104 Squadron		Returned:	15.00

Formation 1

Capt E.J.Garland	2Lt W.E.Bottrill
2Lt P.Hopkinson	2Lt E.D.Barnes
2Lt B.S.Case	2Lt H.Bridger
2Lt C.Workman	Lt L.R.Chandler
2Lt S.T.Crowe	2Lt A.H.Penstone
2Lt J.N.Ogilvie	Sgt W.G.Steward

Formation 2

Lt B.H.Stretton	2Lt H.Grieve
Lt J.R.Tansey	2Lt J.M.Scott
Lt E.A.Forbes	2Lt L.G.Best
2Lt H.D.Arnott	2Lt H.Alexander
2Lt L.Hart	2Lt R.D.Vaughn
2Lt L.C.Pitts	2Lt E.G.Stevens

Again 104 hit Metz railway along with its sister Squadron, No. 99, but it would still not be a combined raid. Captain Garland led out fourteen aircraft which took off five minutes before 99 got back. Climbing to altitude one of the spare aircraft was forced to return with a big end gone leaving the remaining thirteen to head for the lines near Pont-à-Mousson. At the lines the spare machine was signalled away and the twelve crossed. Only a token gesture from German anti-aircraft gunners was seen as the bombers continued straight to Metz.

Over the target at 14.20, six 230lb and twelve 112lb bombs were dropped from 11,500ft all seeming to explode within the triangle. The principal station received a hit, while one 230lb bomb burst on the bridge crossing the railway at the western corner. Four bursts were observed on the western side and three within the triangle; the bridge which was hit was reported as destroyed. Turning for home, six enemy scouts were seen again in the climb trying to intercept the bombers before they re-crossed the lines.

Reaching Verny the fighters eventually caught up but could only fire from long range. Neither side claimed a victory and all twelve bombers landed back at Azelot complete with eighteen photos. The result according to German reports was traffic on one track suspended for an hour, and a goods truck and the glass roof on the goods shed badly damaged.

Leading this raid was the experienced EWART JAMES GARLAND, born in Canada of an Irish father and English mother. The family moved to Melbourne, Australia, where his father was in charge of the Australian branch of the Dunlop Rubber Company. Ewart sheep farmed in Queensland before joining the Royal Flying Corps in September 1915. As a member of the Inns of Court O.T.C., he reported at Oxford on 16 April 1916 for flight training. On the 6th of July he acquired his wings, and joined 10 Squadron on 10th July at Béthune where he became C Flight Commander at the age of twenty. He served with 10 Squadron until July 1917 at which time he was posted to Home Establishment. While serving with 10 Squadron, Garland was Mentioned in Despatches after a solitary bomb raid and artillery shoot, on 7th February. Flying at 3,000ft on a clear and frosty night, he dropped two 112lb bombs on an enemy gun position. Fired at, he climbed to 4,000ft where he directed a 6" battery to fire on the enemy gun position at La Bassée. Due to the ground being covered in snow, Garland could see the artillery shells burst, and reconnaissance photos the following day confirmed the shoot had been successful. Congratulations from Haig and Trenchard followed, with recommendations for an award. Mentioned in Despatches is all Garland got for this unique achievement. After being an instructor at Andover he flew down to Nancy in a Handley Page on 24th August 1918 to join 104 Squadron. While flying during the war he always kept a pocket copy of Shakespeare's works to occupy him, should he be shot down and made prisoner of war.

After the war he was lent a flat in Queen's Gate by Sir Arthur du Cross the then Chairman of the Dunlop Rubber Company. He returned to Brighton, near Melbourne, when news of his father's illness reached him and went back to England where he heard of his father's death and took up a trainee post with Dunlop in Birmingham as a rep. He was soon moved to London where he rubbed shoulders within influential circles; one of his close friends was John Betjeman the Poet Laureate. He married the lady Editor of *Vogue* and they lived in a flat in Brameron Street, Chelsea. The marriage only lasted eighteen months and he later married his second wife Rosalind and moved to Brasted Chart, in Westerham, Kent, in 1938. After WW2 he moved to Brockenhurst in Hampshire where he continued to work for Dunlop. Like many of his generation after the Great War, he never piloted an aircraft again after that conflict.

Target: Triangle of Railways at Metz-Sablon

10th October			Take Off:	12.50
99 Squadron			Returned:	14.40
Formation 1				
Capt W.D.Thom	2Lt M.E.R.Jarvis	D527	/W.I.A.	
2Lt E.J.Kidder	2Lt C.D.Clarke			
2Lt W.Hodder	2Lt J.K.Hall			
2Lt L.B.Duggan	2Lt W.J.Tremellen			
2Lt A.R.Collis	2Lt C.B.Fairhurst		ret e/t	
2Lt L.V.Russell	Sgt S.Beswick			
Formation 2				
Capt W.G.Stevenson	Sgt J.Jones			
2Lt L.S.Springett	2Lt J.C.Barns		ret e/t	
Lt H.S.H.Read	2Lt W.Glew			
2Lt D.F.Brooks	2Lt R.Henderson		ret e/t	
2Lt V.C.Varcoe	2Lt V.J.Fontannaz			
2Lt E.A.Bowyer	Sgt P.A.Cuka		ret e/t	

Once again railways supplying the front were targeted by the DH9s of 99 and 104 Squadrons. Although they would both be hitting the same target, as before it would not be a joint raid. Captain Thom led twelve aircraft to gain height before setting out north towards the lines. Engine trouble which had been virtually non-existent the day before now reared its ugly head and sent four aircraft home. First was 2Lt Springett at 13.10 followed five minutes later by 2Lt Collis. The ten aircraft continued towards the lines where 2Lt Bowyer turned for home followed by 2Lt Brooks.

Crossing the lines at 11,000ft, the eight remaining machines were archied as they followed the Moselle river to Metz. Arriving over Metz at 14.20, five 230lb and six 112lb bombs were dropped as the anti-aircraft fire started to increase. Captain Thom had a narrow escape with a close burst, his observer Jarvis unfortunately being hit and wounded. The machines turned for home and the crews kept their eyes on five enemy aircraft which were lurking to the west of Metz, but no engagement took place and all eight machines landed safely back at Azelot.

Observers reported five explosions on the railway triangle, two on a factory and one on a barracks south-west of the triangle, plus one solitary burst to the south-east. In all sixteen photos were taken and many crews had now got their second raid under their belts. (See page 160 for the damage sustained according to German records.) A bomb exploded outside the army clothing depot causing slight damage. Metz had been receiving attention from night raiders in an all-round attempt at shutting down this vital supply network.

A Handley Page of 216 Squadron had dropped its bombs on the town and one had detonated the powder magazine on Wiese Island, starting a fire which was smouldering for four days. Damage indeed, but whatever the squadrons tried or hit, they could never seem to close down totally this large rail depot so vital to the German war effort.

Note: Aircraft serial numbers are not recorded.

Target: Frescaty Aerodrome

15th October		**Take Off:**	**09.50**
55 Squadron		**Returned:**	**10.55**
Formation 1			
Capt D.R.G.Mackay	2Lt L.J.B.Ward		

After the severe losses at the end of September, 55 Squadron had started to train replacement pilots and observers. A raid on 1st October with 104 Squadron was washed out due to the weather, and three further days of bad weather ensued. Accidents were happening all the time during training. 2Lt F.Seddon and 2Lt R.Kelley were both injured in a training flight on the 6th. More bad weather kept 55 on the ground until the 15th as a solo raid was planned by the experienced crew of 'Jock' Mackay and his observer 2Lt Ward.

Taking off, Mackay flew north from Azelot at about 800ft and picked up the River Moselle which he followed to Nancy. Following the river to the lines he came under accurate archie as he crossed and made his way east of Vittonville. Encountering machine-gun and small arms fire he descended lower in order to find the River Moselle again as the cloud base was now only fifty feet above the tree tops. Following the river he came to the bridge at Ars where the clouds rose again to about 800ft. The railway was followed to the north of Frescaty aerodrome where Mackay throttled back his engine and dove towards it.

Twenty to thirty men were standing near the large Zeppelin hangar on the airfield, oblivious to the imminent danger. They probably mistook Mackay for one of their own. Level with the top of the Zeppelin hangar, and about 30 yards from it, Mackay dropped the first of his two 112lb bombs. Zooming up and making for one of the large hangars on the eastern side of the airfield near the Fort, Mackay dropped his second bomb which entered the hangar through the roof and exploded within. Not finished, Mackay dived and fired at men and horses around the dump on the southern side of the aerodrome; two horses were hit and the rest stampeded.

Running for the lines, Mackay flew a compass course to the River Moselle near Arnaville between 1,000 and 2,500 feet and followed it to the lines. Flying along at 115mph he found it easier to avoid the machine-gun fire as he watched the tracer arcing up to greet him. Large amounts of rifle fire were encountered but much of this was inaccurate. Archie at the lines was a more serious threat but Mackay crossed and followed the river south to Nancy and home.

Mackay wrote at the end of his bomb raid report: "In my opinion only knowledge of the ground made it possible to find the way. I would not advise pilots who do not know the district thoroughly to attempt similar raids". What is interesting is that six copies were ordered to be made, and circulated to the other squadrons. The part quoted above was marked in brackets and was to be left out. Squadron rivalry perhaps or just a case of geeing up the squadrons to bomb despite the weather. Mackay's outstanding raid did not go unnoticed and he was awarded the Distinguished Flying Cross, the citation reading as follows:

Captain Duncan Ronald Gordon Mackay
D.F.C. gazetted 3rd December 1918

An Officer of conspicuous ability and determination, who, during the last four months of the fighting, has taken part in twenty-two bomb raids and three photo reconnaissances, acting as leader on seven occasions. On 15th October he volunteered to carry out a lone bombing attack on an enemy aerodrome; low cloud and mist compelled him to fly at low altitudes varying from 800 to a 1,000ft. Having successfully reached his objective, he obtained two direct hits from a height of forty feet, and stampeded horses with machine-gun fire. The cool courage and marked initiative shown by Captain Mackay in this operation merits high praise.

Target: Triangle of Railways at Metz-Sablon

18th October		**Take Off:**	**13.45**
104 Squadron		**Returned:**	**16.15**
Formation 1			
Capt R.J.Gammon	2Lt H.Grieve		

Lt J.W.Richards	2Lt A.M.Mitchell	D530	/W.I.A.
Lt W.S.Greenwood	2Lt F.W.Aldridge		
Lt H.L.Wren	2Lt J.T.White		photo machine
2Lt I.L.R.Large	Sgt W.H.Ball		
2Lt S.T.Crowe	2Lt A.H.Penstone	D5643	force-landed
2Lt L.C.Pitts	2Lt P.Davey		

Formation 2

Capt E.J.Garland	2Lt W.E.Bottrill		
2Lt B.S.Case	2Lt H.Bridger		
2Lt J.N.Ogilvie	Sgt W.G.Steward		
2Lt P.Hopkinson	2Lt E.D.Barnes		
2Lt C.Workman	2Lt A.B.Rattray		
2Lt H.D.Arnott	2Lt R.D.Vaughn		photo machine

Leaving before 99 Squadron who were also hitting Metz, 104 climbed away led by Captain Gammon. The weather was fair, but there were large banks of cloud to contend with as the machines struggled for height and formation. All engines were running well as the thirteen headed for the lines near Chambley. The spare flown by 2Lt Pitts did not abort, crossing over the lines with the others at 12,000ft and was now amongst a very heavy and accurate barrage which was putting holes in a lot of machines. The two formations flew on towards Metz which was already visible through a gap in the clouds. When nearly overhead at 15.35, the target had disappeared again behind a cloud but Gammon gave the signal and five 230lb and sixteen 112lb bombs were dropped. Observing through a gap in the cloud, five explosions were seen on the railway workshop to the west of the triangle and three within it. More archie greeted the bombers as they left the target area, 2Lt Andrew McGregor Mitchell receiving a lump of anti-aircraft shell in his left elbow. Mitchell kept his machine going and re-crossed the lines with the rest.

Quite a few machines were badly damaged by archie; one flown by 2Lt Crowe had to put down south-west of Flirey, wrecking the machine. Shell splinters had smashed his radiator but both he and his observer were unscathed and walked away from the wreck, on the allied side. No enemy aircraft were seen and Lt Vaughn and 2Lt White between them took eighteen photos.

Reconnaissance

18th October			**Take Off:**	**13.45**
110 Squadron			**Returned:**	**16.30**
Lt R.P.Brailli	2Lt E.W.B.Stevenson	F1032		

Crossed the lines at 15,000ft seeing solid cloud ahead. Flew compass course north-north-east without seeing the ground, reconnaissance abandoned, re-crossed lines at 18,000ft.

Target: Triangle of Railways at Metz-Sablon

18th October		**Take Off:**	**14.00**
99 Squadron		**Returned:**	**16.15**
Formation 1			
Capt W.D.Thom	2Lt H.C.Peat		
2Lt E.J.Kidder	Sgt H.L.Bynon		
2Lt W.Hodder	2Lt N.W.Davidson		ret e/t
2Lt L.B.Duggan	2Lt W.J.Tremellen		
2Lt L.V.Russell	Sgt S.Beswick		ret e/t
2Lt A.R.Collis	Sgt E.V.G.Chalmers		lost in cloud

Formation 2			
Capt H.Sanders	2Lt G.M.Power		
2Lt L.S.Springett	2Lt C.D.Clarke		
Lt H.S.H.Read	2Lt F.P.Regan		ret e/t
2Lt W.H.Warwick	Lt L.H.Burrows		
2Lt E.C.Brown	Lt T.Llewellyn		
2Lt E.A.Bowyer	Sgt P.A.Cuka		

From the 11th to the 17th the weather was too bad for operations due to low cloud, thick mist and rain. The morning of the 18th was fairer but still with an overcast sky and mist patches. Captain Thom would lead the raid to hit Metz-Sablon again, with 104 Squadron also attacking. It would be the seventh visit by the daylight squadrons of the I.A.F. so far this month.

Twelve DH9s climbed away from Azelot and were soon immersed in cloud as they gained altitude. As usual engine trouble would rob the two formations of a full complement of bombers. First to return after fifty minutes was 2Lt Russell with vacuum control problems. Next was a trio of aircraft with engine trouble; first was 2Lt Hodder at 15.15 followed in the next ten minutes by 2Lt Collis with engine trouble and 2Lt Read who became lost in cloud. The remaining eight bombers headed north towards the lines.

Archie was scarce but what did come up was accurate as the two depleted formations flew the now standard route along the Moselle river towards Metz. Overhead the town at 15.40, four 230lb and eight 112lb bombs dropped from 12,500ft. The visibility was poor but hits were observed on the railways. Two enemy aircraft were spotted below the formation but they did not climb to engage. All eight machines returned home complete with nineteen photos despite the weather conditions.

After standing in for Lieutenant-Colonel John Baldwin, Major Pattinson returned from leave on 19th October and became the permanent Commanding Officer of the 41st Wing. Command of 99 Squadron went to Captain Thom.

Reconnaissance

21st October			**Take Off:**	**09.45**
110 Squadron			**Returned:**	**Unknown**
Lt R.P.Brailli	2Lt E.W.B.Stevenson	F1032		

Thick layers of cloud were encountered close to the lines between eight and ten thousand feet. Crossed the lines at 16,000ft with overcast all around. South-west of Metz were a few gaps, and photos were taken wherever there was a gap in the clouds. Continued for another two hours but no further gaps seen.

Target: Deutz near Köln (Cologne)
Secondary Target: Railways at Thionville

21st October			**Take Off:**	**10.20**
55 Squadron			**Returned:**	**13.25**
Formation 1				
Capt J.B.Fox	2Lt J.D.Evans	A7427	photo machine	
2Lt O.E.Miller	Sgt G.F.W.Adams 220131		ret petrol cock	
2Lt G.P.Dymond	2Lt B.H.Du Feu			
2Lt W.F.Smith	2Lt R.Dunn		force-landed	
Lt C.E.Reynolds	2Lt S.Burbidge			
2Lt D.C.Fleischer	2Lt H.B.Mercier		ret e/t	
Formation 2				
Lt D.J.Waterous	2Lt M.E.Barlow			
2Lt F.W.Moulson	2Lt J.H.Adams		ret e/t	
2Lt C.Turner	2Lt C.J.Knight	D9270		
Lt R.F.H.Norman	Sgt E.Clare		/W.I.A.	
2Lt J.D.MacFarlane	2Lt W.H.S.Kingsland		photo machine	
2Lt D.Ramsden	2Lt W.Ward		ret e/t	

Cologne was the target assigned to 55 Squadron on a very cloudy day with large patches of mist. The two formations were made up mostly of inexperienced crews and a long flight to Cologne in bad weather was not the best way of breaking them in.

Captain Fox led twelve aircraft airborne to gain height before heading towards the lines. Whether it was inexperience or wear and tear, aircraft started to return. Engine trouble forced 2Lt Ramsden back after ten minutes followed by 2Lt Moulson after a quarter of an hour. Next to return after an hour and ten minutes was 2Lt Miller with a broken petrol cock; 2Lt Fleischer returned at 11.50 also with engine trouble. The remaining eight bombers crossed the lines at Nomeny at 16,000ft coming under heavy and accurate archie. Steering a course east of Metz, six enemy aircraft engaged the bombers but the attack was not hard pressed and the DH4s continued north-east. Large banks of cloud were encountered and thick mist seen lower down so Fox with depleted numbers and enemy aircraft about decided to bomb Thionville instead. Overhead Thionville at 12.15, four 230lb and six 112lb bombs were dropped from 16,000ft. Two bursts were seen on the railway but the others were unobserved due to cloud cover.

After releasing the bombs the enemy engaged again but still did not press home their attacks. 2Lt Evans claimed a Fokker DVII out of control south-east of Metz at 12.30 in a fight which lasted a quarter of an hour. The bombers were at 17,000ft and Evans watched the enemy aircraft spin down into cloud at 10,000ft; 2Lt Knight also fired at this aircraft. All eight machines reached the lines after firing 2,500 rounds at German aircraft. Captain Fox led the machines back to Azelot, except 2Lt Smith and 2Lt Dunn, who became lost and force-landed; both men may have been injured as they took no further part in operations with 55 Squadron. Another casualty was Sergeant Ernest Clare who was wounded on this day. Whether from archie or machine-gun fire is not clear but this would also be the last operational bombing raid for Clare with 55. A good shot with at least two enemy aircraft to his credit, Clare was awarded the Distinguished Flying Medal, his citation reading as follows:

1st Class Private, A/Sergeant Ernest Clare No. 65289
D.F.M. gazetted 21st September 1918

Has been engaged on seventeen long-distance bombing raids. He has displayed skill and coolness in handling his gun on numerous occasions on which his formation has been attacked by hostile aircraft. Sergeant Clare has rendered valuable services as an observer on photographic reconnaissances as well as on long-distance raids.

Another sergeant on his last operational raid with 55 this day, was GEORGE FREDERICK WILLIAM ADAMS. Born in Lambeth on 16th July 1897, he was an engineer's enameller before the war, whereupon he joined the Royal Naval Air Service, signing up for the duration of the war. His training started on 8th June 1918 at the No.1 Observers School at Hythe. A month later he was at Stonehenge where he was made a Sergeant Mechanic on 17th August. From here he joined 55 Squadron on 28th August 1918. Records show that he joined 49 Squadron on 26th January 1919.

Target: Railways at Köln (Cologne), Coblenz or Ehrang
Secondary Target: Railways and Factories near Frankfurt

21st October			Take Off:	11.10/25
110 Squadron			Returned:	16.45/55
Formation 1				
Maj L.G.S.Reynolds	2Lt M.W.Dunn	F985	P.O.W./P.O.W.	
Lt S.B.Bradley	Sgt A.H.Banks			
2Lt D.B.Aitchison	2Lt E.Bower			
2Lt S.L.Mucklow	2Lt R.Rifkin	F984	P.O.W./P.O.W.	
Lt K.B.Wilkinson	2Lt H.Kettner			
2Lt G.T.Griffith	2Lt E.G.DeCartaret			
Lt A.R.MacDonald	Lt G.H.Tarras	F1028		
Formation 2				
Capt W.E.Windover	2Lt J.A.Simpson	F1005	P.O.W./P.O.W.	
Lt J.McLaren-Pearson	Sgt T.W.Harman 44805	F1029	P.O.W./P.O.W.	
Lt R.Neish	Sgt F.Quilter			
2Lt A.W.R.Evans	Lt R.W.L.Thomson	E8484	P.O.W./P.O.W.	
2Lt P.King	2Lt R.G.Vernon	F1021	P.O.W./D.O.W.	
2Lt J.O.R.S.Saunders	2Lt W.J.Brain	F986	K.I.A./K.I.A.	

Low cloud and mist prevailed on the morning of the 21st, as crews got ready for another attempt to reach Cologne. The two formations started to climb and rendezvoused over the field at the usual 15,000ft before heading off north towards the lines near Château-Salins.

No mention is made of anti-aircraft fire as the two formations crossed the lines at 16,000ft, and headed on a compass course hopefully for Ehrang. Visibility was very hazy, as the two formations followed Major Reynolds on a course, which some described later as erratic. The course to steer had been worked out on the ground before take-off. In the air however, the wind had changed and was now blowing from the west. From letters and reports, it seems that Major Reynolds mistook the River Rhine, for the River Moselle, and thus was way off course. An hour after crossing the lines and steering their heading, the two formations were expected to be over Ehrang. At 13.30 through a gap in the clouds, a town thought to be Treves was spotted five miles to the E.N.E. Other towns could also be picked up occasionally, but a thick layer of haze at about 12,000ft made identification difficult. Reynolds decided to head for Treves and from there proceed towards Ehrang. While heading for Treves, Reynolds decided to try and bomb the more important target which was the bridge at Coblenz. Leaving the Treves area at 13.35, Reynolds led the two formations on a new compass heading for twenty minutes. When Lt Dunn pointed out that they were rather too far south of the Moselle, Reynolds changed course, and headed in a more northerly direction in the hope of reaching Coblenz.

Now at 17,000ft, the two formations were confronted by a great wall of cloud which towered above them. Deciding not to fly through it, Reynolds fired a red Very light, and the two formations closed up and descended. In the descent through the clouds, they lost their leader, and after breaking through at 11,000ft, only Lt Griffith was to be seen. Reynolds gave the 'wash out' signal to Griffith at 9,000ft and continued to descend, in the hope of finding the rest of the squadron. The other machines had overshot their leader in the descent and were now dispersed. Two machines started to climb again, and later bombed a factory and railway before returning to Bettoncourt at 16.45 and 16.55.

Captain Windover, presumably alone, continued to Coblenz. On approaching the town he had his petrol tank pierced by anti-aircraft fire. Landing his aircraft, he tried to plug the hole while Lt Simpson kept approaching Germans at bay with his Lewis gun. Unable to plug the leak, they took off, but eventually ran out of petrol and despite their valiant effort were forced to land on the German side of the lines, to become prisoners of war.

Lt MacDonald, presumably trying to return home, found himself bombing the aerodrome at Boulay from 13,000ft. Whilst on their bombing run they were met by five Fokker DVIIs. The leader of this formation dived at the DH9a whilst firing a long burst. The Fokker then tried three attempts to get in close but was driven off. He stalled underneath the DH9a, and fired short bursts from long range as MacDonald and Tarras climbed away.

Five DH9as made it back across the lines, but not all made it to Bettoncourt. One machine came down near Toul next to an American ammunition dump which almost immediately started to go off. One machine crashed into barbed wire close to the lines near Nancy, while another landed at Preirefite. All three of these machines were reported as landing at 17.30, and may well have re-crossed the lines together.

Although seven machines were lost only one crew was killed. James Oscar Reginald Saunders had joined 110 Squadron on 26th September. Only twenty years of age, he survived less than a month. William John Brain from Stoke-on-Trent, was only nineteen, both men being killed on their first raid. German victories for this day claim only a DH4 at Enslingen with no time given. The victor was Oberleutnant Walther Karjus, Commanding Officer of Jasta 75 who were stationed down near the Swiss border at Habsheim. A holder of the Royal Hohenzollern House Order, Karjus had only one arm and this would be his only victory. With the three other daylight squadrons operating near Metz and Thionville, it would seem that Karjus almost certainly claimed a DH9a of 110 Squadron. Karjus had previously flown in Manfred von Richthofen's unit.

WILLIAM CONRAD WINDOVER was a school teacher before the war in Petrolia, Ontario, Canada. He originally started his training with the R.N.A.S, but was appointed, according to records, to the R.F.C. on 26th February 1917. He had some elementary training in Canada, before leaving from Halifax to arrive in England at the end of April 1917. He then proceeded to the School of Military Aeronautics at Reading reporting on 16th May. No further details could be found, except that he was well liked by his pupils who sent him a set of brushes to clean his boots with. (Or were they trying to tell him something?)

Details of this raid are hard to come by but below is a letter from Major Reynolds giving his version of events.

From Major L.G.S.Reynolds   Baileys Hotel
8th London Regiment & R.A.F. (late 110 sqn)   London, SW7
                                                                                                            28/12/1918

Sir,   **Bomb Raid of 21 Oct 1918**

I beg to submit below a detailed report on the above raid, in which I was leading two formations of 110 squadron, R.A.F., the objective being Coblenz or Ehrang. I regret that ill health since my return from Germany had prevented my sending you this report before.

A copy of the report has been sent to the Air Ministry (Director of Personnel) in amplification of the report made by me on arrival at the Prisoners of War Reception Camp, Ripon.

On the date in question my formation left the ground at 11.30 a.m., and at 12.30 picked up the other formation over the aerodrome at 15,000ft. I flew on the compass course which had been worked out for Ehrang for one hour – when we were due to reach Ehrang – and at 1.30 p.m. picked up Treves about 5 miles to the E.N.E. The day was exceedingly hazy with a layer of cloud, only broken in places, at about 12,000ft; but large towns and rivers could just be picked up from time to time through the gaps.

On sighting Treves I at once headed for the town, my first intention being to bomb Ehrang and return, owing to the poor visibility. Before we reached Treves however I remembered the great importance attached to the bombing of the Coblenz bridge; and as we were due according to within a few minutes up till then – to reach Coblenz at 2 p.m. or soon after, and return to the aerodrome at 4 p.m. or 4.15 p.m., I decided to try to reach the more important objective.

I left Treves about 1.35 p.m., and after flying for about 20 minutes on the compass bearing worked out my observer, Lt M.W.Dunn noticed that we were rather too far south of the Moselle. I accordingly headed a few points more to the North, and suddenly found myself confronted by a great wall of cloud – although we were then at 17,000ft and in practically clean air.

It seemed to me hopeless to try to fly straight through this, and accordingly I decided to go down low, and did so, firing a red light. After a time the formation seems to have lost me – with the exception of one machine, Lt Griffith – and when I found he was the only one actually with me, I signalled to him to 'wash out'. I myself felt it my duty to go right down, in case any other machines should have done so – as I had given the signal to go through the clouds. I cruised round for a time, but found none – the haze was very thick, the ground not being clearly visible from 2,000ft. Knowing however I must be near my objective, and certainly close to the Rhine, I set off again N.E., intending as soon as I struck the river to work up it to Coblenz.

After another 20 minutes there were still no signs of the Rhine, and I was over wooded country exactly like that between the Rhine and Treves. As the bank of cloud that had broken us up appeared to come from the North, and as on our compass course from Treves we had been too far South, I concluded that the wind had veered around to the North (this change of wind had actually occurred on a raid about a week before), and that we were still South of our objective and West of the river. As a matter of fact we must have crossed the Rhine when actually in the cloud bank.

It was then 2.15 p.m., my oxygen had given out shortly after we left Treves, and I decided that it was hopeless to go on, and accordingly turned and flew South-West. At the end of an hour and a quarter I found myself over a large river which I felt sure must be the Rhine, but concluded that we must have got right down to the South near Alsace Lorraine – I had then been flying for about 4 hours, much of it in clouds, and I think the failure of my oxygen supply had affected me. I therefore did not drop my bombs but flew on for home, with a little more West in my bearing, until I found myself about 4.40 p.m. in very hilly country, with dark coming on fast, about 20-30 minutes more petrol, and nothing but hills ahead. There were no signs of war; and I concluded we were in the hilly country by Besancon, and came down as near as possible to a village where there was a clear space. The machine hit a ridge on landing and crashed the undercarriage and propeller, throwing me forward rather violently against the wind screen, so that I was rather badly shaken. My observer got out to ask the name of the village, but had hardly done so when we were surrounded by a mob of people, including some German soldiers who covered us with their rifles from about 30 yards. I was still in the machine and we were unable to destroy it – but we left no papers on board containing any information. The maps had to be left, but they bore only the authorised markings.

We subsequently found that we had landed near a village called Buchenbeuren in Hunsruck; and it is clear that after we left Treves the wind must have veered round not to the North but to the West, and at the same time greatly increased in strength; so that we had been carried far to the East of the Rhine, which we must have crossed when going through the thick clouds. One machine left the formation, apparently with engine trouble, shortly before we reached Treves, and I understand that three others also failed to return.

Deeply as I regret that these losses should have occurred on a raid which I was leading, I still feel that were I again over Treves under similar circumstances I should again make the attempt to reach Coblenz, which I think we should have done but for the dense bank of cloud coming up from just over the Rhine – indeed I understand that Captain Windover was shot down over Coblenz, so that the town was actually reached by some machines of the squadron on this raid.

I am sir,

Your obedient servant

Louis Reynolds Major 8th London Regiment

Target: Triangle of Railways at Metz-Sablon

21st October		**Take Off:**	**14.15**
104 Squadron		**Returned:**	**16.15**

Formation 1

Capt I.W.Leiper	Lt L.G.Best	
2Lt H.D.Arnott	2Lt B.Johnson	
Lt J.R.Tansey	2Lt J.M.Scott	
2Lt L.C.Pitts	2Lt P.Davey	
2Lt P.J.Waller	2Lt R.D.Vaughn	
2Lt L.Hart	2Lt T.Bailey	photo machine
2Lt R.F.Lynch	2Lt E.G.Stevens	

Formation 2

Capt R.J.Gammon	2Lt H.Grieve	
2Lt I.L.R.Large	Sgt W.H.Ball	
Lt H.L.Wren	2Lt J.T.White	
2Lt S.T.Crowe	2Lt A.H.Penstone	photo machine
Lt J.W.Richards	2Lt C.E.Mason	
2Lt B.S.Case	2Lt H.Bridger	
2Lt J.N.Ogilvie	Sgt W.G.Steward	

Yet again Metz was the target for both 99 and 104 Squadrons, on a day that saw all daylight squadrons of the I.A.F targeting vital rail networks. Captain Leiper leading fourteen aircraft took off ten minutes before 99 Squadron and ascended above the field at Azelot. Reaching twelve thousand feet, the two formations, still complete, headed out towards the lines at Pont-à-Mousson.

Normal procedure was for the two spare aircraft to return at the lines, if both formations had a full complement of six bombers each. Whether it was the closeness of the target, or a case of getting maximum ordnance on it is not clear, but all fourteen aircraft crossed the lines coming under moderate archie. Continuing north the bombers flew straight to Metz arriving over the target at 15.50. Also over the target at this time was 99 Squadron who were also bombing from 12,000ft. Twenty-five DH9s at the same altitude must have been a lovely target for the anti-aircraft gunners below. Despite their efforts, the gunners did not deter Captain Leiper as he lined up his two formations well, and seven 230lb and fourteen 112lb bombs hit the mark in and around the triangle. Four explosions were seen on the northern apex of the triangle and one on the eastern side. Three bursts were observed on the tracks on the western side and four bombs exploded on nearby barracks causing several fires. Some bursts were also seen outside the triangle to the west. Three enemy aircraft approached the formations and started to fire from long range. These long-range attacks were directed more at 99 Squadron, and 104 Squadron observers did not bother to return fire.

All fourteen bombers re-crossed the lines and landed five minutes after 99 Squadron, except Lt Large who landed at 16.30, possibly due to enemy anti-aircraft fire although neither crew were wounded. Only ten photos were taken by the two photo machines but with clouds and mist patches there probably wasn't a lot of opportunity. Investigations after the war found that bombs fell mostly on private property causing considerable damage to housing.

Target: Triangle of Railways at Metz-Sablon

21st October		**Take Off:**	**14.25**
99 Squadron		**Returned:**	**16.10**

Formation 1

Capt W.G.Stevenson	Sgt J.Jones

2Lt L.S.Springett	Sgt H.L.Bynon	
Lt H.S.H.Read	2Lt F.P.Regan	
2Lt E.A.Bowyer	Sgt P.A.Cuka	photo machine
2Lt D.F.Brooks	2Lt W.Glew	

Formation 2

Capt H.Sanders	2Lt G.M.Power	
2Lt E.C.Brown	Lt T.Llewellyn	
2Lt W.Hodder	2Lt C.B.Fairhurst	
2Lt W.H.Warwick	Lt L.H.Burrows	
2Lt J.W.F.Merer	2Lt N.W.Davidson	
2Lt L.B.Duggan	2Lt W.J.Tremellen	photo machine

Two days of continued bad weather kept 99 Squadron on the ground. Orders when they came on the 21st were to bomb Metz. The weather on the 21st wasn't much better with an overcast sky and mist patches, but it had improved slightly by the afternoon and eleven DH9s led by Captain Stevenson left for the now familiar target.

Crossing the lines near Pont-à-Mousson the two formations flew up the eastern side of the Moselle river arriving over Metz at 15.50. Six 230lb and ten 112lb bombs were dropped from 12,000ft in very poor visibility. Despite the weather conditions five bursts were seen within the railway triangle, two west and three east of the triangle, and five more were also observed on the nearby barracks. Enemy aircraft were seen south of the town but they did not venture too near. 300 rounds of Lewis ammunition helped keep them away while Sergeant Cuka and 2Lt Tremellen took twelve photos.

All machines re-crossed the lines after following the western bank of the Moselle. Throughout the flight over the lines the German anti-aircraft gunners had put a good deal of exploding metal into the air, some of which came very close, but all machines put down safely at Azelot.

Leading the second formation was HERMAN SANDERS. Born on 27th December 1889, he was originally with the 3rd Battalion Loyal North Lancashire Regiment, before joining the Royal Flying Corps. He was wounded with 99 Squadron on 27th June 1918, on the bombing raid to Thionville. Promoted to Captain on 7th September, his address given during the war was 19 St Denys Road, Southampton. The other leader was the experienced Canadian, WILLIAM GORDON STEVENSON. Born on 2nd December 1893, Stevenson joined 99 Squadron on 16th January 1918 at Old Sarum Airfield. Surviving the war, Stevenson returned to Canada on 2nd April 1919. His home address was given as 2 Hiawatha Avenue, Hanlans Point, Toronto, Ontario, Canada.

Reconnaissance

23rd October		Take Off:	10.20
55 Squadron		**Returned:**	**14.30**
2Lt J.Cunliffe	2Lt G.E.Little		

Crossed lines at Pont-à-Mousson at 19,000ft. Flew over Metz, Montoy, Thionville, Longwy and Longuyon. Re-crossed lines at Verdun. In all fifty-six plates were taken and the reconnaissance was mostly flown at 20,000ft. No record of the aircraft was made.

Target: Deutz (Cologne)
Secondary Target: Railways at Metz-Sablon

23rd October		Take Off:	10.25
55 Squadron		**Returned:**	**12.55**
Formation 1			
Capt D.R.G.Mackay	2Lt H.C.T.Gompertz	photo machine	
2Lt G.T.Richardson	2Lt L.J.B.Ward		
2Lt C.Turner	2Lt C.W.Clutsom		
2Lt O.E.Miller	Sgt A.J.Cousins		

2Lt G.P.Dymond	2Lt B.H.Du Feu		
Lt R.Burgess	2Lt G.H.New		ret with ordnance
Formation 2			
Lt D.J.Waterous	2Lt M.E.Barlow		
Lt C.E.Reynolds	2Lt S.Burbidge	D8386	D.O.W./
Lt R.F.H.Norman	2Lt F.N.Coxhill		photo machine
2Lt C.W.Trimnell	2Lt W.C.Brudenell		
2Lt F.W.Moulson	2Lt J.H.Adams		lost formation
2Lt D.C.Fleischer	2Lt H.B.Mercier		

Along with the other daylight squadrons of the I.A.F., 55 attacked railway junctions in support of the American and French offensives on their part of the front. Captain Mackay led taking two formations of inexperienced crews to Deutz. After gaining height the two groups headed north towards Pont-à-Mousson where they encountered heavy but inaccurate archie as they crossed.

Just before or just after crossing the lines, 2Lt Moulson lost sight of the formation in very hazy conditions and landed safely back at Azelot at 12.05. The remaining eleven continued north following the western bank of the River Moselle towards Metz. Abeam Metz Mackay experienced engine trouble and decided to bomb the town and return home. Over Metz at 12.10, four 230lb and twelve 112lb bombs were dropped from 14,500ft, and four bursts were seen on the western part of the railway triangle.

Turning for home the bombers followed the eastern bank of the Moselle and were shadowed by three enemy scouts. They kept their distance but the observers fired 800 rounds just to be sure as they re-crossed the lines near Pont-à-Mousson. Lt Burgess was still carrying his ordnance which failed to drop but he managed to land safely. Lt Reynolds who was last to land unfortunately crashed and later died of his injuries, but his observer Burbidge survived. Eighteen photos were also taken over the target.

For DONALD JAYNE WATEROUS, born 2nd July 1895, this would be his last raid with 55 Squadron. Joining 55 on 2nd March 1918, Waterous was promoted to Lieutenant on 1st April. On 29th October 1918, he was promoted to Captain and transferred to 110 Squadron, to become a flight leader. He was awarded a D.F.C. while with 55. After the war he stayed with the Royal Air Force and joined 11 Squadron on 15th April 1919. His address given during the war was 507 West 112th Street, New York City.

Lieutenant Donald Jayne Waterous
D.F.C. gazetted 21st September 1918

Has been engaged in twenty-six long-distance bombing raids, and has rendered very valuable services, especially during a raid last month when enemy formations were met in great force. Lieutenant Waterous displays great keenness and determination in his work, and is always ready to volunteer for any difficult task.

CHARLES EDWARD REYNOLDS was born in Sydenham, South-East London on 18th November 1895. He was educated at Dulwich College, and then worked as a Solicitors Clerk in the Strand, from November 1913 to August 1914. On the outbreak of war he enlisted, joining the First Surrey Rifles as a 2Lt on 14th October 1914. Promoted to Lt in March 1916, he took part in operations on the Somme before proceeding to Salonika in March 1917. Transferring to the Royal Flying Corps, he was trained in Egypt, and gained his wings in June 1917. He returned to England to be trained as a bomber pilot, and joined 55 Squadron in March 1918. Wounded on a daylight raid to Cologne on 18th May, he went home and became an instructor at Waddington until fully fit to go back. Returning to 55 Squadron on 10th October from the Air Ministry, he was buried in the I.A.F. Cemetery at Charmes.

Note: Aircraft serial numbers are not recorded for 55 Squadron.

Target: Triangle of Railways at Metz-Sablon

23rd October			**Take Off:**	**10.30**
104 Squadron			**Returned:**	**12.35**

Formation 1

Capt E.J.Garland	2Lt W.E.Bottrill	D3035	
Lt H.L.Wren	2Lt J.T.White	D1050	
2Lt C.Workman	2Lt D.R.Hoon	D3168	
Lt J.H.Cuthbertson	2Lt A.B.Rattray	D3100	photo machine
2Lt R.F.Lynch	Sgt W.G.Steward		crash-landed
2Lt B.S.Case	2Lt H.Bridger	D2932	D.O.W./P.O.W.

Formation 2

Capt I.W.Leiper	2Lt L.G.Best	D3230	
2Lt H.D.Arnott	2Lt B.Johnson	C6191	
Lt J.R.Tansey	2Lt J.M.Scott	D5766	
2Lt P.J.Waller	2Lt R.D.Vaughn		
2Lt L.C.Pitts	2Lt P.Davey	D3248	
2Lt L.Hart	2Lt T.Bailey	D5843	photo machine

A busy Azelot saw 55 Squadron take off first, followed by 104 and 99 five minutes later. Metz-Sablon and its familiar triangle of railways was the target for all three Squadrons. Captain Garland led fourteen aircraft in a climb above the field levelling out at 11,500ft. One of the spare aircraft returned at 11.45 with engine trouble as the remaining thirteen headed for the lines at Nomeny.

Archie was light as the second spare aircraft turned away, and the twelve remaining bombers headed north towards Metz. Lt Lynch was soon forced to return after crossing the lines, his radiator starting to leak. He managed to make Azelot but unfortunately crashed on landing; both Lynch and Steward escaped injury and were back on operations on the 27th. Over Courcelles a formation of four Pfalz scouts was seen waiting for the bombers to approach. These four scouts followed the two bomber formations to the target which was reached at 12.05. As they dropped five 230lb and twelve 112lb bombs, two of the four fighters attacked from the rear. Then eight more enemy scouts, from the direction of Conflans, also attacked but from the front. As the fight grew in momentum another three scouts joined the mêlée making fifteen in all. Several aircraft were claimed by observers; 2Lt White fired 250 rounds at one with a red fuselage, and blue and red striped undersurfaces on his lower wing. This scout entered a spin down to a thousand feet, and was seen to crash near Augny by 2Lt Rattray, who was also firing at it. Another aircraft was claimed as shot down out of control by White although from combat reports it looks like most of the observers were firing at this particular aircraft. William Bottrill fired nearly four hundred rounds at a Pfalz which dived then stalled and spun to within three thousand feet of the ground. The aircraft seen crashing by observers may have been 2Lt Bernard Sydney Case, and his observer 2Lt Harold Bridger who were shot down over the target and seen to crash after spinning down. Case and Bridger were both wounded and became prisoners of war, although Case unfortunately died of his wounds the day before the Armistice.

The scout pilots were particularly aggressive, positioning themselves between the lines and the two formations, diving and firing from the front then attacking from behind once they zoomed back up to the bombers' height. Despite these tactics the remaining ten machines returned to Azelot after firing 2,450 rounds of Lewis, and they also bought back eighteen photos.

Aggressive tactics like these usually meant a Jasta was attacking, and in this case it was Jasta 18. Leutnant Kurt Monnington received confirmation for a DH9 down at Fourasse Wood at 13.15. Leutnant Prahlow of Kest 3 claimed a DH9 down at Frescaty at 13.05; also claiming a DH9 at 13.05 was Vizefeldwebel Trautmann of Jasta 64 at Metz-Sablon for his third victory. All three were awarded victories although only one DH9 had been shot down on the German side. German time was now one hour ahead of British time so Prahlow and Trautmann have the better claim although Monnington had shot down five DH9s and a DH4 already. Prahlow looks as if he was with the four aircraft over Courcelles, with the airfield of Kest 3 at Morchingen nearby. Trautmann may have been with the enemy aircraft from the west (or Conflans as the observers reported it), which was near Tichemont, the airfield Jasta 64 had moved into on the 10th of October to share with Jasta 15. Jasta 18 and Kurt Monnington were still flying out of Montingen near Metz where he had flown from for his last six victories out of a total of eight; these six bombers were all from the I.A.F. Monnington's claim may have been upheld due to Collis and Clarke of 99 Squadron, who force-landed at a French aerodrome after being pursued by a single enemy scout all the way to the lines. If German front line observers had seen an enemy aircraft leave formation, and head down, after being attacked they may well have reported it as destroyed, this may be why Monnington claimed his DH9 ten minutes later, when Case and Bridger were definitely seen going down over the target at 12.05 British time. 2Lt Bridger was wounded in one of his arms, reports do not say which. Bernard Sydney Case, aged nineteen from Thornton Heath in Surrey, died from his wounds on 10th November 1918, and was buried at Ars-sur-Moselle.

Target: Triangle of Railways at Metz-Sablon

23rd October			**Take Off:**	**10.30**
99 Squadron			**Returned:**	**12.50**
Formation 1				
Capt W.D.Thom	2Lt R.Henderson			
2Lt E.C.Brown	Lt T.Llewellyn			
2Lt W.Hodder	Lt L.H.Burrows	5650		
2Lt L.B.Duggan	2Lt W.J.Tremellen		photo machine	
2Lt L.V.Russell	Sgt S.Beswick			
2Lt A.R.Collis	2Lt C.D.Clarke		W.I.A./	
Formation 2				
Capt W.G.Stevenson	Sgt J.Jones			
2Lt L.S.Springett	2Lt J.G.Nagle			
Lt H.S.H.Read	2Lt F.P.Regan		ret e/t	
2Lt V.C.Varcoe	2Lt V.J.Fontannaz			
Lt C.E.W.Thresher	Sgt P.A.Cuka			
Lt F.K.Crosbie-Choppin	2Lt A.T.Bowyer		photo machine	

Metz-Sablon was once more the target for 99 Squadron, the fifth time this month. Recent opposition had been light from the German Air Service, but anti-aircraft fire was still very active and sometimes accurate, keeping pilots and observers on their toes. The new Commanding Officer, Captain Thom, led twelve DH9s skyward and climbed for height before setting out for the lines. Nearing the top of his climb, Lt Read left and headed for Azelot with an overheating engine, landing safely at 11.35. The remaining eleven headed north for the lines.

Archie was quite active but its range was out as the bombers headed north towards the familiar town of Metz. The weather was good and the visibility fair as they arrived at 12.02. From 12,000ft six 230lb and ten 112lb bombs headed down towards the triangle of railways. All bomb impacted in and around the target area with six on the triangle, two on a railway north of the triangle and two west of it. After leaving the target fourteen enemy aircraft attacked, painted black and white. These aircraft were Pfalz scouts and closed to within 300 yards of the formations and exchanged fire with the observers. At 12.15 one of the fighters entered a vertical dive trailing smoke. 2Lt Hodder claimed this aircraft but it appears that all the observers were firing at it.

One of the Germans followed the two groups all the way to the lines but caused no damage. 99 were not unscathed, however, and 2Lt Collis was forced to land his machine at a French aerodrome, after being wounded by machine-gun fire. The remaining ten machines landed back at Azelot complete with sixteen photos and after firing three thousand rounds of ammunition.

German reports state that five bombs fell on the shunting station causing damage to tracks, while another hit the gas works but did no damage. The remaining bombs fell on private property causing considerable damage.

Note: Serial numbers for aircraft were not recorded.

Reconnaissance

23rd October			**Take Off:**	**11.38**
110 Squadron			**Returned:**	**Unknown**
2Lt D.P.James	2Lt A.R.Wylde	F1011		

Crossed the lines at 18,000ft and headed towards Kaiserslautern, then flew over Bitche and on towards Buhl. Before Buhl could be photographed, engine trouble forced James to return and they re-crossed the lines at 20,000ft with twenty-five photos taken. During their reconnaissance they were accurately archied near Kaiserslautern, and saw two enemy aircraft about 3,000ft below. No other movements by road or rail were seen.

Reconnaissance

27th October			Take Off:	12.10
110 Squadron			Returned:	Unknown
2Lt D.P.James	2Lt A.R.Wylde	F1054		

Buhl was the target for this reconnaissance four days later, and James and Wylde crossed the lines at 18,000ft heading east. There was a layer of cloud at around 10,000ft, with mist patches lower down near ground level. Over Buhl eleven plates were exposed and two enemy aircraft were seen on the ground; one enemy aircraft was observed climbing up but was of no danger to the DH9a. The archie was accurate and heavy over Buhl but no hits were recorded on the aircraft. The crew also reported seeing two trains leaving Sarrebourg station.

Target: Railway Junction at Ecouvier
Secondary Target: Frescaty Aerodrome

27th October		Take Off:	12.15
104 Squadron		Returned:	14.05
Formation 1			
Capt E.J.Garland	2Lt W.E.Bottrill		
Lt J.W.Richards	2Lt E.G.Stevens	ret e/t	
Lt H.L.Wren	2Lt J.T.White		
2Lt S.T.Crowe	2Lt A.H.Penstone	photo machine	
2Lt R.F.Lynch	Sgt G.A.Smith		
Lt J.R.Tansey	2Lt J.M.Scott		
Formation 2			
Capt R.J.Gammon	Lt W.Grieve	ret e/t	
2Lt L.Hart	2Lt T.Bailey	ret with leader	
2Lt P.J.Waller	2Lt R.D.Vaughn		
2Lt C.Workman	2Lt C.C.Blizard	force-landed e/t	
2Lt J.N.Ogilvie	Sgt W.G.Steward		
Lt J.H.Cuthbertson	2Lt A.B.Rattray	photo machine	

Stopping rail transport of supplies was still the priority for the I.A.F. and with this in mind 104 were tasked with bombing the rail junction at Ecouvier. Fourteen machines led by Captain Garland took off and started to climb over Azelot, in cloudy weather with bad visibility. Engine trouble just after take-off robbed the second formation of 2Lt Workman and Lt Blizard who force-landed just outside the aerodrome; both were unharmed. Captain Gammon was also experiencing engine trouble and put back down at Azelot at 12.50. 2Lt Hart also returned behind his leader thinking the raid was a wash out. One of the spare aircraft also returned with engine trouble as the remaining eleven continued to climb before heading for the front.

Crossing the lines the two formations received very little in the way of archie as they tried to find their target in amongst the cloud. Cloud was the main problem and Lt Richards returned being unable to keep up with the others after becoming separated. The other spare machine also returned when it lost contact with the formations; both machines landed back at base at 13.50. Now leading eight machines Captain Garland searched for Ecouvier but could not find it, but he had seen Frescaty aerodrome and decided to bomb that instead. At 13.30 three 230lb and ten 112lb bombs fell away from 10,000ft. The Zeppelin hangar was nearly hit as two 230lb bombs exploded in front of it, four bursts were seen on the landing ground while another four were observed to detonate near hangars at the northern part of the aerodrome near some woods.

The weather was so bad that 2Lts Penstone and Rattray didn't bother to take any pictures to or from the target. The eight bombers returned to Azelot and landed safely without seeing any enemy aircraft during the entire trip.

Lt CHARLES CECIL BLIZARD who was back from leave, came from Putney in London. Blizard, born 21st November 1897, was a student at Mill Hill School between 1910 and 1915 from where he joined the 20th Battalion of the Middlesex Regiment. He attended the 4th Army Signal School in 1917 before joining the Royal Flying Corp to become an observer. Joining 104 Squadron in April 1918, he flew out with the Squadron on 19th May 1918 to Azelot. He claimed five enemy aircraft by the war's end, two destroyed and three out of control. He left the Royal Air Force on 19th June 1919, and was still living in Putney when World War Two broke out.

Target: Railways at Longuyon
Secondary Target: Frescaty Aerodrome

27th October		Take Off:	12.25
99 Squadron		Returned:	14.00

Formation 1

Capt W.D.Thom	2Lt R.Henderson	
2Lt V.C.Varcoe	2Lt V.J.Fontannaz	
Lt H.S.H.Read	2Lt F.P.Regan	
2Lt L.B.Duggan	2Lt W.J.Tremellen	photo machine
2Lt L.V.Russell	Sgt S.Beswick	ret e/t big end
Lt C.E.W.Thresher	2Lt W.Glew	

Formation 2

Capt W.G.Stevenson	2Lt G.M.Power	
2Lt E.C.Brown	Lt T.Llewellyn	
2Lt H.E.King	2Lt E.Smith	
2Lt W.A.Warwick	Lt L.H.Burrows	ret e/t
2Lt J.W.F.Merer	2Lt N.W.Davidson	
2Lt L.S.Springett	2Lt J.G.Nagle	

After three days of bad weather since the 24th, operations resumed with 99 Squadron scheduled to bomb the railway junction at Longuyon. With large formations of cloud and poor visibility, twelve DH9s took off led by the experienced Captains Thom and Stevenson. Engine trouble claimed two aircraft before the lines were reached; first to return from the second formation was 2Lt King whose engine kept cutting out, followed by 2Lt Russell who had a big end go, but both machines made it back to Azelot.

A token amount of archie came up as the ten bombers crossed the lines at 12,000ft. Once over it was impossible to see Longuyon, so he turned towards Metz in the hope of seeing a target through gaps in the clouds. South-west of Metz at 13.35, Captain Thom spotted Frescaty aerodrome through a gap and made for it. Followed by the rest of his formation they released four 230lb and two 112lb bombs from 12,000ft. Bursts were seen on the aerodrome with three reported explosions in the middle of the landing ground. The second group were unable to locate this target and re-crossed the lines after closing with the first formation.

All ten machines returned to Azelot, the second formation bringing their ordnance back with them. Despite the weather 2Lt Tremellen took seven photos. These photos were an important part of bombing operations not only for damage assessment but for intelligence purposes. Photos taken by 104 Squadron on 10th October showed a DH4, 9 or 9a on the road next to the railway line at Frescaty aerodrome. I.A.F. intelligence covering the layout of airfields was pretty good. Frescaty was reported as having two large Zeppelin hangars, one large aeroplane hangar, and eighteen tents next to a clump of trees on the western side of the airfield. Intelligence also knew that the living quarters were on the northern side of the airfield behind the Zeppelin hangars. Units based here according to I.A.F. Intelligence in October were Jasta 84, and Flieger-Abteilung 242.

Note: Serial numbers for 99 Squadron aircraft on this raid were not recorded.

Target: Railway Junction at Ecouvier
Secondary Target: Morhange Aerodrome

28th October		Take Off:	13.50
104 Squadron		Returned:	16.00

Formation 1

Capt I.W.Leiper	2Lt L.G.Best	
2Lt H.D.Arnott	2Lt B.Johnson	
Lt J.R.Tansey	2Lt J.M.Scott	
2Lt P.J.Waller	2Lt R.D.Vaughn	photo machine
2Lt L.Hart	2Lt T.Bailey	
2Lt J.N.Ogilvie	Sgt W.G.Steward [1]	
2Lt L.C.Pitts	Sgt W.G.Steward [1]	

Formation 2

Lt W.S.Greenwood	Lt W.Grieve	
Lt J.W.Richards	2Lt E.G.Stevens	
2Lt I.L.R.Large	Sgt W.H.Ball	D5773
Lt H.L.Wren	2Lt J.T.White	D1050
2Lt S.T.Crowe	2Lt A.H.Penstone	
2Lt P.Hopkinson	2Lt E.D.Barnes	photo machine
2Lt A.Hemingway	Sgt G.A.Smith	

Operations were put on hold in the morning as Azelot was enshrouded in thick mist. This started to clear by early afternoon and planes were readied for another attempt at reaching Ecouvier. Although the mist had cleared the sky was still full of large banks of cloud, as Captain Leiper led fourteen aircraft to gain height over the airfield. The climb to altitude went well and all fourteen aircraft headed off towards the lines. Before crossing, both formations flew through a mass of leaflets at 10,000ft. Upon landing these were found to be propaganda leaflets with a message of peace from "The German People".

Crossing the trenches, archie put up a slight barrage, but the fourteen bombers continued on towards Ecouvier, with the exception of 2Lt Hemingway who became separated and had no option but to try and find his way back to Azelot. With heavy cloud it was impossible to find Ecouvier, so Captain Leiper decided to bomb the aerodrome at Morhange which was visible to the east. Arriving over the target at 15.25, five 230lb and sixteen 112lb bombs were toggled from 11,000ft. A direct hit on a hangar with a 230lb bomb was seen which started a fire. Three other bursts were spotted around the hangars and six between the hangars and the railway which rang along the southern side of the aerodrome. Another solitary burst was seen on a road on the eastern side of the aerodrome, while four bursts were observed outside the aerodrome at the south-east corner. Four enemy aircraft were over the target, two of which attacked. Sergeant Ball fired at one of these attacking scouts sending one down out of control. Vizefeldwebel Andreas Emele, of Jasta 80b, was killed during combat with a DH9 over Grémecey on this day. Born in Ringingen on 28th May 1896, he joined Jasta 80b on 23rd August 1918. It looks almost certain that Emele was the victim of Sergeant Ball's Lewis guns. In all 1,250 rounds of Lewis were fired by the observers.

All thirteen aircraft re-crossed the lines, putting down safely at Azelot only ten minutes after 2Lt Hemingway, eight photos were taken by 2Lt Barnes and 2Lt Vaughn.

Note: Aircraft serial numbers for this raid were not recorded.

Target: Railways at Longuyon
Secondary Target: Morhange Aerodrome

28th October		Take Off:	14.05
99 Squadron		Returned:	15.55

Formation 1

Capt W.G.Stevenson	Sgt J.Jones
2Lt V.C.Varcoe	2Lt V.J.Fontannaz

---

[1] According to records Sergeant W.G.Steward is down as flying with both 2Lt Ogilvie, and 2Lt Pitts. Who flew with whom is not clear, and obviously there is another observer's name missing due to an error in the records.

Lt H.S.H.Read	2Lt F.P.Regan	ret e/t
Lt F.K.Crosbie-Choppin	2Lt H.O.Brown	photo machine
2Lt E.A.Bowyer	Sgt P.A.Cuka	
Lt C.E.W.Thresher	2Lt W.Glew	

Formation 2

Capt H.Sanders	2Lt G.M.Power	
2Lt E.C.Brown	Lt T.Llewellyn	
2Lt H.E.King	2Lt E.Smith	
2Lt W.A.Warwick	Lt L.H.Burrows	
2Lt L.V.Russell	Sgt S.Beswick	
2Lt L.B.Duggan	2Lt W.J.Tremellen	photo machine

Longuyon was again the target for 99 on another day of cloud and mist. By early afternoon this mist had cleared leaving dense cloud and bad visibility. Formations led by Captains Stevenson and Sanders took off to gain height before setting out towards the lines. Engine trouble forced Lt Read to return before crossing as the eleven bombers pressed on to try and reach Longuyon.

Anti-aircraft fire was minimal as it had been the day before, as the bombers searched for their target through the clouds. Longuyon was again obscured by cloud, so Captain Stevenson led the two groups east towards Morhange aerodrome. Overhead at 15.30, seven 230lb and eight 112lb bombs were dropped from 12,000ft with good results. Hits were reported on a single hangar while three bursts were seen on the southern corner of the airfield. Four more explosions were also recorded on the sidings south of the airfield. Enemy aircraft which had been lacking lately arrived in the form of five scouts. Of the five which shadowed the two formations, only one closed to within firing distance although this was still from long range.

All eleven machines returned to Azelot after firing 2,100 rounds; 2Lts Brown and Tremellen had also been busy taking nineteen photos over the target.

According to some reports, Captain Thom took off in a DH9a on this day with three 112lb bombs on board. Flying at 15,000ft, he dropped them on Frescaty, scoring a hit on a hangar next to the woods alongside the aerodrome.

Lt Hugh Stanley Hely Read who returned with engine trouble, was born on 17th November 1898. He studied at Magdalen College School, Oxford, between September 1908 and December 1916. He joined 103 Squadron on 6th May 1918, but quickly moved to No.11 TDS on the 16th. On 24th June he joined 107 Squadron, but moved again to 109 Squadron on 27th July, where he became a full Lieutenant the following day. Exactly one month later he joined 99 Squadron. The family address during the war was 195 Leffley Road, Oxford.

Intelligence regarding Morhange reported that two reconnaissance units were operating from the 12th of October, these being Flieger-Abteilung 257 and Flieger-Abteilung 100.

Note: Again 99 Squadron stopped recording aircraft serial numbers on raids.

Target: Railways at Longuyon

29th October		**Take Off:**	**10.35**
99 Squadron		**Returned:**	**14.00**

Formation 1

Capt W.D.Thom	Sgt J.Jones	
2Lt V.C.Varcoe	2Lt V.J.Fontannaz	
Lt H.S.H.Read	2Lt F.P.Regan	force-landed
Lt F.K.Crosbie-Choppin	2Lt A.T.Bowyer	photo machine
2Lt E.A.Bowyer	Sgt P.A.Cuka	
Lt C.E.W.Thresher	2Lt W.Glew	

Formation 2

Capt H.Sanders	2Lt G.M.Power

2Lt E.C.Brown	Lt T.Llewellyn	
2Lt H.E.King	2Lt E.Smith	
2Lt W.A.Warwick	Lt L.H.Burrows	
2Lt J.W.F.Merer	2Lt N.W.Davidson	
2Lt L.B.Duggan	2Lt W.J.Tremellen	photo machine

It was hoped that with better weather conditions, Longuyon would be reached on the third attempt although the visibility was still pretty poor. Captain Thom led out twelve DH9s as they climbed for height and headed out towards Verdun. All engines were running well and for a change all twelve crossed the lines near Verdun, receiving slight but accurate archie as they did so.

Heading north they flew over Mangiennes to arrive over Longuyon at 12.55. Firing a white Very light Captain Thom initiated the dropping of eight 230lb and eight 112lb bombs from 12,500ft. Only six bursts were seen and these were to the west of the town, as trouble arrived in the form of fourteen enemy aircraft. Although strong in number only three of these attacked as the two formations headed for home. Lt Read was having trouble with his aircraft, but whether it was engine trouble, enemy machine-gun fire or archie is not clear.

All twelve re-crossed the lines but only eleven reached Azelot. Read was last seen on the allied side preparing to put his aircraft down. As he was back in action two days later and Regan was also back in action in November, it appears neither were wounded or injured. Both observers had been busy with their cameras taking twenty-seven photos between them. The observers reported seeing rolling stock for two trains in the sidings at Longuyon, and one train leaving the station heading north-west. Although they fired 2,700 rounds, it looks as if the German Air Service were reluctant to mix it, and the engagement such as it was looks as though it was fought only at long range.

Target: Railway Junction at Ecouvier
Secondary Target: Jametz Aerodrome

29th October			**Take Off:**	**10.50**
104 Squadron			**Returned:**	**14.00**
Formation 1				
Capt E.J.Garland	2Lt W.E.Bottrill	D3035		
2Lt C.Workman	Lt C.C.Blizard	D3168		
Lt A.Hemingway	Sgt G.A.Smith			
Lt J.H.Cuthbertson	2Lt A.B.Rattray	D5786	photo machine	
2Lt P.Hopkinson	2Lt E.D.Barnes	D487		
2Lt L.Hart	2Lt T.Bailey	E8859	force-landed	
2Lt P.J.Waller	2Lt R.W.Lewin	D5843	W.I.A./	
Formation 2				
Capt I.W.Leiper	2Lt L.G.Best	D3230	W.I.A./	
Lt J.R.Tansey	2Lt J.M.Scott	D5766	force-landed	
2Lt L.C.Pitts	2Lt P.Davey	D3248		
2Lt H.D.Arnott	2Lt B.Johnson	E8978	K.I.A./K.I.A.	
2Lt J.N.Ogilvie	Sgt W.G.Steward	D5773		
Lt H.L.Wren	2Lt J.T.White	D1050	photo machine	

Ecouvier was on the menu again for 104, although the weather was still gloomy with lots of cloud and bad visibility. Thirteen machines took off, led by Captain Garland, and started to gain height over Azelot. Reaching 10,000ft, the machines headed for the lines at Regnéville near Verdun, which were crossed with little trouble from German anti-aircraft gunners.

Once over the two formations headed straight for the objective, only to find it completely covered by cloud. Captain Garland therefore decided to bomb the aerodrome at Jametz, just south-west of Montmédy. Over the aerodrome at 12.45, five 230lb and sixteen 112lb bombs were dropped from 10,000ft. Ten bursts were seen on trenches surrounding the airfield. Attention however was focused on twenty enemy scouts climbing up to meet the two formations; a baptism of fire was about to occur for some of the more inexperienced crews. The engagement started over the aerodrome where 2Lt Arnott and 2Lt Johnson were seen going down in flames. Captain Garland who had spotted the enemy aircraft previously climbing up as they crossed the lines, kept a watchful eye as they closed in on the bombers. Preparing for action he and his observer Bottrill, were soon in the thick of it. A Pfalz dived under the second formation and came up firing at the first. Bottrill fired his twin Lewis guns and watched as pieces came off the Pfalz scout, before it broke up in the air. Bottrill fired at another fighter which spun away for 4,000ft. 2Lt White also fired at a Pfalz scout which he saw spin away for 2,000ft.

More enemy aircraft joined the fight and from combat reports it would seem between thirty and forty German aircraft were engaged. Most combat reports record the aircraft as Pfalz scouts and Fokker DVIIs; some scouts were armed with four front-firing machine guns according to the bomb raid report on the engagement. Sergeant Steward claimed a Fokker DVII out of control after firing two bursts at it. Also claiming a Fokker DVII out of control was 2Lt Rattray who fired at a lead Fokker which spun away for 4,000ft. In all he saw three gaggles of ten enemy aircraft. Lt Blizard fired at twelve different aircraft at long range, the nearest Fokker to him received forty rounds and was seen to spin for 3,000ft. Also in the first formation was 2Lt Barnes who fired thirty rounds at a Pfalz, and watched it stall before turning over on its back falling for 4,000ft. Barnes reported that he saw three enemy aircraft going down and one DH9. This running fight continued to the lines at Argonne Wood, but 104 were not unscathed. Several machines were badly shot up, and two had wounded on board.

Captain Leiper had been wounded and put his machine down at Clermont. Also forced to land at this time at St.Mihiel was 2Lt P.J.Waller and Lt Lewin. Waller was wounded and was treated in a French hospital nearby. Also coming down at St.Mihiel was 2Lt Hart and 2Lt Bailey, neither of whom were wounded. One other machine was missing but was later found at Laheycourt just north-west of Bar-le-Duc. The occupants Lt Tansey and 2Lt Scott were unharmed and on the Allied side of the lines. The combat was a tremendous one and although only eight machines made it back to Azelot, only two men were killed and two wounded. Considering the amount of opposition the pilots showed great determination and courage in staying in formation, for usually once they became separated machines seldom got back in one piece. Usually one of the crew was dead, almost always the observer judging from previous raids. Keeping formation had stopped a repeat of the catastrophe of 15th September.

Several sources suggest Leutnant Georg Meyer, Staffelführer of Jasta 37, as the victor of Arnott and Johnson. This is unlikely as Jasta 37 were at Villers-sur-Nicole on the German 2nd Army Front, well to the north. Claims for Arnott and Johnson come from the two Jastas both operating out of Preutin aerodrome on the German 5th Army Front. Leutnant Max Näther of Jasta 62 claimed three victories this day. His first was a Spad, the second was a DH9 at Sivry, and the third was a DH4 at Montfaucon. Also claiming a DH4, this time west of Sivry was Unteroffizier Rozmiarek also of Jasta 62. Leutnant Selzer, Leutnant Dangers, Senior Unteroffizier Weidner, Oberleutnant Theodor Camman all of Jasta 74 bought down aircraft on this part of the front, but unfortunately for historians the aircraft types were not given. Allied losses regarding bombers on this part of the front were a DH4 of the 135th US Aero, and Arnott and Johnson. With the information available both Jastas engaged 104 Squadron, but who exactly got who is not clear and with some machines seen going down behind allied lines, it will probably remain that way. Harold Dwight Arnott from Toronto, Ontario in Canada was twenty-three. He was buried along with Benjamin Johnson, aged twenty-one in Montcornet Cemetery. Johnson was from Schull, County Cork in Ireland and had already been wounded on 31st July 1918.

Note: Aircraft serial numbers are from combat reports.

Target: Railways at Ehrang or Longuyon

29th October		**Take Off:**	**11.25**
55 Squadron		**Returned:**	**14.40**
Formation 1			
Capt J.B.Fox	Lt J.Parke	photo machine	
2Lt G.P.Dymond	2Lt B.H.Du Feu		
Lt S.L.Dowswell	2Lt J.D.Evans		
2Lt C.W.Trimnell	2Lt W.C.Brudenell	ret e/t	
2Lt J.D.MacFarlane	2Lt W.H.S.Kingsland		
2Lt R.Burgess	2Lt G.H.New		
Formation 2			
Capt W.J.Pace	Lt D.W.Stewart		

2Lt G.T.Richardson	2Lt L.J.B.Ward	D8384
Lt R.F.H.Norman	2Lt F.N.Coxhill	
2Lt W.H.Thomas	2Lt J.Mitchell	force-landed
2Lt D.C.Fleischer	2Lt H.B.Mercier	photo machine
2Lt H.A.Griffiths	2Lt H.W.Robinson	

Railway lines in the German Army rear were detailed as targets for 55 Squadron. Ehrang was approximately seventy miles in a straight line from Verdun while Longuyon was approximately twenty-five miles north of it. Captain Fox would be leading and he decided to bomb Longuyon due to the very thick haze and large detached formations of cloud. Leaving Azelot the machines gained height, and after an hour 2Lt Trimnell returned with engine trouble. The remaining eleven bombers headed for Verdun where they crossed the lines at 16,500ft under considerable and penetrating archie fire.

The archie was indeed accurate, 2Lt Thomas having to force-land at Sandaucourt with a punctured radiator. The remaining ten flew west of Spincourt to Longuyon noticing four Fokker DVII below them. They failed to intercept however, and Longuyon was reached at 13.45. Dropping four 230lb and twelve 112lb bombs the machines turned for home, the crews observing five explosions on the railway lines and several on houses near the station.

Heading straight for Verdun, the formations were intercepted by six Fokker DVIIs which despite their number kept their distance and fired from long range. The nearest Fokker which was about 400 yards away nose dived and did not recover after concentrated fire from all the observers. All ten DH4s landed safely back at base with twenty photos of the target. German losses on this day amounted to two pilots but on different fronts; this does not mean however that aircraft were not hit. The observers of 55 fired nearly two thousand rounds during this engagement, and the German aircraft may well have been damaged and simply landed and were repaired with no loss being recorded as the pilot was unhurt.

This was Lieutenant Joshua Parke's last raid with 55. He originally served with the Durham Light Infantry, and joined 55 after his observer training on 14th August 1917. He earned a D.F.C. while with 55, the citation reading as follows:

Lt Joshua Parke
D.F.C. gazetted 21st September 1918

This officer has taken part in 40 long-distance day bomb raids and photographic reconnaissances. His work as an observer has been consistently good, and he displays great gallantry and determination, notably in a bombing raid when he was observer to the leader of our second formation.

JOHN BERTRAM FOX was born on 24th July 1893. His father was in the Indian Civil Service with the title of Assistant Postmaster General of Ceylon. Fox was schooled at St. Edward's School, Newara, Elyia, in Ceylon between 1902 and 1905. In 1906 he went to Scotland and studied English, Maths, Greek, Dynamics, Latin and Drawing at the Dollar Academy, Dollar in Scotland. After leaving Dollar he became a bank clerk. When war broke out he joined the 1st Canadian Division as a private in the machine-gun section.

Note: Serial numbers do not exist for aircraft on this raid.

Reconnaissance

29th October			**Take Off:**	**12.00**
110 Squadron			**Returned:**	**Unknown**
Lt K.B.Wilkinson	Sgt A.H.Banks	F1060		

This crew were tasked with finding a supposedly new aerodrome at Thal but this could not be found. Operating at 20,000ft four plates were exposed over Sarrebourg and eight over Buhl. A new aerodrome under construction was spotted west-south-west of Buhl and two plates taken of this.

This was the only reconnaissance mission flown by KENNETH BRUCE WILKINSON. Born on 24th September 1898 in Toronto, Canada, he attended the University of Toronto as a student, until September 1916 when he enlisted. He was at the Royal Naval College Greenwich in March 1918, and was later known to be flying at R.A.F. Eastchurch. He joined 110 Squadron on 31st August 1918. Proud of his Naval past, he still wore his Naval jacket and topcoat whilst serving in the newly formed R.A.F. After war's end he flew postal duties for the army of occupation, before leaving for Canada on 30th June 1919. The family address during the war was 31 Wells Street, Toronto, Canada.

Target: Buhl Aerodrome

30th October			Take Off:	14.30
99 Squadron			Returned:	16.30

Formation 1

Capt W.D.Thom	Sgt J.Jones		ret e/t water leak
2Lt L.V.Russell	Sgt S.Beswick		did not follow
Lt C.E.W.Thresher	2Lt W.Glew		did not follow
Lt F.K.Crosbie-Choppin	2Lt A.T.Bower		ret e/t plugs

Formation 2

Capt H.Sanders	2Lt G.M.Power	B9394	
2Lt J.W.F.Merer	2Lt N.W.Davidson	D3270	
2Lt H.E.King	2Lt E.Smith	D529	
2Lt W.A.Warwick	Lt L.H.Burrows	D3042	
2Lt D.C.Bain	2Lt R.Mugford		ret e/t overheating
2Lt L.B.Duggan	2Lt W.J.Tremellen	C6210	photo machine

Buhl aerodrome, home to Jasta 39 and Jasta 78, was the target as ten DH9s headed out for the long trip to the east. Shortly after taking off, Captain Thom heard a knocking sound coming from his engine. He also noticed a water leak and turned back, landing safely at Azelot at 14.55. Lt Crosbie-Choppin took over the lead of the first formation as height was gained. The second group lost 2Lt Bain whose engine was overheating; he landed safely back at Azelot at 15.50, followed then by Lt Crosbie-Choppin who returned with plug trouble. Lt Thresher and 2Lt Russell tried to formate with the second bunch but failed and returned home leaving the second group now numbering five, to cross the lines just east of Lunéville.

Archie was slight but accurate as the five bombers went over the lines heading for Avricourt, which was noted as having large amounts of rolling stock in the sidings, with a train seen leaving going north-east. The bombers pressed on led by Captain Sanders. Overhead at 15.50 four 230lb and two 112lb bombs fell from 12,000ft. Explosions were not observed due to the presence of eight enemy aircraft. Three of these aircraft were reported as Pfalz scouts which attacked from the left rear of the single formation. All the observers fired short bursts except for 2Lt Power who fired long bursts from his twin Lewis guns and watched as one of the Pfalz headed down in a straight nose dive, emitting smoke as it went. As well as firing at enemy aircraft 2Lt Wilfred Tremellen was also trying to operate his camera. Two Pfalz attacked and despite him firing his twin Lewis guns, the de Havilland was hit and suddenly awash in petrol from the punctured gravity tank. Blinded by the fuel, his pilot 2Lt Duggan, momentarily lost control and collided with another machine. Managing to regain control, the only apparent damage was to an aileron. The German scout however, taking advantage of the situation, was firing from below the bomber, the blind spot. Tremellen was still returning fire when 'Huntley and Palmer' (his guns had 'H' and 'P' stamped on them) both jammed. Realising the game was up he was astonished to see the German scout turn away evidently hit. This scout was again hit by Power and was later claimed as driven down out of control. Tremellen was not finished and fired Very lights at the remaining German scout near his machine (very risky when soaked in petrol) until Duggan got their machine back in formation. Tremellen carried spare parts for his guns but trying to rectify stoppages in combat was difficult, especially in a strong slipstream. Manhandling twin Lewis guns also took a lot of brawn, and it was a case of quickly moving one gun with probably more accuracy or slowly moving two but with greater fire power.

The same route was flown back to Azelot and all machines landed safely except Duggan and Tremellen. Just as they approached to land the damaged aileron controls finally gave way on their riddled bomber sending it skidding into the ground. Both men escaped unharmed from amongst the pile of fabric and wood, and both would be down to fly again the next day. Hopefully, Tremellen would have an easier time on his fourteenth operational raid. Duggan survived the war but while flying DH9 E8563, he hit some trees killing himself and his observer, 2Lt E.E.Bricknell, on 20th December 1918. Like so many survivors of the war, he was killed in an accident after it.

Target: Cologne (Deutz)
Secondary Target: Bonn, Frescaty Aerodrome, Treves

31st October		Take Off:	**11.40**
55 Squadron		Returned:	**16.20**
Formation 1			
Capt D.R.G.Mackay	2Lt H.C.T.Gompertz	photo machine	
Lt S.L.Dowswell	2Lt M.E.Barlow		
2Lt D.C.Fleischer	2Lt H.B.Mercier		
2Lt C.W.Trimnell	2Lt W.C.Brudenell	ret e/t	
2Lt O.E.Miller	Sgt A.J.Cousins		
2Lt W.D.C.Hutton	2Lt R.Dunn	lost formation	
Formation 2			
Lt J.Cunliffe	2Lt G.E.Little		
2Lt C.Turner	2Lt C.W.Clutsom	could not keep up	
Lt R.F.H.Norman	2Lt F.N.Coxhill	petrol problem	
2Lt H.A.Griffiths	2Lt H.W.Robinson	ret e/t	
2Lt R.Burgess	2Lt G.H.New	could not keep up	
2Lt W.H.Thomas	2Lt J.Mitchell		

Cologne was again the target for 55 Squadron, the third time this month, on this rather misty day with low clouds. A late morning start saw twelve DH4s take off to bomb a target approximately 160 miles over the lines. An attack on railway lines nearer the immediate front or just behind would have probably helped the war effort more, while a drop in the morale of the enemy population was all that would be gained from a target like Cologne. With minimum time to gain height before crossing the lines, twelve DH4s headed north to cross just west of Pont-à-Mousson at 15,500ft.

Engine trouble, and probably inexperience, would rob Mackay of four aircraft within an hour and a half of take-off. First to return at 12.40 was 2Lt Hutton who lost the formations, followed by 2Lt Griffiths who returned at 13.00 with engine trouble. Engine trouble brought 2Lt Trimnell back at 13.15 followed by 2Lt Burgess at 13.40 who could not keep up. As these machines returned the rest were flying west of the Moselle river until they reached Treves. Before Treves was reached, 2Lt Turner who was unable to keep pace, turned and bombed Frescaty aerodrome instead. Turner landed just after Burgess and reported his bombs exploding near the large Zeppelin hangar. From Treves the remaining seven DH4s headed north towards Bonn and Cologne beyond. Thirty miles north of Treves, Lt Norman left the formation and turned back. When crossing the lines earlier, Lt Norman had noticed problems with the flow of his petrol, and had continued on but decided that it was now or never regarding getting home. After dropping his bombs on Treves station, he climbed in his now lighter aircraft and re-crossed the lines at 21,500ft. Flying higher used less petrol and enemy aircraft would have a harder job trying to intercept him; Norman touched down at Azelot at 15.50. The single formation of six bombers reached Bonn at 14.10 where Mackay decided to bomb instead, due to the bad weather ahead, and his fears about fuel and re-crossing the lines. Dropping their ordnance from 16,400ft, eight bursts were seen in the centre of the town either side of the railway.

Turning for home one enemy aircraft was spotted over Cologne but it turned away after seeing the bombers. The weather had turned and the six aircraft were forced to fly a compass heading to the Moselle river. Flying south following the right bank of the Moselle, the formation flew through rain until they reached Pont-à-Mousson at 16.00, at 16,000ft. All six machines landed safely back at Azelot twenty minutes later, except Lt Dowswell who appears to have got lost and landed at 16.40. In all fourteen photos had been taken by 2Lts Gompertz and Coxhill, and one 230lb and ten 112lb bombs had been dropped on the various targets. Opposition for the entire raid was the one enemy aircraft seen over Cologne, and two more over Metz on the outward leg which turned and flew away.

Investigations after the war confirmed the observers' reports. All bombs had fallen just south of the central railway line running through the centre of town, with one bursting actually on the line itself. In all twenty-nine people were killed, thirty-seven severely injured, and twenty slightly injured; several houses had also been hit during the raid. Other sources suggest that the heavy casualties were due to the late warnings of the raid and that the streets were full of people, with one bomb falling on a number of them waiting to get into a tram-car.

Note: Aircraft serial numbers are not recorded for this raid.

Target: Buhl Aerodrome

31st October		**Take Off:**	**12.25**
104 Squadron		**Returned:**	**14.55**
Formation 1			
Capt R.J.Gammon	2Lt H.Grieve		
Lt J.W.Richards	2Lt E.G.Stevens		
Lt H.L.Wren	2Lt W.H.Tresham		
Lt J.Wrighton	Sgt W.H.Ball	ret e/t	
2Lt L.C.Pitts	2Lt H.Alexander		
Formation 2			
Capt E.J.Garland	2Lt W.E.Bottrill		
2Lt P.Hopkinson	2Lt E.D.Barnes		
2Lt J.N.Ogilvie	Sgt W.G.Steward		
2Lt B.F.Ross	2Lt L.W.Launchbury	ret e/t	
Lt J.H.Cuthbertson	2Lt A.B.Rattray		
Lt A.Hemingway	Sgt G.A.Smith	photo machine	

Ordered to attack Buhl aerodrome, 104 was in company with 99 Squadron who had gone for Buhl the previous day. Captain Gammon led the two formations against this home airfield of Jasta 39 and Jasta 78. Leading eleven DH9s, Gammon gained height above Azelot and headed out east for the lines near Blâmont. Engine trouble sent both Lt Ross and Lt Wrighton back home with both landing at 13.40 as the others crossed the lines.

Moderate amounts of archie greeted the crews as they continued east, flying over Lorquin and on to Buhl. Over Buhl at 14.15, two 230lb and fourteen 112lb bombs were let go from 12,000ft, ten bursts being observed on the aerodrome between the large hangar and the small sheds at the north-western corner of the field.

Two enemy aircraft were seen as the crews were half way home, but they failed to catch the bombers and all nine re-crossed the lines at Blâmont. Despite Lt Wrighton returning early in the other photo machines, Sgt Smith still managed to take eighteen photos.

Note: Aircraft serial numbers were not recorded for this raid.

Target: Buhl Aerodrome

31st October		**Take Off:**	**12.45**
99 Squadron		**Returned:**	**15.05**
Formation 1			
Capt W.D.Thom	Sgt J.Jones	ret e/t	
Lt H.S.H.Read	2Lt R.Mugford		
Lt C.E.W.Thresher	2Lt W.Glew	ret e/t	
2Lt L.B.Duggan	2Lt W.J.Tremellen	photo machine	
2Lt L.V.Russell	Sgt S.Beswick		
Formation 2			
Capt H.Sanders	2Lt G.M.Power		
2Lt H.E.King	2Lt E.Smith		
Lt F.K.Crosbie-Choppin	2Lt A.T.Bower		
2Lt W.A.Warwick	Lt L.H.Burrows		

Captain Thom would again lead 99 to Buhl with Captain Sanders heading the second formation. Whilst climbing to altitude two aircraft had to return. First was Captain Thom who landed safely at 14.35, followed by 2Lt Thresher, both with engine trouble. The remaining aircraft made one formation led by Captain Sanders and headed east towards the lines.

The archie which did greet the bombers as they crossed was way off the mark, and the single group of seven headed east towards the target. Over Buhl at 14.25 four 230lb and six 112lb bombs were dropped from 11,000ft. Tremellen who had cheated death the previous day was again busy with his camera, taking sixteen photos. Bursts were observed around the aerodrome with six on the south-east corner of the field, one on a hangar, one on the canal near a bridge and two on the road behind the row of hangars. Although the visibility was poor, two enemy aircraft were seen at about 1,000ft. Whether the observers opened up at these, or just blazed away over the aerodrome is not clear, but they fired about a thousand rounds all the same.

All seven bombers made it back to Azelot and finished a good month for 99 considering the losses they had suffered in the previous months.

CHAPTER 7

OPERATIONS – NOVEMBER 1918

Target: Avricourt Railway Junction

2nd November			**Take Off:**	**11.50**
99 Squadron			**Returned:**	**13.40**
Capt H.Sanders	2Lt G.M.Power	F967		

The weather on the 1st had been dud, but on the 2nd was slightly better, although still not good enough to get twelve aircraft across in formation to a target. The junction of Avricourt, about seven miles behind the lines, was detailed to be hit in support of allied ground forces. Captain Sanders and 2Lt Power decided they could reach the target despite the weather and took off with three 112lb bombs.

After take-off it was apparent that the cloud base was only a thousand feet off the ground. Sanders flew low towards the lines and received very little in the way of archie as they crossed. Although archie had given them an easy time, machine-gun fire from the ground was accurate as they made their way towards the target. The cloud base was higher on the German side, and Sanders managed to get up to 2,500ft as he approached. Over the junction at 13.15, two 112lb bombs were dropped which impacted just west of it. Receiving more machine-gun fire, Sanders dropped his last bomb on what looked like a small ammunition dump west of the junction. It was an ammunition dump and a huge explosion was the result as Sanders headed for the lines. No enemy aircraft were seen the entire trip and Sanders landed safely back at base, or so the bomb raid report says.

However, the wing report tells a different story. DH9a F967 was badly shot up and Sanders crash-landed at Azelot. Sanders himself was unhurt and Power received facial injuries which ended his war.

GEORGE HERBERT POWER was born on 17th November 1895, in Royton, Lancashire. After leaving school he went to work for the Higginshaw Gas Works as a clerk. Aged sixteen he enlisted in the Lancashire Fusiliers Territorial Force and was posted to the 6th Battalion. Promoted to Lance Corporal on May 1st 1914, the Battalion moved to Alexandria in September. Promoted to Corporal in May 1915, he received a gun-shot wound to the left shoulder while serving at Gallipoli. On October 13th he received a temporary commission as a 2nd Lt in the 24th Service Battalion (the 'Oldham Pals'). Posted to the 27th , then the 21st Battalion Manchester Regiment, he proceeded to France on November 10th 1915. While serving with the 21st Battalion at High Wood on the Somme, he received a gun-shot wound to the stomach. While being treated in Hospital at Southampton he was promoted to Lt on February 9th 1917. Returning to his Battalion he was then promoted Acting Captain between 11th November and 10th December 1917. He left the Battalion in Italy on 20th February 1918, and commenced his observer training at No. 1 School of Aeronautics at Reading. On the unemployed list in February 1919, he was Commissioned Lt with 6th Battalion Lancashire Fusiliers in July 1920. Leaving the Army in 1923, he again joined up in 1939 serving as a Captain in the 39th Searchlight Regiment in Northern England on airfield defence. In March 1940 he relinquished his commission on enlistment in the ranks with the 8th Battalion The Border Regiment. By July he had reached the rank of Lt. In December 1941 he embarked for India where he was seconded to the 2nd Ghurkha Rifles. After a spell at Lahore University OTC in March 1944, he held various appointments with South-East Asia Command before returning to the UK in June 1947. He relinquished his commission with the rank of Lieutenant Colonel in 1954 aged 59. George Herbert Power died in Southampton General Hospital aged eighty in 1976. While serving with 99 Squadron he liked to drop empty beer bottles on enemy soldiers "because the noise got the German soldiers running all ways".

KEITH DOUGLAS MARSHALL was to see his award of the D.F.C. gazetted this month. Born on 5th January 1897 in Tara, Ontario, in Canada, he was a grain buyer in Winnipeg before the war. Marshall was one of the original members of 99 Squadron who proceeded overseas in April 1918. On the 11th of March 1919 he joined 123 Squadron, Canadian Air Force, flying light bombers. His citation read as follows:

Lieutenant Keith Douglas Marshall
D.F.C. gazetted 3rd November 1918

A very skilful, and determined air fighter, who has been engaged in twenty-one successful bombing operations since 1st May, 1918. Lieutenant Marshall was the leader of a formation recently detailed to attack an enemy aerodrome, which resulted in the destruction of three enemy machines and eight hangars; no casualties were sustained by his party. This officer was engaged a few days later in a combined attack on a great enemy war factory. Just as the bombs were falling an enemy formation of fifteen machines appeared, and Lieutenant Marshall, as leader, turned quickly in their direction, which disconcerted the enemy so completely that they at once scattered and were unable to reform. During the progress of this bombing expedition thirty-two enemy aircraft were encountered.

Target: Buhl Aerodrome

| 3rd November | | Take Off: | 09.50 |
| 99 Squadron | | Returned: | 12.05 |

Formation 1

Capt W.D.Thom	2Lt J.C.Barns	
2Lt L.B.Duggan	2Lt W.J.Tremellen	
2Lt H.E.King	2Lt C.B.Fairhurst	
2Lt W.A.Warwick	Lt L.H.Burrows	photo machine
2Lt L.V.Russell	Sgt S.Beswick	
2Lt J.W.F.Merer	2Lt N.W.Davidson	

Formation 2

Capt W.G.Stevenson	Sgt J.Jones	
Lt W.C.Jeffries	Sgt E.V.G.Chalmers	ret vac control
Lt H.S.H.Read	2Lt J.E.Nagle	
2Lt C.Lambe	Lt T.Llewellyn	
Lt C.E.W.Thresher	2Lt W.Glew	bombed with 104
Lt F.K.Crosbie-Choppin	2Lt A.T.Bower	photo machine

Azelot, despite the weather, was a hive of activity with all three squadrons getting ready for take-off. Captains Thom and Stevenson led twelve DHs against Buhl aerodrome, if they could see it through the large cloud formations. After gaining height the two formations headed out east towards the lines at Blâmont. Engine trouble forced the two reserve machines to return, followed by Lt Jeffries who landed at 12.05 with vacuum control problems. Lt Thresher, who took off late at 10.30, attempted to catch up with the second formation, couldn't, so joined 104 Squadron who were trying to find Lorquin through the clouds.

Captain Thom led ten machines over the lines little troubled by archie and headed east towards the River Rhine. Despite the large formations of cloud, the bombers arrived over Buhl at 11.25. From 12,000ft, six 230lb and eight 112lb bombs were dropped, three bursts being seen on or near the Zeppelin hangar while another three burst on the landing ground in front of the aircraft hangars. Observers also reported three bursts in the village east of the aerodrome.

The two formations turned for home seeing eight enemy aircraft. Shots were exchanged at long range but no serious engagement took place. The route home went over Lorquin and then Blâmont where the lines were re-crossed. With the weather so bad only six photos were taken, but 1,200 rounds of Lewis were fired by the observers.

Note: 99 Squadron failed to record aircraft serials on this raid in their bomb raid report.

Target: Buhl Aerodrome
Secondary Target: Railway Sidings and Ammunition Dump at Lorquin

3rd November			Take Off:	09.50
104 Squadron			Returned:	12.00

Formation 1

Capt E.J.Garland	2Lt W.E.Bottrill	
2Lt J.N.Ogilvie	Sgt W.G.Steward	
2Lt A.Hemingway	Sgt G.A.Smith	
2Lt B.F.Ross	2Lt L.W.Launchbury	photo machine
2Lt L.C.Pitts	2Lt P.Davey	
Lt J.H.Cuthbertson	2Lt A.B.Rattray	

Formation 2

Capt R.J.Gammon	2Lt H.Grieve	ret pilot sick
Lt J.Wrighton	Sgt W.H.Ball	ret e/t
2Lt S.T.Crowe	2Lt A.H.Penstone	
Lt H.L.Wren	2Lt W.H.Tresham	
Lt J.W.Richards	2Lt E.G.Stevens	
Lt J.R.Tansey	2Lt H.Alexander	ret not keep up

With heavy cloud and an overcast sky, Captain Garland led thirteen machines away from Azelot to bomb Buhl aerodrome. Within twenty minutes of taking off, the spare machine returned with engine trouble, followed by Lt Tansey at 10.50, being unable to keep up. Also returning with engine trouble was Lt Wrighton at 11.10. The two formations continued on and crossed the lines near Blâmont at 11.10.

Archie was very slight as the two formations flew a compass course over cloud towards Sarrebourg. Sarrebourg was obscured by cloud as was the Rhine valley but Garland still looked for a clearing which would allow him to find the target. After much searching, he headed for a clearing which turned out to be over Lorquin, just south of Sarrebourg. Before Lorquin was reached, Captain Gammon became sick and was forced to abort to Azelot; he landed safely at 11.50. Through a gap Garland spotted the railway sidings and a dump and fired a white Very light signalling the two formations to drop their bombs. Seven 230lb and four 112lb bombs were dropped from 10,000ft at 11.20. Two bursts were seen on the railway the rest being obscured by cloud.

Leaving the target area Garland set a compass course back to Azelot where all machines landed safely at midday. No enemy aircraft were seen and no photos were taken.

Note: Aircraft serial numbers are not recorded for this raid.

Target: Railways at Köln (Cologne)
Secondary Target: Sidings at Sarrebourg

3rd November			Take Off:	10.10
55 Squadron			Returned:	13.30

Formation 1

Capt W.J.Pace	Lt D.W.Stewart		photo machine
2Lt G.T.Richardson	2Lt W.H.S.Kingsland		
2Lt D.C.Fletcher	2Lt H.B.Mercier	B7812	W.I.Acc/K.I.Acc
2Lt H.A.Griffiths	2Lt H.W.Robinson		
2Lt R.Burgess	2Lt G.H.New		
2Lt W.D.C.Hutton	2Lt R.Dunn		ret couldn't climb

Formation 2

Lt S.L.Dowswell	2Lt M.E.Barlow	
Lt R.F.H.Norman	Col C.L.Courtney	
2Lt G.Gorrill	2Lt F.N.Coxhill	
2Lt C.W.Trimnell	2Lt W.C.Brudenell	
2Lt W.H.Thomas	2Lt J.Mitchell	photo machine
2Lt F.W.Moulson	2Lt J.D.Adams	ret not keep up

The weather at the start of November was mainly overcast with rain and mist, and on the 3rd it was no better. Cologne was the target as the crews prepared for the three hundred-mile round trip. Opposition hopefully would be light regarding the German Air Service but one could never anticipate. Captain William John Pace, now the proud owner of a D.F.C. was leading. Twelve DH4s rolled forward and took off. Cologne began to look highly unlikely as the two formations continued up through different layers of cloud. Unlikely even to get to the lines was more on the mind of 2Lts Hutton, Gorrill and Moulson who all kept falling behind their respective groups. Hutton was the first to return at 11.35 after his machine would just not climb, Gorrill at 11.40 unable to keep up, while Moulson returned at 11.55. Despite the cloud all men got their machines back down safely at Azelot.

Heading for the lines Captain Pace noticed complete cloud cover over Metz and to the north and north-east. Cologne was now out of the question so both formations followed their leader east to cross the lines near Arracourt. Archie was weak, as the bombers headed south-east over Zabern towards the Rhine valley, where conditions looked slightly better. Two enemy aircraft seen near the lines as they crossed chose not to follow. Once past Sarrebourg the ground was completely covered by cloud so Pace turned the two formations around and lined up to bomb the railway sidings at Sarrebourg. Overhead at 15,500ft, four 230lb and ten 112lb bombs were dropped at 12.15. Only one explosion was observed due to the cloud cover, this bomb exploding on one of the railway tracks. Also near Sarrebourg at this time were seven Fokker DVIIs although they did not attempt to engage and the two formations climbed to 16,000ft and headed for the lines at Blâmont.

Coming in to land, 2Lt Fletcher crashed just outside the aerodrome. Fletcher was seriously injured, his observer, Herbert Blennerhass Mercier of the Royal Irish Rifles was killed; he was only twenty. Eleven photos were taken, and two hundred rounds of Lewis fired presumably at enemy aircraft at long range.

Captain William John Pace came from Edmonton in Canada and was a civil engineer for Northern Railways in Canada between 1911 and 1914. He was killed in a motor accident on 24 June 1919 aged twenty-seven. His Distinguished Flying Cross citation read as follows:

Lieutenant William John Pace
D.F.C. gazetted 2nd November 1918

Since this officer joined his Squadron in March last he has carried out five photographic reconnaissances and has taken part in thirty-two bombing raids. His work has been distinguished throughout by keenness, efficiency and determination. When attacked by hostile planes he has invariably shown coolness and initiative, never hesitating to assist weaker pilots in critical situations. On photographic reconnaissances he has rendered most valuable service.

Reconnaissance

3rd November			**Take Off:**	**10.30**
55 Squadron			**Returned:**	**13.20**
Capt D.R.G.Mackay	2Lt H.C.T.Gompertz	F5725		

Crossing the lines at Pont-à-Mousson at 19,000ft, Mackay and Gompertz headed north towards Metz. Approaching Metz, Gompertz observed eight red and white Fokker DVIIs splitting up, and manoeuvring for a favourable position to attack. The Fokkers, most probably from Jasta 18, could not gain sufficient height and after Gompertz fired one hundred rounds at the nearer ones, they could all be seen spiralling down and apparently landing. From Metz the bomber headed towards Montoy aerodrome with increasingly worsening conditions. After photographing Montoy, Gompertz noticed five machines he thought were single-seaters climbing very fast. These craft were in formation and flew underneath the DH4, still climbing. At about 1,300ft below his DH4, Gompertz fired ninety rounds into the formation, and watched as his rounds struck the aircraft which was positioned number two. Gompertz fired yet more rounds as the formation dispersed in different directions, all except the number two aircraft. This machine descended almost vertically into the clouds "with a kind of blur behind it" as Gompertz put it. He wasn't sure if it was smoke or petrol as visibility was poor but he claimed it as out of control upon landing. The cloud had now rendered reconnaissance impractical and Mackay turned for home. While heading for the lines five more Fokker DVIIs were spotted, three were red and white and two were red all over; these Fokkers were flying in formation but did not try to attack. Gompertz when making out his combat report positioned the fallen enemy aircraft between Metz and Montoy; he also commented that these aircraft were larger then normal enemy single-seat scouts.

Target: Morhange Aerodrome

5th November
110 Squadron

| | | | Take Off: | 11.50 |
| | | | Returned: | Unknown |

Formation 1

Capt D.J.Waterman	2Lt C.C.Carlon	E9711	
Lt M.L.T.Leroy	2Lt W.L.Beck	E704	
2Lt S.C.Henderson	Lt M.C.Trench	F1023	
Lt S.B.Bradley	Sgt A.H.Banks	F1060	
Lt K.B.Wilkinson	2Lt H.M.Keltsuse	F1015	
2Lt D.B.Aitchison	2Lt D.Bower	F996	

Formation 2

Lt W.Armstrong	Sgt W.G.Ambler	F1011	
Lt L.R.Haskell	Lt H.Hinchcliffe	E9722	
2Lt H.P.Gardner	Lt A.S.Robertson	F1028	
2Lt G.A.Wacker	Lt D.Martin	E8482	
2Lt R.R.Spencer	2Lt G.A.Livett	F1032	
2Lt W.L.Carroll	2Lt J.M.Theaker	E8481	

Morhange aerodrome was the target for 110 Squadron on their first show since the terrible losses on the 5th of October. Many new faces had arrived on the Squadron and a short flight to Morhange, just over the lines, would be good experience for the crews, many of whom had never seen combat. Long-range raids into Germany would rest solely on the shoulders of 55 Squadron for the foreseeable future. Morhange according to I.A.F. intelligence was occupied by Kest 3 which was now Jasta 83, (other Kest units from the 30th of October were also made into Jastas) and the 100th Bavarian and 257th Reconnaissance Flights. It was quite a large aerodrome with two very large hangars, six smaller hangars running north-west alongside a railway track and several buildings running north-east alongside a road. This target would receive considerable attention from I.A.F. units over the final days of the war.

The weather was fine, but visibility was only moderate due to haze as Captain Waterman led twelve DH9as into the air. Height was gained over Bettoncourt before the two formations headed east towards Lunéville and then north crossing the lines near Hampont.

Archie was light as they went over but on reaching Dieuze a heavy and accurate barrage caught the two formations at 16,400ft. Continuing north they reached Morhange at 13.15 and dropped five 230lb and eleven 112lb bombs. Targeting was accurate as four bombs hit the railway line, three exploded on hangars alongside the railway while four burst on the north-east corner of the aerodrome amongst some hangars. Enemy aircraft were spotted but did not close and the two formations flew directly south crossing the lines at Château-Salins.

Target: Morhange Aerodrome
Secondary Target: Buhl Aerodrome

6th November
104 Squadron

| | | | Take Off: | 12.00 |
| | | | Returned: | 14.30 |

Formation 1

Lt J.W.Richards	2Lt E.G.Stevens	D526	W.I.A./W.I.A.
2Lt J.Wrighton	Sgt W.H.Ball	D5773	
2Lt W.B.Henderson	2Lt W.J.Sutherland		
2Lt S.T.Crowe	2Lt A.H.Penstone		ret e/t
2Lt B.H.Stretton	2Lt H.Grieve	E8972	
2Lt H.L.Wren	2Lt W.H.Tresham	D1050	P.O.W./P.O.W.

Formation 2

Lt J.K.Cuthbertson	2Lt A.B.Rattray		
2Lt P.Hopkinson	Lt C.C.Blizard	D487	
2Lt J.N.Ogilvie	Sgt W.G.Steward		
2Lt B.F.Ross	2Lt L.W.Launchbury		
2Lt F.Wallis	2Lt R.D.Vaughn		
2Lt A.Hemingway	Sgt G.A.Smith	D3101	K.I.A./K.I.A.

A combined raid with 99 Squadron to bomb the aerodromes at Morhange and Lellingham, was detailed for 104 Squadron. Lt Richards led the first formation, and Lt Cuthbertson the second as twelve DH9s took off and started to climb into a cloudy sky. As arranged 99 would be the lead Squadron although 104 took off according to reports, twenty minutes before them. Of the twelve aircraft only 2Lt Crowe returned with engine trouble at 12.45, the rest met 99 Squadron over Lunéville at 11,000ft as arranged.

Archie was heavy and accurate as they crossed the lines at Blâmont at 13.50. Cloud cover obscured everything near the lines so Captain Thom led both Squadrons east towards the secondary target of Buhl aerodrome. Just before reaching it, the sight of between twenty and thirty scouts greeted the crews as they followed 99 Squadron into the fray. Sergeant Ball was first to claim one after firing a long burst at a Fokker DVII which entered a steep spiral and caught fire. With the ensuing fight Ball was unable to see if it crashed. Lt Blizard was also in the thick of it firing at up to fifteen different scouts at long range. One of these scouts closed to within 150 yards. Blizard fired eighty rounds at it and watched as it stalled and then entered a spin. He followed as long as he could before other enemy aircraft caught his attention. He also noticed a scout going down in flames; both Blizard and Ball claimed these scouts at 14.00 before reaching the target. Arriving over Buhl at 14.10, seven 230lb and eight 112lb bombs were dropped from 11,000ft. One 112lb bomb scored a direct hit on a hangar on the north-eastern side of the aerodrome while another burst on the landing ground; other hits were not observed due to the air battle.

A course was steered west-south-west as the two formations left the target area still heavily engaged by up to thirty scouts which were mostly Fokker DVIIs and Pfalz. With this amount of enemy aircraft casualties were inevitable. First to leave formation was 2Lt Hemingway who was seen going down by other observers in an out of control spin. The second to leave was 2Lt Wren, with a shot radiator; he was last spotted being followed down by three scouts by observers of 99 Squadron. The fighting continued to the lines where 2Lt Grieve claimed a Fokker DVII out of control at 14.10 near Lorquin. This scout had ventured to within fifty yards of Grieve who hit it with a burst, and it was seen to spin for two thousand feet before Grieve was distracted by more scouts.

The lines were re-crossed near Blâmont and all nine surviving aircraft landed safely back at Azelot. Lt Richards and his observer 2Lt Stevens, were helped from their cockpits as both had been hit in their left legs by machine-gun fire. Wren and Tresham became prisoners of war. Wren had been wounded badly in the thigh, and his immediate treatment was not very good. Tresham was also wounded in the hand. Hemingway and Smith were killed. In all 3,400 rounds had been fired but no photos taken for obvious reasons. What is interesting is that 104 managed to overtake 99 Squadron on the return leg although they bombed the target five minutes later.

Doing the damage again were Jasta 39 stationed at Buhl. The pilots claimed three DH9s, two near Buhl and one at Ibingen. Vizefeldwebel Hanz Nülle claimed his tenth and eleventh victories with a DH9 at Buhl and another at Ibingen. The other victor was Unteroffizier Krüchelsdorf who claimed a DH9 at Buhl for his one and only victory of the war. All three were claimed at 15.00 German time which was one hour ahead of British, times and locations match but who actually got whom is unclear. In all 104 Squadron were awarded one destroyed and two out of control although German records suggest no fatal casualties on this date. Arnold Hemingway, aged nineteen from Yorkshire, and George Arnold Smith, aged twenty, from Bradford in Yorkshire, were both buried at Sarralbe.

Note: Aircraft serial numbers were not recorded, serial numbers mentioned are from combat reports.

Target: Lellingham Aerodrome
Secondary Target: Buhl Aerodrome

6th November 99 Squadron			Take Off: Returned:	12.20 14.45
Formation 1				
Capt W.D.Thom	2Lt J.G.Nagle			
2Lt V.C.Varcoe	Sgt H.L.Bynon			
Lt H.S.H.Read	2Lt F.P.Regan		ret e/t	
Lt F.K.Crosbie-Choppin	2Lt A.T.Bower	D544	photo machine	
2Lt L.V.Russell	Sgt S.Beswick	D1008	W.I.A./	
2Lt C.E.W.Thresher	2Lt W.Glew	C3040	P.O.W./D.O.W.	

Formation 2

Capt H.Sanders	2Lt J.C.Barns		ret hit by archie
2Lt L.B.Duggan	2Lt W.J.Tremellen		
2Lt H.E.King	Lt T.Llewellyn	D3270	
2Lt W.A.Warwick	Lt L.H.Burrows	B9394	
Lt W.C.Jeffries	Sgt E.V.G.Chalmers	D5650	
2Lt G.R.A.Dick	2Lt E.Smith	C6210	photo machine

The aerodrome at Lellingham near Lorquin, was the target for 99 Squadron on a cloudy and misty day. Captain Thom was leading as twelve DH9s circled above Azelot gaining height, and at 11,000ft the two formations headed for the lines near Badonviller. While climbing Lt Read noticed his engine getting hotter and hotter, and he was forced to abort, landing safely at 13.30.

As the lines were reached, heavy and accurate archie greeted the bombers as they crossed. Captain Sanders had a lucky escape as shell fragments from exploding archie pierced his petrol tank. With his machine quickly becoming awash in petrol, Sanders had no choice but to return to Azelot landing safely at 14.15. Now down to ten Captain Thom set about trying to find Lellingham aerodrome through the clouds and mist. Flying between Cirey and Lorquin just over the lines, Lellingham couldn't be seen so Thom headed east towards Buhl. Reaching here at 14.05, six 230lb, six 112lb and five 50lb bombs fell from 11,000ft. Three bursts were observed on or near the large hangar at the northern end of the aerodrome, while three bursts were also seen on the road next to the large hangar. Attention quickly turned to twenty German scouts which now turned towards the bombers.

Attacks were mostly made against the second formation and Lt Llewellyn soon had three scouts on his tail. He fired a whole drum at the nearest and watched as it side-slipped steeply, issuing thick smoke for about 4,000ft. Lt Burrows also fired at a scout which came up on the right-hand side of the second formation. Burrows fired and watched as the enemy scout dived and caught fire about 3,000ft below the formation, it continued down and crashed in a wood south of Arzviller. It wasn't all one way traffic. 2Lt Smith watched as a DH9 went down with two Pfalz scouts in tow just after leaving the target area. The engagement continued as 99 headed towards the lines. In the first formation 2Lt Nagle fired at a scout which came under their aircraft from the right to attack the second formation behind them. His fire hit the scout which entered a spin, and was seen going down smoking for about 4,000ft. Also firing at enemy aircraft was 2Lt Bower. This scout entered a spin and was seen to crash into a field near a wood south-west of the target. All of these aircraft shot down were confirmed by other observers, however some claims were obviously for the same aircraft although the official tally according to the bomb raid report was one destroyed and two driven down out of control; all scouts claimed were Pfalz.

These engagements continued near to the lines which were re-crossed at Blâmont. All nine made it back to Azelot, although 2Lt Russell had a lucky escape after a splinter from an exploding anti-aircraft shell cut his face. In all 2,690 rounds were fired during the engagement while twenty-four photos had been taken. Thresher and Glew, both wounded, were taken prisoner. Thresher had a slight wound to the hand while Glew unfortunately died of his wounds the next day. The victor of Thresher and Glew was either Vizefeldwebel Hanz Nülle, or Unteroffizier Krüchelsdorf both of Jasta 39. Both of these men claimed a DH9 at Buhl at 15.00 German time which was one hour ahead of British time. As mentioned earlier the other machine which went down at Buhl was from 104 Squadron who were flying behind 99 Squadron, and bombed Buhl five minutes after. Jasta 39 claimed three DH9s in total. This would seem to tally up with the two lost by 104, and the single lost by 99. Although several claims were made by different observers, no German casualties this day were recorded amongst the Jastas, at least, no fatalities. William Glew came from Howden in Yorkshire, he was eighteen and was buried at Sarralbe.

Target: The Burbach Works at Saarbrücken

6th November			**Take Off:**	**12.30**
55 Squadron			**Returned:**	**15.15**

Formation 1

Capt J.B.Fox	Lt J.Parke	A7427	
Lt S.L.Dowswell	2Lt M.E.Barlow		
2Lt G.T.Richardson	2Lt L.J.B.Ward	D8384	P.O.W./D.O.W.
Lt R.F.H.Norman	Capt J.F.W.Tanqueray	B7933	photo machine
2Lt R.Burgess	2Lt G.H.New		
2Lt G.Gorrill	2Lt W.H.S.Kingsland		

A single formation led by Captain Fox was tasked with hitting the Burbach works near Saarbrücken. This was one of the largest manufactures of armour plate and was well defended by twenty 10.5 cm anti-aircraft guns. The bombers took off and gained height except for 2Lt Gorrill who was having trouble getting airborne and who finally took off after the other five had left. The weather was again very cloudy with mist and rain showers. Gorrill hunted in amongst the cloud formations but could not find the others. Captain Fox led the formation through several layers of thin cloud up to 15,000ft where he turned for the Fôret de Parroy.

The lines were crossed over the forest at 15,500ft, and a compass course steered towards Saarbrücken. Gorrill was still unable to locate the formation so made his own way over the lines. Spotting the aerodrome at Hattigny, he dropped his 230lb bomb watching it explode beside a hangar. He then turned for home and landed back at Azelot at 14.35. Fox continued on his course until he came to a clear patch in the overcast at Bensdorf. This clearing in the cloud continued all the way to Saarbrücken which was reached at 14.00. From 16,000ft three 230lb and four 112lb bombs were dropped through a very heavy and accurate barrage of archie. One bomb was seen to explode on the sidings and another on the factory adjoining the station. Once clear of the barrage, thirty enemy aircraft attacked. Suddenly Fokker DVIIs were everywhere and a large fight soon started. Captain John Tanqueray described the Fokkers as having grey wings, and either red or yellow tails, some also had two white stripes across the centre of the top wing. One of these Fokkers dived at Tanqueray's machine and opened fire at two hundred yards. Tanqueray held his fire until the Fokker was one hundred yards away then fired thirty rounds. The Fokker turned over and entered a spin and a series of somersaults; it was last seen still falling three thousand feet below. Also in the thick of it was Lt Parke, who described the Fokkers as having white and yellow tails. Firing fifty rounds at a Fokker attacking another machine in his formation, he watched as his tracers entered the cockpit. The Fokker stalled and then dived which turned into a spin. The enemy aircraft continued to spin for about six thousand feet where it broke up in the air. Parke fired eighty rounds at another Fokker attacking the formation and watched as his tracers hit the engine and the fuselage. This enemy aircraft stalled and entered a spin and was last seen spinning below the formation where it was lost in the haze; these combats took place at 14,500ft. The reason for the drop in altitude was to gain speed so as to enter a large formation of clouds as soon as possible.

When the clouds were reached the enemy aircraft broke off their attack and all four bombers re-crossed the lines at 14,000ft at Arracourt. The last time Richardson and Ward were seen was just before the formation entered cloud. Their DH4 was losing height slowly below the formation, but what was more worrying was that they were streaming petrol. In all the observers had fired 2,930 rounds of Lewis and despite the attention of enemy aircraft, Captain Tanqueray had taken ten photos. Many machines were riddled and 55 did well to stay together and get home; clouds which were often the enemy were this day the saviour.

Vizefeldwebel Brüchner of Jasta 78 had a DH4 confirmed at St Georg-Ibingen at 15.00 German time, for his one and only victory of the war. What is certain is that apart from Jasta 78, Jasta 39 also engaged 55 Squadron, these two Jastas also engaged 99 Squadron who were attacking Buhl aerodrome. Geoffrey Taswell Richardson was a student at Trinity College, Cambridge, before the war. Born 5th March 1897, he came from Trewollack, Bodmin, in Cornwall. He was repatriated to England from the General Hospital at Rouen, to the Prince of Wales Hospital on 27th January 1919. Richardson had joined 55 Squadron on 14th June 1918. Lewis John Beer Ward died from his wounds. The official date at first was 2nd January 1919, but this was later changed to death accepted as having occurred in action on or soon after 6th November 1918.

After the war civilian reports noted that seven bombs fell on the outskirts of the Burbach works, just north of the station causing slight damage. Two other bombs fell in the suburb of St.Johann resulting in considerable damage to private property.

Target: Bensdorf Railway Station

9th November		Take Off:	11.30
55 Squadron		Returned:	12.45
Formation 1			
Capt D.R.G.Mackay	2Lt H.C.T.Gompertz		

Another solo assault by the experienced 'Jock' Mackay, would hopefully take him to Bensdorf railway station near Morhange. After taking off Mackay headed for the lines at Arracourt at 1,500ft.

Receiving some fire as they crossed the lines, Mackay climbed his machine up to 3,000ft, heading north-north-east towards Morhange flying above the overcast. When he thought he was over Morhange, he descended through the cloud coming out at approximately 500ft to get his bearings. After about a minute,

Mackay picked up the railway line which ran east towards Bensdorf, and followed it. Overhead the aerodrome at Bensdorf there seemed little activity and the only aircraft seen was a Rumpler poking out of a hangar entrance. Tracers arched up towards Mackay as he headed off towards the railway station nearby. Attacking from the north Mackay noticed three trains in the station. The first was a covered goods train facing east containing soldiers and materials. Some of the soldiers on this train started to fire at Mackay, others began to run. The two other trains were facing east and west and looked like passenger trains; Mackay also noticed what looked like a dump full of material, mostly wood. Mackay dropped one 112lb bomb which burst on the tracks, slightly to the east of the station between the two passenger trains. He dropped one of his 40lb phosphorous bombs on the dump which exploded and started a fire. Mackay had been receiving accurate fire while in the target area and he quickly left climbing to 2,000ft and steering a course south-west. Gompertz had also been busy firing 150 rounds of Lewis at different targets. Re-crossing the lines at Sornéville Mackay landed safely back at Azelot.

According to his report Mackay also had another 112lb bomb and another 40lb phosphorous on board but no mention is made of where they fell. Mackay and Gompertz would team up again on the 10th, as part of the last bombing raid carried out by 55 Squadron in the Great War.

Note: The aircraft serial number was not recorded.

Target: Transport at Château-Salins

9th November		**Take Off:**	**11.45**
99 Squadron		**Returned:**	**14.10/15.40**
Formation 1			
Maj C.R.Cox	2Lt J.B.Fairhurst	landed at Toul	
Capt W.D.Thom	2Lt J.G.Nagle		
2Lt L.B.Duggan	2Lt W.J.Tremellen		

Since the 6th, low cloud and mist had limited 99 Squadron to local practice flights in some of their DH9as. The morning of the 9th again presented an overcast sky with cloud reported as low as 200ft in some areas. Despite these conditions three DH9as were wheeled out and loaded with bombs. All three took off and were soon lost to sight as they headed out north-west towards the lines at Château-Salins.

Major Cox was still unsure of the local terrain, having only arrived on the 4th of November to take over command of the Squadron from Captain Thom. After flying around and becoming lost, Major Cox put his machine down at Toul aerodrome at 15.35. Captain Thom and 2Lt Duggan continued on separately towards Château-Salins. Thom arrived at 12.50 dropping two of his 112lb bombs on motor transport, and his third 112lb bomb fell further up the road on horse drawn transport. Despite the cloud cover and low height, Thom and Nagle came under heavy and accurate fire from both archie and ground troops. The second machine flown by 2Lt Duggan dropped his two 230lb bombs on the railway lines south of Château-Salins scoring two direct hits.

The return journey was more eventful for both crews as they tried to find Azelot through the cloud and mist. Duggan touched down at 14.10, while Thom landed at 15.40.

CLAUDE RUSSELL COX was born on 9th July 1893. His father was a clerk for the London and Brazilian Bank in Buenos Aires, Argentina and rose to Manager when the bank became the Anglo-South American Bank in Rosario. A student at Churches College, Petersfield, between September 1905 and July 1907, Claude served in the College's Cadet Corps for two years. Moving to Argentina in 1908 he went to study engineering at the National College in Buenos Aires. He returned to England on 20th March 1915 and joined the 7th Battalion Dorsetshire Regiment. He applied for training with the Royal Flying Corps and joined 22 Squadron on 2nd August 1916 flying FE2bs. Back to England on rest, he was posted to No.9 Training Squadron at Norwich on 6th November 1917 as an instructor. Cox served here until he returned to operations with 99 Squadron in late 1918.

Target: Railway Sidings at Lorquin and Racécourt

9th November		**Take Off:**	**14.50**
104 Squadron		**Returned:**	**15.45**

Formation 1

Capt E.J.Garland	2Lt W.E.Bottrill	
Lt B.H.Stretton	2Lt H.Grieve	
Lt J.R.Tansey	2Lt R.W.Lewin	landed Tantonville
Capt J.Cunliffe	2Lt J.T.White	ret with bombs
2Lt W.B.Henderson	2Lt R.D.Vaughn	landed Essey

A day of low cloud, rain, and mist patches greeted the pilots and observers of 104 Squadron. Although the weather grounded formations of bombers individual raids were mounted by the more experienced crews. First away at 14.50 was Captain Garland, shortly followed by Lt Stretton, both heading up towards the overcast.

Garland carried on up and through heading east towards the lines at 4,000ft flying on a compass heading. Sighting Lorquin and its railway and dump, he descended and dropped four 50lb bombs. Four bursts were observed in a field twenty yards from the sidings and dump. Garland immediately climbed for the sanctuary of the clouds after receiving a fair amount of ground fire. He flew a reciprocal heading and landed safely back at Azelot at 15.45.

Stretton had chosen to fly beneath the cloud which started at about 1,200ft. He flew directly to the triangle of railways south of Racécourt and dropped four 50lb bombs. The sidings were full of rolling stock and Stretton watched as one of his bombs impacted within the sidings, another bomb fell twenty-five yards from the sidings while the other two were not seen to explode. Receiving heavy fire from the ground, he turned for home still under the clouds, and landed safely back at Azelot at 15.45 also.

Next to leave Azelot at 14.50 was Lt Tansey. Conditions however had worsened and unable to find the front lines he turned for home. Azelot was now obscured and after forty minutes he finally put down at Tantonville. Next away was Captain Cunliffe who took off at 15.00. Again the weather prevented any offensive action and he landed back at base at 15.50. Last to attempt a raid was 2Lt Henderson who took off at 15.30 and headed up into the overcast. Unable to find the lines also he was forced to return home, if he could find it. After much searching and probably lack of petrol he force-landed at Essey three kilometres from Nancy. The Adjutant at 104 was not too hopeful of their return and initially posted them as missing.

Reconnaissance/Bomb Raid

9th November			**Take Off:**	**Unknown**
110 Squadron			**Returned:**	**Unknown**
Capt J.L.M.de C Hughes- Chamberlain	2Lt A.R.Wylde	E704		

This aircraft went out on a solo bombing and reconnaissance mission but Hughes-Chamberlain was unable to find the target due to the cloud. Flying between 300ft and 2,500ft he had crossed the lines at Bezange-la-Grande and then flew along the trenches German side up to Château-Salins. Unable to find any targets they flew a heading of 350° for fifteen minutes but found no targets. Upon landing Hughes-Chamberlain reported the German trenches as being evacuated.

Target: Morhange Aerodrome

10th November			**Take Off:**	**11.00**
110 Squadron			**Returned:**	**Unknown**

Formation 1

Capt D.J.Waterman	2Lt C.C.Carlon	F1065
Lt S.B.Bradley	Sgt A.H.Banks	F1060
Lt M.L.T.Leroy	2Lt W.L.Beck	E9722
2Lt S.C.Henderson	Lt M.C.French	E8482
2Lt D.B.Aitchison	2Lt D.Bower	F996

Formation 2
Capt J.L.M. de C Hughes-
   Chamberlain   2Lt A.R.Wylde   F1011
2Lt A.R.S.Proctor   2Lt L.R.Robins   E703
Lt R.Neish   Sgt F.Quilter   F1023
2Lt R.D.V.Howard   2Lt R.W.Jones   F1032
2Lt W.J.Sanderson   2Lt F.H.Wilcockson   F1054
2Lt W.L.Carroll   2Lt J.M.Theaker   E8481

Morhange was the target again for 110, as well as 99 and 104 Squadrons. The weather was cloudy in the morning but this cleared, leaving large banks of clouds with clear patches and good visibility. Captain Waterman led again with Captain Hughes-Chamberlain at the head of the second group. The two formations took off and started to gain height before heading out north towards Château-Salins.

   Crossing over the lines archie was quiet as the bombers proceeded towards Morhange. Overhead at 12.30, seven 230lb and seven 112lb bombs were dropped from 17,500ft by the first formation and 18,000ft by the second. No record is given of bomb bursts but observers fired between one and three drums of Lewis ammunition at about a dozen large aircraft seen on the aerodrome near hangars. Several of these aircraft started to take off as the bombers appeared. Both groups headed straight for the lines re-crossing at Château-Salins; no enemy aircraft were seen in the air except for those seen taking off. All machines returned to Bettoncourt.

Leading the second formation on his one and only raid with the Squadron was JOHN LLOYD MELVILLE DE COSIGNY HUGHES-CHAMBERLAIN. Born on the 15th of January 1896 at 42 Worton Road, Hove, he attended St.Edward's School, Oxford, when his parents moved to Arncott House, also in Oxford. When war broke out he lived at 236 Barcombe Avenue in Streatham Hill, London. He joined the 2nd Battalion the Suffolk Regiment and was a temporary 2nd Lieutenant attached to the Army Cyclist Corps. Swapping his bicycle for wings, he joined the Royal Flying Corps and first served with 11 Squadron in 1916 on FE2bs. On 13th May 1916 he was sent home to learn to fly at Christ Church, Oxford. In the summer of 1917 he was flying RE8s with No.7 Squadron, being wounded on 27 July. He joined 110 Squadron in October 1918 and remained in the R.A.F. where by 1937 he was a Wing Commander.

WILLIAM JOHN (JACK) SANDERSON was born in Lakewood, Ohio, U.S.A. on November 24th 1898. He was raised on a farm outside London, Ontario, Canada, from where he joined the 9th Battalion Canadian Railway Troops on the outbreak of war. He was sent to France in 1916, where he successfully applied for a transfer to the Royal Flying Corps. Transferred to England for pilot training, he was sent to 110 Squadron where his only bombing raid appeared to be on 10th November. He stayed with the Squadron flying mail for the British Army of Occupation in Germany, until 110 disbanded and he returned to his father's farm in Canada.

   In 1928 the London Flying Club was formed. Completion of an instructors course saw him become the flying club's instructor. A chance meeting with Major R.H.Fleet, President of Consolidated Aircraft Corporation in New York invoked a career change. He became the Canadian representative for the company and began demonstrating Fleet 2 aircraft in Canada. When manufacturing began in Fort Erie, Ontario, he became General Manager and test pilot and became recognized as one of the best aerobatic pilots in the country. He was appointed to the Board of Directors of the Commercial Air Transport and Manufacturers Association of Canada, in November 1937. In October 1939, he was asked to head the Aircraft Division Defence Purchasing Board, and with its reorganization in April 1940, he was appointed Director of Aircraft Supply. After helping with the British Commonwealth Air Training Plan he returned to Fleet Aircraft in October 1940. At war's end he returned to Toronto after a stint in America, and set up Sanderson-Acfield Aircraft Limited, and continued as a Cessna sales agency. At 65 he did a season of amphibious flying in Newfoundland. He moved to British Columbia in 1967 where he qualified on helicopters and retired. He died in Vancouver, British Columbia on 22nd January 1984.

Target: Deutz Factory at Köln (Cologne)
Secondary Target: Railway Sidings at Ehrang

| 10th November | | | Take Off: | 11.55 |
| 55 Squadron | | | Returned: | 15.15/ 30 |

Formation 1

Capt D.R.G.Mackay	2Lt H.C.T.Gompertz	F5725	D.O.W./P.O.W.
Lt S.L.Dowswell	2Lt M.E.Barlow		
2Lt W.H.Thomas	2Lt J.D.Adams		
2Lt C.W.Trimnell	2Lt W.C.Brudenell		
2Lt P.Girvin	2Lt W.Ward		ret lost formation
2Lt H.A.Griffiths	2Lt H.W.Robinson		

Formation 2

Capt W.J.Pace	Lt D.W.Stewart	
Lt R.F.H.Norman	Capt J.F.D.Tanqueray	
2Lt R.Burgess	2Lt G.H.New	
2Lt W.D.C.Hutton	2Lt R.Dunn	
2Lt O.E.Miller	Sgt A.J.Cousins	photo machine
2Lt L.Ramsden	2Lt J.Motion	

Cologne was once again the assigned target for 55 on what proved to be their last raid of the war. Talk of an Armistice was rife but until word came, operations carried on. All that could be hoped for with the end in sight was that one would survive. The experienced and well-liked twenty-three-year old 'Jock' Mackay would lead. Twelve DH4s roared over Azelot and started to climb in amongst the layers of cloud and haze. While in the climb over Toul, 2Lt Girvin was seen to fall out of formation and had still not arrived at Azelot when the others returned. At 15,000ft the two formations headed for the lines just west of Chambley.

Once over the lines the bombers headed over Conflans, east of Metz, and continued north-east towards Briey. To the east over Metz eight enemy aircraft could be seen, but they did not follow and Mackay led the eleven bombers on over Esch and on to Trier. This whole route had been flown under exceptionally heavy and accurate archie, as in some defiant gesture from a nation about to capitulate. Cloud cover to the north persuaded Mackay to bomb the sidings at Ehrang just north of their position. At 13.45 five 230lb and twelve 112lb bombs were dropped from 15,500ft. Observations were difficult due to the cloud and mist but two bursts were seen on the railway tracks as the formations headed south-west for Saarburg. Still the archie came heavy and accurate as the formations flew over Remich and Esch. For 2Lt Gompertz, a lesson in landing a DH4 presented itself as Mackay in the front seat, suddenly badly wounded by a shell splinter, let go of the controls. All the pilots watched as their leader's machine descended in a slow glide between Thionville and Metz. The formations carried on over Audun-les-Romans and crossed the lines near Gondrecourt. They became separated amongst cloud as they descended, but all returned to Azelot, the last, 2Lt Trimnell, landing at 15.30. Mackay had been flying one photo machine while Sergeant Cousins in the other had taken seven photos. Mackay and Gompertz were down on the German side and both prisoners of war. Unfortunately the much respected Mackay died of his wounds the following day, the day the war ended; Gompertz was not wounded and was repatriated after the war.

DUNCAN RONALD GORDON MACKAY was born in Inverness on 30th September 1895. He was educated at Brandon School, Painswick Road in Cheltenham, before going on to Cheltenham College, attending between 1909 and 1914. From college he joined the 2nd (Public Schools) Battalion of the Royal Fusiliers being commissioned into the 13th Battalion Argyll and Sutherland Highlanders on 2nd June 1916. From here he joined the Royal Flying Corps and served with 55 Squadron where he was wounded on 23rd April 1917. He is buried in the military plot at Joeuf Communal Cemetery, Meurthe-et-Moselle in France. His parents at his time of death were living at Gatehouse, Midhurst in Sussex.

HARRY CHRISTOPHER TRAVERS GOMPERTZ came from Ilfracombe, South Devon. Born on 25th May 1898, he attended Winchester College where he excelled in his studies. Commissioned as a 2Lt in the Royal Field Artillery on 26th June 1917, he joined the R.F.C. in August. Confirmed as an observer officer on 26th June, he flew most of his operations with Mackay while with 55. He was repatriated on 29th November 1918, and left the R.A.F. on 28th January 1919. Gompertz was wounded while with 55 (30th August) and was fortunate to survive the war, having a collection of bullet holes in his Sidcot suit by the war's end. His father was the Honourable Mr Justice Gompertz of the Supreme Court in Hong Kong.

Target: Morhange Aerodrome

10th November		Take Off:	12.25
99 Squadron		Returned:	15.05

Formation 1

Capt W.G.Stevenson	2Lt F.P.Regan	
2Lt W.T.Jones	2Lt N.W.Davidson	
2Lt H.W.Atherton	Sgt P.A.Cuka	ret not keep up
Lt F.K.Crosbie-Choppin	2Lt A.T.Bower	photo machine
2Lt C.Lambe	2Lt R.Mugford	ret e/t
Lt W.C.Jeffries	Sgt E.V.G.Chalmers	

Formation 2

Maj C.R.Cox	2Lt J.G.Nagle	
2Lt L.B.Duggan	2Lt W.J.Tremellen	ret engine seized
2Lt H.E.King	Lt T.Llewellyn	
2Lt M.J.Poulton	2Lt J.L.M.Oliphant	ret not keep up
2Lt W.A.Warwick	Lt L.H.Burrows	
2Lt G.R.A.Dick	2Lt E.Smith	ret obs sick

Many new faces were among the thirteen pilots and observers lined up for the raid on Morhange aerodrome just over the lines. Captain Stevenson led all thirteen machines away with the new Commanding Officer at the head of the second formation. The weather was cloudy in the morning, although it had started to clear, and by the time 99 took off, it had cleared significantly so finding the target shouldn't have been a problem. The real problem would be getting the new inexperienced crews to the target. First to return at 14.15 was 2Lt Lambe followed by 2Lt Poulton. Lambe, a mechanical engineer, had an overheating engine while Poulton could not keep formation. Poulton was on his first raid since returning from hospital after his crash on the 25th of September. Another two machines returned at 14.35, those of 2Lt Atherton who could not keep up with the others and the more experienced 2Lt Duggan whose engine seized up. With a sick observer 2Lt Dick was forced to return at 14.55 followed by the spare aircraft also. From a total of thirteen aircraft, Captain Stevenson led only seven in a single group over the lines at Château-Salins coming under heavy and accurate archie as they did so.

Arriving over Morhange at 14.30, four 230lb and six 112lb bombs were dropped from 11,000ft. Four direct hits were observed on a hangar next to a railway line and a road, while two bursts were seen on the railway itself. One bomb was seen to explode close to eight machines parked in front of the hangars, while three bombs exploded on the landing ground.

The machines re-crossed the lines at Château-Salins and landed safely back at Azelot at 14.30. Throughout the raid eight enemy aircraft were seen but did not engage, and observers fired 1,020 rounds of Lewis but claimed no victories. 2Lt Bower took four photos and reported two trains at Morhange going in opposite directions.

Target: Morhange Aerodrome
Secondary Target: Ammunition Dump at Sarrebourg

10th November		Take Off:	13.00
104 Squadron		Returned:	15.00

Formation 1

| Capt J.Cunliffe | Lt C.C.Blizard |

Lt P.C.Saxby	Sgt W.H.Ball	ret e/t
2Lt G.Wilby	2Lt H.V.Westwood	
2Lt S.T.Crowe	2Lt G.C.Graham	ret not climb
2Lt J.N.Ogilvie	Sgt W.G.Steward	
2Lt R.F.Lynch	Sgt H.Parkin	

Formation 2

Capt C.H.Sands	2Lt T.Bailey		
2Lt L.C.Pitts	2Lt P.Davey		
Lt B.H.Stretton	2Lt H.Grieve		
2Lt F.Wallis	2Lt C.B.Parker		
2Lt N.de Gersigny	2Lt R.D.Vaughn		
2Lt W.B.Henderson	2Lt W.J.Sutherland		ret e/t
Capt E.J.Garland	2Lt W.E.Bottrill	F1867 DH10	

Again Morhange was the target, and again 104 would follow 99 formating. Two formations of six led by Captain Cunliffe and Captain Sands took off to gain height behind the already formating 99 Squadron. Returning in the photo machine from the second formation was 2Lt Henderson with engine trouble; he landed at Azelot at 13.25. First to return from the first formation at 13.45 was Lt Saxby on his first raid with the Squadron, he also had engine trouble. A third machine returned at 14.05 being unable to climb, this was flown by Lt Crowe and was the other photo machine. The remaining nine bombers joined up behind 99 Squadron at 11,000ft, and crossed the lines near Château-Salins coming under moderate and fairly accurate archie.

Arriving over Morhange at 14.30, three 230lb, eight 112lb and eight 50lb bombs went down from 11,000ft. Ten bursts were observed in all. Two bombs exploded on the centre of the aerodrome, one direct hit was seen on the railway line south-west of the aerodrome, and a solitary bomb burst on a hangar at the north end. Two bombs blew up two huts on the south-west corner, causing fires, while a further four bombs just missed the railway line also in the south-west corner of the field. Enemy aircraft arrived in the shape of seven scouts but the gap was not closed, and fire was only exchanged at long range. The nine bombers re-crossed the lines and landed safely back at Azelot at 15.00. One thousand rounds were expended but no photos were taken as both photo machines had already returned.

Although not on an operational raid this day, Ewart Garland was aloft in a recent arrival to the Squadron in the shape of the new De Havilland 10. Destined to replace the unreliable DH9, 104 Squadron had received DH10 F1867 in late September or early October 1918. Fitted with two American Liberty 12 engines, Garland was on a test flight with William Bottrill in the back seat as they headed towards the lines. There is no bomb raid report regarding this flight but mention is made in the fascinating diary written by Garland. Although capable of carrying six 230lb bombs it is unlikely that six were carried, especially on a practice or test flight. What we do know is that they dropped their bombs on an ammunition dump near Sarrebourg just west of Saverne. On his return Bottrill fired at four enemy scouts with his twin Lewis guns. Fortunately he missed as the German scouts turned out to be French Spads. They returned safely and there ended the only operational raid carried out by a DH10 in the Great War. Below is how Garland described it in his diary: *'(Sun) Well! The war seems to continue – there was a raid on a Hun aerodrome and one of our machines was lost. I took up the D.H.10 and went to bomb Sarrebourg aerodrome on my own – I'd dropped my bombs and was coming back at 100m.p.h. when four scouts dived around us. – Bottrill let off a few bursts from his double-barrell Lewis, and suddenly we realized they were French Spads! Lucky we didn't shoot them down or they shoot us, as the D.H.10 was not known and the Spads undoubtedly mistook us for a Hun bomber. The Spad chaps didn't report us for firing at them as far as we know, so all's well that ends well! What might have made things worse is that I was not supposed to take the D.H.10 on a job but wanted to use it "on active service" on the last day of the war'.*

The missing aircraft would seem to be that of Mackay and Gompertz from 55, all other aircraft making it back to Azelot this day. DH10 F1867 had been flown by Major Quinnell on 30th September. With a full load including bombs, camera, two observers and oxygen cylinders, making a combined weight of 1,800lbs, the performance with this maximum load was reported as poor. Garland first flew the D.H.10 on 30th October, and was asked to demonstrate this aircraft for Trenchard, during a visit by 'Boom & Co' (as they were known) on 5th November. Unfortunately the DH10 got stuck in the mud, but he did fly it on the 6th with Bottrill and White as observers.

CHAPTER 8

SUMMARY

The results achieved by the daylight bomber squadrons of the I.A.F. cannot just be gauged merely by looking at the damage done to targets and casualties on both sides. Although significant in determining the effect of a bomber force, these points alone cannot tell the whole story.

In the beginning the Strategic Council was realistic in what they thought the I.A.F. could achieve by day and by night in 1918. The task they gave Trenchard` was "the breakdown of the German Army in Germany, its Government, and the crippling of its sources of supply". With this in mind two alternative plans were devised.

(i) A sustained and continuous attack on one large centre after another until each centre was destroyed, and the industrial population largely displaced to other towns.

(ii) To attack as many of the large industrial centres as it was possible to reach with the machines at his disposal.

Trenchard decided on plan two for the following reasons:

It was not possible with the forces at his disposal, to do sufficient material damage so as to destroy completely the industrial centres in question. His second reason was that even if the I.A.F. had grown larger (as was the plan), it would not have been possible to accomplish the task unless the war had lasted another four or five years, due to the obvious limitations on long-distance bombing and the weather. By attacking as many towns as could be reached, he hoped to spread fear amongst the German populace, which would hopefully disrupt war production. Trenchard chose to attack German aerodromes containing bomber aircraft, in the added hope that these units could be knocked out before they inflicted any damage to his own squadrons. The Kest and Jasta aerodromes were also to be attacked, due to the mounting casualties inflicted by these units. It was well known in allied intelligence that rolling stock was in short supply in Germany. Trenchard hoped that attacking railways on a regular basis would disrupt war supplies, and also seriously deplete the number of goods trains and wagons in use. Another reason Trenchard chose the second idea was the amount of aircraft, men and materials, which Germany would have to take from the Western Front, and spread over a large area to protect vital industries. Taking these points into consideration, the air war against German industry began, and results were recorded in Air Ministry reports compiled in August 1919.

Aerodromes

When investigators from the Air Ministry arrived in the Lorraine area, most aerodromes had been dismantled by the local population, presumably for the wood. However, talking to local civilians, a comprehensive idea of what happened was recorded. On the whole little destruction was done to individual hangars in regard to destroying them. Lots of hangars were reported as being struck by bomb splinters, however this was hard to determine as German-built hangars had easily replaceable units, being constructed mostly of wood panelling. Any machines inside these hangars hit by bomb splinters, would have been out of action or even struck off strength. A few hangars still remained un-repaired, with machines still inside. These machines were completely splattered with holes and were found not worth repairing. Air Ministry analysis concluded that for every raid at least two enemy machines were damaged.

Of all the aerodromes attacked during I.A.F. operations, Boulay was damaged the most. Civilians stated that at one time or another each hangar had received a direct hit. Frescaty aerodrome was little damaged except for one of the longer hangars, east of the Zeppelin shed, which received a direct hit. A single bomb had pierced the roof and exploded on the concrete floor below. The crater was negligible, but all walls and the rest of the roof were bespattered with bomb splinters. (This hangar was most probably hit by Captain Mackay on 15th October on a solo bombing raid with 2Lt Ward, see chapter 8). Morhange aerodrome was also damaged but not to the same extent as Boulay. One long hangar and three small hangars had been burnt out, and subsequently replaced. At Buhl, home to three of the Jastas inflicting serious casualties to the I.A.F., more damage was done to unoccupied hangars than to those occupied. The southern part of the aerodrome was unoccupied and was still being finished when the Armistice was signed. Several workshops had been damaged from time to time, but no hangars looked as if they had received a direct hit. Again all small hangars had been removed by the time the Air Ministry arrived. All landing grounds were well covered in bomb craters, which obviously hampered operations.

It can be said from the information gathered that although buildings and materials were not extensively destroyed, bombing the aerodromes had severely hampered the enemy's ability to strike back. Many units, most noticeably the German bomber units, had their operations severely curtailed. Emergency landing grounds were built as a haven for German aircraft. However as these were discovered by reconnaissance aircraft, so they were bombed forcing aircraft to move again. A good example of this was Boulay which was first bombed in June. From here machines were moved to Freisdorf, which in turn was bombed, forcing a further move to Lellingham. Again bombed, machines moved to Ruplingen where the ground was unsuitable and no hangars were available. The unsuitability of this aerodrome resulted in many crashes. In all, the bombing of aerodromes by day and by night, considering the technical limitations of the time, was a success.

Railways

Closing the railway network down was virtually impossible. Cutting the major lines and destruction of locomotive engines and rolling stock however, was within the limitations of the technology available. Two main stations received the brunt of I.A.F. attacks. Thionville station linked the German northern armies with the armies of the Alsace. The other main station which was singled out was Metz-Sablon. Metz, as well as being a vital link in the chain, also had four large blast furnaces on its line. These four furnaces (Maizières-les-Metz, Hagondange, Uckange, and the Carlshutte works) were crucial to the German war effort, regarding output of steel and iron for war production. They had also to be constantly supplied with coke.

To analyse the railway offensive each station must be dealt with on an individual basis. Metz-Sablon had every locomotive shed and workshop hit several times. Every line had been hit and repaired, as well as every building in the station triangle.

Thionville on the other hand had escaped without a direct hit on its locomotive sheds or its passenger station. The goods yard however had been severely damaged on occasions, and the dislocation of traffic owing to its strategic position, had caused far more delays in the delivery of war supplies.

Little or no damage was recorded at smaller stations such as Karlsruhe, Offenburg, Saarbrücken, Darmstadt, Coblenz, Treves, Luxembourg, Arnaville, Courcelles, Conflans, Ars and Audun. However these stations were affected by alarms, being central to most of the bomber routes taken into Germany. These alarms forced traffic to stop for a considerable amount of time, or to be diverted.

The German authorities took the threat of I.A.F. bombers very seriously, and put into effect several counter measures to ease railway congestion. No train was permitted to remain in a main station for more than ten minutes. If a train was delayed except for an air raid warning, it would be shunted out of the station. As soon as an alarm was given, all trains, except troop and express trains, in the area affected at once stopped, and did not move until the 'All Clear' was given. Troop and express trains were allowed to proceed but only at a reduced speed. Several branch lines were constructed near major stations to divert traffic in case of an alarm. At smaller stations where this wasn't possible shunting yards were enlarged. At all-important stations (Metz, Thionville) large concrete shelters were constructed with ample room for all employees. A lot of these shelters were built amongst the lines and sidings so personnel could get under cover in the shortest possible time. These large shelters had a bursting platform on top. The interiors were divided into several compartments so as to localize the effects of a bomb should the shelter be penetrated. Other shelters were no more than holes covered with iron rails with earth piled on top. At other stations authorities were slow in the construction of shelters and this caused much dissatisfaction among the railway employees and troops. At Metz, Thionville, Bingen, Coblenz and Cologne, the Eisenbahn Truppe (specially selected troops from the infantry with a knowledge of the railways) were in charge of supervising the traffic, working signals and repairing any damaged tracks. When serious damage was done whole garrisons were called in to assist. After the raid on 16th July at Thionville, the Eisenbahn garrison was doubled, and this became standard at the other major stations and remained so until the Armistice.

German officials when questioned, summed up the bombing of railways as "annoying". Air Ministry officials concluded that raids had been too frequent to allow the German officials to belittle the bombing. Raids such as on 16th July had left an impression on the minds of officials never to be forgotten. In all the

German officials considered themselves to have been lucky regarding the amount of damage caused, in comparison to the large amount of raids carried out. While they concluded that bomb dropping accuracy had been moderate, all officials agreed though, that the bombing of locomotive sheds and workshops severely hampered their operations. Most engines and rolling stock which were hit were written off. The German authorities admitted that the damage had been constantly recurrent, with serious consequences on occasions. The morale of the local population and railway workers had been severely hit.

Blast Furnaces

The directors of several works did not attach much importance to the air raids. With a few exceptions material damage had not affected output, and was repaired almost immediately. In very few cases did work have to be stopped completely. Morale among workers was considered to be low because of the constant alarms. Output however, was not affected and very few workers left the works during the war, because of the bombing. Bomb dropping was reported as "very erratic both by day and by night" and workers were unsure of what part of the works was the target. Some complained of a lack of raw materials, especially coke, and were warned that this difficulty would continue and increase. A study of the plans of several works revealed several hits within the perimeter. But only in a few cases were vital points hit. Some figures suggest a 10% decrease in production due to the bombing. However, this could be caused more by the disruption to the railway system then to damage to the blast furnaces themselves. Before I.A.F. operations began, planners knew how hard it would be to knock out a blast furnace, due to the small and very few critical elements in their construction. Workers' morale had been affected, but not to the extent of other targets. Overall damage to production can therefore be said to be negligible.

Despite apparent disregard for I.A.F. attacks, several counter-measures were taken by the directors of several works. At Dillingen for instance, thirty-five air raid shelters were erected, while at the Carlshutte works at Thionville, forty-five shelters were built. Efforts were also made to protect vital buildings and pipes from damage. Several roofs were reinforced with earth piled on top. Dummy works were constructed at Bous and Volklingen in an attempt to fool allied airmen. At Bous the spoof works was located on a slag heap 1,000 metres to the north-east of the Mannesmann works. This consisted of several lights and masonry. The dummy factory at Volklingen, just north of Saarbrücken, was constructed along the same lines, and was placed 2,000 metres north of the Rochtingen works. Both proved unsuccessful receiving a couple of bombs each, while the works they were meant to protect were still bombed. The building of these dummy works started in the winter of 1917-1918, and goes some way to emphasise the German forward-thinking regarding protection of vital war industries.

Chemical Works

The Badische Anilin and Soda Fabrik and the Oppau works were the only chemical factories bombed. The Director, Herr Julius, stated that the damage both from a military and destructive point of view had been small. A large proportion of the bombs falling within the factory perimeters had burst between buildings, doing little or no damage. Some pipes were damaged by splinters, but any signs of extensive damage or repairs were not seen by the Air Ministry team sent to investigate. Chief engineers at both works said that damage caused had never been of such a formidable nature, that repairs could not be effected, nor had output stopped. The Oppau works was once stopped for repairs, but the Badische Anilin and Soda Fabrik works had never shut down. Alarms by night caused most disruptions, but these shortfalls in production were quickly made up although this entailed extra labour and of course cost. It is interesting to note that factory officials knew that bombers by day always attacked from the east (except on 7 September 1918 when they came from the south). At night, attacks always came from the north or east, routes well known to the anti-aircraft batteries and searchlights. Officials believed that the token amount of destruction at both works, was due to the excellent barrages put up by anti-aircraft batteries. Unless repeated attacks around the clock were flown against these large works, there was little hope of shutting them down. Even if enough bombers could be found, and accuracy improved, the task would have still been virtually impossible with the bombs available at the time. The offensive against these factories was a failure, but this was due to the limitations of the time regarding aircraft, bomb sights and bombs.

Industrial Centres

Large towns such as Cologne, Frankfurt and Mannheim were targeted by the I.A.F. for their railway stations as well as various factories. The material damage done to these various targets was minimal, whereas damage to the morale of the local populations was considerable. With bombs falling wide of the mark in these built-up towns, rich and poor areas were being hit causing widespread panic amongst all walks of society. In some towns the health of the population deteriorated as they spent nights in cellars and dugouts. Letters taken from German prisoners often told of the panic at home: "If the raids are by day much time is lost in taking cover, and if by night their sleep is broken, and this tires them for work if the raids are frequent. Besides this makes them more tired of the war than they already are". Once it was clear to the people of these towns that the raids would continue, they sought compensation from the local authorities. Eventually the authorities gave in and a form was produced to be filled in by anyone suffering damage to property due to air raids. Any claim below 15,000 marks was to be paid by the local authority immediately. However claims were seldom settled quickly, and this was another source of dissatisfaction among the populace. Reports of unrest due to late payments were recorded at Ludwigshafen and Saarbrücken. Any claim over 15,000 marks would be settled at a later date. The Air Ministry came to the conclusion that the morale of the German population suffered greatly from these attacks deep into Germany. British Intelligence knew of the dissatisfaction amongst the civilians, borne out by a letter found in the Public Record Office, at Kew, while researching this book.

The Under Secretary of State for Foreign Affairs presents his compliments to the Secretary of the Air Ministry and is directed by Mr. Secretary Balfour to state, for the Air Council's information, that his Majesty's Minister at the Hague has reported that according to various sources the despondency in Germany is at the present moment intense: and that this would be greatly increased by air raids on German towns and that the moment would appear to demand the exercise of this method of warfare to its utmost extent.

Foreign Office
September 10th, 1918

Conversely many accounts were also recorded stating the resolve of people to keep fighting, and air raids only stiffened this resolve further. As World War Two was to prove, bombing of civilians, for example, during the London Blitz, and later the bombing of Germany, could not subdue a nation and stop it fighting. There is no doubt that the bombing of large towns did lower the morale of the population in general, but whether this helped bring the war to a quicker end is open to speculation. From a perspective of damage to targets within, or near these towns, the I.A.F. raids could be said to have none or very little effect.

Overall the results achieved by the daylight squadrons of the I.A.F., do not make good reading, especially if looked at purely from the viewpoint of destruction wrought. However, the I.A.F. which operated during those five months of 1918, was only a small proportion of what was planned to become an inter-allied strategic force, involving squadrons from both France and America in a combined effort against Germany and her war production. Had this happened, the experience gained by the crews of the I.A.F. would have been invaluable. A breakdown of raids carried out in June, July and August gave the Air Staff in London the news they had anticipated. Trenchard was not an advocate of strategic bombing and directives from the Air Ministry were not being followed regarding targets. The chemical industry received only 14% of raids in June, 9.5% in July and 8% in August. Iron and steel production received 13.3% in June, 9% in July and 7% in August. Aerodromes on the other hand scored 13.3%, 28% and 49% respectively in the same period. Railways received the most attention with 55% in June, 46% in July and 31% in August. Trenchard was chastised by his superiors at the Air Ministry, but objectives and targeting were firmly in his hands as the figures show. His policy of attacking aerodromes was probably the most successful out of the target groups attacked by the I.A.F. However, casualties from enemy airmen continued to be severe, and the German Jasta and Kest units put up strong opposition until the Armistice.

The railways, which was Trenchard's other main target, escaped relatively unscathed despite receiving most of the attention in these three months. Two schools of thought prevailed regarding the I.A.F. Trenchard, who was to become commander of the Inter-Allied Bombing Force, (on paper anyway) was a keen advocate of aircraft supporting the Army in the field. Sykes and Weir at the Air Ministry, were advocates of strategic bombing but did not sacrifice aircraft support for the Army in favour of strengthening the I.A.F. These two schools of thought continued until the end of the war, and after; with Trenchard quoting "Thus the Independent Force comes to an end. A more gigantic waste of effort and personnel there has never been in any war". Rather a harsh criticism, but in some respects true. The bombing once finished had very little effect on Germany's ability to fight. Sykes and Weir were visionaries. What they put in place came to fruition in another war, with vast changes in technology and superior aircraft. Whether results would have been better with more aircraft, as envisioned, is hard to say. Bombing from aircraft was still in its infancy, more squadrons would have increased the destructive ability of the I.A.F. but it is unlikely that any part of the German war effort would have been destroyed.

Undoubtedly bad weather over France seriously handicapped and affected the I.A.F.'s ability to reach its assigned targets. Had better weather prevailed, more positive results would have been achieved. Improved methods of navigation and bomb aiming too would have helped. Had long-range fighters been available, this may well have reduced the appalling casualty rate. The I.A.F. perhaps, was ahead of its time but was the forerunner of things to come in a far more devastating war.

APPENDIX A

BOMBS

As can be seen from the summary, damage to targets, when hit, could be said to be disappointing. Air Ministry officials looked into this and came up with the following conclusions.

The 230lb and 112lb bombs

Whenever these bombs had penetrated a building prior to exploding, the effects had been good. Even against some of the strongest built buildings, marks had been left. In cases where bombs had detonated well outside buildings, the explosions had been good with much damage, but in nearly all cases, the force of the blast had been vertical with little or no horizontal effect. Effects against blast furnaces and factories such as the Badische Aniline and Soda Fabrik proved disappointing. The buildings and machinery were so solidly built that in some cases, 230lb bombs had telescoped and consequently not exploded. A case of this was at Hagondange when a 230lb bomb pierced the roof of the Central Power Station and struck one of the alternator armatures. The bomb was telescoped and the fuse shot back into the bomb. Most of these bombs however had not penetrated targets, and exploded almost on impact and caused little damage. Some 230lb bombs were tried with delayed action fuses, but these also failed to penetrate many buildings and exploded outside. The effect of these two bombs was fairly satisfactory, but their blast was too localized with not enough destructive or penetrative power.

The 40lb and 25lb bombs

The 40lb bombs were in most places supposed to be filled with asphyxiating gas. The effect on buildings and streets had been slight, but the decline in morale produced by this bomb had been great. The 40lb phosphorous bombs had little or no effect unless they penetrated a building, which was rare. Reports also suggested that the fires these bombs caused were easily extinguished. The use of this bomb was justified more on its affect on the population than on material. The opinion expressed of the 25lb bomb was that it was useless. The damage caused had been negligible, and directors at the Badische Aniline and Soda Fabrik said they feared anti-aircraft blinds more. These 25lb bombs may well have been useless against buildings, but the author feels their effects may well have been greater against softer targets such as airfields.

Blinds

The most disturbing find made by Air Ministry investigators, were the amount of bombs which failed to detonate. These failures were recorded on railways, industrial centres and blast furnaces. The only redeeming fact is that in many cases these 'blinds' penetrated buildings. Many records showed that in some raids a quarter, a third, or even two thirds failed to explode. German records also showed that many of these bombs were apparently faultless, so it remains something of a mystery why they didn't detonate. On nearly every raid 230lb, 112lb, and 40lb bombs were recorded as blinds, or duds.

APPENDIX B

APPENDIX B

OFFICIAL FIGURES FOR RAIDS,
BOMB TONNAGE AND RECONNAISSANCES

June 1918

Squadron	Raids	Germany	Recon	Bomb Weight	230lb	112lb	25lb	40lb Phos
55	16	10	9	32,792lbs	18	211	188	8
99	16	6	–	30,170lbs	63	140	–	–
104	11	4	–	24,199lbs	20	112	239	27

July 1918

Squadron	Raids	Germany	Recon	Bomb Weight	230lb	112lb	25lb	40lb Phos
55	16	11	16	35,700lbs	38	185	184	41
99	13	8	–	21,878lbs	41	104	32	–
104	6	2	–	8,436lbs	18	33	24	–

August 1918

Squadron	Raids	Germany	Recon	Bomb Weight	230lb	112lb	25lb	40lb Phos
55	14	9	15	25,950lbs	13	190	48	12
99	6	1	–	10,743lbs	25	39	25	–
104	6	4	–	15,000lbs	40	50	8	–

September 1918

Squadron	Raids	Germany	Recon	Bomb Weight	230lb	112lb	25lb	40lb Phos
55	9	5	17	17,600lbs	40	75	–	–
99	14	1	–	29,118lbs	60	114	102	–
104	11	1	–	25,820lbs	58	90	25	–
110	4	2	–	11,702lbs	9	86	–	–

October 1918

Squadron	Raids	Germany	Recon	Bomb Weight	230lb	112lb	25lb	40lb Phos
55	4	1	5	8,154lbs	15	42	–	–
99	10	–	–	20,596lbs	54	73	–	–
104	10	–	–	26,720lbs	48	140	–	–
110	3	3	4	5,872lbs	8	36	–	–

November 1918

Squadron	Raids	Germany	Recon	Bomb Weight	230lb	112lb	25lb	40lb Phos
55	3	2	1	6,206lbs	13	28	–	2
99	3	–	–	7,532lbs	19	26	–	5x50lb
104	3	–	–	6,950lbs	17	20	–	16x50lb
110	2	–	–	4,776lbs	12	18	–	–

OFFICIAL FIGURES FOR AIRCRAFT
DESTROYED OR OUT OF CONTROL

June 1918

Squadron	Destroyed	Out of Control
55	1	3
99	1	4
104	5	7

July 1918

Squadron	Destroyed	Out of Control
55	1	3
99	5	4
104	1	3

August 1918

Squadron	Destroyed	Out of Control
55	6	9
99	–	–
104	13	8

September 1918

Squadron	Destroyed	Out of Control
55	4	2
99	3	3
104	5	3
110	–	6

October 1918

Squadron	Destroyed	Out of Control
55	–	2
99	–	2
104	5	6
110	–	4

November 1918

Squadron	Destroyed	Out of Control
55	1	3
99	2	1
104	1	–
110	–	–

THE COST

Date	Squadron	Name	Casualty Type	Aircraft Serial	Pilot/ Observer
8th June	104	R.K.Pollard	W.I.A.	D1674	Obs
13th June	55	W.Legge	K.I.A.	A7466	Pil
13th June	55	A.Mckenzie	K.I.A.	A7466	Obs
13th June	104	W.J.Rivett–Carnac	W.I.A.	C6267	Pil
13th June	104	W.E.Flexman	D.O.W.	C6267	Obs
24th June	104	O.J.Lange	W.I.A.	D7229	Pil
24th June	104	G.A.Smith	W.I.A.	D7229	Obs
24th June	104	M.J.Ducray	W.I.A.	D1674	Pil
24th June	104	K.C.B.Woodman	W.I.A.	D1674	Obs
25th June	104	S.C.M.Pontin	P.O.W.	C2170	Pil
25th June	104	J.Arnold	P.O.W.	C2170	Obs
25th June	104	A.W.Robertson	W.I.A.	D1675	Pil
25th June	104	E.W.Mundy	W.I.A.	C6260	Pil
25th June	104	H.A.B.Jackson	D.O.W.	C6260	Obs
25th June	99	N.S.Harper	K.I.A.	D5570	Pil
25th June	99	D.G.Benson	K.I.A.	D5570	Obs
25th June	99	W.W.L.Jenkin	D.O.W.	C6149	Obs
25th June	55	G.A.Sweet	K.I.A.	B7866	Pil
25th June	55	C.R.F.Goodyear	K.I.A.	B7866	Obs
26th June	104	C.G.Jenyns	P.O.W.	C6256	Pil
26th June	104	H.C.Davis	K.I.A.	C6256	Obs
26th June	55	F.F.H.Bryan	P.O.W.	A8073	Pil
26th June	55	A.Boocock	P.O.W.	A8073	Obs
27th June	99	E.A.Chapin	K.I.A.	D1669	Pil
27th June	99	T.W.Wiggins	K.I.A.	D1669	Obs
27th June	99	H.Sanders	W.I.A.	C1670	Pil
30th June	104	W.L.Deetjen	K.I.A.	C5720	Pil
30th June	104	M.H.Cole	K.I.A.	C5270	Obs
30th June	104	O.J.Lange	W.I.A.	D1729	Pil
30th June	104	V.G.McCabe	W.I.A.	D1729	Obs
1st July	99	R.F.Connell	W.I.A.	C6278	Obs
1st July	104	R.H.Wetherall	W.I.A.	–	Obs
1st July	104	T.L.McConchie	P.O.W.	C6307	Pil
1st July	104	K.C.B.Woodman	P.O.W.	C6307	Obs
1st July	104	G.C.Body	P.O.W.	C6262	Pil
1st July	104	W.G.Norden	P.O.W.	C6262	Obs
5th July	99	W.D.Thom	W.I.A.	C6202	Pil
5th July	99	C.G.Claye	K.I.A.	C6202	Obs
7th July	104	A.Moore	P.O.W.	D2868	Pil
7th July	104	F.P.Cobden	K.I.A.	D2868	Obs
7th July	104	M.J.Ducray	P.O.W.	D2878	Pil
7th July	104	N.H.Wildig	K.I.A.	D2878	Obs

7th July	104	A.H.Morgan	W.I.A.	D5658	Obs
16th July	55	W.H.Currie	D.O.W.	D8392	Obs
20th July	99	T.K.Ludgate	W.I.A.	C6149	Obs
20th July	99	F.G.Thompson	P.O.W.	D1679	Pil
20th July	99	S.C.Thornley	P.O.W	D1679	Obs
20th July	55	F.E.Nash	W.I.A.	A7876	Pil
20th July	55	W.E.Baker	K.I.A.	A7876	Obs
20th July	55	J.S.Pollock	D.O.W.	A7427	Obs
20th July	55	A.S.Keep	W.I.A,	A7427	Pil
20th July	55	C.Young	K.I.A.	D9275	Pil
20th July	55	R.A.Butler	K.I.A.	D9275	Obs
30th July	99	G.Martin	W.I.A.	C6210	Pil
30th July	99	S.G.Burton	K.I.A.	C6210	Obs
30th July	99	P.Dietz	K.I.A.	D7223	Pil
30th July	99	H.W.Batty	K.I.A.	D7223	Obs
30th July	55	R.R.S.Barker	W.I.A.	–	Obs
30th July	55	E.R.Beesly	W.I.A.	–	Obs
31st July	99	M.T.S.Papenfus	P.O.W.	D3039	Pil
31st July	99	A.L.Benjamin	P.O.W.	D3039	Obs
31st July	99	S.M.Black	P.O.W.	C6278	Pil
31st July	99	E.Singleton	P.O.W.	C6278	Obs
31st July	99	F.Smith	P.O.W.	D1029	Pil
31st July	99	K.H.Ashton	P.O.W.	D1029	Obs
31st July	99	E.L.Doidge	K.I.A.	C6145	Pil
31st July	99	H.T.Melville	K.I.A.	C6145	Obs
31st July	99	W.J.Garrity	P.O.W.	C6196	Pil
31st July	99	G.H.Stephenson	P.O.W.	C6196	Obs
31st July	99	T.M.Ritchie	P.O.W.	C6149	Pil
31st July	99	L.W.G.Stagg	K.I.A.	C6149	Obs
31st July	99	L.V.Dennis	K.I.A.	D1032	Pil
31st July	99	F.W.Wooley	K.I.A.	D1032	Obs
31st July	104	B.Johnson	W.I.A.	–	Obs
1st August	104	A.Haines	W.I.A.	–	Pil
1st August	104	W.H.Goodale	K.I.A.	D2960	Pil
1st August	104	L.C.Prentice	K.I.A.	D2960	Obs
11th August	104	J.E.Parke	P.O.W.	D501	Pil
11th August	104	W.W.Bradford	P.O.W.	D501	Obs
12th August	55	E.R.Stewart	K.I.A.	B3957	Obs
12th August	104	G.H.Patman	P.O.W.	D3084	Pil
12th August	104	J.M.S.McPherson	P.O.W.	D3084	Obs
12th August	104	O.F.Meyer	P.O.W.	D2931	Pil
12th August	104	A.C.Wallace	P.O.W.	D2931	Obs
13th August	55	E.P.Critchley	W.I.A.	F5700	Pil
13th August	55	S.E.Lewis	K.I.A.	F5700	Obs
13th August	104	H.P.G.Leyden	K.I.A.	D7229	Pil
13th August	104	A.L.Windridge	K.I.A.	D7229	Obs
13th August	104	E.C.Clarke	K.I.A.	D3088	Pil
13th August	104	J.L.C.Sutherland	D.O.W.	D3088	Obs
13th August	104	F.H.Beaufort	K.I.A.	D2881	Pil
13th August	104	H.O.Bryant	K.I.A.	D2881	Obs
13th August	104	J.C.Uhlman	W.I.A.	F5844	Pil
13th August	104	P.Sutherland	D.O.W.	F5844	Obs
16th August	55	A.G.Roberts	W.I.A.	F5703	Obs
16th August	55	J.Campbell	P.O.W.	A7813	Pil
16th August	55	J.R.Fox	D.O.W.	A7813	Obs
16th August	55	N.Wallace	W.I.A.	D8388	Obs

16th August	55	J.B.McIntyre	K.I.A.	A7781	Pil
16th August	55	H.H.Bracher	K.I.A.	A7781	Obs
16th August	55	E.A.Brownhill	K.I.A.	D9273	Pil
16th August	55	W.T.Madge	K.I.A.	D9273	Obs
22nd August	104	J.B.Home–Hay	P.O.W.	D1729	Pil
22nd August	104	W.T.Smith	P.O.W.	D1729	Obs
22nd August	104	E.Cartwright	K.I.A.	D5729	Pil
22nd August	104	A.G.L.Mullen	K.I.A.	D5729	Obs
22nd August	104	W.Moorhouse	K.I.A.	–	Obs
22nd August	104	E.A.Mckay	P.O.W.	D2812	Pil
22nd August	104	R.A.C.Brie	P.O.W.	D2812	Obs
22nd August	104	R.Searle	P.O.W.	D1048	Pil
22nd August	104	C.G.Pickard	K.I.A.	D1048	Obs
22nd August	104	G.H.B.Smith	P.O.W.	C2179	Pil
22nd August	104	W.Harrop	P.O.W.	C2179	Obs
22nd August	104	J.Valentine	P.O.W.	C6202	Pil
22nd August	104	C.G.Hitchcock	P.O.W.	C6202	Obs
22nd August	104	H.P.Wells	P.O.W.	D2917	Pil
22nd August	104	J.J.Redfield	P.O.W.	D2917	Obs
25th August	55	J.A.Lee	K.I.A.	A2131	Obs
25th August	55	A.S.Allan	D.O.W.	B3967	Obs
30th August	99	C.G.Russell	K.I.A.	D3215	Obs
30th August	55	P.J.Cunningham	K.I.A.	A7783	Pil
30th August	55	J.G.Quinton	D.O.W.	A7783	Obs
30th August	55	T.H.Laing	K.I.A.	A7972	Pil
30th August	55	T.F.L.Myring	K.I.A.	A7972	Obs
30th August	55	H.H.Doehler	P.O.W.	A7708	Pil
30th August	55	A.S.Papworth	P.O.W.	A7708	Obs
30th August	55	H.C.T.Gompertz	W.I.A.	A8069	Obs
30th August	55	W.W.Tanney	P.O.W.	A7589	Pil
30th August	55	A.J.C.Gormley	P.O.W.	A7589	Obs
30th August	55	C.E.Thorp	D.O.W.	F5711	Obs
30th August	55	R.I.A.Hickes	K.I.A.	D8396	Pil
30th August	55	T.A.Jones	K.I.A.	D8396	Obs
4th September	104	F.H.J.Denney	W.I.A.	B9355	Obs
7th September	99	G.Broadbent	P.O.W.	D2916	Pil
7th September	99	M.A.Dunn	P.O.W.	D2916	Obs
7th September	104	W.E.Reast	D.O.W.	D7318	Obs
7th September	104	E.Mellor	K.I.A.	D3268	Pil
7th September	104	J.Bryden	K.I.A.	D3268	Obs
7th September	104	J.E.Kemp	P.O.W.	B7653	Pil
7th September	104	E.B.Smailes	D.O.W.	B7653	Obs
7th September	104	W.E.L.Courtney	P.O.W.	D7210	Pil
7th September	104	A.R.Sabey	D.O.W.	D7210	Obs
13th September	99	F.A.Wood	K.I.A.	D3218	Pil
13th September	99	C.Bridgett	K.I.A.	D3218	Obs
13th September	99	H.S.Notley	W.I.A.	D1668	Obs
13th September	99	J.L.Hunter	W.I.A.	B9347	Pil
13th September	99	E.E.Crosby	K.I.A.	D1670	Pil
13th September	99	C.P.Wogan-Browne	K.I.A.	D1670	Obs
13th September	104	T.J.Bond	D.O.W.	D1050	Obs
14th September	99	W.E.Ogilvy	P.O.W.	D3264	Pil
14th September	99	G.A.Shipton	P.O.W.	D3264	Obs
14th September	99	J.G.Dennis	W.I.A.	D3215	Pil
14th September	99	H.G.Ramsay	W.I.A.	D3215	Obs
14th September	104	G.H.Knight	W.I.A.	D5581	Pil

15th September	104	L.G.Hall	D.O.W.	D3245	Pil
15th September	104	W.D.Evans	P.O.W.	D3245	Obs
15th September	104	A.A.Baker	W.I.A.	D532	Pil
15th September	104	H.E.Tonge	W.I.A.	D532	Obs
15th September	104	A.D.MacKenzie	K.I.A.	D3263	Pil
15th September	104	C.E.Bellord	K.I.A.	D3263	Obs
15th September	104	W.E.Jackson	D.O.W.	D3211	Obs
15th September	104	R.H.Rose	P.O.W.	D7205	Pil
15th September	104	E.L.Baddeley	P.O.W.	D7205	Obs
16th September	55	W.E.Johns	P.O.W.	F5712	Pil
16th September	55	A.E.Amey	K.I.A.	F5712	Obs
16th September	110	H.Kettener	W.I.A.	E8434	Obs
16th September	110	A.Haigh	K.I.A.	E8410	Pil
16th September	110	J.West	K.I.A.	E8410	Obs
16th September	110	H.V.Brisbin	P.O.W.	F997	Pil
16th September	110	R.S.Lipsett	P.O.W.	F997	Obs
25th September	55	J.B.Dunn	K.I.A.	D8356	Pil
25th September	55	H.S.Orange	K.I.A.	D8356	Obs
25th September	55	R.V.Gordon	D.O.W.	D8365	Pil
25th September	55	G.S.Barber	K.I.A.	D8386	Obs
25th September	55	E.Wood	W.I.A.	D8392	Pil
25th September	55	J.T.L.Attwood	K.I.A.	–	Obs
25th September	55	G.B.Dunlop	P.O.W.	F5714	Pil
25th September	55	A.C.Heyes	P.O.W.	F5714	Obs
25th September	55	R.C.Pretty	P.O.W.	D8388	Pil
25th September	55	G.R.Bartlett	P.O.W.	D8388	Obs
25th September	55	A.J.Robinson	K.I.A.	D8413	Pil
25th September	55	H.R.Burnett	K.I.A.	D8413	Obs
25th September	99	M.J.Poulton	W.I.A.	C2197	Pil
25th September	99	J.L.M.Oliphant	W.I.A.	D3270	Obs
25th September	110	A.Lindley	P.O.W.	F1030	Pil
25th September	110	C.R.Gross	P.O.W.	F1030	Obs
25th September	110	H.J.Cockman	W.I.A.	F1000	Pil
25th September	110	L.S.Brooke	K.I.A.	F992	Pil
25th September	110	A.Provan	K.I.A.	F992	Obs
25th September	110	R.F.Casey	W.I.A.	F993	Obs
25th September	110	W.H.Neighbour	K.I.A.	E8420	Obs
25th September	110	C.B.E.Lloyd	P.O.W.	E9660	Pil
25th September	110	H.J.C.Elwig	P.O.W.	E9660	Obs
25th September	110	H.W.Tozer	K.I.A.	E8422	Pil
25th September	110	W.Platt	K.I.A.	E8422	Obs
26th September	104	O.L.Malcolm	K.I.A.	D7232	Pil
26th September	104	G.V.Harper	K.I.A.	D7232	Obs
26th September	99	P.E.Welchman	D.O.W.	B9347	Pil
26th September	99	T.H.Swann	P.O.W.	B9347	Obs
26th September	99	S.McKeever	W.I.A.	B9366	Pil
26th September	99	J.W.Howard	K.I.A.	D544	Obs
26th September	99	C.R.G.Abrahams	K.I.A.	C6272	Pil
26th September	99	C.H.Sharp	K.I.A.	C6272	Obs
26th September	99	L.G.Stern	K.I.A.	D5573	Pil
26th September	99	F.O.Cook	K.I.A.	D5573	Obs
26th September	99	S.C.Gilbert	K.I.A.	E632	Pil
26th September	99	R.Buckby	K.I.A.	E632	Obs
26th September	99	W.H.Gillett	P.O.W.	D3213	Pil
26th September	99	H.Crossley	P.O.W.	D3213	Obs
5th October	110	C.J.H.May	W.I.A.	F1036	Obs

5th October	110	D.P.Davies	P.O.W.	E8439	Pil
5th October	110	H.M.Speagell	P.O.W.	E8439	Obs
5th October	110	A.Brandrick	P.O.W.	F980	Pil
5th October	110	H.C.Eyre	K.I.A.	F980	Obs
5th October	110	A.G.Inglis	P.O.W.	F1010	Pil
5th October	110	W.G.L.Bodley	P.O.W.	F1010	Obs
5th October	110	R.C.P.Ripley	K.I.A.	E8421	Pil
5th October	110	F.S.Towler	K.I.A.	E8421	Obs
10th October	99	M.E.R.Jarvis	W.I.A.	D527	Obs
18th October	104	A.M.Mitchell	W.I.A.	D530	Obs
21st October	55	E.Clare	W.I.A.	B7933	Obs
21st October	110	L.G.S.Reynolds	P.O.W.	F985	Pil
21st October	110	M.W.Dunn	P.O.W.	F985	Obs
21st October	110	S.L.Mucklow	P.O.W.	F984	Pil
21st October	110	R.Rifkin	P.O.W.	F984	Obs
21st October	110	W.E.Windover	P.O.W.	F1005	Pil
21st October	110	J.A.Simpson	P.O.W.	F1005	Obs
21st October	110	J.McLaren–Pearson	P.O.W.	F1029	Pil
21st October	110	T.W.Harman	P.O.W.	F1029	Obs
21st October	110	A.W.R.Evans	P.O.W.	E8484	Pil
21st October	110	R.W.L.Thomson	P.O.W.	E8484	Obs
21st October	110	P.King	P.O.W.	F1021	Pil
21st October	110	R.G.Vernon	D.O.W.	F1021	Obs
21st October	110	J.O.R.S.Saunders	K.I.A.	F986	Pil
21st October	110	W.J.Brain	K.I.A.	F986	Obs
23rd October	55	C.E.Reynolds	D.O.W.	D8386	Pil
23rd October	104	B.S.Case	D.O.W.	D2932	Pil
23rd October	104	H.Bridger	P.O.W.	D2932	Obs
23rd October	99	A.R.Collis	W.I.A.	B9394	Pil
29th October	104	P.J.Waller	W.I.A.	D5843	Pil
29th October	104	I.W.Leiper	W.I.A.	D3230	Pil
29th October	104	H.D.Arnott	K.I.A.	E8978	Pil
29th October	104	B.Johnson	K.I.A.	E8978	Obs
6th November	104	J.W.Richards	W.I.A.	D526	Pil
6th November	104	E.G.Stevens	W.I.A.	D526	Obs
6th November	104	H.L.Wren	P.O.W.	D1050	Pil
6th November	104	W.H.Tresham	P.O.W.	D1050	Obs
6th November	104	A.Hemingway	K.I.A.	D3101	Pil
6th November	104	G.A.Smith	K.I.A.	D3101	Obs
6th November	99	L.V.Russell	W.I.A.	D1008	Pil
6th November	99	C.E.W.Thresher	P.O.W.	C3040	Pil
6th November	99	W.Glew	D.O.W.	C3040	Obs
6th November	55	G.T.Richardson	P.O.W.	D8384	Pil
6th November	55	L.J.B.Ward	D.O.W.	D8384	Obs
10th November	55	D.R.G.Mackay	D.O.W.	F5725	Pil
10th November	55	H.C.T.Gompertz	P.O.W.	F5725	Obs

SELECT BIBLIOGRAPHY

Air Ministry: Results of Air Raids on Germany; October 1918 & August 1919
First of the Many: Alan Morris; Jarrolds Publishers Ltd: 1968
From Many Angles: Sir Frederick Sykes; George G Harrap & Co 1942
History of 99 Squadron Independent Force: L.A.Pattinson; W.Heffer & Sons Ltd 1920
Pioneer Pilot: William Armstrong; Blandford Press Ltd 1952
Sir Frederick Sykes and the Air Revolution 1912-1918: Eric Ash; Frank Cass Publishers 1999
The Chronicles of 55 Squadron RFC & RAF: L.Miller 1919
The D.H.4 / D.H.9 File: Ray Sturtivant & Gordon Page; Air-Britain (Historians) Ltd 1999
The Jasta Pilots: Norman Franks, Frank Bailey & Rick Duiven; Grub Street 1996
The Legacy of Lord Trenchard: H.R.Allen; Cassell 1972
The Origins of Strategic Bombing; Neville Jones; William Kimber & Co Ltd 1973
The Sky Their Battlefield: Trevor Henshaw; Grub Street 1995
Trenchard man of vision; Andrew Boyle; 1962

Various issues of *Cross & Cockade* GB, *Cross & Cockade Journal* (US), *Popular Flying*, *Wings*, *R.A.F. Quarterly*, AIR 1 files from the Public Records Office at Kew; Records held at R.A.F. Museum at Hendon; Records held at the Imperial War Museum London.

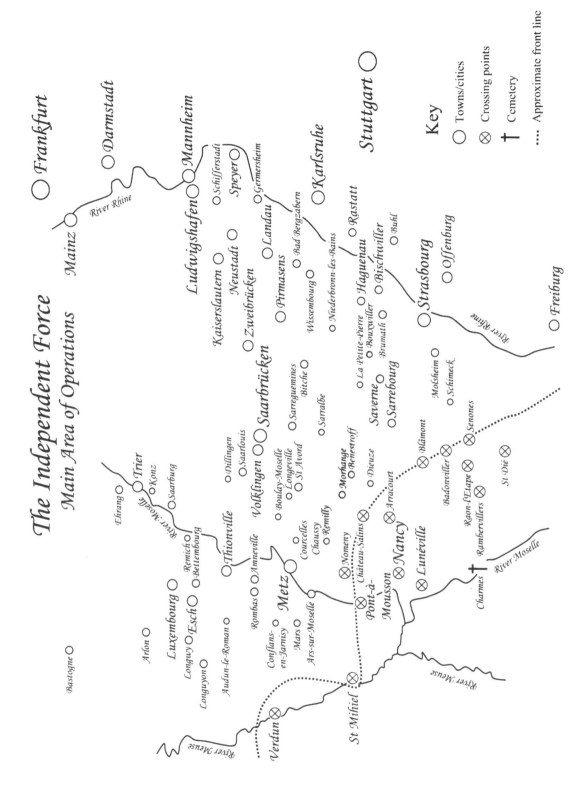

The Independent Force
Main Area of Operations

Bastogne

Arlon

Luxembourg
Longwy Esch
Longuyon
Audun-le-Roman

Ehrang

Trier
Konz
Saarburg

Remich
Bettembourg

Rombas Amneville

Thionville

Conflans-
en-Jarnisy
Mars
Ars-sur-Moselle

Metz

Boulay-Moselle
Longeville
St Avold

Courcelles
Chaussy
Remilly

Dillingen
Saarlouis

Volklingen

Saarbrücken

Sarreguemines
Bitche
Sarralbe

Morhange
Benestroff
Dieuze

Nomeny
Château-Salins
Pont-à-Mousson
Arracourt

Nancy

Lunéville

Blâmont

St Mihiel

Verdun

River Meuse

River Moselle

River Meuse

Charmes
Rambervillers

River Moselle

Badonviller

Raon-l'Etape
Senones

St Dié

Frankfurt

Darmstadt

Mainz

River Rhine

Ludwigshafen Mannheim

Schifferstadt
Speyer
Germersheim

Kaiserslautern
Neustadt
Landau

Zweibrücken

Pirmasens

Wissembourg

Bad Bergzabern

Niederbronn-les-Bains

Karlsruhe

Rastatt

La Petite-Pierre
Haguenau
Bouxwiller Bischwiller
Brumath Buhl

Saverne

Sarrebourg

Molsheim

Schirmeck

Strasbourg

Offenburg

River Rhine

Freiburg

Stuttgart

Key

○ Towns/cities

⊗ Crossing points

✝ Cemetery

···· Approximate front line

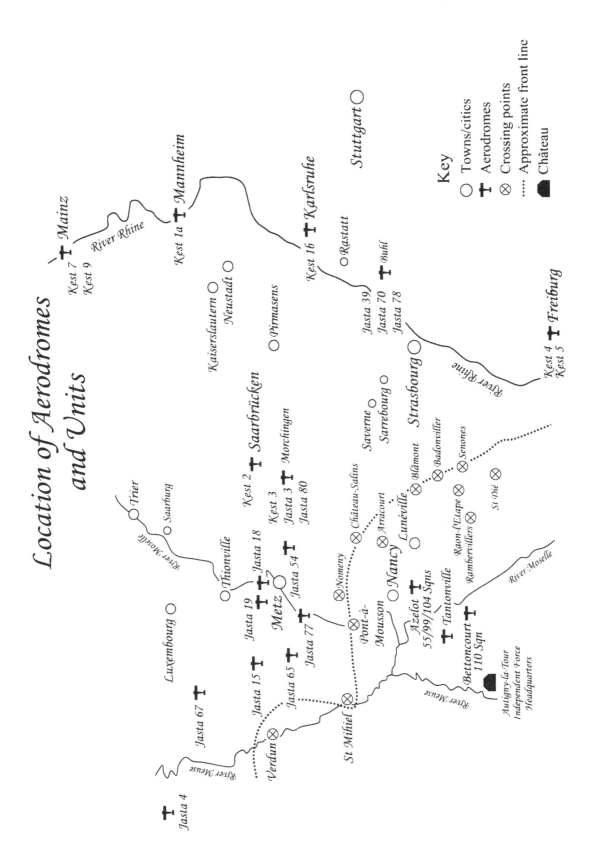

Location of Aerodromes and Units

Key

- ◯ Towns/cities
- ✝ Aerodromes
- ⊗ Crossing points
- ⋯ Approximate front line
- ◼ Château

Jasta 4

River Meuse

Luxembourg ◯

Trier ◯

River Moselle

Saarburg

Thionville ◯

Jasta 67

✝ Jasta 15

✝ Jasta 19

Metz ◯

Jasta 65 ✝

Jasta 77 ✝

Jasta 18 ✝

Jasta 54 ✝

Verdun ⊗

St Mihiel ⊗

Pont-à-Mousson ⊗

⊗ Nomeny

Château-Salins ⊗

Arracourt ⊗

Nancy ◯

Azelot ✝
55/99/104 Sqns

Tantonville ✝

Bettoncourt ✝
110 Sqn

Autigny-la-Tour
Independent Force
Headquarters

River Meuse

River Moselle

Mainz ✝
Kest 7
Kest 9

River Rhine

Mannheim ✝
Kest 1a

Kaiserslautern ◯

Neustadt ◯

Pirmasens ◯

Saarbrücken ✝
Kest 2

Kest 3 ✝
Jasta 3 ✝
Jasta 80

Morchingen

Karlsruhe ✝
Kest 16

Rastatt ◯

Buhl ✝
Jasta 39
Jasta 70
Jasta 78

Stuttgart ◯

Saverne ◯
Sarrebourg ◯

Strasbourg ◯

Blâmont ⊗
Lunéville ⊗
Badonviller ⊗
Senones ⊗

Raon-l'Etape ⊗
Rambervillers ⊗
St Dié ⊗

River Rhine

Freiburg ✝
Kest 4
Kest 5

INDEX

The following index is selective due to the amount of names repeated in this book. Pilots and observers are only listed where either their medal citation, or biography, is mentioned. Place names such as Metz, are mentioned only if they appear as either a primary or secondary target. German pilots are mentioned for research reasons.